1997 SUPPLEMENT

to

ELEMENTS

OF

CIVIL PROCEDURE

CASES AND MATERIALS

By

MAURICE ROSENBERG

Harold R. Medina Professor of Procedural Jurisprudence Emeritus,
Columbia University

HANS SMIT

Stanley H. Fuld Professor of Law
Director, Parker School of Foreign and Comparative Law,
Columbia University

ROCHELLE COOPER DREYFUSS

Professor of Law, New York University
Director, Engelberg Center on Innovation Law and Policy

FIFTH EDITION

Westbury, New York
THE FOUNDATION PRESS, INC.
1997

PREFACE

As we stated in the Preface to our 1996 Supplement, the courts are fashioning limitations on the uses of the class action. In a most significant decision, *Amechem v. Windsor,* the Supreme Court has now voiced its views on one of the most far-reaching of these decisions. The implications on past and future cases, including the Tobacco Settlement, are explored in the Notes following this decision. Two important Supreme court decisions on standing, *Bennett v. Spear* and *Ranies v. Byrd* (the line-item veto case), have been substituted for the *Lujan* case, and a new decision on mootness has also been added (*Arizona for Official English v. Arizona*). Interesting *Erie* questions are addressed in *Henderson v U.S.* and *Yamaha Motors v. Calhoun.* And questions of subject matter competence (diversity and supplemental) are treated in *Strate v. A-1 Contractors, Caterpillar v. Lewis,* and *Peacock v. Thomas.*

The right to trial by jury has also received additional attention. In *Markman v. Westview Instruments Inc.,* the Court delineated the role of the jury in patent infringement cases, and, in *Gasperini v. Center for Humanities,* it ruled, in a decision with *Erie* implications, that state standards could be accommodated in reviewing a federal jury's award in a diversity case.

The res judicata effect of a class action judgment on federal claims is the focus of *Richards v. Jefferson County, Alabama.* The collateral order doctrine receives another look in *Quackenbush v. Allstate Insurance Co.*

All in all, the 1996 Term has produced a bountiful harvest of procedural decisions, all of which are included in this Supplement.

Because some of the most important decisions were not rendered until the very end of the Term, we decided to defer publication of the next edition of our casebook until next year. In that edition, we contemplate giving more detailed consideration to where recent developments, including the burgeoning of rocket dockets, are likely to lead.

HANS SMIT
ROCHELLE COOPER DREYFUSS

New York
July, 1997

*

TABLE OF CONTENTS

vi

TABLE OF CASES

Principal cases are in italic type. Non-principal cases are in roman type. References are to Pages.

TABLE OF CASES

1997 SUPPLEMENT

to

ELEMENTS

OF

CIVIL PROCEDURE

CASES AND MATERIALS

*

Part II

TRANSLATING RIGHTS INTO REMEDIES

Chapter Two

ACCESS TO COURT AND LAWYER

SECTION 2. ACCESS TO COURT

[Insert on page 55, at the end of the Notes:]

(3) In M.L.B. v. S.L.J., ___ U.S. ___, 117 S.Ct. 555, 136 L.Ed.2d 473 (1996), the majority, per Justice Ginsburg, ruled that a mother whose parental rights had been terminated could not constitutionally be required to pay fees in the amount of $2,352.36 as a condition to her being able to appeal from a lower court's decision, rendered on what the lower court characterized as "clear and convincing evidence." Justice Ginsburg stressed that access to court decisions "reflect both equal protection and due process concerns."

Justice Kennedy concurred, writing that "due process is quite a sufficient basis for our holding." Justices Rehnquist, Scalia, and Thomas dissented.

(4) Is access to court constitutionally guaranteed only in family and personal relations cases?

(5) May, in the principal case, the mother constitutionally be assessed the fees involved at the end of the appeal?

Chapter Three

FINAL REMEDIES

SECTION 2. HISTORICAL BACKGROUND: AMERICAN

[Insert on page 78, at the end of Section 2:]

The Federal Rules of Civil Procedure have been amended on a number of occasions. The latest amendments are referenced in this Supplement at relevant points.

SECTION 3. REMEDIES TODAY

B. MONEY JUDGMENT

[Insert at page 81, in lieu of Note (5):]

(5) On several occasions in recent years, the Supreme Court has considered whether there is any constitutional limitation on the amount of money a judge or a jury may award as punitive damages. In Bankers Life and Casualty Co. v. Crenshaw, 486 U.S. 71, 108 S.Ct. 1645, 100 L.Ed.2d 62 (1988), the Court held this question presented an issue of "moment and difficulty," but declined to decide it; in Browning–Ferris Industries of Vermont v. Kelco Disposal, Inc., 492 U.S. 257, 109 S.Ct. 2909, 106 L.Ed.2d 219 (1989), the Court ruled that the Excessive Fines Clause of the Eighth Amendment did not limit the amount of punitive damages a nongovernmental plaintiff may be awarded, and left to another day the question whether the Due Process Clause applied.

That day came in Pacific Mutual Life Ins. Co. v. Haslip, 499 U.S. 1, 111 S.Ct. 1032, 113 L.Ed.2d 1 (1991). The Court held that "the common-law method for assessing punitive damages does not in itself violate due process," id. at 17, 111 S.Ct. at 1043, 113 L.Ed.2d at 19, but that "unlimited jury discretion—or unlimited judicial discretion ... may invite extreme results that jar one's constitutional sensibilities," id. at 18, 111 S.Ct. at 1043, 113 L.Ed. at 20. The Court reviewed the procedures used in Pacific Mutual's case and found them satisfactory. The award amounted to more than 4 times the compensatory damages and more than 200 times Haslip's out-of-pocket loss. The Supreme Court had another chance to consider this issue in TXO Production Corp. v. Alliance Resources Corp., but the Court again refrained from announcing a constitutional test, 509 U.S. 443, 113 S.Ct. 2711, 125 L.Ed.2d 366 (1993) (punitive award was over 526 times as large as actual damages award). Howev-

2

er, in Honda Motor Co. v. Oberg, 512 U.S. 415, 114 S.Ct. 2331, 129 L.Ed.2d 336 (1994), the court emphasized the importance of *procedural* protections by reversing an award that could not, under relevant state law, be subjected to judicial review. See Hart, The Constitutionality of Punitive Damages: Pacific Mutual Life Insurance Co. v. Haslip, 21 Cum.L.Rev. 585 (1990). See also Cutter, TXO Production Corp. v. Alliance Resources Corp.: A Failure to Create True Constitutional Protection Against Excessive Punitive Damages, 44 Cath.U.L.Rev. 631 (1995); Franco, TXO Production Corporation v. Alliance Resources Corporation: The United States Supreme Court's Equivocal Reply to the Punitive Damages Predicament, 27 Conn.L.Rev. 735 (1995).

[Insert on page 81, after the notes:]

BMW OF NORTH AMERICA, INC. v. IRA GORE

Supreme Court of the United States, 1996.
___ U.S. ___, 116 S.Ct. 1589, 134 L.Ed.2d 809.

JUSTICE STEVENS delivered the opinion of the Court.*

The Due Process Clause of the Fourteenth Amendment prohibits a State from imposing a " 'grossly excessive' " punishment on a tortfeasor. TXO Production Corp. v. Alliance Resources Corp., 509 U.S. 443, 454, 113 S.Ct. 2711, 2718, 125 L.Ed.2d 366 (1993) (and cases cited). The wrongdoing involved in this case was the decision by a national distributor of automobiles not to advise its dealers, and hence their customers, of predelivery damage to new cars when the cost of repair amounted to less than 3 percent of the car's suggested retail price. The question presented is whether a $2 million punitive damages award to the purchaser of one of these cars exceeds the constitutional limit.

I

In January 1990, Dr. Ira Gore, Jr. (respondent), purchased a black BMW sports sedan for $40,750.88 from an authorized BMW dealer in Birmingham, Alabama. After driving the car for approximately nine months, and without noticing any flaws in its appearance, Dr. Gore took the car to "Slick Finish," an independent detailer, to make it look " 'snazzier than it normally would appear.' " 646 So.2d 619, 621 (Ala. 1994). Mr. Slick, the proprietor, detected evidence that the car had been repainted.[1] Convinced that he had been cheated, Dr. Gore brought suit against petitioner BMW of North America (BMW), the American distributor of BMW automobiles. Dr. Gore alleged, inter alia, that the failure to disclose that the car had been repainted constituted suppression of a material fact.[3] The complaint prayed for $500,000 in compensatory and punitive damages, and costs.

---

* Some footnotes omitted, others renumbered.

1. The top, hood, trunk, and quarter panels of Dr. Gore's car were repainted at BMW's vehicle preparation center in Brunswick, Georgia. The parties presumed that the damage was caused by exposure to acid rain during transit between the manufacturing plant in Germany and the preparation center.

3. Alabama codified its common-law cause of action for fraud in a 1907 statute

At trial, BMW acknowledged that it had adopted a nationwide policy in 1983 concerning cars that were damaged in the course of manufacture or transportation. If the cost of repairing the damage exceeded 3 percent of the car's suggested retail price, the car was placed in company service for a period of time and then sold as used. If the repair cost did not exceed 3 percent of the suggested retail price, however, the car was sold as new without advising the dealer that any repairs had been made. Because the $601.37 cost of repainting Dr. Gore's car was only about 1.5 percent of its suggested retail price, BMW did not disclose the damage or repair to the Birmingham dealer.

Dr. Gore asserted that his repainted car was worth less than a car that had not been refinished. To prove his actual damages of $4,000, he relied on the testimony of a former BMW dealer, who estimated that the value of a repainted BMW was approximately 10 percent less than the value of a new car that had not been damaged and repaired.[4] To support his claim for punitive damages, Dr. Gore introduced evidence that since 1983 BMW had sold 983 refinished cars as new, including 14 in Alabama, without disclosing that the cars had been repainted before sale at a cost of more than $300 per vehicle.[5] Using the actual damage estimate of $4,000 per vehicle, Dr. Gore argued that a punitive award of $4 million would provide an appropriate penalty for selling approximately 1,000 cars for more than they were worth.

In defense of its disclosure policy, BMW argued that it was under no obligation to disclose repairs of minor damage to new cars and that Dr. Gore's car was as good as a car with the original factory finish. It disputed Dr. Gore's assertion that the value of the car was impaired by the repainting and argued that this good-faith belief made a punitive award inappropriate. BMW also maintained that transactions in jurisdictions other than Alabama had no relevance to Dr. Gore's claim.

The jury returned a verdict finding BMW liable for compensatory damages of $4,000. In addition, the jury assessed $4 million in punitive damages, based on a determination that the nondisclosure policy constituted "gross, oppressive or malicious" fraud.[6] See Ala.Code §§ 6–11–20, 6–11–21 (1993).

that is still in effect. Hackmeyer v. Hackmeyer, 268 Ala. 329, 333, 106 So.2d 245, 249 (Ala.1958). The statute provides: "Suppression of a material fact which the party is under an obligation to communicate constitutes fraud. The obligation to communicate may arise from the confidential relations of the parties or from the particular circumstances of the case." Ala. Code § 6–5–102 (1993); see Ala.Code § 4299 (1907).

4. The dealer who testified to the reduction in value is the former owner of [a] Birmingham dealership sued in this action.

He sold the dealership approximately one year before the trial.

5. Dr. Gore did not explain the significance of the $300 cut-off.

6. The jury also found the Birmingham dealership liable for Dr. Gore's compensatory damages and [a] German manufacturer liable for both the compensatory and punitive damages. The dealership did not appeal the judgment against it. The Alabama Supreme Court held that the trial court did not have jurisdiction over the German manufacturer and therefore reversed the judgment against that defendant.

BMW filed a post-trial motion to set aside the punitive damages award. The company introduced evidence to establish that its nondisclosure policy was consistent with the laws of roughly 25 States defining the disclosure obligations of automobile manufacturers, distributors, and dealers. The most stringent of these statutes required disclosure of repairs costing more than 3 percent of the suggested retail price; none mandated disclosure of less costly repairs.[7] Relying on these statutes, BMW contended that its conduct was lawful in these States and therefore could not provide the basis for an award of punitive damages.

BMW also drew the court's attention to the fact that its nondisclosure policy had never been adjudged unlawful before this action was filed. Just months before Dr. Gore's case went to trial, the jury in a similar lawsuit filed by another Alabama BMW purchaser found that BMW's failure to disclose paint repair constituted fraud. Yates v. BMW of North America, Inc., 642 So.2d 937 (Ala.1993).[8] Before the judgment in this case, BMW changed its policy by taking steps to avoid the sale of any refinished vehicles in Alabama and two other States. When the $4 million verdict was returned in this case, BMW promptly instituted a nationwide policy of full disclosure of all repairs, no matter how minor.

In response to BMW's arguments, Dr. Gore asserted that the policy change demonstrated the efficacy of the punitive damages award. He noted that while no jury had held the policy unlawful, BMW had received a number of customer complaints relating to undisclosed repairs and had settled some lawsuits.[9] Finally, he maintained that the disclosure statutes of other States were irrelevant because BMW had failed to offer any evidence that the disclosure statutes supplanted, rather than supplemented, existing causes of action for common-law fraud.

The trial judge denied BMW's post-trial motion, holding, inter alia, that the award was not excessive. On appeal, the Alabama Supreme Court also rejected BMW's claim that the award exceeded the constitutionally permissible amount. 646 So.2d 619 (1994). The court's excessiveness inquiry applied the factors articulated in Green Oil Co. v. Hornsby, 539 So.2d 218, 223–224 (Ala.1989), and approved in Pacific Mut. Life Ins. Co. v. Haslip, 499 U.S. 1, 21–22, 111 S.Ct. 1032, 1045–1046, 113 L.Ed.2d 1 (1991). 646 So.2d, at 624–625. Based on its

7. BMW acknowledged that a Georgia statute enacted after Dr. Gore purchased his car would require disclosure of similar repairs to a car before it was sold in Georgia. Ga.Code Ann. §§ 40–1–5(b)–(e) (1994).

8. While awarding a comparable amount of compensatory damages, the Yates jury awarded no punitive damages at all. In Yates, the plaintiff also relied on the 1983 nondisclosure policy, but instead of offering evidence of 983 repairs costing more than $300 each, he introduced a bulk exhibit containing 5,856 repair bills to show that petitioner had sold over 5,800 new BMW vehicles without disclosing that they had been repaired.

9. Prior to the lawsuits filed by Dr. Yates and Dr. Gore, BMW and various BMW dealers had been sued 14 times concerning presale paint or damage repair. According to the testimony of BMW's in-house counsel at the postjudgment hearing on damages, only one of the suits concerned a car repainted by BMW.

analysis, the court concluded that BMW's conduct was "reprehensible"; the nondisclosure was profitable for the company; the judgment "would not have a substantial impact upon [BMW's] financial position"; the litigation had been expensive; no criminal sanctions had been imposed on BMW for the same conduct; the award of no punitive damages in Yates reflected "the inherent uncertainty of the trial process"; and the punitive award bore a "reasonable relationship" to "the harm that was likely to occur from [BMW's] conduct as well as ... the harm that actually occurred." Id., at 625–627.

The Alabama Supreme Court did, however, rule in BMW's favor on one critical point: The court found that the jury improperly computed the amount of punitive damages by multiplying Dr. Gore's compensatory damages by the number of similar sales in other jurisdictions. Id., at 627. Having found the verdict tainted, the court held that "a constitutionally reasonable punitive damages award in this case is $2,000,000," id., at 629, and therefore ordered a remittitur in that amount.[10] The court's discussion of the amount of its remitted award expressly disclaimed any reliance on "acts that occurred in other jurisdictions"; instead, the court explained that it had used a "comparative analysis" that considered Alabama cases, "along with cases from other jurisdictions, involving the sale of an automobile where the seller misrepresented the condition of the vehicle and the jury awarded punitive damages to the purchaser."[11] Id., at 628. *reduction in damages*

Because we believed that a review of this case would help to illuminate "the character of the standard that will identify constitutionally excessive awards" of punitive damages, see Honda Motor Co. v. Oberg, 512 U.S. ___, ___, ___ S.Ct. ___, ___, ___ L.Ed.2d ___ (1994) (slip op., at 4), we granted certiorari, 513 U.S. ___, 115 S.Ct. 932, 130 L.Ed.2d 879 (1995).

10. The Alabama Supreme Court did not indicate whether the $2 million figure represented the court's independent assessment of the appropriate level of punitive damages, or its determination of the maximum amount that the jury could have awarded consistent with the Due Process Clause.

11. Other than Yates v. BMW of North America, Inc., 642 So.2d 937 (Ala.1993), in which no punitive damages were awarded, the Alabama Supreme Court cited no such cases. In another portion of its opinion, 646 So.2d, at 629, the court did cite five Alabama cases, none of which involved either a dispute arising out of the purchase of an automobile or an award of punitive damages. G.M. Mosley Contractors, Inc. v. Phillips, 487 So.2d 876, 879 (Ala.1986);

Hollis v. Wyrosdick, 508 So.2d 704 (Ala. 1987); Campbell v. Burns, 512 So.2d 1341, 1343 (Ala.1987); Ashbee v. Brock, 510 So.2d 214 (Ala.1987); and Jawad v. Granade, 497 So.2d 471 (Ala.1986). All of these cases support the proposition that appellate courts in Alabama presume that jury verdicts are correct. In light of the Alabama Supreme Court's conclusion that (1) the jury had computed its award by multiplying $4,000 by the number of refinished vehicles sold in the United States and (2) that the award should have been based on Alabama conduct, respect for the error-free portion of the jury verdict would seem to produce an award of $56,000 ($4,000 multiplied by 14, the number of repainted vehicles sold in Alabama).

II

Punitive damages may properly be imposed to further a State's legitimate interests in punishing unlawful conduct and deterring its repetition. Gertz v. Robert Welch, Inc., 418 U.S. 323, 350, 94 S.Ct. 2997, 3012, 41 L.Ed.2d 789 (1974); Newport v. Fact Concerts, Inc., 453 U.S. 247, 266–267, 101 S.Ct. 2748, 2759–2760, 69 L.Ed.2d 616 (1981); Haslip, 499 U.S., at 22, 111 S.Ct., at 1045–1046. In our federal system, States necessarily have considerable flexibility in determining the level of punitive damages that they will allow in different classes of cases and in any particular case. Most States that authorize exemplary damages afford the jury similar latitude, requiring only that the damages awarded be reasonably necessary to vindicate the State's legitimate interests in punishment and deterrence. See TXO, 509 U.S., at 456, 113 S.Ct., at 2719–2720; Haslip, 499 U.S., at 21, 22, 111 S.Ct., at 1045, 1045–1046. Only when an award can fairly be categorized as "grossly excessive" in relation to these interests does it enter the zone of arbitrariness that violates the Due Process Clause of the Fourteenth Amendment. Cf. TXO, 509 U.S., at 456, 113 S.Ct., at 2719–2720. For that reason, the federal excessiveness inquiry appropriately begins with an identification of the state interests that a punitive award is designed to serve. We therefore focus our attention first on the scope of Alabama's legitimate interests in punishing BMW and deterring it from future misconduct.

No one doubts that a State may protect its citizens by prohibiting deceptive trade practices and by requiring automobile distributors to disclose presale repairs that affect the value of a new car. But the States need not, and in fact do not, provide such protection in a uniform manner. Some States rely on the judicial process to formulate and enforce an appropriate disclosure requirement by applying principles of contract and tort law. Other States have enacted various forms of legislation that define the disclosure obligations of automobile manufacturers, distributors, and dealers.[13] The result is a patchwork of rules representing the diverse policy judgments of lawmakers in 50 States.

13. Four States require disclosure of vehicle repairs costing more than 3 percent of suggested retail price. Ariz.Rev.Stat.Ann. § 28–1304.03 (1989); N.C.Gen.Stat. § 20–305.1(d)(5a) (1995); S.C.Code § 56–32–20 (Supp.1995); Va.Code Ann. § 46.2–1571(D) (Supp.1995). An additional three States mandate disclosure when the cost of repairs exceeds 3 percent or $500, whichever is greater. Ala.Code § 8–19–5(22)(c) (1993); Cal.Veh.Code Ann. §§ 9990–9991 (West Supp.1996); Okla.Stat., Tit. 47, § 1112.1 (1991). Indiana imposes a 4 percent disclosure threshold. Ind.Code §§ 9–23–4–4, 9–23–4–5 (1993). Minnesota requires disclosure of repairs costing more than 4 percent of suggested retail price or $500, whichever is greater. Minn.Stat. § 325F.664 (1994).

New York requires disclosure when the cost of repairs exceeds 5 percent of suggested retail price. N.Y.Gen.Bus.Law §§ 396–p(5)(a), (d) (McKinney Supp.1996). Vermont imposes a 5 percent disclosure threshold for the first $10,000 in repair costs and 2 percent thereafter. Vt.Stat.Ann., Tit. 9, § 4087(d) (1993). Eleven States mandate disclosure only of damage costing more than 6 percent of retail value to repair. Ark.Code Ann. § 23–112–705 (1992); Idaho Code § 49–1624 (1994); Ill.Comp.Stat., ch. 815, § 710/5 (1994); Ky.Rev.Stat.Ann. § 100.0101(5) (Baldwin 1988); La.Rev.Stat. Ann. § 32:1260 (Supp.1995); Miss. Motor Vehicle Comm'n, Regulation No. 1 (1992); N.H.Rev.Stat.Ann. § 357–C:5(III)(d) (1995);

That diversity demonstrates that reasonable people may disagree about the value of a full disclosure requirement. Some legislatures may conclude that affirmative disclosure requirements are unnecessary because the self-interest of those involved in the automobile trade in developing and maintaining the goodwill of their customers will motivate them to make voluntary disclosures or to refrain from selling cars that do not comply with self-imposed standards. Those legislatures that do adopt affirmative disclosure obligations may take into account the cost of government regulation, choosing to draw a line exempting minor repairs from such a requirement. In formulating a disclosure standard, States may also consider other goals, such as providing a "safe harbor" for automobile manufacturers, distributors, and dealers against lawsuits over minor repairs.[14]

We may assume, arguendo, that it would be wise for every State to adopt Dr. Gore's preferred rule, requiring full disclosure of every presale repair to a car, no matter how trivial and regardless of its actual impact on the value of the car. But while we do not doubt that Congress has ample authority to enact such a policy for the entire Nation,[15] it is clear that no single State could do so, or even impose its own policy choice on neighboring States. See Bonaparte v. Tax Court, 104 U.S. 592, 594, 26 L.Ed. 845 (1881) ("No State can legislate except with reference to its own jurisdiction.... Each State is independent of all the others in this particular").[16] Similarly, one State's power to impose burdens on the

Ohio Rev.Code Ann. § 4517.61 (1994); R.I.Gen.Laws §§ 31–5.1–18(d), (f) (1995); Wis.Stat. § 218.01(2d)(a) (1994); Wyo.Stat. § 31–16–115 (1994). Two States require disclosure of repairs costing $3,000 or more. See Iowa Code Ann. § 321.69 (Supp.1996); N.D.Admin.Code § 37–09–01–01 (1992). Georgia mandates disclosure of paint damage that costs more than $500 to repair. Ga.Code Ann. §§ 40–1–5(b)–(e) (1994) (enacted after respondent purchased his car). Florida requires dealers to disclose paint repair costing more than $100 of which they have actual knowledge. Fla.Stat. § 320.27(9)(n) (1992). Oregon requires manufacturers to disclose all "post-manufacturing" damage and repairs. It is unclear whether this mandate would apply to repairs such as those at issue here. Ore. Rev.Stat. § 650.155 (1991). Many, but not all, of the statutes exclude from the computation of repair cost the value of certain components—typically items such as glass, tires, wheels and bumpers—when they are replaced with identical manufacturer's original equipment. E.g., Cal.Veh.Code Ann. §§ 9990–9991 (West Supp.1996); Ga.Code Ann. §§ 40–1–5(b)–(e) (1994); Ill.Comp. Stat., ch. 815, § 710/5 (1994); Ky.Rev.Stat.

Ann. § 190.0491(5) (Baldwin 1988); Okla. Stat., Tit. 47, § 1112.1 (1991); Va.Code Ann. § 46.2–1571(D) (Supp.1995); Vt.Stat. Ann., Tit. 9, § 4087(d) (1993).

14. Also, a state legislature might plausibly conclude that the administrative costs associated with full disclosure would have the effect of raising car prices to the State's residents.

15. Federal disclosure requirements are, of course, a familiar part of our law. See, e.g., the Federal Food, Drug, and Cosmetic Act, as added by the Nutrition Labeling and Education Act of 1990, 104 Stat. 2353, 21 U.S.C. § 343; the Truth In Lending Act, 82 Stat. 148, as amended, 15 U.S.C. § 1604; the Securities and Exchange Act of 1934, 48 Stat. 892, 894, as amended, 15 U.S.C. §§ 781–78m; Federal Cigarette Labeling and Advertising Act, 79 Stat. 283, as amended, 15 U.S.C. § 1333; Alcoholic Beverage Labeling Act of 1988, 102 Stat. 4519, 27 U.S.C. § 215.

16. See also Bigelow v. Virginia, 421 U.S. 809, 824, 95 S.Ct. 2222, 2234, 44 L.Ed.2d 600 (1975) ("A State does not acquire power or supervision over the internal affairs of another State merely because the

interstate market for automobiles is not only subordinate to the federal power over interstate commerce, Gibbons v. Ogden, 9 Wheat. 1, 194–196, 6 L.Ed. 23 (1824), but is also constrained by the need to respect the interests of other States, see, e.g., Healy v. Beer Institute, 491 U.S. 324, 335–336, 109 S.Ct. 2491, 2498–2499, 105 L.Ed.2d 275 (1989) (the Constitution has a "special concern both with the maintenance of a national economic union unfettered by state-imposed limitations on interstate commerce and with the autonomy of the individual States within their respective spheres" (footnote omitted)); Edgar v. MITE Corp., 457 U.S. 624, 643, 102 S.Ct. 2629, 2641, 73 L.Ed.2d 269 (1982).

We think it follows from these principles of state sovereignty and comity that a State may not impose economic sanctions on violators of its laws with the intent of changing the tortfeasors' lawful conduct in other States.[17] Before this Court Dr. Gore argued that the large punitive damages award was necessary to induce BMW to change the nationwide policy that it adopted in 1983.[18] But by attempting to alter BMW's nationwide policy, Alabama would be infringing on the policy choices of other States. To avoid such encroachment, the economic penalties that a State such as Alabama inflicts on those who transgress its laws, whether the penalties take the form of legislatively authorized fines or judicially imposed punitive damages, must be supported by the State's interest in protecting its own consumers and its own economy. Alabama may insist that BMW adhere to a particular disclosure policy in that State. Alabama does not have the power, however, to punish BMW for conduct that was lawful where it occurred and that had no impact on

welfare and health of its own citizens may be affected when they travel to that State"); New York Life Ins. Co. v. Head, 234 U.S. 149, 161, 34 S.Ct. 879, 882, 58 L.Ed. 1259 (1914) ("[I]t would be impossible to permit the statutes of Missouri to operate beyond the jurisdiction of that State ... without throwing down the constitutional barriers by which all the States are restricted within the orbits of their lawful authority and upon the preservation of which the Government under the Constitution depends. This is so obviously the necessary result of the Constitution that it has rarely been called in question and hence authorities directly dealing with it do not abound"); Huntington v. Attrill, 146 U.S. 657, 669, 13 S.Ct. 224, 228, 36 L.Ed. 1123 (1892) ("Laws have no force of themselves beyond the jurisdiction of the State which enacts them, and can have extra-territorial effect only by the comity of other States").

17. State power may be exercised as much by a jury's application of a state rule of law in a civil lawsuit as by a statute. See New York Times Co. v. Sullivan, 376 U.S. 254, 265, 84 S.Ct. 710, 718, 11 L.Ed.2d 686 (1964) ("The test is not the form in which state power has been applied but, whatever the form, whether such power has in fact been exercised"); San Diego Building Trades Council v. Garmon, 359 U.S. 236, 247, 79 S.Ct. 773, 780, 3 L.Ed.2d 775 (1959) ("regulation can be as effectively exerted through an award of damages as through some form of preventive relief").

18. Brief for Respondent 11–12, 23, 27–28; Tr. of Oral Arg. 50–54. Dr. Gore's interest in altering the nationwide policy stems from his concern that BMW would not (or could not) discontinue the policy in Alabama alone. Id., at 11. "If Alabama were limited to imposing punitive damages based only on BMW's gain from fraudulent sales in Alabama, the resulting award would have no prospect of protecting Alabama consumers from fraud, as it would provide no incentive for BMW to alter the unitary, national policy of nondisclosure which yielded BMW millions of dollars in profits." Id., at 23. The record discloses no basis for Dr. Gore's contention that

Alabama or its residents.[19]   Nor may Alabama impose sanctions on
BMW in order to deter conduct that is lawful in other jurisdictions.

In this case, we accept the Alabama Supreme Court's interpretation
of the jury verdict as reflecting a computation of the amount of punitive
damages "based in large part on conduct that happened in other jurisdictions." 646 So.2d, at 627. As the Alabama Supreme Court noted,
neither the jury nor the trial court was presented with evidence that any
of BMW's out-of-state conduct was unlawful. "The only testimony
touching the issue showed that approximately 60% of the vehicles that
were refinished were sold in states where failure to disclose the repair
was not an unfair trade practice." Id., at 627, n. 6.[20]   The Alabama
Supreme Court therefore properly eschewed reliance on BMW's out-of-
state conduct, id., at 628, and based its remitted award solely on conduct
that occurred within Alabama.[21]   The award must be analyzed in the
light of the same conduct, with consideration given only to the interests
of Alabama consumers, rather than those of the entire Nation. When
the scope of the interest in punishment and deterrence that an Alabama
court may appropriately consider is properly limited, it is apparent—for
reasons that we shall now address—that this award is grossly excessive.

III

Elementary notions of fairness enshrined in our constitutional jurisprudence dictate that a person receive fair notice not only of the conduct
that will subject him to punishment but also of the severity of the
penalty that a State may impose.[22]   Three guideposts, each of which

---

BMW could not comply with Alabama's law
without changing its nationwide policy.

19. See Bordenkircher v. Hayes, 434
U.S. 357, 363, 98 S.Ct. 663, 668, 54 L.Ed.2d
604 (1978) ("To punish a person because
he has done what the law plainly allows
him to do is a due process violation of the
most basic sort"). Our cases concerning
recidivist statutes are not to the contrary.
Habitual offender statutes permit the sentencing court to enhance a defendant's
punishment for a crime in light of prior
convictions, including convictions in foreign
jurisdictions. See e.g., Ala.Code § 13A–5–9
(1994); Cal.Penal Code Ann. §§ 667.5(f),
668 (West Supp.1996); Ill.Comp.Stat., ch.
720, § 5/33B–1 (1994); N.Y.Penal Law
§§ 70.04, 70.06, 70.08, 70.10 (McKinney
1987 and Supp.1996); Tex.Penal Code Ann.
§ 12.42 (1994 and Supp.1995–1996). A
sentencing judge may even consider past
criminal behavior which did not result in a
conviction and lawful conduct that bears on
the defendant's character and prospects for
rehabilitation. Williams v. New York, 337
U.S. 241, 69 S.Ct. 1079, 93 L.Ed. 1337
(1949). But we have never held that a
sentencing court could properly punish lawful conduct. This distinction is precisely
the one we draw here. See n. 21, infra.

20. Given that the verdict was based in
part on out-of-state conduct that was lawful
where it occurred, we need not consider
whether one State may properly attempt to
change a tortfeasors' unlawful conduct in
another State.

21. Of course, the fact that the Alabama
Supreme Court correctly concluded that it
was error for the jury to use the number of
sales in other States as a multiplier in computing the amount of its punitive sanction
does not mean that evidence describing out-
of-state transactions is irrelevant in a case
of this kind. To the contrary, as we stated
in TXO Production Corp. v. Alliance Resources Corp., 509 U.S. 443, 462, n. 28, 113
S.Ct. 2711, 2722, n. 28, 125 L.Ed.2d 366
(1993), and discuss more fully infra, at 16–
19, such evidence is relevant to the determination of the degree of reprehensibility of
the defendant's conduct.

22. See Miller v. Florida, 482 U.S. 423,
107 S.Ct. 2446, 96 L.Ed.2d 351 (1987) (Ex
Post Facto Clause violated by retroactive
imposition of revised sentencing guidelines

indicates that BMW did not receive adequate notice of the magnitude of the sanction that Alabama might impose for adhering to the nondisclosure policy adopted in 1983, lead us to the conclusion that the $2 million award against BMW is grossly excessive: the degree of reprehensibility of the nondisclosure; the disparity between the harm or potential harm suffered by Dr. Gore and his punitive damages award; and the difference between this remedy and the civil penalties authorized or imposed in comparable cases. We discuss these considerations in turn.

Degree of Reprehensibility

Perhaps the most important indicium of the reasonableness of a punitive damages award is the degree of reprehensibility of the defendant's conduct.[23] As the Court stated nearly 150 years ago, exemplary damages imposed on a defendant should reflect "the enormity of his offense." Day v. Woodworth, 13 How. 363, 371, 14 L.Ed. 181 (1852). See also St. Louis, I.M. & S.R. Co. v. Williams, 251 U.S. 63, 66–67, 40 S.Ct. 71, 73, 64 L.Ed. 139 (1919) (punitive award may not be "wholly disproportioned to the offense"); Browning–Ferris Industries of Vt., Inc. v. Kelco Disposal, Inc., 492 U.S. 257, 301, 109 S.Ct. 2909, 2934, 106 L.Ed.2d 219 (1989) (O'Connor, J., concurring in part and dissenting in part) (reviewing court "should examine the gravity of the defendant's conduct and the harshness of the award of punitive damages").[24] This principle reflects the accepted view that some wrongs are more blameworthy than others. Thus, we have said that "nonviolent crimes are less serious than crimes marked by violence or the threat of violence." Solem v. Helm, 463 U.S. 277, 292–293, 103 S.Ct. 3001, 3011, 77 L.Ed.2d 637 (1983). Similarly, "trickery and deceit", TXO, 509 U.S., at 462, 113 S.Ct., at 2722, are more reprehensible than negligence. In TXO, both the West Virginia Supreme Court and the Justices of this Court placed

that provided longer sentence for defendant's crime); Bouie v. City of Columbia, 378 U.S. 347, 84 S.Ct. 1697, 12 L.Ed.2d 894 (1964) (retroactive application of new construction of statute violated due process); id., at 350–355, 84 S.Ct., at 1701–1703 (citing cases); Lankford v. Idaho, 500 U.S. 110, 111 S.Ct. 1723, 114 L.Ed.2d 173 (1991) (due process violated because defendant and his counsel did not have adequate notice that judge might impose death sentence). The strict constitutional safeguards afforded to criminal defendants are not applicable to civil cases, but the basic protection against "judgments without notice" afforded by the Due Process Clause, Shaffer v. Heitner, 433 U.S. 186, 217, 97 S.Ct. 2569, 2587, 53 L.Ed.2d 683 (1977) (Stevens, J., concurring in judgment), is implicated by civil penalties.

23. "The flagrancy of the misconduct is thought to be the primary consideration in determining the amount of punitive damages." Owen, A Punitive Damages Overview: Functions, Problems and Reform, 39 Vill.L.Rev. 363, 387 (1994).

24. The principle that punishment should fit the crime "is deeply rooted and frequently repeated in common-law jurisprudence." Solem v. Helm, 463 U.S. 277, 284, 103 S.Ct. 3001, 3006, 77 L.Ed.2d 637 (1983). See Burkett v. Lanata, 15 La.Ann. 337, 339 (1860) (punitive damages should be "commensurate to the nature of the offence"); Blanchard v. Morris, 15 Ill. 35, 36 (1853) ("[W]e cannot say [the exemplary damages] are excessive under the circumstances; for the proofs show that threats, violence, and imprisonment, were accompanied by mental fear, torture, and agony of mind"); Louisville & Northern R. Co. v. Brown, 127 Ky. 732, 749, 106 S.W. 795, 799 (1908) ("We are not aware of any case in which the court has sustained a verdict as large as this one unless the injuries were permanent").

special emphasis on the principle that punitive damages may not be "grossly out of proportion to the severity of the offense." [25]   Id., at 453, 482, 113 S.Ct., at 2718, 2733. Indeed, for Justice Kennedy, the defendant's intentional malice was the decisive element in a "close and difficult" case. Id., at 468, 113 S.Ct., at 2725.[26]

In this case, none of the aggravating factors associated with particularly reprehensible conduct is present. The harm BMW inflicted on Dr. Gore was purely economic in nature. The presale refinishing of the car had no effect on its performance or safety features, or even its appearance for at least nine months after his purchase. BMW's conduct evinced no indifference to or reckless disregard for the health and safety of others. To be sure, infliction of economic injury, especially when done intentionally through affirmative acts of misconduct, id., at 453, 113 S.Ct., at 2717–2718, or when the target is financially vulnerable, can warrant a substantial penalty. But this observation does not convert all acts that cause economic harm into torts that are sufficiently reprehensible to justify a significant sanction in addition to compensatory damages.

Dr. Gore contends that BMW's conduct was particularly reprehensible because nondisclosure of the repairs to his car formed part of a nationwide pattern of tortious conduct. Certainly, evidence that a defendant has repeatedly engaged in prohibited conduct while knowing or suspecting that it was unlawful would provide relevant support for an argument that strong medicine is required to cure the defendant's disrespect for the law. See id., at 462, n. 28, 113 S.Ct., at 2722, n. 28. Our holdings that a recidivist may be punished more severely than a first offender recognize that repeated misconduct is more reprehensible than an individual instance of malfeasance. See Gryger v. Burke, 334 U.S. 728, 732, 68 S.Ct. 1256, 1258–1259, 92 L.Ed. 1683 (1948).

In support of his thesis, Dr. Gore advances two arguments. First, he asserts that the state disclosure statutes supplement, rather than supplant, existing remedies for breach of contract and common-law fraud. Thus, according to Dr. Gore, the statutes may not properly be viewed as immunizing from liability the nondisclosure of repairs costing less than the applicable statutory threshold. Brief for Respondent 18–19. Second, Dr. Gore maintains that BMW should have anticipated that its failure to disclose similar repair work could expose it to liability for fraud. Id., at 4–5.

We recognize, of course, that only state courts may authoritatively construe state statutes. As far as we are aware, at the time this action was commenced no state court had explicitly addressed whether its

25. Pacific Mut. Life Ins. Co. v. Haslip, 499 U.S. 1, 22, 111 S.Ct. 1032, 1045, 113 L.Ed.2d 1 (1991).

26. The dissenters also recognized that "TXO's conduct was clearly wrongful, cal-culated, and improper...."   TXO, 509 U.S., at 482, 113 S.Ct., at 2733 (O'Connor, J., dissenting).

State's disclosure statute provides a safe harbor for nondisclosure of presumptively minor repairs or should be construed instead as supplementing common-law duties.[27]   A review of the text of the statutes, however, persuades us that in the absence of a state-court determination to the contrary, a corporate executive could reasonably interpret the disclosure requirements as establishing safe harbors.   In California, for example, the disclosure statute defines "material" damage to a motor vehicle as damage requiring repairs costing in excess of 3 percent of the suggested retail price or $500, whichever is greater.   Cal.Veh.Code Ann. § 9990 (West Supp.1996).   The Illinois statute states that in cases in which disclosure is not required, "nondisclosure does not constitute a misrepresentation or omission of fact."   Ill.Comp.Stat., ch. 815, § 710/5 (1994).[28]   Perhaps the statutes may also be interpreted in another way. We simply emphasize that the record contains no evidence that BMW's decision to follow a disclosure policy that coincided with the strictest extant state statute was sufficiently reprehensible to justify a $2 million award of punitive damages.

Dr. Gore's second argument for treating BMW as a recidivist is that the company should have anticipated that its actions would be considered fraudulent in some, if not all, jurisdictions.   This contention overlooks the fact that actionable fraud requires a material misrepresenta-

27. In Jeter v. M & M Dodge, Inc., 634 So.2d 1383 (La.App.1994), a Louisiana court of appeals suggested that the Louisiana disclosure statute functions as a safe harbor.   Finding that the cost of repairing presale damage to the plaintiff's car exceeded the statutory disclosure threshold, the court held that the disclosure statute did not provide a defense to the action.   Id., at 1384.   During the pendency of this litigation, Alabama enacted a disclosure statute which defines "material" damage to a new car as damage requiring repairs costing in excess of 3 percent of suggested retail price or $500, whichever is greater.   Ala.Code § 8–19–5(22) (1993).   After its decision in this case, the Alabama Supreme Court stated in dicta that the remedies available under this section of its Deceptive Trade Practices Act did not displace or alter preexisting remedies available under either the common law or other statutes.   Hines v. Riverside Chevrolet–Olds, Inc., 655 So.2d 909, 917, n. 2 (Ala.1994).   It refused, however, to "recognize, or impose on automobile manufacturers, a general duty to disclose every repair of damage, however slight, incurred during the manufacturing process."   Id., at 921.   Instead, it held that whether a defendant has a duty to disclose is a question of fact "for the jury to determine."   Id., at 918.   In reaching that conclusion it overruled two earlier decisions that seemed to indicate that as a matter of law there was no disclosure obligation in cases comparable to this one.   Id., at 920 (overruling Century 21–Reeves Realty, Inc. v. McConnell Cadillac, Inc., 626 So.2d 1273 (Ala.1993), and Cobb v. Southeast Toyota Distributors, Inc., 569 So.2d 395 (Ala. 1990)).

28. See also Ariz.Rev.Stat.Ann. § 28–1304.03 (1989) ("[I]f disclosure is not required under this section, a purchaser may not revoke or rescind a sales contract due solely to the fact that the new motor vehicle was damaged and repaired prior to completion of the sale"); Ind.Code § 9–23–4–5 (1993) (providing that "[r]epaired damage to a customer-ordered new motor vehicle not exceeding four percent (4%) of the manufacturer's suggested retail price does not need to be disclosed at the time of sale"); N.C.Gen.Stat. § 20–305.1(e) (1993) (requiring disclosure of repairs costing more than 5 percent of suggested retail price and prohibiting revocation or rescission of sales contract on the basis of less costly repairs); Okla.Stat., Tit. 47, § 1112.1 (1991) (defining "material" damage to a car as damage requiring repairs costing in excess of 3 percent of suggested retail price or $500, whichever is greater).

tion or omission.[29] This qualifier invites line drawing of just the sort engaged in by States with disclosure statutes and by BMW. We do not think it can be disputed that there may exist minor imperfections in the finish of a new car that can be repaired (or indeed, left unrepaired) without materially affecting the car's value.[30] There is no evidence that BMW acted in bad faith when it sought to establish the appropriate line between presumptively minor damage and damage requiring disclosure to purchasers. For this purpose, BMW could reasonably rely on state disclosure statutes for guidance. In this regard, it is also significant that there is no evidence that BMW persisted in a course of conduct after it had been adjudged unlawful on even one occasion, let alone repeated occasions.[31]

Finally, the record in this case discloses no deliberate false statements, acts of affirmative misconduct, or concealment of evidence of improper motive, such as were present in Haslip and TXO. Haslip, 499 U.S., at 5, 111 S.Ct., at 1036, TXO, 509 U.S., at 453, 113 S.Ct., at 2717–2718. We accept, of course, the jury's finding that BMW suppressed a material fact which Alabama law obligated it to communicate to prospective purchasers of repainted cars in that State. But the omission of a material fact may be less reprehensible than a deliberate false statement, particularly when there is a good-faith basis for believing that no duty to disclose exists.

That conduct is sufficiently reprehensible to give rise to tort liability, and even a modest award of exemplary damages, does not establish the high degree of culpability that warrants a substantial punitive damages award. Because this case exhibits none of the circumstances ordinarily associated with egregiously improper conduct, we are persuaded that BMW's conduct was not sufficiently reprehensible to warrant imposition of a $2 million exemplary damages award.

Ratio

The second and perhaps most commonly cited indicium of an unreasonable or excessive punitive damages award is its ratio to the actual harm inflicted on the plaintiff. See TXO, 509 U.S., at 459, 113 S.Ct., at 2721; Haslip, 499 U.S., at 23, 111 S.Ct., at 1046. The principle that exemplary damages must bear a "reasonable relationship" to compensa-

29. Restatement (Second) of Torts § 538 (1977); W. Keeton, D. Dobbs, R. Keeton, & D. Owen, Prosser and Keeton on Law of Torts § 108 (5th ed. 1984).

30. The Alabama Supreme Court has held that a car may be considered "new" as a matter of law even if its finish contains minor cosmetic flaws. Wilburn v. Larry Savage Chevrolet, Inc., 477 So.2d 384 (Ala. 1985). We note also that at trial respondent only introduced evidence of undisclosed paint damage to new cars repaired at a cost of $300 or more. This decision suggests that respondent believed that the jury might consider some repairs too de minimis to warrant disclosure.

31. Before the verdict in this case, BMW had changed its policy with respect to Alabama and two other States. Five days after the jury award, BMW altered its nationwide policy to one of full disclosure.

tory damages has a long pedigree.[32] Scholars have identified a number of early English statutes authorizing the award of multiple damages for particular wrongs. Some 65 different enactments during the period between 1275 and 1753 provided for double, treble, or quadruple damages.[33] Our decisions in both Haslip and TXO endorsed the proposition that a comparison between the compensatory award and the punitive award is significant.

In Haslip we concluded that even though a punitive damages award of "more than 4 times the amount of compensatory damages," might be "close to the line," it did not "cross the line into the area of constitutional impropriety." Haslip, 499 U.S., at 23–24, 111 S.Ct., at 1046. TXO, following dicta in Haslip, refined this analysis by confirming that the proper inquiry is " 'whether there is a reasonable relationship between the punitive damages award and the harm likely to result from the defendant's conduct as well as the harm that actually has occurred.' " TXO, 509 U.S., at 460, 113 S.Ct., at 2721 (emphasis in original), quoting Haslip, 499 U.S., at 21, 111 S.Ct., at 1045. Thus, in upholding the $10 million award in TXO, we relied on the difference between that figure and the harm to the victim that would have ensued if the tortious plan had succeeded. That difference suggested that the relevant ratio was not more than 10 to 1.[34]

The $2 million in punitive damages awarded to Dr. Gore by the Alabama Supreme Court is 500 times the amount of his actual harm as

32. See, e.g., Grant v. McDonogh, 7 La. Ann. 447, 448 (1852) ("[E]xemplary damages allowed should bear some proportion to the real damage sustained"); Saunders v. Mullen, 66 Iowa 728, 729, 24 N.W. 529 (1885) ("When the actual damages are so small, the amount allowed as exemplary damages should not be so large"); Flannery v. Baltimore & Ohio R. Co., 15 D.C. 111, 125 (1885) (when punitive damages award "is out of all proportion to the injuries received, we feel it our duty to interfere"); Houston & Texas Central R. Co. v. Nichols, 9 Am. & Eng.R.R.Cas. 361, 365 (Tex.1882) ("Exemplary damages, when allowed, should bear proportion to the actual damages sustained"); McCarthy v. Niskern, 22 Minn. 90, 91–92 (1875) (punitive damages "enormously in excess of what may justly be regarded as compensation" for the injury must be set aside "to prevent injustice").

33. Owen, supra n. 23, at 368, and n. 23. One English statute, for example, provides that officers arresting persons out of their jurisdiction shall pay double damages. 3 Edw., I., ch. 35. Another directs that in an action for forcible entry or detainer, the plaintiff shall recover treble damages. 8 Hen. VI, ch. 9, § 6. Present-day federal law allows or mandates imposition of multiple damages for a wide assortment of of-fenses, including violations of the antitrust laws, see § 4 of the Clayton Act, 38 Stat. 731, as amended, 15 U.S.C. § 15, and the Racketeer Influenced and Corrupt Organizations Act, see 18 U.S.C. § 1964, and certain breaches of the trademark laws, see § 35 of the Trademark Act of 1946, 60 Stat. 439, as amended, 15 U.S.C. § 1117, and the patent laws, see 66 Stat. 813, 35 U.S.C. § 284.

34. "While petitioner stresses the shocking disparity between the punitive award and the compensatory award, that shock dissipates when one considers the potential loss to respondents, in terms of reduced or eliminated royalties payments, had petitioner succeeded in its illicit scheme. Thus, even if the actual value of the 'potential harm' to respondents is not between $5 million and $8.3 million, but is closer to $4 million, or $2 million, or even $1 million, the disparity between the punitive award and the potential harm does not, in our view, 'jar one's constitutional sensibilities.' " TXO, 509 U.S., at 462, 113 S.Ct., at 2722, quoting Pacific Mut. Life Ins. Co. v. Haslip, 499 U.S., at 18, 111 S.Ct., at 1043.

determined by the jury.[35] Moreover, there is no suggestion that Dr. Gore or any other BMW purchaser was threatened with any additional potential harm by BMW's nondisclosure policy. The disparity in this case is thus dramatically greater than those considered in Haslip and TXO.[36]

Of course, we have consistently rejected the notion that the constitutional line is marked by a simple mathematical formula, even one that compares actual and potential damages to the punitive award. TXO, 509 U.S., at 458, 113 S.Ct., at 2720.[37] Indeed, low awards of compensatory damages may properly support a higher ratio than high compensatory awards, if, for example, a particularly egregious act has resulted in only a small amount of economic damages. A higher ratio may also be justified in cases in which the injury is hard to detect or the monetary value of noneconomic harm might have been difficult to determine. It is appropriate, therefore, to reiterate our rejection of a categorical approach. Once again, "we return to what we said ... in Haslip: 'We need not, and indeed we cannot, draw a mathematical bright line between the constitutionally acceptable and the constitutionally unacceptable that would fit every case. We can say, however, that [a] general concer[n] of reasonableness ... properly enter[s] into the constitutional calculus.' " TXO, 509 U.S., at 458, 113 S.Ct., at 2720 (quoting Haslip, 499 U.S., at 18, 111 S.Ct., at 1043). In most cases, the ratio will be within a constitutionally acceptable range, and remittitur will not be justified on this basis. When the ratio is a breathtaking 500 to 1, however, the award must surely "raise a suspicious judicial eyebrow." TXO, 509 U.S., at 482, 113 S.Ct., at 2732 (O'Connor, J., dissenting).

Sanctions for Comparable Misconduct

Comparing the punitive damages award and the civil or criminal penalties that could be imposed for comparable misconduct provides a third indicium of excessiveness. As Justice O'Connor has correctly observed, a reviewing court engaged in determining whether an award of punitive damages is excessive should "accord 'substantial deference' to legislative judgments concerning appropriate sanctions for the conduct at issue." Browning–Ferris Industries of Vt., Inc. v. Kelco Disposal, Inc., 492 U.S., at 301, 109 S.Ct., at 2934 (O'Connor, J., concurring in part and dissenting in part). In Haslip, 499 U.S., at 23, 111 S.Ct., at 1046, the

---

35. Even assuming each repainted BMW suffers a diminution in value of approximately $4,000, the award is 35 times greater than the total damages of all 14 Alabama consumers who purchased repainted BMW's.

36. The ratio here is also dramatically greater than any award that would be permissible under the statutes and proposed statutes summarized in the appendix to Justice Ginsburg's dissenting opinion. Post, at 1618–1620.

37. Conceivably the Alabama Supreme Court's selection of a 500 to 1 ratio was an application of Justice Scalia's identification of one possible reading of the plurality opinion in TXO: any future due process challenge to a punitive damages award could be disposed of with the simple observation that "this is no worse than TXO." 509 U.S., at 472, 113 S.Ct., at 2727 (Scalia, J., concurring in judgment). As we explain in the text, this award is significantly worse than the award in TXO.

Court noted that although the exemplary award was "much in excess of the fine that could be imposed," imprisonment was also authorized in the criminal context.[38] In this case the $2 million economic sanction imposed on BMW is substantially greater than the statutory fines available in Alabama and elsewhere for similar malfeasance.

The maximum civil penalty authorized by the Alabama Legislature for a violation of its Deceptive Trade Practices Act is $2,000;[39] other States authorize more severe sanctions, with the maxima ranging from $5,000 to $10,000.[40] Significantly, some statutes draw a distinction between first offenders and recidivists; thus, in New York the penalty is $50 for a first offense and $250 for subsequent offenses. None of these statutes would provide an out-of-state distributor with fair notice that the first violation—or, indeed the first 14 violations—of its provisions might subject an offender to a multimillion dollar penalty. Moreover, at the time BMW's policy was first challenged, there does not appear to have been any judicial decision in Alabama or elsewhere indicating that application of that policy might give rise to such severe punishment.

The sanction imposed in this case cannot be justified on the ground that it was necessary to deter future misconduct without considering whether less drastic remedies could be expected to achieve that goal. The fact that a multimillion dollar penalty prompted a change in policy sheds no light on the question whether a lesser deterrent would have adequately protected the interests of Alabama consumers. In the absence of a history of noncompliance with known statutory requirements, there is no basis for assuming that a more modest sanction would not have been sufficient to motivate full compliance with the disclosure requirement imposed by the Alabama Supreme Court in this case.

---

38. Although the Court did not address the size of the punitive damages award in Silkwood v. Kerr–McGee Corp., 464 U.S. 238, 104 S.Ct. 615, 78 L.Ed.2d 443 (1984), the dissenters commented on its excessive character, noting that the "$10 million [punitive damages award] that the jury imposed is 100 times greater than the maximum fine that may be imposed ... for a single violation of federal standards" and "more than 10 times greater than the largest single fine that the Commission has ever imposed." Id., at 263, 104 S.Ct., at 629 (Blackmun, J., dissenting). In New York Times Co. v. Sullivan, 376 U.S. 254, 84 S.Ct. 710, 11 L.Ed.2d 686 (1964), the Court observed that the punitive award for libel was "one thousand times greater than the maximum fine provided by the Alabama criminal statute," and concluded that the "fear of damage awards under a rule such as that invoked by the Alabama courts here may be markedly more inhibiting than the fear of prosecution under a criminal statute." Id., at 277, 84 S.Ct., at 724.

39. Ala.Code § 8–19–11(b) (1993).

40. See, e.g., Ark.Code Ann. § 23–112–309(b) (1992) (up to $5,000 for violation of state Motor Vehicle Commission Act that would allow suspension of dealer's license; up to $10,000 for violation of Act that would allow revocation of dealer's license); Fla.Stat. § 320.27(12) (1992) (up to $1,000); Ga.Code Ann. §§ 40–1–5(g), 10–1–397(a) (1994 and Supp.1996) (up to $2,000 administratively; up to $5,000 in superior court); Ind.Code Ann. § 9–23–6–4 (1993) ($50 to $1,000); N.H.Rev.Stat.Ann. §§ 357–C:15, 651:2 (1995 and Supp.1995) (corporate fine of up to $20,000); N.Y.Gen.Bus.Law § 396–p(6) (McKinney Supp.1995) ($50 for first offense; $250 for subsequent offenses).

IV

We assume, as the juries in this case and in the Yates case found, that the undisclosed damage to the new BMW's affected their actual value. Notwithstanding the evidence adduced by BMW in an effort to prove that the repainted cars conformed to the same quality standards as its other cars, we also assume that it knew, or should have known, that as time passed the repainted cars would lose their attractive appearance more rapidly than other BMW's. Moreover, we of course accept the Alabama courts' view that the state interest in protecting its citizens from deceptive trade practices justifies a sanction in addition to the recovery of compensatory damages. We cannot, however, accept the conclusion of the Alabama Supreme Court that BMW's conduct was sufficiently egregious to justify a punitive sanction that is tantamount to a severe criminal penalty.

The fact that BMW is a large corporation rather than an impecunious individual does not diminish its entitlement to fair notice of the demands that the several States impose on the conduct of its business. Indeed, its status as an active participant in the national economy implicates the federal interest in preventing individual States from imposing undue burdens on interstate commerce. While each State has ample power to protect its own consumers, none may use the punitive damages deterrent as a means of imposing its regulatory policies on the entire Nation.

As in Haslip, we are not prepared to draw a bright line marking the limits of a constitutionally acceptable punitive damages award. Unlike that case, however, we are fully convinced that the grossly excessive award imposed in this case transcends the constitutional limit.[41] Whether the appropriate remedy requires a new trial or merely an independent determination by the Alabama Supreme Court of the award necessary to vindicate the economic interests of Alabama consumers is a matter that should be addressed by the state court in the first instance.

The judgment is reversed, and the case is remanded for further proceedings not inconsistent with this opinion.

It is so ordered.

Justice Breyer, with whom Justice O'Connor and Justice Souter join, concurring.

The Alabama state courts have assessed the defendant $2 million in "punitive damages" for having knowingly failed to tell a BMW automo-

---

41. Justice Ginsburg expresses concern that we are "the only federal court policing" this limit. Post, at 1617. The small number of punitive damages questions that we have reviewed in recent years, together with the fact that this is the first case in decades in which we have found that a punitive damages award exceeds the constitutional limit, indicates that this concern is at best premature. In any event, this consideration surely does not justify an abdication of our responsibility to enforce constitutional protections in an extraordinary case such as this one.

bile buyer that, at a cost of $600, it had repainted portions of his new $40,000 car, thereby lowering its potential resale value by about 10%. The Court's opinion, which I join, explains why we have concluded that this award, in this case, was "grossly excessive" in relation to legitimate punitive damages objectives, and hence an arbitrary deprivation of life, liberty, or property in violation of the Due Process Clause. See TXO Production Corp. v. Alliance Resources Corp., 509 U.S. 443, 453, 454, 113 S.Ct. 2711, 2718, 125 L.Ed.2d 366 (1993) (A "grossly excessive" punitive award amounts to an "arbitrary deprivation of property without due process of law") (plurality opinion). Members of this Court have generally thought, however, that if "fair procedures were followed, a judgment that is a product of that process is entitled to a strong presumption of validity." Id., at 457, 113 S.Ct., at 2720. See also Pacific Mut. Life Ins. Co. v. Haslip, 499 U.S. 1, 40–42, 111 S.Ct. 1032, 1054–1056, 113 L.Ed.2d 1 (1991) (Kennedy, J., concurring in judgment). And the Court also has found that punitive damages procedures very similar to those followed here were not, by themselves, fundamentally unfair. Id., at 15–24, 111 S.Ct., at 1041–1047. Thus, I believe it important to explain why this presumption of validity is overcome in this instance.

The reason flows from the Court's emphasis in Haslip upon the constitutional importance of legal standards that provide "reasonable constraints" within which "discretion is exercised," that assure "meaningful and adequate review by the trial court whenever a jury has fixed the punitive damages," and permit "appellate review [that] makes certain that the punitive damages are reasonable in their amount and rational in light of their purpose to punish what has occurred and to deter its repetition." Id., at 20–21, 111 S.Ct., at 1045. See also id., at 18, 111 S.Ct., at 1043 ("[U]nlimited jury discretion—or unlimited judicial discretion for that matter—in the fixing of punitive damages may invite extreme results that jar one's constitutional sensibilities").

This constitutional concern, itself harkening back to the Magna Carta, arises out of the basic unfairness of depriving citizens of life, liberty, or property, through the application, not of law and legal processes, but of arbitrary coercion. Daniels v. Williams, 474 U.S. 327, 331, 106 S.Ct. 662, 665, 88 L.Ed.2d 662 (1986); Dent v. West Virginia, 129 U.S. 114, 123, 9 S.Ct. 231, 233–234, 32 L.Ed. 623 (1889). Requiring the application of law, rather than a decisionmaker's caprice, does more than simply provide citizens notice of what actions may subject them to punishment; it also helps to assure the uniform general treatment of similarly situated persons that is the essence of law itself. See Railway Express Agency, Inc. v. New York, 336 U.S. 106, 112, 69 S.Ct. 463, 466–467, 93 L.Ed. 533 (1949) (Jackson, J., concurring) ("[T]here is no more effective practical guaranty against arbitrary and unreasonable government than to require that the principles of law which officials would impose upon a minority must be imposed generally").

Legal standards need not be precise in order to satisfy this constitutional concern. See Haslip, supra, at 20, 111 S.Ct., at 1044 (comparing punitive damages standards to such legal standards as "reasonable care," "due diligence," and "best interests of the child") (internal quotation marks omitted). But they must offer some kind of constraint upon a jury or court's discretion, and thus protection against purely arbitrary behavior. The standards the Alabama courts applied here are vague and open-ended to the point where they risk arbitrary results. In my view, although the vagueness of those standards does not, by itself, violate due process, see Haslip, supra, it does invite the kind of scrutiny the Court has given the particular verdict before us. See id., at 18, 111 S.Ct., at 1043 ("[C]oncerns of ... adequate guidance from the court when the case is tried to a jury properly enter into the constitutional calculus"); TXO, supra, at 475, 113 S.Ct., at 2729 ("[I]t cannot be denied that the lack of clear guidance heightens the risk that arbitrariness, passion, or bias will replace dispassionate deliberation as the basis for the jury's verdict") (O'Connor, J., dissenting). This is because the standards, as the Alabama Supreme Court authoritatively interpreted them here, provided no significant constraints or protection against arbitrary results. ...

The upshot is that the rules that purport to channel discretion in this kind of case, here did not do so in fact. That means that the award in this case was both (a) the product of a system of standards that did not significantly constrain a court's, and hence a jury's, discretion in making that award; and (b) was grossly excessive in light of the State's legitimate punitive damages objectives.

The first of these reasons has special importance where courts review a jury-determined punitive damages award. That is because one cannot expect to direct jurors like legislators through the ballot box; nor can one expect those jurors to interpret law like judges, who work within a discipline and hierarchical organization that normally promotes roughly uniform interpretation and application of the law. Yet here Alabama expects jurors to act, at least a little, like legislators or judges, for it permits them, to a certain extent, to create public policy and to apply that policy, not to compensate a victim, but to achieve a policy-related objective outside the confines of the particular case.

To the extent that neither clear legal principles, nor fairly obvious historical or community-based standards (defining, say, especially egregious behavior) significantly constrain punitive damages awards, is there not a substantial risk of outcomes so arbitrary that they become difficult to square with the Constitution's assurance, to every citizen, of the law's protection? The standards here, as authoritatively interpreted, in my view, make this threat real and not theoretical. And, in these unusual circumstances, where legal standards offer virtually no constraint, I believe that this lack of constraining standards warrants this Court's detailed examination of the award.

The second reason—the severe disproportionality between the award and the legitimate punitive damages objectives—reflects a judgment about a matter of degree. I recognize that it is often difficult to determine just when a punitive award exceeds an amount reasonably related to a State's legitimate interests, or when that excess is so great as to amount to a matter of constitutional concern. Yet whatever the difficulties of drawing a precise line, once we examine the award in this case, it is not difficult to say that this award lies on the line's far side. The severe lack of proportionality between the size of the award and the underlying punitive damages objectives shows that the award falls into the category of "gross excessiveness" set forth in this Court's prior cases.

These two reasons taken together overcome what would otherwise amount to a "strong presumption of validity." TXO, 509 U.S., at 457, 113 S.Ct., at 2720. And, for those two reasons, I conclude that the award in this unusual case violates the basic guarantee of nonarbitrary governmental behavior that the Due Process Clause provides.   . . .

JUSTICE SCALIA, with whom JUSTICE THOMAS joins, dissenting.

Today we see the latest manifestation of this Court's recent and increasingly insistent "concern about punitive damages that 'run wild.'" Pacific Mut. Life Ins. Co. v. Haslip, 499 U.S. 1, 18, 111 S.Ct. 1032, 1043, 113 L.Ed.2d 1 (1991). Since the Constitution does not make that concern any of our business, the Court's activities in this area are an unjustified incursion into the province of state governments.   . . .

II

One might understand the Court's eagerness to enter this field, rather than leave it with the state legislatures, if it had something useful to say. In fact, however, its opinion provides virtually no guidance to legislatures, and to state and federal courts, as to what a "constitutionally proper" level of punitive damages might be.   . . .

The relationship between judicial application of the new "guideposts" and jury findings poses a real problem for the Court, since as a matter of logic there is no more justification for ignoring the jury's determination as to how reprehensible petitioner's conduct was (i.e., how much it deserves to be punished), than there is for ignoring its determination that it was reprehensible at all (i.e., that the wrong was willful and punitive damages are therefore recoverable). That the issue has been framed in terms of a constitutional right against unreasonably excessive awards should not obscure the fact that the logical and necessary consequence of the Court's approach is the recognition of a constitutional right against unreasonably imposed awards as well. The elevation of "fairness" in punishment to a principle of "substantive due process" means that every punitive award unreasonably imposed is unconstitutional; such an award is by definition excessive, since it attaches a penalty to conduct undeserving of punishment. Indeed, if the

Court is correct, it must be that every claim that a state jury's award of compensatory damages is "unreasonable" (because not supported by the evidence) amounts to an assertion of constitutional injury. See TXO, supra, at 471, 113 S.Ct., at 2727 (Scalia, J. concurring in judgment). And the same would be true for determinations of liability. By today's logic, every dispute as to evidentiary sufficiency in a state civil suit poses a question of constitutional moment, subject to review in this Court. That is a stupefying proposition.

For the foregoing reasons, I respectfully dissent.

JUSTICE GINSBURG, with whom THE CHIEF JUSTICE joins, dissenting.

The Court, I am convinced, unnecessarily and unwisely ventures into territory traditionally within the States' domain, and does so in the face of reform measures recently adopted or currently under consideration in legislative arenas. The Alabama Supreme Court, in this case, endeavored to follow this Court's prior instructions; and, more recently, Alabama's highest court has installed further controls on awards of punitive damages .... I would therefore leave the state court's judgment undisturbed, and resist unnecessary intrusion into an area dominantly of state concern. ....

B

The Court finds Alabama's $2 million award not simply excessive, but grossly so, and therefore unconstitutional. The decision leads us further into territory traditionally within the States' domain, and commits the Court, now and again, to correct "misapplication of a properly stated rule of law." But cf. S.Ct. Rule 10 ("A petition for a writ of certiorari is rarely granted when the asserted error consists of erroneous factual findings or the misapplication of a properly stated rule of law."). The Court is not well equipped for this mission. Tellingly, the Court repeats that it brings to the task no "mathematical formula," ante, at 1602, no "categorical approach," ante, at 1602, no "bright line," ante, at 1604. It has only a vague concept of substantive due process, a "raised eyebrow" test, see ante, at 1603, as its ultimate guide.

In contrast to habeas corpus review under 28 U.S.C. § 2254, the Court will work at this business alone. It will not be aided by the federal district courts and courts of appeals. It will be the only federal court policing the area. The Court's readiness to superintend state court punitive damages awards is all the more puzzling in view of the Court's longstanding reluctance to countenance review, even by courts of appeals, of the size of verdicts returned by juries in federal district court proceedings. See generally 11 C. Wright, A. Miller, & M. Kane, Federal Practice and Procedure § 2820 (2d ed. 1995). And the reexamination prominent in state courts [1] and in legislative arenas, see Appendix, infra, ... serves to underscore why the Court's enterprise is undue.

---

1. See, e.g., Distinctive Printing and Packaging Co. v. Cox, 232 Neb. 846, 857, 443 N.W.2d 566, 574 (1989) (per curiam) ("[P]unitive, vindictive, or exemplary dam-

For the reasons stated, I dissent from this Court's disturbance of the judgment the Alabama Supreme Court has made.

APPENDIX TO DISSENTING OPINION OF GINSBURG, J. STATE LEGISLATIVE ACTIVITY REGARDING PUNITIVE DAMAGES

State legislatures have in the hopper or have enacted a variety of measures to curtail awards of punitive damages. At least one state legislature has prohibited punitive damages altogether, unless explicitly provided by statute. See N.H.Rev.Stat.Ann. § 507:16 (1994). We set out in this appendix some of the several controls enacted or under consideration in the States. The measures surveyed are: (1) caps on awards; (2) provisions for payment of sums to state agencies rather than to plaintiffs; and (3) mandatory bifurcated trials with separate proceedings for punitive damages determinations.

I. Caps on Punitive Damages Awards

• Colorado—Colo.Rev.Stat. §§ 13–21–102(1)(a) and (3) (1987) (as a main rule, caps punitive damages at amount of actual damages).

• Connecticut—Conn.Gen.Stat. § 52–240b (1995) (caps punitive damages at twice compensatory damages in products liability cases).

• Delaware—H.R. 237, 138th Gen.Ass. (introduced May 17, 1995) (would cap punitive damages at greater of three times compensatory damages, or $250,000).

• Florida—Fla.Stat. §§ 768.73(1)(a) and (b) (Supp.1992) (in general, caps punitive damages at three times compensatory damages).

• Georgia—Ga.Code Ann. § 51–12–5.1 (Supp.1995) (caps punitive damages at $250,000 in some tort actions; prohibits multiple awards stemming from the same predicate conduct in products liability actions).

• Illinois—H. 20, 89th Gen.Ass.1995–1996 Reg.Sess. (enacted Mar. 9, 1995) (caps punitive damages at three times economic damages).

ages contravene Neb. Const. art. VII, § 5, and thus are not allowed in this jurisdiction."); Santana v. Registrars of Voters of Worcester, 398 Mass. 862, 502 N.E.2d 132 (1986) (punitive damages are not permitted, unless expressly authorized by statute); Fisher Properties, Inc. v. Arden–Mayfair, Inc., 106 Wash.2d 826, 852, 726 P.2d 8, 23 (1986) (en banc) (same). In Life Ins. Co. of Georgia v. Johnson, No. 1940357 (Nov. 17, 1995), the Alabama Supreme Court revised the State's regime for assessments of punitive damages. Henceforth, trials will be bifurcated. Initially, juries will be instructed to determine liability and the amount of compensatory damages, if any; also, the jury is to return a special verdict on the question whether a punitive damages award is warranted. If the jury answers yes to the punitive damages question, the trial will be resumed for the presentation of evidence and instructions relevant to the amount appropriate to award as punitive damages. After postverdict trial court review and subsequent appellate review, the amount of the final punitive damages judgment will be paid into the trial court. The trial court will then order payment of litigation expenses, including the plaintiff's attorney fees, and instruct the clerk to divide the remainder equally between the plaintiff and the State General Fund. The provision for payment to the State General Fund is applicable to all judgments not yet satisfied, and therefore would apply to the judgment in Gore's case.

• Indiana—H. 1741, 109th Reg.Sess. (enacted Apr. 26, 1995) (caps punitive damages at greater of three times compensatory damages, or $50,000).

• Kansas—Kan.Stat.Ann. §§ 60–3701(e) and (f) (1994) (in general, caps punitive damages at lesser of defendant's annual gross income, or $5 million).

• Maryland—S. 187, 1995 Leg.Sess. (introduced Jan. 27, 1995) (in general, would cap punitive damages at four times compensatory damages).

• Minnesota—S. 489, 79th Leg.Sess., 1995 Reg.Sess. (introduced Feb. 16, 1995) (would require reasonable relationship between compensatory and punitive damages).

• Nevada—Nev.Rev.Stat. § 42.005(1) (1993) (caps punitive damages at three times compensatory damages if compensatory damages equal $100,000 or more, and at $300,000 if the compensatory damages are less than $100,000).

• New Jersey—S. 1496, 206th Leg., 2d Ann.Sess. (1995) (caps punitive damages at greater of five times compensatory damages, or $350,-000, in certain tort cases).

• North Dakota—N.D.Cent.Code § 32–03.2–11(4) (Supp.1995) (caps punitive damages at greater of two times compensatory damages, or $250,000).

• Oklahoma—Okla Stat., Tit. 23, §§ 9.1(B)–(D) (Supp.1996) (caps punitive damages at greater of $100,000, or actual damages, if jury finds defendant guilty of reckless disregard; and at greatest of $500,000, twice actual damages, or the benefit accruing to defendant from the injury-causing conduct, if jury finds that defendant has acted intentionally and maliciously).

• Texas—S. 25, 74th Reg.Sess. (enacted Apr. 20, 1995) (caps punitive damages at twice economic damages, plus up to $750,000 additional noneconomic damages).

• Virginia—Va.Code Ann. § 8.01–38.1 (1992) (caps punitive damages at $350,000).

II. ALLOCATION OF PUNITIVE DAMAGES TO STATE AGENCIES

• Arizona—H.R. 2279, 42d Leg., 1st Reg.Sess. (introduced Jan. 12, 1995) (would allocate punitive damages to a victims' assistance fund, in specified circumstances).

• Florida—Fla.Stat. §§ 768.73(2)(a)–(b) (Supp.1992) (allocates 35% of punitive damages to General Revenue Fund or Public Medical Assistance Trust Fund); see Gordon v. State, 585 So.2d 1033, 1035–1038 (Fla.App.1991), aff'd, 608 So.2d 800 (Fla.1992) (upholding provision against due process challenge).

• Georgia—Ga.Code Ann. § 51–12–5.1(e)(2) (Supp.1995) (allocates 75% of punitive damages, less a proportionate part of litigation costs, including counsel fees, to state treasury); see Mack Trucks, Inc. v. Conkle, 263 Ga. 539, 540–543, 436 S.E.2d 635, 637–639 (Ga.1993) (upholding provision against constitutional challenge).

• Illinois—Ill.Comp.Stat. ch. 735, § 5/2–1207 (1994) (permits court to apportion punitive damages among plaintiff, plaintiff's attorney, and Illinois Department of Rehabilitation Services).

• Indiana—H. 1741, 109th Reg.Sess. (enacted Apr. 26, 1995) (subject to statutory exceptions, allocates 75% of punitive damages to a compensation fund for violent crime victims).

• Iowa—Iowa Code § 668A.1(2)(b) (1987) (in described circumstances, allocates 75% of punitive damages, after payment of costs and counsel fees, to a civil reparations trust fund); see Shepherd Components, Inc. v. Brice Petrides–Donohue & Assoc., Inc., 473 N.W.2d 612, 619 (Iowa 1991) (upholding provision against constitutional challenge).

• Kansas—Kan.Stat.Ann. § 60–3402(e) (1994) (allocates 50% of punitive damages in medical malpractice cases to state treasury).

• Missouri—Mo.Rev.Stat. § 537.675 (1994) (allocates 50% of punitive damages, after payment of expenses and counsel fees, to Tort Victims' Compensation Fund).

• Montana—H. 71, 54th Leg.Sess. (introduced Jan. 2, 1995) (would allocate 48% of punitive damages to state university system and 12% to school for the deaf and blind).

• New Jersey—S. 291, 206th Leg., 1994–1995 1st Reg.Sess. (introduced Jan. 18, 1994); A. 148, 206th Leg., 1994–1995 1st Reg.Sess. (introduced Jan. 11, 1994) (would allocate 75% of punitive damages to New Jersey Health Care Trust Fund).

• New Mexico—H. 1017, 42d Leg., 1st Sess. (introduced Feb. 16, 1995) (would allocate punitive damages to Low–Income Attorney Services Fund).

• Oregon—S. 482, 68th Leg.Ass. (enacted July 19, 1995) (amending Ore.Rev.Stat. §§ 18.540 and 30.925, and repealing Ore.Rev.Stat. § 41.315) (allocates 60% of punitive damages to Criminal Injuries Compensation Account).

• Utah—Utah Code Ann. § 78–18–1(3) (1992) (allocates 50% of punitive damages in excess of $20,000 to state treasury).

III. MANDATORY BIFURCATION OF LIABILITY AND PUNITIVE DAMAGES DETERMINATIONS

• California—Cal.Civ.Code Ann. § 3295(d) (West Supp.1995) (requires bifurcation, on application of defendant, of liability and damages phases of trials in which punitive damages are requested).

- Delaware—H.R. 237, 138th Gen.Ass. (introduced May 17, 1995) (would require, at request of any party, a separate proceeding for determination of punitive damages).

- Georgia—Ga.Code Ann. § 51–12–5.1(d) (Supp.1995) (in all cases in which punitive damages are claimed, liability for punitive damages is tried first, then amount of punitive damages).

- Illinois—H. 20, 89th Gen.Assembly, 1995–1996 Reg.Sess. (enacted Mar. 9, 1995) (mandates, upon defendant's request, separate proceeding for determination of punitive damages).

- Kansas—Kan.Stat.Ann. § 60–3701(a)–(b) (1994) (trier of fact determines defendant's liability for punitive damages, then court determines amount of such damages).

- Missouri—Mo.Rev.Stat. §§ 510.263(1) and (3) (1994) (mandates bifurcated proceedings, on request of any party, for jury to determine first whether defendant is liable for punitive damages, then amount of punitive damages).

- Montana—Mont.Code Ann. § 27–1–221(7) (1995) (upon finding defendant liable for punitive damages, jury determines the amount in separate proceeding).

- Nevada—Nev.Rev.Stat. § 42.005(3) (1993) (if jury determines that punitive damages will be awarded, jury then determines amount in separate proceeding).

- New Jersey—N.J.Stat.Ann. §§ 2A:58C–5(b) and (d) (West 1987) (mandates separate proceedings for determination of compensatory and punitive damages).

- North Dakota—N.D.Cent.Code § 32.03.2–11(2) (Supp.1995) (upon request of either party, trier of fact determines whether compensatory damages will be awarded before determining punitive damages liability and amount).

- Ohio—Ohio Rev.Code Ann. § 2315.21(C)(2) (1995) (if trier of fact determines that defendant is liable for punitive damages, court determines the amount of those damages).

- Oklahoma—Okla.Stat., Tit. 23, §§ 9.1(B)–(D) (Supp.1995–1996) (requires separate jury proceedings for punitive damages); S. 443, 45th Leg., 1st Reg.Sess. (introduced Jan. 31, 1995) (would require courts to strike requests for punitive damages before trial, unless plaintiff presents prima facie evidence at least 30 days before trial to sustain such damages; provide for bifurcated jury trial on request of defendant; and permit punitive damages only if compensatory damages are awarded).

- Virginia—H. 1070, 1994–1995 Reg.Sess. (introduced Jan. 25, 1994) (would require separate proceedings in which court determines that punitive damages are appropriate and trier of fact determines amount of punitive damages).

NOTES

(1) Eight days after the principal case was decided, the Supreme Court rendered decisions in six punitive damages cases: Fraidin v. Weitzman, ___ U.S. ___, 116 S.Ct. 1846, 134 L.Ed.2d 948 (1996), Honda v. Oberg, ___ U.S. ___, 116 S.Ct. 1847, 134 L.Ed.2d 948 (1996), Wolfberg v. Greenberg, ___ U.S. ___, 116 S.Ct. 12, 132 L.Ed.2d 897 (1995), Apache Corp. v. Moore, ___ U.S. ___, 116 S.Ct. 901, 133 L.Ed.2d 835 (1996), Ford v. Sperau, ___ U.S. ___, 116 S.Ct. 1843, 134 L.Ed.2d 945 (1996), and Oxy USA Inc. v. Continental Trend, ___ U.S. ___, 116 S.Ct. 1843, 134 L.Ed.2d 945 (1996). In three, it vacated for reconsideration in the light of the principal cases; in the other three, it denied *certiorari*.

(2) What do you think of the criteria considered by the Court? Would you apply different or additional ones? Should the Court have ruled that, in determining the appropriate measure of punishment, only the repainting of the car at issue and not that of any other car should be considered?

(3) What about the notion that any punitive damages awarded, after deduction of an award of costs, including a reasonable attorney's fee (if deemed appropriate), should go to the state?

(4) Or should the legislature put a general cap on punitive damages—for example, by limiting them to a legislatively prescribed multiple of compensatory damages?

(5) Civil law countries do not permit the award of punitive damages as such, except in very limited legislatively defined circumstances, but leave the courts considerable freedom in determining the amount of damages. It has been noted that civil law courts use this freedom by awarding larger amounts in cases in which the conduct of the wrongdoer was particularly reprehensible. However, if the civil law court states that it took the reprehensible character of the conduct into account, its judgment will be reversed on appeal. Should the same regime be adopted in the United States, especially since juries have considerable leeway in finding the amount of compensatory damages?

(6) To what extent does the award of punitive damages put American producers at a competitive disadvantage with producers elsewhere when they are sued for defects of products marketed outside the United States? Should there be a statutory *forum non conveniens* rule for such cases? See Texas Civ. Practice & Remedies Code Section 71.031(a)(3) (1985).

(7) If you were asked to draw a federal statute dealing comprehensively with the award of punitive damages, what provisions would you put into it? Would a proposal of such a general statute have a greater chance of political survival than the recently proposed statute dealing with security frauds alone? See Private Securities Litigation Reform Act of 1995, P.L. 104–67, 1995 HR 1058, 109 Stat. 737.

(8) In Gasperini v. Center for Humanities, Inc., ___ U.S. ___, 116 S.Ct. 2211, 135 L.Ed.2d 659 (1996), the Court considered two other aspects of the excessiveness problem. In this diversity action, a jury returned a verdict of $450,000 to a journalist whose 300 photographic slides were lost. Because the case was tried under New York law, the Second Circuit applied a N.Y. State tort reform statute which requires courts to determine whether such verdicts "deviat[e] materially from what would be reasonable compensation." The court found the award unreasonable and ordered a new trial unless Gasperini agreed to accept $100,-

000. The Supreme Court first addressed the question whether New York's review procedure was applicable in federal court. It held that under Erie Railroad Co. v. Tompkins, 304 U.S. 64, 58 S.Ct. 817, 82 L.Ed. 1188 (1938), discussed in Chapter Seven, infra, it was applicable. Next, the Court considered whether this review was barred by the Seventh Amendment's reexamination clause. Reasoning that trial court review was "in keeping with historic understanding" of the Seventh Amendment, the Court held that the statutory procedure should be applied at trial, but that federal appellate courts can determine only whether the trial court abused it discretion. See p. 228 infra.

F. ATTORNEY'S FEES

[Insert at page 118, following Note (10):]

(11) The prevailing American rule of not requiring the loser to pay the winner's attorney's fees indubitably has led to the commencement of lawsuits that would not have been brought if the loser were required to pay the attorney's fees of the winner. Among these lawsuits are those seeking to stifle public criticism, commonly called Slapps (strategic lawsuits against public participation). Such suits have prompted enactment of anti-Slapp laws in such states as California, Delaware, Massachusetts, Minnesota, Nebraska, Nevada, New York, Rhode Island and Washington. Other states are considering adoption of such laws. Anti–Slapp laws typically provide for the successful defendant to recover attorney's fees or even punitive damages. On these developments, see Pring, G. & Canan, P., Slapps: Getting Sued for Speeding Out Temple University Press (1944). For some examples of Slapps, see Miller, J., States Have to Keep Plaintiffs from Using Courts to Muzzle Critics, N.Y. Times, June 11, 1996, A22.

Chapter Four

PROVISIONAL REMEDIES

SECTION 2. ATTACHMENT AND GARNISHMENT

[Insert on page 145, after the Notes:]

CONNECTICUT v. DOEHR

Supreme Court of the United States, 1991.
501 U.S. 1, 111 S.Ct. 2105, 115 L.Ed.2d 1.

JUSTICE WHITE delivered an opinion, Parts I, II, and III of which are the opinion of the Court.*

This case requires us to determine whether a state statute that authorizes prejudgment attachment of real estate without prior notice or hearing, without a showing of extraordinary circumstances, and without a requirement that the person seeking the attachment post a bond, satisfies the Due Process Clause of the Fourteenth Amendment. We hold that, as applied to this case, it does not.

I

On March 15, 1988, Petitioner John F. DiGiovanni submitted an application to the Connecticut Superior Court for an attachment in the amount of $75,000 on respondent Brian K. Doehr's home in Meridan, Connecticut. DiGiovanni took this step in conjunction with a civil action for assault and battery that he was seeking to institute against Doehr in the same court. The suit did not involve Doehr's real estate nor did DiGiovanni have any pre-existing interest either in Doehr's home or any of his other property.

Connecticut law authorizes prejudgment attachment of real estate without affording prior notice or the opportunity for a prior hearing to the individual whose property is subject to the attachment. The State's prejudgment remedy statute provides, in relevant part:

"The court or a judge of the court may allow the prejudgment remedy to be issued by an attorney without hearing as provided in sections 52–278c and 52–278d upon verification by oath of the plaintiff or of some competent affiant, that there is probable cause to sustain the validity of the plaintiff's claims and (1) that the prejudgment remedy requested is for an attachment of real property...."

---

* Footnotes omitted.

29

The statute does not require the plaintiff to post a bond to insure the payment of damages that the defendant may suffer should the attachment prove wrongfully issued or the claim prove unsuccessful.

As required, DiGiovanni submitted an affidavit in support of his application. In five one-sentence paragraphs, DiGiovanni stated that the facts set forth in his previously submitted complaint were true; that "I was willfully, wantonly and maliciously assaulted by the defendant, Brian K. Doehr"; that "[s]aid assault and battery broke my left wrist and further caused an ecchymosis to my right eye, as well as other injuries"; and that "I have further expended sums of money for medical care and treatment." The affidavit concluded with the statement, "In my opinion, the foregoing facts are sufficient to show that there is probable cause that judgment will be rendered for the plaintiff."

On the strength of these submissions the Superior Court judge, by an order dated March 17, found "probable cause to sustain the validity of the plaintiff's claim" and ordered the attachment on Doehr's home "to the value of $75,000." The sheriff attached the property four days later, on March 21. Only after this did Doehr receive notice of the attachment. He also had yet to be served with the complaint, which is ordinarily necessary for an action to commence in Connecticut.... As the statute further required, the attachment notice informed Doehr that he had the right to a hearing: (1) to claim that no probable cause existed to sustain the claim; (2) to request that the attachment be vacated, modified, or that a bond be substituted; or (3) to claim that some portion of the property was exempt from execution. Conn.Gen.Stat. § 52–278e(b) (1991). Rather than pursue these options, Doehr filed suit against DiGiovanni in Federal District Court, claiming that § 52–278e(a)(1) was unconstitutional under the Due Process Clause of the Fourteenth Amendment. The District Court upheld the statute and granted summary judgment in favor of DiGiovanni.... [T]he Second Circuit reversed....

II

With this case we return to the question of what process must be afforded by a state statute enabling an individual to enlist the aid of the State to deprive another of his or her property by means of the prejudgment attachment or similar procedure. Our cases reflect the numerous variations this type of remedy can entail.

* * *

These cases "underscore the truism that '[d]ue process, unlike some legal rules, is not a technical conception with a fixed content unrelated to time, place and circumstances.'" Mathews v. Eldridge, [424 U.S. 319,] 334, [96 S.Ct. 893,] 902 [(1976)] (quoting Cafeteria Workers v. McElroy, 367 U.S. 886, 895, 81 S.Ct. 1743, 1748, 6 L.Ed.2d 1230 (1961)). In *Mathews,* we drew upon our prejudgment remedy decisions to determine what process is due when the government itself seeks to effect a deprivation on its own initiative. *Mathews,* 424 U.S., at 334, 96 S.Ct., at 902. That analysis resulted in the now familiar threefold inquiry requiring consideration of "the private interest that will be affected by the official action"; "the risk of an erroneous deprivation of such interest through the procedures used, and the probable value, if any, of additional or substitute safeguards"; and lastly "the Government's interest, including the function involved and the fiscal and administrative burdens that the additional or substitute procedural requirement would entail." Id., at 335, 96 S.Ct., at 903.

Here the inquiry is similar but the focus is different. Prejudgment remedy statutes ordinarily apply to disputes between private parties rather than between an individual and the government. Such enactments are designed to enable one of the parties to "make use of state procedures with the overt, significant assistance of state officials," and they undoubtedly involve state action "substantial enough to implicate the Due Process Clause." Tulsa Professional Collection Services, Inc. v. Pope, 485 U.S. 478, 486, 108 S.Ct. 1340, 1345, 99 L.Ed.2d 565 (1988). Nonetheless, any burden that increasing procedural safeguards entails primarily affects not the government, but the party seeking control of the other's property. See Fuentes v. Shevin, supra, 407 U.S. [67,] 99–101, 92 S.Ct. [1983,] 2003–2005 [(1972)] (WHITE, J., dissenting). For this type of case, therefore, the relevant inquiry requires, as in *Mathews,* first, consideration of the private interest that will be affected by the prejudgment measure; second, an examination of the risk of erroneous deprivation through the procedures under attack and the probable value of additional or alternative safeguards; and third, in contrast to *Mathews,* principal attention to the interest of the party seeking the prejudgment remedy, with, nonetheless, due regard for any ancillary interest the government may have in providing the procedure or forgoing the added burden of providing greater protections.

We now consider the *Mathews* factors in determining the adequacy of the procedures before us, first with regard to the safeguards of notice and a prior hearing, and then in relation to the protection of a bond.

III

We agree with the Court of Appeals that the property interests that attachment affects are significant. For a property owner like Doehr, attachment ordinarily clouds title; impairs the ability to sell or otherwise alienate the property; taints any credit rating; reduces the chance of obtaining a home equity loan or additional mortgage; and can even place an existing mortgage in technical default where there is an insecurity clause. Nor does Connecticut deny that any of these consequences occurs. Instead, the State correctly points out that these effects do not amount to a complete, physical, or permanent deprivation of real property; their impact is less than the perhaps temporary total deprivation of household goods or wages.... But the Court has never held that only such extreme deprivations trigger due process concern. See Buchanan v. Warley, 245 U.S. 60, 74, 38 S.Ct. 16, 18, 62 L.Ed. 149 (1917). To the contrary, our cases show that even the temporary or partial impairments to property rights that attachments, liens, and similar encumbrances entail are sufficient to merit due process protection. Without doubt, state procedures for creating and enforcing attachments, as with liens, "are subject to the strictures of due process." Peralta v. Heights Medical Center, Inc., 485 U.S. 80, 85, 108 S.Ct. 896, 899, 99 L.Ed.2d 75 (1988) (citing *Mitchell,* supra, 416 U.S., at 604, 94 S.Ct., at 1898; Hodge v. Muscatine County, 196 U.S. 276, 281, 25 S.Ct. 237, 239, 49 L.Ed. 477 (1905)).

We also agree with the Court of Appeals that the risk of erroneous deprivation that the State permits here is substantial. By definition, attachment statutes premise a deprivation of property on one ultimate factual contingency—the award of damages to the plaintiff which the defendant may not be able to satisfy.... For attachments before judgment, Connecticut mandates that this determination be made by means of a procedural inquiry that asks whether "there is probable cause to sustain the validity of the plaintiff's claim." Conn.Gen.Stat. § 52–278e(a). The statute elsewhere defines the validity of the claim in terms of the likelihood "that judgment will be rendered in the matter in favor of the plaintiff." Conn.Gen.Stat. § 52–278c(a)(2) (1991).... What probable cause means in this context, however, remains obscure. The State initially took the position, as did the dissent below, that the statute requires a plaintiff to show the objective likelihood of the suit's success. Brief for Petitioner 12.... DiGiovanni, citing ambiguous state cases, reads the provision as requiring no more than that a plaintiff demonstrate a subjective good faith belief that the suit will succeed. Brief for Respondent 25–26.... At oral argument, the State shifted its position to argue that the statute requires something akin to the plaintiff stating a claim with sufficient facts to survive a motion to dismiss.

We need not resolve this confusion since the statute presents too great a risk of erroneous deprivation under any of these interpretations. If the statute demands inquiry into the sufficiency of the complaint, or, still less, the plaintiff's good-faith belief that the complaint is sufficient, requirement of a complaint and a factual affidavit would permit a court to make these minimal determinations. But neither inquiry adequately reduces the risk of erroneous deprivation. Permitting a court to authorize attachment merely because the plaintiff believes the defendant is liable, or because the plaintiff can make out a facially valid complaint, would permit the deprivation of the defendant's property when the claim would fail to convince a jury, when it rested on factual allegations that were sufficient to state a cause of action but which the defendant would dispute, or in the case of a mere good-faith standard, even when the complaint failed to state a claim upon which relief could be granted. The potential for unwarranted attachment in these situations is self-evident and too great to satisfy the requirements of due process absent any countervailing consideration.

Even if the provision requires the plaintiff to demonstrate, and the judge to find, probable cause to believe that judgment will be rendered in favor of the plaintiff, the risk of error was substantial in this case. As the record shows, and as the State concedes, only a skeletal affidavit need be and was filed. The State urges that the reviewing judge normally reviews the complaint as well, but concedes that the complaint may also be conclusory. It is self-evident that the judge could make no realistic assessment concerning the likelihood of an action's success based upon these one-sided, self-serving, and conclusory submissions. And as the Court of Appeals said, in a case like this involving an alleged assault, even a detailed affidavit would give only the plaintiff's version of the confrontation. Unlike determining the existence of a debt or delinquent payments, the issue does not concern "ordinarily uncomplicated matters that lend themselves to documentary proof." *Mitchell*, 416 U.S., at 609, 94 S.Ct., at 1901. The likelihood of error that results illustrates that "fairness can rarely be obtained by secret, one-sided determination of facts decisive of rights.... [And n]o better instrument has been devised for arriving at truth than to give a person in jeopardy of serious loss notice of the case against him and an opportunity to meet it." Joint Anti–Fascist Refugee Committee v. McGrath, 341 U.S. 123, 170–172, 71 S.Ct. 624, 647–649, 95 L.Ed. 817 (1951) (Frankfurter, J., concurring).

What safeguards the State does afford do not adequately reduce this risk. Connecticut points out that the statute also provides an "expeditiou[s]" postattachment adversary hearing, § 52–278e(c); notice for such a hearing, § 52–278e(b); judicial review of an adverse decision, § 52–278l(a); and a double damages action if the original suit is commenced without probable cause, § 52–568(a)(1). Similar considerations were present in *Mitchell* where we upheld Louisiana's sequestration statute despite the lack of predeprivation notice and hearing. But in *Mitchell*, the plaintiff had a vendor's lien to protect, the risk of error was minimal because the likelihood of recovery involved uncomplicated matters that lent themselves to documentary proof, *Mitchell*, supra, 416 U.S., at 609–610, 94 S.Ct., at 1901, and plaintiff was required to put up a bond. None of these factors diminishing the need for a predeprivation hearing is present in this case. It is true that a later hearing might negate the presence of probable cause, but this would not cure the temporary deprivation that an earlier hearing might have prevented. "The Fourteenth Amendment draws no bright lines around three-day, 10–day or 50–day deprivations of property. Any significant taking of property by the State is within the purview of the Due Process Clause." *Fuentes*, 407 U.S., at 86, 92 S.Ct., at 1997.

Finally, we conclude that the interests in favor of an ex parte attachment, particularly the interests of the plaintiff, are too minimal to supply such a consideration here. Plaintiff had no existing interest in Doehr's real estate when he sought the attachment. His only interest in attaching the property was to ensure the availability of assets to satisfy his judgment if he prevailed on the merits of his action. Yet there was no allegation that Doehr was about to transfer or encumber his real estate or take any other action during the pendency of the action that would render his real estate unavailable to satisfy a judgment. Our cases have recognized such a properly supported claim would be an exigent circumstance permitting postponing any notice or hearing until after the attachment is effected. See *Mitchell,* supra, 416 U.S., at 609, 94 S.Ct., at 1901; *Fuentes,* supra, 407 U.S., at 90–92, 92 S.Ct., at 1999–2000.... Absent such allegations, however, the plaintiff's interest in attaching the property does not justify the burdening of Doehr's ownership rights without a hearing to determine the likelihood of recovery.

* * *

IV

A

Although a majority of the Court does not reach the issue, Justices Marshall, Stevens, O'Connor, and I deem it appropriate to consider whether due process also requires the plaintiff to post a bond or other security in addition to requiring a hearing or showing of some exigency.

As noted, the impairments to property rights that attachments affect merit due process protection. Several consequences can be severe, such as the default of a homeowner's mortgage. In the present context, it need only be added that we have repeatedly recognized the utility of a bond in protecting property rights affected by the mistaken award of prejudgment remedies.... Without a bond, at the time of attachment, the danger that these property rights may be wrongfully deprived remains unacceptably high even with such safeguards as a hearing or exigency requirement. The need for a bond is especially apparent where extraordinary circumstances justify an attachment with no more than the plaintiff's ex parte assertion of a claim....

But the need for a bond does not end here. A defendant's property rights remain at undue risk even when there has been an adversarial hearing to determine the plaintiff's likelihood of recovery. At best, a court's initial assessment of each party's case cannot produce more than an educated prediction as to who will win. This is especially true when, as here, the nature of the claim makes any accurate prediction elusive....

The State stresses its double damages remedy for suits that are commenced without probable cause. Conn.Gen.Stat. § 52–568(a)(1). This remedy, however, fails to make up for the lack of a bond. As an initial matter, the meaning of "probable cause" in this provision is no more clear here than it was in the attachment provision itself.... Problems persist even if the plaintiff's ultimate failure permits recovery. At best a defendant must await a decision on the merits of the plaintiff's complaint, even assuming that a § 52–568(a)(1) action may be brought as a counterclaim.... Settlement, under Connecticut law, precludes seeking the damages remedy, a fact that encourages the use of attachments as a tactical device to pressure an opponent to capitulate. Blake v. Levy, 191 Conn. 257, 464 A.2d 52 (1983). An attorney's advice that there is probable cause to commence an action constitutes a complete defense, even if the advice was unsound or erroneous. Vandersluis v. Weil, 176 Conn. 353, 361, 407 A.2d 982, 987 (1978). Finally, there is no guarantee that the original plaintiff will have adequate assets to satisfy an award that the defendant may win.

* * *

[Concurring opinions omitted.]

NOTE

The right to notice and a hearing under the Due Process clause was revisited in Gilbert v. Homar, ___ U.S. ___, 117 S.Ct. 1807, 138 L.Ed.2d 120 (1997), in which a police officer at a state university was suspended without pay before a hearing. The Court ruled the suspension constitutionally unobjectionable. Is there a special rule in cases in which a public authority takes action without prior notice or hearing?

Part III

THE LOCUS AND SCOPE OF SUIT: WHICH COURTS, LAW AND LITIGANTS?

Chapter Five

JUSTICIABILITY

SECTION 2.   STANDING

[Substitute at page 156 for United States v. SCRAP:]

BENNETT v. SPEAR

Supreme Court of the United States, 1997.*
___ U.S. ___, 117 S.Ct. 1154, 137 L.Ed.2d 281.

JUSTICE SCALIA delivered the opinion of the Court.

This is a challenge to a biological opinion issued by the Fish and Wildlife Service in accordance with the Endangered Species Act of 1973 (ESA), 87 Stat. 884, as amended, 16 U.S.C. § 1531 et seq., concerning the operation of the Klamath Irrigation Project by the Bureau of Reclamation, and the project's impact on two varieties of endangered fish. The question for decision is whether the petitioners, who have competing economic and other interests in Klamath Project water, have standing to seek judicial review of the biological opinion under the citizen-suit provision of the ESA, § 1540(g)(1), and the Administrative Procedure Act (APA), 80 Stat. 392, as amended, 5 U.S.C. § 701 et seq.

I

The ESA requires the Secretary of the Interior to promulgate regulations listing those species of animals that are "threatened" or "endangered" under specified criteria, and to designate their "critical habitat." 16 U.S.C. § 1533. The ESA further requires each federal agency to "insure that any action authorized, funded, or carried out by such agency ... is not likely to jeopardize the continued existence of any endangered species or threatened species or result in the destruction or

---

* All footnotes but one omitted; the one retained has been renumbered.

36

adverse modification of habitat of such species which is determined by the Secretary ... to be critical." § 1536(a)(2). If an agency determines that action it proposes to take may adversely affect a listed species, it must engage in formal consultation with the Fish and Wildlife Service, as delegate of the Secretary, ibid.; 50 CFR § 402.14 (1995), after which the Service must provide the agency with a written statement (the Biological Opinion) explaining how the proposed action will affect the species or its habitat, 16 U.S.C. § 1536(b)(3)(A). If the Service concludes that the proposed action will "jeopardize the continued existence of any [listed] species or result in the destruction or adverse modification of [critical habitat]," § 1536(a)(2), the Biological Opinion must outline any "reasonable and prudent alternatives" that the Service believes will avoid that consequence, § 1536(b)(3)(A). Additionally, if the Biological Opinion concludes that the agency action will not result in jeopardy or adverse habitat modification, or if it offers reasonable and prudent alternatives to avoid that consequence, the Service must provide the agency with a written statement (known as the "Incidental Take Statement") specifying the "impact of such incidental taking on the species," any "reasonable and prudent measures that the [Service] considers neces-sary or appropriate to minimize such impact," and setting forth "the terms and conditions ... that must be complied with by the Federal agency ... to implement [those measures]." § 1536(b)(4).

The Klamath Project, one of the oldest federal reclamation schemes, is a series of lakes, rivers, dams and irrigation canals in northern California and southern Oregon. The project was undertaken by the Secretary of the Interior pursuant to the Reclamation Act of 1902, 32 Stat. 388, as amended, 43 U.S.C. § 371 et seq., and the Act of Feb. 9, 1905, 33 Stat. 714, and is administered by the Bureau of Reclamation, which is under the Secretary's jurisdiction. In 1992, the Bureau notified the Service that operation of the project might affect the Lost River Sucker *(Deltistes luxatus)* and Shortnose Sucker *(Chasmistes brevirostris)*, species of fish that were listed as endangered in 1988, see 53 Fed.Reg. 27130–27133 (1988). After formal consultation with the Bureau in accordance with 50 CFR § 402.14 (1995), the Service issued a Biological Opinion which concluded that the " 'long-term operation of the Klamath Project was likely to jeopardize the continued existence of the Lost River and shortnose suckers.' " The Biological Opinion identified "reasonable and prudent alternatives" the Service believed would avoid jeopardy, which included the maintenance of minimum water levels on Clear Lake and Gerber reservoirs. The Bureau later notified the Service that it intended to operate the project in compliance with the Biological Opinion.

Petitioners, two Oregon irrigation districts that receive Klamath Project water and the operators of two ranches within those districts, filed the present action against the director and regional director of the Service and the Secretary of the Interior. Neither the Bureau nor any of its officials is named as defendant. The complaint asserts that the Bureau "has been following essentially the same procedures for storing and releasing water from Clear Lake and Gerber reservoirs throughout the twentieth century," ... that "[t]here is no scientifically or commercially available evidence indicating that the populations of endangered suckers in Clear Lake and Gerber reservoirs have declined, are declining, or will decline as a result" of the Bureau's operation of the Klamath Project, ... that "[t]here is no commercially or scientifically available evidence indicating that the restrictions on lake levels imposed in the Biological Opinion will have any beneficial effect on the ... populations of suckers in Clear Lake and Gerber reservoirs," ... and that the Bureau nonetheless "will abide by the restrictions imposed by the Biological Opinion," ...

Petitioners' complaint included three claims for relief that are relevant here. The first and second claims allege that the Service's jeopardy determination with respect to Clear Lake and Gerber reservoirs, and the ensuing imposition of minimum water levels, violated § 7 of the ESA, 16 U.S.C. § 1536. The third claim is that the imposition of minimum water elevations constituted an implicit determination of critical habitat for the suckers, which violated § 4 of the ESA, 16 U.S.C. § 1533(b)(2), because it failed to take into consideration the designation's economic impact. Each of the claims also states that the relevant action violated the APA's prohibition of agency action that is "arbitrary, capricious, an abuse of discretion, or otherwise not in accordance with law." 5 U.S.C. § 706(2)(A).

The complaint asserts that petitioners' use of the reservoirs and related waterways for "recreational, aesthetic and commercial purposes, as well as for their primary sources of irrigation water" will be "irreparably damaged" by the actions complained of, ... and that the restrictions on water delivery "recommended" by the Biological Opinion "adversely affect plaintiffs by substantially reducing the quantity of available irrigation water," .... In essence, petitioners claim a competing interest in the water the Biological Opinion declares necessary for the preservation of the suckers.

The District Court dismissed the complaint for lack of jurisdiction. It concluded that petitioners did not have standing because their "recreational, aesthetic, and commercial interests ... do not fall within the zone of interests sought to be protected by ESA." ... The Court of Appeals for the Ninth Circuit affirmed. Bennett v. Plenert, 63 F.3d 915 (1995). It held that the "zone of interests" test limits the class of persons who may obtain judicial review not only under the APA, but also under the citizen-suit provision of the ESA, 16 U.S.C. § 1540(g), and that "only plaintiffs who allege an interest in the *preservation* of endangered species fall within the zone of interests protected by the ESA," 63 F.3d, at 919 (emphasis in original). We granted certiorari. 517 U.S. ___, 116 S.Ct. 1316, 134 L.Ed.2d 469 (1996).

In this Court, petitioners raise two questions: first, whether the prudential standing rule known as the "zone of interests" test applies to claims brought under the citizen-suit provision of the ESA, and second, if so, whether petitioners have standing under that test notwithstanding that the interests they seek to vindicate are economic rather than environmental. In this Court, the Government has made no effort to defend the reasoning of the Court of Appeals. Instead, it advances three alternative grounds for affirmance: (1) that petitioners fail to meet the standing requirements imposed by Article III of the Constitution; (2) that the ESA's citizen-suit provision does not authorize judicial review of the types of claims advanced by petitioners; and (3) that judicial review is unavailable under the APA because the Biological Opinion does not constitute final agency action.

II

We first turn to the question the Court of Appeals found dispositive: whether petitioners lack standing by virtue of the zone-of-interests test. Although petitioners contend that their claims lie both under the ESA and the APA, we look first at the ESA because it may permit petitioners to recover their litigation costs, see 16 U.S.C. § 1540(g)(4), and because the APA by its terms independently authorizes review only when "there is no other adequate remedy in a court," 5 U.S.C. § 704.

The question of standing "involves both constitutional limitations on federal-court jurisdiction and prudential limitations on its exercise." Warth v. Seldin, 422 U.S. 490, 498, 95 S.Ct. 2197, 2205, 45 L.Ed.2d 343 (1975) (citing Barrows v. Jackson, 346 U.S. 249, 73 S.Ct. 1031, 97 L.Ed. 1586 (1953)). To satisfy the "case" or "controversy" requirement of Article III, which is the "irreducible constitutional minimum" of standing, a plaintiff must, generally speaking, demonstrate that he has suffered "injury in fact," that the injury is "fairly traceable" to the actions of the defendant, and that the injury will likely be redressed by a favorable decision. Lujan v. Defenders of Wildlife, 504 U.S. 555, 560–561, 112 S.Ct. 2130, 2136–2137, 119 L.Ed.2d 351 (1992); Valley Forge Christian College v. Americans United for Separation of Church and State, Inc., 454 U.S. 464, 471–472, 102 S.Ct. 752, 757–759, 70 L.Ed.2d 700 (1982). In addition to the immutable requirements of Article III, "the federal judiciary has also adhered to a set of prudential principles that bear on the question of standing." Id., at 474–475, 102 S.Ct., at 760. Like their constitutional counterparts, these "judicially self-imposed limits on the exercise of federal jurisdiction," Allen v. Wright, 468 U.S. 737, 751, 104 S.Ct. 3315, 3324, 82 L.Ed.2d 556 (1984), are "founded in concern about the proper—and properly limited—role of the courts in a democratic society," Warth, supra, at 498, 95 S.Ct., at 2205; but unlike their constitutional counterparts, they can be modified or abrogated by Congress, see 422 U.S., at 501, 95 S.Ct., at 2206. Numbered among these prudential requirements is the doctrine of particular concern in this case: that a plaintiff's grievance must arguably fall within the zone of interests protected or regulated by the statutory provision or constitutional guarantee invoked in the suit. See Allen, supra, at 751, 104 S.Ct., at 3324; Valley Forge, supra, at 474–475, 102 S.Ct., at 759–760.

The "zone of interests" formulation was first employed in Association of Data Processing Service Organizations, Inc. v. Camp, 397 U.S. 150, 90 S.Ct. 827, 25 L.Ed.2d 184 (1970). There, certain data processors sought to invalidate a ruling by the Comptroller of the Currency authorizing national banks to sell data processing services on the ground that it violated, inter alia, § 4 of the Bank Service Corporation Act of 1962, 76 Stat. 1132, which prohibited bank service corporations from engaging in "any activity other than the performance of bank services for banks." The Court of Appeals had held that the banks' data-processing competitors were without standing to challenge the alleged violation of § 4. In reversing, we stated the applicable prudential standing requirement to be "whether the interest sought to be protected by the complainant is arguably within the zone of interests to be protected or regulated by the statute or constitutional guarantee in question." Data Processing, supra, at 153, 90 S.Ct., at 830. *Data Processing,* and its companion case, Barlow v. Collins, 397 U.S. 159, 90 S.Ct. 832, 25 L.Ed.2d 192 (1970), applied the zone-of-interests test to suits under the APA, but later cases have applied it also in suits not involving review of federal administrative action, see Dennis v. Higgins, 498 U.S. 439, 449, 111 S.Ct. 865, 871, 112 L.Ed.2d 969 (1991); Boston Stock Exchange v. State Tax Comm'n, 429 U.S. 318, 320–321, n. 3, 97 S.Ct. 599, 602–603, n. 3, 50 L.Ed.2d 514 (1977); see also Note, A Defense of the "Zone of Interests" Standing Test, 1983 Duke L.J. 447, 455–456, and nn. 40–49 (1983) (cataloging lower court decisions), and have specifically listed it among other prudential standing requirements of general application, see, e.g., Allen, supra, at 751, 104 S.Ct., at 3324; Valley Forge, supra, at 474–475, 102 S.Ct., at 759–760. We have made clear, however, that the breadth of the zone of interests varies according to the provisions of law at issue, so that what comes within the zone of interests of a statute for purposes of obtaining judicial review of administrative action under the " 'generous review provisions' " of the APA may not do so for other purposes, Clarke v. Securities Industry Assn., 479 U.S. 388, 400, n. 16, 107 S.Ct. 750, 757, n. 16, 93 L.Ed.2d 757 (1987) (quoting Data Processing, supra, at 156, 90 S.Ct., at 831).

Congress legislates against the background of our prudential standing doctrine, which applies unless it is expressly negated. See Block v. Community Nutrition Institute, 467 U.S. 340, 345–348, 104 S.Ct. 2450, 2453–2455, 81 L.Ed.2d 270 (1984). Cf. Associated Gen. Contractors of Cal., Inc. v. Carpenters, 459 U.S. 519, 532–533, and n. 28, 103 S.Ct. 897, 906, and n. 28, 74 L.Ed.2d 723 (1983). The first question in the present case is whether the ESA's citizen-suit provision, set forth in pertinent part in the margin,[1] negates the zone-of-interests test (or, perhaps more accurately, expands the zone of interests). We think it does. The first operative portion of the provision says that "any person may commence a civil suit"—an authorization of remarkable breadth when compared with the language Congress ordinarily uses. Even in some other environmental statutes, Congress has used more restrictive formulations, such as "[any person] having an interest which is or may be adversely affected," 33 U.S.C. § 1365(g) (Clean Water Act); see also 30 U.S.C. § 1270(a) (Surface Mining Control and Reclamation Act) (same); "[a]ny person suffering legal wrong," 15 U.S.C. § 797(b)(5) (Energy Supply and Environmental Coordination Act); or "any person having a valid legal interest which is or may be adversely affected . . . whenever such action constitutes a case or controversy," 42 U.S.C. § 9124(a) (Ocean Thermal Energy Conversion Act). And in contexts other than the environment, Congress has often been even more restrictive. In statutes concerning unfair trade practices and other commercial matters, for example, it has authorized suit only by "[a]ny person injured in his business or property," 7 U.S.C. § 2305(c); see also 15 U.S.C. § 72 (same), or only by "competitors, customers, or subsequent purchasers," § 298(b).

Our readiness to take the term "any person" at face value is greatly augmented by two interrelated considerations: that the overall subject matter of this legislation is the environment (a matter in which it is common to think all persons have an interest) and that the obvious purpose of the particular provision in question is to encourage enforcement by so-called "private attorneys general"—evidenced by its elimination of the usual amount-in-controversy and diversity-of-citizenship re-

---

1. "Except as provided in paragraph (2) of this subsection any person may commence a civil suit on his own behalf—

"(A) to enjoin any person, including the United States and any other governmental instrumentality or agency (to the extent permitted by the eleventh amendment to the Constitution), who is alleged to be in violation of any provision of this chapter or regulation issued under the authority thereof; or

. . .

"(C) against the Secretary where there is alleged a failure of the Secretary to perform any act or duty under section 1533 of this title which is not discretionary with the Secretary. The district courts shall have jurisdiction, without regard to the amount in controversy or the citizenship of the parties, to enforce any such provision or regulation, or to order the Secretary to perform such act or duty, as the case may be. . . .

(2)(A) No action may be commenced under subparagraph (1)(A) of this section—

"(i) prior to sixty days after written notice of the violation has been given to the Secretary, and to any alleged violator of any such provision or regulation;

"(ii) if the Secretary has commenced action to impose a penalty pursuant to subsection (a) of this section; or

"(iii) if the United States has commenced and is diligently prosecuting a criminal action . . . to redress a violation of any such provision or regulation.

. . .

"(3)(B) In any such suit under this subsection in which the United States is not a party, the Attorney General, at the request of the Secretary, may intervene on behalf of the United States as a matter of right.

"(4) The court, in issuing any final order in any suit brought pursuant to paragraph (1) of this subsection, may award costs of litigation (including reasonable attorney and expert witness fees) to any party, whenever the court determines such award is appropriate." 16 U.S.C. § 1540(g).

quirements, its provision for recovery of the costs of litigation (including even expert witness fees), and its reservation to the Government of a right of first refusal to pursue the action initially and a right to intervene later. Given these factors, we think the conclusion of expanded standing follows a fortiori from our decision in Trafficante v. Metropolitan Life Ins. Co., 409 U.S. 205, 93 S.Ct. 364, 34 L.Ed.2d 415 (1972), which held that standing was expanded to the full extent permitted under Article III by a provision of the Civil Rights Act of 1968 that authorized "[a]ny person who claims to have been injured by a discriminatory housing practice" to sue for violations of the Act. There also we relied on textual evidence of a statutory scheme to rely on private litigation to ensure compliance with the Act. See id., at 210–211, 93 S.Ct., at 367–368. The statutory language here is even clearer, and the subject of the legislation makes the intent to permit enforcement by everyman even more plausible.

It is true that the plaintiffs here are seeking to prevent application of environmental restrictions rather than to implement them. But the "any person" formulation applies to all the causes of action authorized by § 1540(g)—not only to actions against private violators of environmental restrictions, and not only to actions against the Secretary asserting underenforcement under § 1533, but also to actions against the Secretary asserting overenforcement under § 1533. As we shall discuss below, the citizen-suit provision does favor environmentalists in that it covers all private violations of the Act but not all failures of the Secretary to meet his administrative responsibilities; but there is no textual basis for saying that its expansion of standing requirements applies to environmentalists alone. The Court of Appeals therefore erred in concluding that petitioners lacked standing under the zone-of-interests test to bring their claims under the ESA's citizen-suit provision.

III

The Government advances several alternative grounds upon which it contends we may affirm the dismissal of petitioners' suit. Because the District Court and the Court of Appeals found the zone-of-interests ground to be dispositive, these alternative grounds were not reached below. A respondent is entitled, however, to defend the judgment on any ground supported by the record, see Ponte v. Real, 471 U.S. 491, 500, 105 S.Ct. 2192, 2197, 85 L.Ed.2d 553 (1985); Matsushita Elec. Industrial Co. v. Epstein, 516 U.S. ___, ___, n. 5, 116 S.Ct. 873, 880, n. 5, 134 L.Ed.2d 6 (1996). The asserted grounds were raised below, and have been fully briefed and argued here; we deem it an appropriate exercise of our discretion to consider them now rather than leave them for disposition on remand.

A

The Government's first contention is that petitioners' complaint fails to satisfy the standing requirements imposed by the "case" or "controversy" provision of Article III. This "irreducible constitutional minimum" of standing requires: (1) that the plaintiff have suffered an "injury in fact"—an invasion of a judicially cognizable interest which is (a) concrete and particularized and (b) actual or imminent, not conjectural or hypothetical; (2) that there be a causal connection between the injury and the conduct complained of—the injury must be fairly traceable to the challenged action of the defendant, and not the result of the independent action of some third party not before the court; and (3) that it be likely, as opposed to merely speculative, that the injury will be redressed by a favorable decision. Defenders of Wildlife, 504 U.S., at 560–561, 112 S.Ct., at 2136–2137.

Petitioners allege, among other things, that they currently receive irrigation water from Clear Lake, that the Bureau "will abide by the restrictions imposed by the Biological Opinion," App. to Pet. for Cert. 32, and that "[t]he restrictions on lake levels imposed in the Biological Opinion adversely affect [petitioners] by substantially reducing the quantity of available irrigation water," id., at 40. The Government contends, first, that these allegations fail to satisfy the "injury in fact" element of Article III standing because they demonstrate only a diminution in the *aggregate* amount of available water, and do not necessarily establish (absent information concerning the Bureau's water allocation practices) that the *petitioners* will receive less water. This contention overlooks, however, the proposition that each element of Article III standing "must be supported in the same way as any other matter on which the plaintiff bears the burden of proof, i.e., with the manner and degree of evidence required at the successive stages of the litigation." Defenders of Wildlife, supra, at 561, 112 S.Ct., at 2136. Thus, while a plaintiff must "set forth" by affidavit or other evidence "specific facts," to survive a motion for summary judgment, Fed. Rule Civ. Proc. 56(e), and must ultimately support any contested facts with evidence adduced at trial, "[a]t the pleading stage, general factual allegations of injury resulting from the defendant's conduct may suffice, for on a motion to dismiss we 'presum[e] that general allegations embrace those specific facts that are necessary to support the claim.' " Defenders of Wildlife, supra, at 561, 112 S.Ct., at 2137 (quoting Lujan v. National Wildlife Federation, 497 U.S. 871, 889, 110 S.Ct. 3177, 3189, 111 L.Ed.2d 695 (1990)). Given petitioners' allegation that the amount of available water will be reduced and that they will be adversely affected thereby, it is easy to presume specific facts under which petitioners will be injured—for example, the Bureau's distribution of the reduction pro rata among its customers. The complaint alleges the requisite injury in fact.

The Government also contests compliance with the second and third Article III standing requirements, contending that any injury suffered by petitioners is neither "fairly traceable" to the Service's Biological Opinion, nor "redressable" by a favorable judicial ruling, because the "action agency" (the Bureau) retains ultimate responsibility for determining

whether and how a proposed action shall go forward. See 50 CFR
§ 402.15(a) (1995) ("Following the issuance of a biological opinion, the
Federal agency shall determine whether and in what manner to proceed
with the action in light of its section 7 obligations and the Service's
biological opinion"). "If the petitioners have suffered injury," the Government contends, "the proximate cause of their harm is an (as yet
unidentified) decision by the Bureau regarding the volume of water
allocated to petitioners, not the biological opinion itself." ... This
wrongly equates injury "fairly traceable" to the defendant with injury as
to which the defendant's actions are the very last step in the chain of
causation. While, as we have said, it does not suffice if the injury
complained of is " 'th[e] result [of] the *independent* action of some third
party not before the court,' " Defenders of Wildlife supra, at 560–561,
112 S.Ct., at 2136 (emphasis added) (quoting Simon v. Eastern Ky.
Welfare Rights Organization, 426 U.S. 26, 41–42, 96 S.Ct. 1917, 1926, 48
L.Ed.2d 450 (1976)), that does not exclude injury produced by determinative or coercive effect upon the action of someone else.

By the Government's own account, while the Service's Biological
Opinion theoretically serves an "advisory function," 51 Fed.Reg. 19928
(1986), in reality it has a powerful coercive effect on the action agency:

> "The statutory scheme ... presupposes that the biological opinion
> will play a central role in the action agency's decisionmaking pro-
> cess, and that it will typically be based on an administrative record
> that is fully adequate for the action agency's decision insofar as ESA
> issues are concerned.... [A] federal agency that chooses to deviate
> from the recommendations contained in a biological opinion bears
> the burden of 'articulat[ing] in its administrative record its reasons
> for disagreeing with the conclusions of a biological opinion,' 51
> Fed.Reg. 19,956 (1986). In the government's experience, action
> agencies very rarely choose to engage in conduct that the Service
> had concluded is likely to jeopardize the continued existence of a
> listed species." ...

What this concession omits to say, moreover, is that the action agency
must not only articulate its reasons for disagreement (which ordinarily
requires species and habitat investigations that are not within the action
agency's expertise), but that it runs a substantial risk if its (inexpert)
reasons turn out to be wrong. A Biological Opinion of the sort rendered
here alters the legal regime to which the action agency is subject. When
it "offers reasonable and prudent alternatives" to the proposed action, a
Biological Opinion must include a so-called "Incidental Take Statement"—a written statement specifying, among other things, those "measures that the [Service] considers necessary or appropriate to minimize
[the action's impact on the affected species]" and the "terms and
conditions ... that must be complied with by the Federal agency ... to
implement [such] measures." 16 U.S.C. § 1536(b)(4). Any taking that is
in compliance with these terms and conditions "shall not be considered

to be a prohibited taking of the species concerned" § 1536(*o*)(2). Thus, the Biological Opinion's Incidental Take Statement constitutes a permit authorizing the action agency to "take" the endangered or threatened species so long as it respects the Service's "terms and conditions." The action agency is technically free to disregard the Biological Opinion and proceed with its proposed action, but it does so at its own peril (and that of its employees), for "any person" who knowingly "takes" an endangered or threatened species is subject to substantial civil and criminal penalties, including imprisonment. See §§ 1540(a) and (b) (authorizing civil fines of up to $25,000 per violation and criminal penalties of up to $50,000 and imprisonment for one year); see also Babbitt v. Sweet Home Chapter, Communities for Great Ore., 515 U.S. ___, ___, 115 S.Ct. 2407, 2418, 132 L.Ed.2d 597 (1995) (upholding interpretation of the term "take" to include significant habitat degradation).

The Service itself is, to put it mildly, keenly aware of the virtually determinative effect of its biological opinions. The Incidental Take Statement at issue in the present case begins by instructing the reader that any taking of a listed species is prohibited unless "such taking is in compliance with this incidental take statement," and warning that "[t]he measures described below are nondiscretionary, and must be taken by [the Bureau]." Given all of this, and given petitioners' allegation that the Bureau had, until issuance of the Biological Opinion, operated the Klamath Project in the same manner throughout the twentieth century, it is not difficult to conclude that petitioners have met their burden—which is relatively modest at this stage of the litigation—of alleging that their injury is "fairly traceable" to the Service's Biological Opinion and that it will "likely" be redressed—i.e., the Bureau will not impose such water level restrictions—if the Biological Opinion is set aside.

B

Next, the Government contends that the ESA's citizen-suit provision does not authorize judicial review of petitioners' claims. The relevant portions of that provision provide that

"any person may commence a civil suit on his own behalf—

"(A) to enjoin any person, including the United States and any other governmental instrumentality or agency ... who is alleged to be in violation of any provision of this chapter or regulation issued under the authority thereof; or

. . .

"(C) against the Secretary [of Commerce or the Interior] where there is alleged a failure of the Secretary to perform any act or duty under section 1533 of this title which is not discretionary with the Secretary." 16 U.S.C. § 1540(g)(1).

The Government argues that judicial review is not available under subsection (A) because the Secretary is not "in violation" of the ESA, and under subsection (C) because the Secretary has not failed to perform any nondiscretionary duty under § 1533.

1

Turning first to subsection (C): that it covers only violations of § 1533 is clear and unambiguous. Petitioners' first and second claims, which assert that the Secretary has violated § 1536, are obviously not reviewable under this provision. However, as described above, the third claim alleges that the Biological Opinion implicitly determines critical habitat without complying with the mandate of § 1533(b)(2) that the Secretary "tak[e] into consideration the economic impact, and any other relevant impact, of specifying any particular area as critical habitat." This claim does come within subsection (C).

The Government seeks to avoid this result by appealing to the limitation in subsection (C) that the duty sought to be enforced not be "discretionary with the Secretary." But the terms of § 1533(b)(2) are plainly those of obligation rather than discretion: "The Secretary *shall* designate critical habitat, and make revisions thereto, . . . on the basis of the best scientific data available and after taking into consideration the economic impact, and any other relevant impact, of specifying any particular area as critical habitat." (Emphasis added.) It is true that this is followed by the statement that, except where extinction of the species is at issue, "[t]he Secretary *may* exclude any area from critical habitat if he determines that the benefits of such exclusion outweigh the benefits of specifying such area as part of the critical habitat." Ibid. (emphasis added). However, the fact that the Secretary's ultimate decision is reviewable only for abuse of discretion does not alter the categorical *requirement* that, in arriving at his decision, he "tak[e] into consideration the economic impact, and any other relevant impact," and use "the best scientific data available." Ibid. It is rudimentary administrative law that discretion as to the substance of the ultimate decision does not confer discretion to ignore the required procedures of decisionmaking. See SEC v. Chenery Corp., 318 U.S. 80, 94–95, 63 S.Ct. 454, 462–463, 87 L.Ed. 626 (1943). Since it is the omission of these required procedures that petitioners complain of, their § 1533 claim is reviewable under § 1540(g)(1)(C).

2

Having concluded that petitioners' § 1536 claims are not reviewable under subsection (C), we are left with the question whether they are reviewable under subsection (A), which authorizes injunctive actions against any person "who is alleged to be in violation" of the ESA or its implementing regulations. The Government contends that the Secretary's conduct in implementing or enforcing the ESA is not a "violation" of the ESA within the meaning of this provision. In its view,

§ 1540(g)(1)(A) is a means by which private parties may enforce the substantive provisions of the ESA against regulated parties—both private entities and Government agencies—but is not an alternative avenue for judicial review of the Secretary's implementation of the statute. We agree.

The opposite contention is simply incompatible with the existence of § 1540(g)(1)(C), which expressly authorizes suit against the Secretary, but only to compel him to perform a nondiscretionary duty under § 1533. That provision would be superfluous—and, worse still, its careful limitation to § 1533 would be nullified—if § 1540(g)(1)(A) permitted suit against the Secretary for *any* "violation" of the ESA. It is the " 'cardinal principle of statutory construction' . . . [that] [i]t is our duty 'to give effect, if possible, to every clause and word of a statute' . . . rather than to emasculate an entire section." United States v. Menasche, 348 U.S. 528, 538, 75 S.Ct. 513, 520, 99 L.Ed. 615 (1955) (quoting NLRB v. Jones & Laughlin Steel Corp., 301 U.S. 1, 30, 57 S.Ct. 615, 621, 81 L.Ed. 893 (1937), and Montclair v. Ramsdell, 107 U.S. 147, 152, 2 S.Ct. 391, 395, 27 L.Ed. 431 (1883)). Application of that principle here clearly requires us to conclude that the term "violation" does not include the Secretary's failure to perform his duties as administrator of the ESA.

Moreover, the ESA uses the term "violation" elsewhere in contexts in which it is most unlikely to refer to failure by the Secretary or other federal officers and employees to perform their duties in administering the Act. Section 1540(a), for example, authorizes the Secretary to impose substantial civil penalties on "[a]ny person who knowingly violates . . . any provision of [the ESA]," and entrusts the Secretary with the power to "remi[t] or mitigat[e]" any such penalty. We know of no precedent for applying such a provision against those who administer (as opposed to those who are regulated by) a substantive law. Nor do we think it likely that the statute meant to subject the Secretary, his officers and employees to criminal liability under § 1540(b), which makes it a crime for "[a]ny person [to] knowingly violat[e] any provision of [the ESA]," or that § 1540(e)(3), which authorizes law enforcement personnel to "make arrests without a warrant for any violation of [the ESA]," was intended to authorize warrantless arrest of the Secretary or his delegates for "knowingly" failing to use the best scientific data available.

Finally, interpreting the term "violation" to include any errors on the part of the Secretary in administering the ESA would effect a wholesale abrogation of the APA's "final agency action" requirement. Any procedural default, even one that had not yet resulted in a final disposition of the matter at issue, would form the basis for a lawsuit. We are loathe to produce such an extraordinary regime without the clearest of statutory direction, which is hardly present here.

Viewed in the context of the entire statute, § 1540(g)(1)(A)'s reference to any "violation" of the ESA cannot be interpreted to include the

Secretary's maladministration of the Act. Petitioners' claims are not subject to judicial review under § 1540(g)(1)(A).

IV

The foregoing analysis establishes that the principal statute invoked by petitioners, the ESA, does authorize review of their § 1533 claim, but does not support their claims based upon the Secretary's alleged failure to comply with § 1536. To complete our task, we must therefore inquire whether these § 1536 claims may nonetheless be brought under the Administrative Procedure Act, which authorizes a court to "set aside agency action, findings, and conclusions found to be ... arbitrary, capricious, an abuse of discretion, or otherwise not in accordance with law," 5 U.S.C. § 706.

A

No one contends (and it would not be maintainable) that the causes of action against the Secretary set forth in the ESA's citizen-suit provision are exclusive, supplanting those provided by the APA. The APA, by its terms, provides a right to judicial review of all "final agency action for which there is no other adequate remedy in a court," 5 U.S.C. § 704, and applies universally "except to the extent that—(1) statutes preclude judicial review; or (2) agency action is committed to agency discretion by law," § 701(a). Nothing in the ESA's citizen-suit provision expressly precludes review under the APA, nor do we detect anything in the statutory scheme suggesting a purpose to do so. And any contention that the relevant provision of 16 U.S.C. § 1536(a)(2) is discretionary would fly in the face of its text, which uses the imperative "shall."

In determining whether the petitioners have standing under the zone-of-interests test to bring their APA claims, we look not to the terms of the ESA's citizen-suit provision, but to the substantive provisions of the ESA, the alleged violations of which serve as the gravamen of the complaint. See National Wildlife Federation, 497 U.S., at 886, 110 S.Ct., at 3187. The classic formulation of the zone-of-interests test is set forth in Data Processing, 397 U.S., at 153, 90 S.Ct., at 830: "whether the interest sought to be protected by the complainant is arguably within the zone of interests to be protected or regulated by the statute or constitutional guarantee in question." The Court of Appeals concluded that this test was not met here, since petitioners are neither directly regulated by the ESA nor seek to vindicate its overarching purpose of species preservation. That conclusion was error.

Whether a plaintiff's interest is "arguably ... protected ... by the statute" within the meaning of the zone-of-interests test is to be determined not by reference to the overall purpose of the Act in question (here, species preservation), but by reference to the particular provision of law upon which the plaintiff relies. It is difficult to understand how the Ninth Circuit could have failed to see this from our cases. In Data Processing itself, for example, we did not require that the plaintiffs' suit vindicate the overall purpose of the Bank Service Corporation Act of 1962, but found it sufficient that their commercial interest was sought to be protected by the anti-competition limitation contained in § 4 of the Act—the specific provision which they alleged had been violated. See Data Processing, supra, at 155–156, 90 S.Ct., at 830–831. As we said with the utmost clarity in National Wildlife Federation, "the plaintiff must establish that the injury he complains of . . . falls within the 'zone of interests' sought to be protected *by the statutory provision whose violation forms the legal basis for his complaint*." National Wildlife Federation, supra, at 883, 110 S.Ct., at 3186 (emphasis added). See also Air Courier Conference v. Postal Workers, 498 U.S. 517, 523–524, 111 S.Ct. 913, 917–918, 112 L.Ed.2d 1125 (1991) (same).

In the claims that we have found not to be covered by the ESA's citizen-suit provision, petitioners allege a violation of § 7 of the ESA, 16 U.S.C. § 1536, which requires, inter alia, that each agency "use the best scientific and commercial data available," § 1536(a)(2). Petitioners contend that the available scientific and commercial data show that the continued operation of the Klamath Project will not have a detrimental impact on the endangered suckers, that the imposition of minimum lake levels is not necessary to protect the fish, and that by issuing a Biological Opinion which makes unsubstantiated findings to the contrary the defendants have acted arbitrarily and in violation of § 1536(a)(2). The obvious purpose of the requirement that each agency "use the best scientific and commercial data available" is to ensure that the ESA not be implemented haphazardly, on the basis of speculation or surmise. While this no doubt serves to advance the ESA's overall goal of species preservation, we think it readily apparent that another objective (if not indeed the primary one) is to avoid needless economic dislocation produced by agency officials zealously but unintelligently pursuing their environmental objectives. That economic consequences are an explicit concern of the Act is evidenced by § 1536(h), which provides exemption from § 1536(a)(2)'s no-jeopardy mandate where there are no reasonable and prudent alternatives to the agency action and the benefits of the agency action clearly outweigh the benefits of any alternatives. We believe the "best scientific and commercial data" provision is similarly intended, at least in part, to prevent uneconomic (because erroneous) jeopardy determinations. Petitioners' claim that they are victims of such a mistake is plainly within the zone of interests that the provision protects.

B

The Government contends that petitioners may not obtain judicial review under the APA on the theory that the Biological Opinion does not constitute "final agency action," 5 U.S.C. § 704, because it does not conclusively determine the manner in which Klamath Project water will be allocated:

"Whatever the practical likelihood that the [Bureau] would adopt the reasonable and prudent alternatives (including the higher lake levels) identified by the Service, the Bureau was not legally obligated to do so. Even if the Bureau decided to adopt the higher lake levels, moreover, nothing in the biological opinion would constrain the [Bureau's] discretion as to how the available water should be allocated among potential users." ...

This confuses the question of whether the Secretary's action is final with the separate question of whether the petitioners' harm is "fairly traceable" to the Secretary's action (a question we have already resolved against the Government, see supra, at Part III–A). As a general matter, two conditions must be satisfied for agency action to be "final": First, the action must mark the "consummation" of the agency's decisionmaking process, Chicago & Southern Air Lines, Inc. v. Waterman S.S. Corp., 333 U.S. 103, 113, 68 S.Ct. 431, 437, 92 L.Ed. 568 (1948)—it must not be of a merely tentative or interlocutory nature. And second, the action must be one by which "rights or obligations have been determined," or from which "legal consequences will flow," Port of Boston Marine Terminal Assn. v. Rederiaktiebolaget Transatlantic, 400 U.S. 62, 71, 91 S.Ct. 203, 209, 27 L.Ed.2d 203 (1970). It is uncontested that the first requirement is met here; and the second is met because, as we have discussed above, the Biological Opinion and accompanying Incidental Take Statement alter the legal regime to which the action agency is subject authorizing it to take the endangered species if (but only if) it complies with the prescribed conditions. In this crucial respect the present case is different from the cases upon which the Government relies, Franklin v. Massachusetts, 505 U.S. 788, 112 S.Ct. 2767, 120 L.Ed.2d 636 (1992), and Dalton v. Specter, 511 U.S. 462, 114 S.Ct. 1719, 128 L.Ed.2d 497 (1994). In the former case, the agency action in question was the Secretary of Commerce's presentation to the President of a report tabulating the results of the decennial census; our holding that this did not constitute "final agency action" was premised on the observation that the report carried "no direct consequences" and served "more like a tentative recommendation than a final and binding determination." 505 U.S., at 798, 112 S.Ct., at 2774. And in the latter case, the agency action in question was submission to the President of base closure recommendations by the Secretary of Defense and the Defense Base Closure and Realignment Commission; our holding that this was not "final agency action" followed from the fact that the recommendations were in no way binding on the President, who had absolute discretion to accept or reject them. 511 U.S., at 470, 114 S.Ct., at 1725. Unlike the reports in Franklin and Dalton, which were purely advisory and in no way affected the legal rights of the relevant actors, the Biological Opinion at issue here has direct and appreciable legal consequences.

* * *

The Court of Appeals erred in affirming the District Court's dismissal of petitioners' claims for lack of jurisdiction. Petitioners' complaint alleges facts sufficient to meet the requirements of Article III standing, and none of their ESA claims is precluded by the zone-of-interests test. Petitioners' § 1533 claim is reviewable under the ESA's citizen-suit provision, and petitioners' remaining claims are reviewable under the APA.

The judgment of the Court of Appeals is reversed, and the case is remanded for further proceedings consistent with this opinion.

It is so ordered.

RAINES v. BYRD

Supreme Court of the United States, 1997.
___ U.S. ___, 117 S.Ct. 2312, ___ L.Ed.3d ___*

CHIEF JUSTICE REHNQUIST delivered the opinion of the Court.

The District Court for the District of Columbia declared the Line Item Veto Act unconstitutional. On this direct appeal, we hold that appellees lack standing to bring this suit, and therefore direct that the judgment of the District Court be vacated and the complaint dismissed.

I

The appellees are six Members of Congress, four of whom served as Senators and two of whom served as Congressmen in the 104th Congress (1995–1996). On March 27, 1996, the Senate passed a bill entitled the Line Item Veto Act by a vote of 69–31. All four appellee Senators voted "nay." 142 Cong. Rec. S2995. The next day, the House of Representatives passed the identical bill by a vote of 232–177. Both appellee Congressmen voted "nay." Id., at H2986. On April 4, 1996, the President signed the Line Item Veto Act (Act) into law. Pub.L. 104–130, 110 Stat. 1200, codified at 2 U.S.C.A. § 691 et seq. (Supp.1997). The Act went into effect on January 1, 1997. See Pub.L. 104–130, § 5. The next day, appellees filed a complaint in the District Court for the District of Columbia against the two appellants, the Secretary of the Treasury and the Director of the Office of Management and Budget, alleging that the Act was unconstitutional.

The provisions of the Line Item Veto Act do not use the term "veto." Instead, the President is given the authority to "cancel" certain spending and tax benefit measures after he has signed them into law. Specifically, the Act provides:

"[T]he President may, with respect to any bill or joint resolution that has been signed into law pursuant to Article I, section 7, of the Constitution of the United States, cancel in whole—(1) any dollar

---

* Some footnotes omitted; others renumbered.

amount of discretionary budget authority; (2) any item of new direct spending; or (3) any limited tax benefit; if the President—

"(A) determines that such cancellation will—(i) reduce the Federal budget deficit; (ii) not impair any essential Government functions; and (iii) not harm the national interest; and

"(B) notifies the Congress of such cancellation by transmitting a special message . . . within five calendar days (excluding Sundays) after the enactment of the law [to which the cancellation applies]." § 691(a) (some indentations omitted).

The President's "cancellation" under the Act takes effect when the "special message" notifying Congress of the cancellation is received in the House and Senate. With respect to dollar amounts of "discretionary budget authority," a cancellation means "to rescind." § 691e(4)(A). With respect to "new direct spending" items or "limited tax benefit[s]," a cancellation means that the relevant legal provision, legal obligation, or budget authority is "prevent[ed] . . . from having legal force or effect." §§ 691e(4)(B), (C).

The Act establishes expedited procedures in both Houses for the consideration of "disapproval bills," § 691d, bills or joint resolutions which, if enacted into law by the familiar procedures set out in Article I, § 7 of the Constitution, would render the President's cancellation "null and void," § 691b(a). "Disapproval bills" may only be one sentence long and must read as follows after the enacting clause: "That Congress disapproves of cancellations _____ as transmitted by the President in a special message on _____ regarding _____." § 691e(6)(C). (The blank spaces correspond to the cancellation reference numbers as set out in the special message, the date of the President's special message, and the public law number to which the special message relates, respectively. Ibid.)

The Act provides that "[a]ny Member of Congress or any individual adversely affected by [this Act] may bring an action, in the United States District Court for the District of Columbia, for declaratory judgment and injunctive relief on the ground that any provision of this part violates the Constitution." § 692(a)(1). Appellees brought suit under this provision, claiming that "[t]he Act violates Article I" of the Constitution. Complaint ¶ 17. Specifically, they alleged that the Act "unconstitutionally expands the President's power," and "violates the requirements of bicameral passage and presentment by granting to the President, acting alone, the authority to 'cancel' and thus repeal provisions of federal law." Ibid. They alleged that the Act injured them "directly and concretely . . . in their official capacities" in three ways:

"The Act . . . (a) alter[s] the legal and practical effect of all votes they may cast on bills containing such separately vetoable items, (b) divest[s] the [appellees] of their constitutional role in the repeal of legislation, and (c) alter[s] the constitutional balance of powers between the Legislative and Executive Branches, both with respect to measures containing separately vetoable items and with respect to other matters coming before Congress." Id., ¶ 14.

Appellants moved to dismiss for lack of jurisdiction, claiming (among other things) that appellees lacked standing to sue and that their claim was not ripe. Both sides also filed motions for summary judgment on the merits.

On April 10, 1997, the District Court (i) denied appellants' motion to dismiss, holding that appellees had standing to bring this suit and that their claim was ripe, and (ii) granted appellees' summary judgment motion, holding that the Act is unconstitutional. 956 F.Supp. 25. As to standing, the court noted that the Court of Appeals for the District of Columbia "has repeatedly recognized Members' standing to challenge measures that affect their constitutionally prescribed lawmaking powers." Id., at 30 (citing, e.g., Michel v. Anderson, 14 F.3d 623, 625 (C.A.D.C.1994); Moore v. U.S. House of Representatives, 733 F.2d 946, 950–952 (C.A.D.C.1984)). See also 956 F.Supp., at 31 ("[T]he Supreme Court has never endorsed the [Court of Appeals'] analysis of standing in such cases"). The court held that appellees' claim that the Act "dilute[d] their Article I voting power" was sufficient to confer Article III standing: "[Appellees'] votes mean something different from what they meant before, for good or ill, and [appellees] who perceive it as the latter are thus 'injured' in a constitutional sense whenever an appropriations bill comes up for a vote, whatever the President ultimately does with it.... Under the Act the dynamic of lawmaking is fundamentally altered. Compromises and trade-offs by individual lawmakers must take into account the President's item-by-item cancellation power looming over the end product." Ibid.

The court held that appellees' claim was ripe even though the President had not yet used the "cancellation" authority granted him under the Act: "Because [appellees] now find themselves in a position of unanticipated and unwelcome subservience to the President before and after they vote on appropriations bills, Article III is satisfied, and this Court may accede to Congress' directive to address the constitutional cloud over the Act as swiftly as possible." Id., at 32 (referring to § 692(a)(1), the section of the Act granting Members of Congress the right to challenge the Act's constitutionality in court). On the merits, the court held that the Act violated the Presentment Clause, Art. I, § 7, cl. 2, and constituted an unconstitutional delegation of legislative power to the President. 956 F.Supp., at 33, 35, 37–38.

The Act provides for a direct, expedited appeal to this Court. § 692(b) (direct appeal to Supreme Court); § 692(c) ("It shall be the duty of ... the Supreme Court of the United States to advance on the docket and to expedite to the greatest possible extent the disposition of any [suit challenging the Act's constitutionality] brought under [§ 3(a) of the Act]''). On April 18, eight days after the District Court issued its order, appellants filed a jurisdictional statement asking us to note probable jurisdiction, and on April 21, appellees filed a memorandum in response agreeing that we should note probable jurisdiction. On April 23, we did so. 520 U.S. ___, 117 S.Ct. 1489, 137 L.Ed.2d 699 (1997). We established an expedited briefing schedule and heard oral argument on May 27. We now hold that appellees have no standing to bring this suit, and therefore direct that the judgment of the District Court be vacated and the complaint dismissed.

II

Under Article III, § 2 of the Constitution, the federal courts have jurisdiction over this dispute between appellants and appellees only if it is a "case" or "controversy." This is a "bedrock requirement." Valley Forge Christian College v. Americans United for Separation of Church and State, Inc., 454 U.S. 464, 471, 102 S.Ct. 752, 758, 70 L.Ed.2d 700 (1982). As we said in Simon v. Eastern Ky. Welfare Rights Organization, 426 U.S. 26, 37, 96 S.Ct. 1917, 1924, 48 L.Ed.2d 450 (1976), "No principle is more fundamental to the judiciary's proper role in our system of government than the constitutional limitation of federal-court jurisdiction to actual cases or controversies."

One element of the case-or-controversy requirement is that appellees, based on their complaint, must establish that they have standing to sue. Lujan v. Defenders of Wildlife, 504 U.S. 555, 561, 112 S.Ct. 2130, 2136–2137, 119 L.Ed.2d 351 (1992).... The standing inquiry focuses on whether the plaintiff is the proper party to bring this suit.... To meet the standing requirements of Article III, "[a] plaintiff must allege personal injury fairly traceable to the defendant's allegedly unlawful conduct and likely to be redressed by the requested relief." Allen v. Wright, 468 U.S. 737, 751, 104 S.Ct. 3315, 3324, 82 L.Ed.2d 556 (1984).... We have consistently stressed that a plaintiff's complaint must establish that he has a "personal stake" in the alleged dispute, and that the alleged injury suffered is particularized as to him, see Lujan ... (to have standing, the plaintiff must have suffered a "particularized" injury, which means that "the injury must affect the plaintiff in a personal and individual way"); Bender v. Williamsport Area School Dist., 475 U.S. 534, 543–544, 106 S.Ct. 1326, 1332, 89 L.Ed.2d 501 (1986) (school board member who "has no personal stake in the outcome of the litigation" has no standing).

We have also stressed that the alleged injury must be legally and judicially cognizable. This requires, among other things, that the plaintiff have suffered "an invasion of a legally protected interest which is ... concrete and particularized," Lujan, 504 U.S., at 560, 112 S.Ct., at 2136, and that the dispute is "traditionally thought to be capable of resolution through the judicial process," Flast v. Cohen, 392 U.S. 83, 97, 88 S.Ct. 1942, 1951, 20 L.Ed.2d 947 (1968).

We have always insisted on strict compliance with this jurisdictional standing requirement. See, e.g, ibid. (under Article III, "federal courts may exercise power only 'in the last resort, and as a necessity' "). And our standing inquiry has been especially rigorous when reaching the merits of the dispute would force us to decide whether an action taken by one of the other two branches of the Federal Government was unconstitutional. See, e.g., Bender, supra, at 542, 106 S.Ct., at 1331–1332; Valley Forge, supra, at 473–474, 102 S.Ct., at 759–760. As we said in Allen, supra, at 752, 104 S.Ct., at 3325, "the law of Art. III standing is built on a single basic idea—the idea of separation of powers." In the light of this overriding and time-honored concern about keeping the Judiciary's power within its proper constitutional sphere,[1] we must put aside the natural urge to proceed directly to the merits of this important dispute and to "settle" it for the sake of convenience and efficiency. Instead, we must carefully inquire as to whether appellees have met their burden of establishing that their claimed injury is personal, particularized, concrete, and otherwise judicially cognizable.

III

We have never had occasion to rule on the question of legislative standing presented here. In Powell v. McCormack, 395 U.S. 486, 496, 512–514, 89 S.Ct. 1944, 1950–1951, 1959–1960, 23 L.Ed.2d 491 (1969), we held that a Member of Congress' constitutional challenge to his exclusion from the House of Representatives (and his consequent loss of salary) presented an Article III case or controversy. But Powell does not help appellees. First, appellees have not been singled out for specially unfavorable treatment as opposed to other Members of their respective bodies. Their claim is that the Act causes a type of institutional injury (the diminution of legislative power), which necessarily damages all Members of Congress and both Houses of Congress equally. See n. 2, infra. Second, appellees do not claim that they have been deprived of something to which they personally are entitled—such as their seats as Members of Congress after their constituents had elected them. Rather, appellees' claim of standing is based on a loss of political power, not loss of any private right, which would make the injury more concrete. Unlike the injury claimed by Congressman Adam Clayton Powell, the injury claimed by the Members of Congress here is not claimed in any private capacity but solely because they are Members of Congress. See Complaint ¶ 14 (purporting to sue "in their official capacities"). If one of the Members were to retire tomorrow, he would no longer have a claim; the claim would be possessed by his successor instead. The claimed injury thus runs (in a sense) with the Member's seat, a seat which the Member

1. It is settled that Congress cannot erase Article III's standing requirements by statutorily granting the right to sue to a plaintiff who would not otherwise have standing. Gladstone, Realtors v. Village of Bellwood, 441 U.S. 91, 100, 99 S.Ct. 1601, 1608, 60 L.Ed.2d 66 (1979). We acknowledge, though, that Congress' decision to grant a particular plaintiff the right to challenge an act's constitutionality (as here, see § 692(a)(1), supra, at ___) eliminates any prudential standing limitations and significantly lessens the risk of unwanted conflict with the Legislative Branch when that plaintiff brings suit. See, e.g., Bennett v. Spear, 520 U.S. ___, ___, ___ 117 S.Ct. 1154, 1162–1163, 137 L.Ed.2d 281 (1997).

holds (it may quite arguably be said) as trustee for his constituents, not as a prerogative of personal power. See The Federalist No. 62, p. 378 (J. Madison) (C. Rossiter ed. 1961).

The one case in which we have upheld standing for legislators (albeit state legislators) claiming an institutional injury is Coleman v. Miller, 307 U.S. 433, 59 S.Ct. 972, 83 L.Ed. 1385 (1939). Appellees, relying heavily on this case, claim that they, like the state legislators in Coleman, "have a plain, direct and adequate interest in maintaining the effectiveness of their votes," id., at 438, 59 S.Ct., at 975, sufficient to establish standing. In Coleman, 20 of Kansas' 40 State Senators voted not to ratify the proposed "Child Labor Amendment" to the Federal Constitution. With the vote deadlocked 20–20, the amendment ordinarily would not have been ratified. However, the State's Lieutenant Governor, the presiding officer of the State Senate, cast a deciding vote in favor of the amendment, and it was deemed ratified (after the State House of Representatives voted to ratify it). The 20 State Senators who had voted against the amendment, joined by a 21st State Senator and three State House Members, filed an action in the Kansas Supreme Court seeking a writ of mandamus that would compel the appropriate state officials to recognize that the legislature had not in fact ratified the amendment. That court held that the members of the legislature had standing to bring their mandamus action, but ruled against them on the merits. See id., at 436–437, 59 S.Ct., at 974–975.

This Court affirmed. By a vote of 5–4, we held that the members of the legislature had standing. In explaining our holding, we repeatedly emphasized that if these legislators (who were suing as a bloc) were correct on the merits, then their votes not to ratify the amendment were deprived of all validity:

"Here, the plaintiffs include twenty senators, whose votes against ratification have been overridden and virtually held for naught although if they are right in their contentions their votes would have been sufficient to defeat ratification. We think that these senators have a plain, direct, and adequate interest in maintaining the effectiveness of their votes." Id., at 438, 59 S.Ct., at 975 (emphasis added).

"[T]he twenty senators were not only qualified to vote on the question of ratification but their votes, if the Lieutenant Governor were excluded as not being a part of the legislature for that purpose, would have been decisive in defeating the ratifying resolution." Id., at 441, 59 S.Ct., at 976 (emphasis added).

"[W]e find no departure from principle in recognizing in the instant case that at least the twenty senators whose votes, if their contention were sustained, would have been sufficient to defeat the resolution ratifying the proposed constitutional amendment, have an interest in the controversy which, treated by the state court as a basis for entertaining and deciding the federal questions, is sufficient to give the Court jurisdiction to review that decision." Id., ... at 446, 59 S.Ct., at 979 (emphasis added).

It is obvious, then, that our holding in Coleman stands for the proposition that legislators whose votes would have been sufficient to defeat (or enact) a specific legislative act have standing to sue if that legislative action goes into effect (or does not go into effect), on the ground that their votes have been completely nullified.

It should be equally obvious that appellees' claim does not fall within our holding in Coleman, as thus understood. They have not alleged that they voted for a specific bill, that there were sufficient votes to pass the bill, and that the bill was nonetheless deemed defeated. In the vote on the Line Item Veto Act, their votes were given full effect. They simply lost that vote. Nor can they allege that the Act will nullify their votes in the future in the same way that the votes of the Coleman legislators had been nullified. In the future, a majority of Senators and Congressmen can pass or reject appropriations bills; the Act has no effect on this process. In addition, a majority of Senators and Congressmen can vote to repeal the Act, or to exempt a given appropriations bill (or a given provision in an appropriations bill) from the Act; again, the Act has no effect on this process. Coleman thus provides little meaningful precedent for appellees' argument.

Nevertheless, appellees rely heavily on our statement in Coleman that the Kansas senators had "a plain, direct, and adequate interest in maintaining the effectiveness of their votes." Appellees claim that this statement applies to them because their votes on future appropriations bills (assuming a majority of Congress does not decide to exempt those bills from the Act) will be less "effective" than before, and that the "meaning" and "integrity" of their vote has changed. . . . The argument goes as follows. Before the Act, Members of Congress could be sure that when they voted for, and Congress passed, an appropriations bill that included funds for Project X, one of two things would happen: (i) the bill would become law and all of the projects listed in the bill would go into effect, or (ii) the bill would not become law and none of the projects listed in the bill would go into effect. Either way, a vote for the appropriations bill meant a vote for a package of projects that were inextricably linked. After the Act, however, a vote for an appropriations bill that includes Project X means something different. Now, in addition to the two possibilities listed above, there is a third option: the bill will become law and then the President will "cancel" Project X.

Even taking appellees at their word about the change in the "meaning" and "effectiveness" of their vote for appropriations bills which are subject to the Act, we think their argument pulls Coleman too far from its moorings. Appellees' use of the word "effectiveness" to link their argument to Coleman stretches the word far beyond the sense in which the Coleman opinion used it. There is a vast difference between the level of vote nullification at issue in Coleman and the abstract dilution of institutional legislative power that is alleged here. To uphold standing here would require a drastic extension of Coleman. We are unwilling to take that step. . . .

IV

In sum, appellees have alleged no injury to themselves as individuals (contra Powell), the institutional injury they allege is wholly abstract and widely dispersed (contra Coleman), and their attempt to litigate this dispute at this time and in this form is contrary to historical experience. We attach some importance to the fact that appellees have not been authorized to represent their respective Houses of Congress in this action, and indeed both Houses actively oppose their suit. . . . We also note that our conclusion neither deprives Members of Congress of an adequate remedy (since they may repeal the Act or exempt appropriations bills from its reach), nor forecloses the Act from constitutional challenge (by someone who suffers judicially cognizable injury as a result of the Act). Whether the case would be different if any of these circumstances were different we need not now decide.

We therefore hold that these individual members of Congress do not have a sufficient "personal stake" in this dispute and have not alleged a sufficiently concrete injury to have established Article III standing.[2] The judgment of the District Court is vacated, and the case is remanded with instructions to dismiss the complaint for lack of jurisdiction.

It is so ordered.

JUSTICE SOUTER, concurring in the judgment, with whom JUSTICE GINSBURG joins, concurring.

JUSTICE STEVENS, dissenting.

JUSTICE BREYER, dissenting.

NOTES

(1) Note that Justice Scalia distinguishes constitutional from prudential elements in the concept of standing and seeks to define the constitutional elements. When you apply this analysis to other cases, which were decided on purely constitutional grounds? From what source derive the courts the authority to develop prudential standing rules?

(2) In Air Courier Conf. of America v. American Postal Workers Union, 498 U.S. 517, 111 S.Ct. 913, 112 L.Ed.2d 1125 (1991), the Supreme Court explored the meaning of "zone of interest," holding that postal employees were not within

---

2. In addition, it is far from clear that this injury is "fairly traceable" to appellants, as our precedents require, since the alleged cause of appellees' injury is not appellants' exercise of legislative power but the actions of their own colleagues in Congress in passing the Act. Cf. Holtzman v. Schlesinger, 484 F.2d 1307, 1315 (C.A.2 1973) ("Representative Holtzman . . . has not been denied any right to vote on [the war in Cambodia] by any action of the defendants [Executive Branch officials]. . . . The fact that her vote was ineffective was due to the contrary votes of her colleagues and not the defendants herein").

the zone for challenging a rulemaking that resulted in the suspension of the Postal Service's statutory monopoly on international remailing.

SECTION 4. MOOT, HYPOTHETICAL, AND ABSTRACT QUESTIONS

[Insert at page 176, after Note (4):]

(5) To what extent is the doctrine of mootness constitutionally based? See Lee, Deconstitutionalizing Justiciability: The Example of Mootness, 105 Harv. L.Rev. 903 (1991); Watson, Mootness and the Constitution, 86 Nw.U.L.Rev. 143 (1991).

[Insert on page 176, before *Aetna:*]

U.S. BANCORP MORTGAGE COMPANY v. BONNER MALL PARTNERSHIP

Supreme Court of the United States, 1994.
513 U.S. 18, 115 S.Ct. 386, 130 L.Ed.2d 233.

JUSTICE SCALIA delivered the opinion of the Court.

The question in this case is whether appellate courts in the federal system should vacate civil judgments of subordinate courts in cases that are settled after appeal is filed or certiorari sought.

I

In 1984 and 1985, Northtown Investments built the Bonner Mall in Bonner County, Idaho, with financing from a bank in that State. In 1986, respondent Bonner Mall Partnership (Bonner) acquired the mall, while petitioner U.S. Bancorp Mortgage Co. (Bancorp) acquired the loan and mortgage from the Idaho bank. In 1990, Bonner defaulted on its real-estate taxes and Bancorp scheduled a foreclosure sale.

The day before the sale, Bonner filed a petition under Chapter 11 of the Bankruptcy Code, 11 U.S.C. § 1101 et seq., in the United States Bankruptcy Court for the District of Idaho. It filed a reorganization plan that depended on the "new value exception" to the absolute priority rule. Bancorp moved to suspend the automatic stay of its foreclosure imposed by 11 U.S.C. § 362(a), arguing that Bonner's plan was unconfirmable as a matter of law for a number of reasons, including unavailability of the new value exception. The Bankruptcy Court eventually granted the motion, concluding that the new value exception had not survived enactment of the Bankruptcy Code. The court stayed its order pending an appeal by Bonner. The United States District Court for the District of Idaho reversed, In re Bonner Mall Partnership, 142 B.R. 911 (1992); Bancorp took an appeal in turn, but the Court of Appeals for the Ninth Circuit affirmed, In re Bonner Mall Partnership, 2 F.3d 899 (1993).

Bancorp then petitioned for a writ of certiorari. After we granted the petition, 510 U.S. ___, 114 S.Ct. 681, 126 L.Ed.2d 648 (1994), and received briefing on the merits, Bancorp and Bonner stipulated to a consensual plan of reorganization, which received the approval of the Bankruptcy Court. The parties agreed that confirmation of the plan constituted a settlement that mooted the case. Bancorp, however, also requested that we exercise our power under 28 U.S.C. § 2106 to vacate the judgment of the Court of Appeals. Bonner opposed the motion. We set the vacatur question for briefing and argument. 511 U.S. ___, 114 S.Ct. 1367, 128 L.Ed.2d 44 (1994).

II

Respondent questions our power to entertain petitioner's motion to vacate, suggesting that the limitations on the judicial power conferred by Article III, see U.S. Const., Art. III, § 1, "may, at least in some cases, prohibit an act of vacatur when no live dispute exists due to a settlement that has rendered a case moot." Brief for Respondent 21 (emphasis in original).

The statute that supplies the power of vacatur provides: "The Supreme Court or any other court of appellate jurisdiction may affirm, modify, vacate, set aside or reverse any judgment, decree, or order of a court lawfully brought before it for review, and may remand the cause and direct the entry of such appropriate judgment, decree, or order, or require such further proceedings to be had as may be just under the circumstances." 28 U.S.C. § 2106. Of course no statute could authorize a federal court to decide the merits of a legal question not posed in an Article III case or controversy. For that purpose, a case must exist at all the stages of appellate review. Preiser v. Newkirk, 422 U.S. 395, 401, 95 S.Ct. 2330, 2334, 45 L.Ed.2d 272 (1975); Mills v. Green, 159 U.S. 651, 653, 16 S.Ct. 132, 133, 40 L.Ed. 293 (1895). But reason and authority refute the quite different notion that a federal appellate court may not take any action with regard to a piece of litigation once it has been determined that the requirements of Article III no longer are (or indeed never were) met. That proposition is contradicted whenever an appellate court holds that a district court lacked Article III jurisdiction in the first instance, vacates the decision, and remands with directions to dismiss. In cases that become moot while awaiting review, respondent's logic would hold the Court powerless to award costs, e.g., Heitmuller v. Stokes, 256 U.S. 359, 362–363, 41 S.Ct. 522, 523–524, 65 L.Ed. 990 (1921), or even to enter an order of dismissal.

Article III does not prescribe such paralysis. "If a judgment has become moot [while awaiting review], this Court may not consider its merits, but may make such disposition of the whole case as justice may require." Walling v. Reuter, Inc., 321 U.S. 671, 677, 64 S.Ct. 826, 829, 88 L.Ed. 1001 (1944). As with other matters of judicial administration and practice "reasonably ancillary to the primary, dispute-deciding function" of the federal courts, Chandler v. Judicial Council of Tenth Circuit, 398 U.S. 74, 111, 90 S.Ct. 1648, 1667, 26 L.Ed.2d 100 (1970) (Harlan, J., concurring in denial of writ), Congress may authorize us to enter orders necessary and appropriate to the final disposition of a suit that is before us for review. See Mistretta v. United States, 488 U.S. 361, 389–390, 109 S.Ct. 647, 663–664, 102 L.Ed.2d 714 (1989); see also id., at 417, 109 S.Ct., at 678 (Scalia, J., dissenting).

III

The leading case on vacatur is United States v. Munsingwear, Inc., 340 U.S. 36, 71 S.Ct. 104, 95 L.Ed. 36 (1950), in which the United States sought injunctive and monetary relief for violation of a price control regulation. The damages claim was held in abeyance pending a decision on the injunction. The District Court held that the respondent's prices complied with the regulations and dismissed the complaint. While the United States' appeal was pending, the commodity at issue was decontrolled; at the respondent's request, the case was dismissed as moot, a disposition in which the United States acquiesced. The respondent then obtained dismissal of the damages action on the ground of res judicata, and we took the case to review that ruling. The United States protested the unfairness of according preclusive effect to a decision that it had tried to appeal but could not. We saw no such unfairness, reasoning that the United States should have asked the Court of Appeals to vacate the District Court's decision before the appeal was dismissed. We stated that "[t]he established practice of the Court in dealing with a civil case from a court in the federal system which has become moot while on its way here or pending our decision on the merits is to reverse or vacate the judgment below and remand with a direction to dismiss." Id., at 39, 71 S.Ct., at 106. We explained that vacatur "clears the path for future relitigation of the issues between the parties and eliminates a judgment, review of which was prevented through happenstance." Id., at 40, 71 S.Ct., at 107. Finding that the United States had "slept on its rights," id., at 41, 71 S.Ct., at 107, we affirmed.

The parties in the present case agree that vacatur must be decreed for those judgments whose review is, in the words of Munsingwear, " 'prevented through happenstance' "—that is to say, where a controversy presented for review has "become moot due to circumstances unattributable to any of the parties." Karcher v. May, 484 U.S. 72, 82, 83, 108 S.Ct. 388, 391, 98 L.Ed.2d 327 (1987). They also agree that vacatur must be granted where mootness results from the unilateral action of the party who prevailed in the lower court. The contested question is whether courts should vacate where mootness results from a settlement. The centerpiece of petitioner's argument is that the Munsingwear procedure has already been held to apply in such cases. Munsingwear's description of the "established practice" (the argument runs) drew no distinctions between categories of moot cases; opinions in later cases granting vacatur have reiterated the breadth of the rule, see, e.g., Great

Western Sugar Co. v. Nelson, 442 U.S. 92, 93, 99 S.Ct. 2149, 2150, 60 L.Ed.2d 735 (1979) (per curiam); and at least some of those cases specifically involved mootness by reason of settlement, see, e.g., Lake Coal Co. v. Roberts & Schaefer Co., 474 U.S. 120, 106 S.Ct. 553, 88 L.Ed.2d 418 (1985) (per curiam).

But Munsingwear, and the post-Munsingwear practice, cannot bear the weight of the present case. To begin with, the portion of Justice Douglas' opinion in Munsingwear describing the "established practice" for vacatur was dictum; all that was needful for the decision was (at most) the proposition that vacatur should have been sought, not that it necessarily would have been granted. Moreover, as Munsingwear itself acknowledged, see 340 U.S., at 40, n. 2, 71 S.Ct., at 107, n. 2, the "established practice" (in addition to being unconsidered) was not entirely uniform, at least three cases having been dismissed for mootness without vacatur within the four Terms preceding Munsingwear. See, e.g., Schenley Distilling Corp. v. Anderson, 333 U.S. 878, 68 S.Ct. 914, 92 L.Ed. 1154 (1948) (per curiam). Nor has the post-Munsingwear practice been as uniform as petitioner claims. See, e.g., Allen & Co. v. Pacific Dunlop Holdings, Inc., 510 U.S. ___, 114 S.Ct. 1146, 127 L.Ed.2d 454 (1994); Minnesota Newspaper Assn., Inc. v. Postmaster General, 488 U.S. 998, 109 S.Ct. 632, 102 L.Ed.2d 766 (1989); St. Luke's Federation of Nurses and Health Professionals v. Presbyterian/St. Luke's Medical Center, 459 U.S. 1025, 103 S.Ct. 433, 74 L.Ed.2d 522 (1982). Of course all of those decisions, both granting vacatur and denying it, were per curiam, with the single exception of Karcher v. May, supra, in which we declined to vacate. This seems to us a prime occasion for invoking our customary refusal to be bound by dicta, e.g., McCray v. Illinois, 386 U.S. 300, 312, n. 11, 87 S.Ct. 1056, 1063, n. 11, 18 L.Ed.2d 62 (1967), and our customary skepticism towards per curiam dispositions that lack the reasoned consideration of a full opinion, see Edelman v. Jordan, 415 U.S. 651, 670–671, 94 S.Ct. 1347, 1359–1360, 39 L.Ed.2d 662 (1974). Today we examine vacatur once more in the light shed by adversary presentation.

The principles that have always been implicit in our treatment of moot cases counsel against extending Munsingwear to settlement. From the beginning we have disposed of moot cases in the manner " 'most consonant to justice' ... in view of the nature and character of the conditions which have caused the case to become moot." United States v. Hamburg–Amerikanische Packetfahrt–Actien Gesellschaft, 239 U.S. 466, 477–478, 36 S.Ct. 212, 216–217, 60 L.Ed. 387 (1916) (quoting South Spring Hill Gold Mining Co. v. Amador Medean Gold Mining Co., 145 U.S. 300, 302, 12 S.Ct. 921, 921, 36 L.Ed. 712 (1892)). The principal condition to which we have looked is whether the party seeking relief from the judgment below caused the mootness by voluntary action. See Hamburg–Amerikanische Packetfahrt–Actien Gesellschaft, supra, 239 U.S., at 478, 36 S.Ct., at 217 (remanding a moot case for dismissal because "the ends of justice exact that the judgment below should not be permitted to stand when without any fault of the [petitioner] there is no power to review it upon the merits"); Heitmuller v. Stokes, 256 U.S., at 362, 41 S.Ct., at 523–524 (remanding for dismissal because "without fault of the plaintiff in error, the defendant in error, after the proceedings below, ... caus[ed] the case to become moot").

The reference to "happenstance" in Munsingwear must be understood as an allusion to this equitable tradition of vacatur. A party who seeks review of the merits of an adverse ruling, but is frustrated by the vagaries of circumstance, ought not in fairness be forced to acquiesce in the judgment. See Hamburg–Amerikanische Packetfahrt–Actien Gesellschaft, supra, 239 U.S., at 477–478, 36 S.Ct., at 216–217. The same is true when mootness results from unilateral action of the party who prevailed below. See Walling, 321 U.S., at 675, 64 S.Ct., at 828; Heitmuller, supra, 256 U.S. at 362, 41 S.Ct., at 523–524. Where mootness results from settlement, however, the losing party has voluntarily forfeited his legal remedy by the ordinary processes of appeal or certiorari, thereby surrendering his claim to the equitable remedy of vacatur. The judgment is not unreviewable, but simply unreviewed by his own choice. The denial of vacatur is merely one application of the principle that "[a] suitor's conduct in relation to the matter at hand may disentitle him to the relief he seeks." Sanders v. United States, 373 U.S. 1, 17, 83 S.Ct. 1068, 1078, 10 L.Ed.2d 148 (1963) (citing Fay v. Noia, 372 U.S. 391, 438, 83 S.Ct. 822, 848, 9 L.Ed.2d 837 (1963)).

In these respects the case stands no differently than it would if jurisdiction were lacking because the losing party failed to appeal at all. In Karcher v. May, 484 U.S. 72, 108 S.Ct. 388, 98 L.Ed.2d 327 (1987), two state legislators, acting in their capacities as presiding officers of the legislature, appealed from a federal judgment that invalidated a state statute on constitutional grounds. After the jurisdictional statement was filed the legislators lost their posts, and their successors in office withdrew the appeal. Holding that we lacked jurisdiction for want of a proper appellant, we dismissed. The legislators then argued that the judgments should be vacated under Munsingwear. But we denied the request, noting that "[t]his controversy did not become moot due to circumstances unattributable to any of the parties. The controversy ended when the losing party—the [State] Legislature—declined to pursue its appeal. Accordingly, the Munsingwear procedure is inapplicable to this case." Karcher, 484 U.S., at 83, 108 S.Ct., at 391. So too here.

It is true, of course, that respondent agreed to the settlement that caused the mootness. Petitioner argues that vacatur is therefore fair to respondent, and seeks to distinguish our prior cases on that ground. But that misconceives the emphasis on fault in our decisions. That the parties are jointly responsible for settling may in some sense put them on even footing, but petitioner's case needs more than that. Respondent won below. It is petitioner's burden, as the party seeking relief from the status quo of the appellate judgment, to demonstrate not merely equivalent responsibility for the mootness, but equitable entitlement to the extraordinary remedy of vacatur. Petitioner's voluntary forfeiture of review constitutes a failure of equity that makes the burden decisive, whatever respondent's share in the mooting of the case might have been.

As always when federal courts contemplate equitable relief, our holding must also take account of the public interest. "Judicial precedents are presumptively correct and valuable to the legal community as a whole. They are not merely the property of private litigants and should stand unless a court concludes that the public interest would be served by a vacatur." Izumi Seimitsu Kogyo Kabushiki Kaisha v. U.S. Philips Corp., 510 U.S. ___, ___, 114 S.Ct. 425, 428, 126 L.Ed.2d 396 (1993) (Stevens, J., dissenting). Congress has prescribed a primary route, by appeal as of right and certiorari, through which parties may seek relief from the legal consequences of judicial judgments. To allow a party who steps off the statutory path to employ the secondary remedy of vacatur as a refined form of collateral attack on the judgment would—quite apart from any considerations of fairness to the parties—disturb the orderly operation of the federal judicial system. Munsingwear establishes that the public interest is best served by granting relief when the demands of "orderly procedure," 340 U.S., at 41, 71 S.Ct., at 107, cannot be honored; we think conversely that the public interest requires those demands to be honored when they can.

Petitioner advances two arguments meant to justify vacatur on systemic grounds. The first is that appellate judgments in cases that we have consented to review by writ of certiorari are reversed more often than they are affirmed, are therefore suspect, and should be vacated as a sort of prophylactic against legal error. It seems to us inappropriate, however, to vacate mooted cases, in which we have no constitutional power to decide the merits, on the basis of assumptions about the merits. Second, petitioner suggests that "[v]acating a moot decision, and thereby leaving an issue . . . temporarily unresolved in a Circuit, can facilitate the ultimate resolution of the issue by encouraging its continued examination and debate." Brief for Petitioner 33. We have found, however, that debate among the courts of appeal sufficiently illuminates the questions that come before us for review. The value of additional intra-circuit debate seems to us far outweighed by the benefits that flow to litigants and the public from the resolution of legal questions.

A final policy justification urged by petitioner is the facilitation of settlement, with the resulting economies for the federal courts. But while the availability of vacatur may facilitate settlement after the judgment under review has been rendered and certiorari granted (or appeal filed), it may deter settlement at an earlier stage. Some litigants, at least, may think it worthwhile to roll the dice rather than settle in the district court, or in the court of appeals, if, but only if, an unfavorable outcome can be washed away by a settlement-related vacatur. And the judicial economies achieved by settlement at the district-court level are ordinarily much more extensive than those achieved by settlement on appeal. We find it quite impossible to assess the effect of our holding, either way, upon the frequency or systemic value of settlement.

Although the case before us involves only a motion to vacate, by reason of settlement, the judgment of a court of appeals (with, of course, the consequential vacation of the underlying judgment of the district court), it is appropriate to discuss the relevance of our holding to motions at the court of appeals level for vacatur of district-court judgments. Some opinions have suggested that vacatur motions at that level should be more freely granted, since district-court judgments are subject to review as of right. See, e.g., Manufacturers Hanover Trust Co. v. Yanakas, 11 F.3d 381, 384 (C.A.2 1993). Obviously, this factor does not affect the primary basis for our denying vacatur. Whether the appellate court's seizure of the case is the consequence of an appellant's right or of a petitioner's good luck has no bearing upon the lack of equity of a litigant who has voluntarily abandoned review. If the point of the proposed distinction is that district-court judgments, being subject to review as of right, are more likely to be overturned and hence presumptively less valid: We again assert the inappropriateness of disposing of cases, whose merits are beyond judicial power to consider, on the basis of judicial estimates regarding their merits. Moreover, as petitioner's own argument described two paragraphs above points out, the reversal rate for cases in which this Court grants certiorari (a precondition for our vacatur) is over 50%—more than double the reversal rate for appeals to the courts of appeal. See Jill E. Fisch, Rewriting History: The Propriety of Eradicating Prior Decisional Law Through Settlement and Vacatur, 76 Cornell L.Rev. 589, 595, n. 25 (1991) (citing studies).

We hold that mootness by reason of settlement does not justify vacatur of a judgment under review. This is not to say that vacatur can never be granted when mootness is produced in that fashion. As we have described, the determination is an equitable one, and exceptional circumstances may conceivably counsel in favor of such a course. It should be clear from our discussion, however, that those exceptional circumstances do not include the mere fact that the settlement agreement provides for vacatur—which neither diminishes the voluntariness of the abandonment of review nor alters any of the policy considerations we have discussed. Of course even in the absence of, or before considering the existence of, extraordinary circumstances, a court of appeals presented with a request for vacatur of a district-court judgment may remand the case with instructions that the district court consider the request, which it may do pursuant to Federal Rule of Civil Procedure 60(b).

* * *

Petitioner's motion to vacate the judgment of the Court of Appeals for the Ninth Circuit is denied. The case is dismissed as moot. See this Court's Rule 46.

It is so ordered.

NOTES

(1) Why did Bancorp want the judgment of the Court of Appeals to be vacated? If not vacated, would it retain its force for *res judicata* and *stare decisis* purposes? How could such force affect Bancorp?

(2) What lesson do you draw from this case? Could the settlement agreement have required vacatur of the Court of Appeals' judgment?

ARIZONANS FOR OFFICIAL ENGLISH v. ARIZONA

Supreme Court of the United States, 1997.
___ U.S. ___, 117 S.Ct. 1055, 137 L.Ed.2d 170.

JUSTICE GINSBURG delivered the opinion of the Court.

Federal courts lack competence to rule definitively on the meaning of state legislation, see, e.g., Reetz v. Bozanich, 397 U.S. 82, 86–87, 90 S.Ct. 788, 790, 25 L.Ed.2d 68 (1970), nor may they adjudicate challenges to state measures absent a showing of actual impact on the challenger, see, e.g., Golden v. Zwickler, 394 U.S. 103, 110, 89 S.Ct. 956, 960–961, 22 L.Ed.2d 113 (1969). The Ninth Circuit, in the case at hand, lost sight of these limitations. The initiating plaintiff, Maria–Kelly F. Yniguez, sought federal-court resolution of a novel question: the compatibility with the Federal Constitution of a 1988 amendment to Arizona's Constitution declaring English "the official language of the State of Arizona"—"the language of . . . all government functions and actions." Ariz. Const., Art. XXVIII, §§ 1(1), 1(2). Participants in the federal litigation, proceeding without benefit of the views of the Arizona Supreme Court, expressed diverse opinions on the meaning of the amendment.

Yniguez commenced and maintained her suit as an individual, not as a class representative. A state employee at the time she filed her complaint, Yniguez voluntarily left the State's employ in 1990 and did not allege she would seek to return to a public post. Her departure for a position in the private sector made her claim for prospective relief moot. Nevertheless, the Ninth Circuit held that a plea for nominal damages could be read into Yniguez's complaint to save the case, and therefore pressed on to an ultimate decision. A three-judge panel of the Court of Appeals declared Article XXVIII unconstitutional in 1994, and a divided en banc court, in 1995, adhered to the panel's position.

The Ninth Circuit had no warrant to proceed as it did. The case had lost the essential elements of a justiciable controversy and should not have been retained for adjudication on the merits by the Court of Appeals. We therefore vacate the Ninth Circuit's judgment, and remand the case to that court with directions that the action be dismissed by the

District Court. We express no view on the correct interpretation of Article XXVIII or on the measure's constitutionality....

NOTE

1. Could the principal case have been decided on the exception to the mootness doctrine that moot cases that are likely to be repeated are justiciable? Note that Justice Ginsburg, when an advocate, had persuaded the Court to decide the case of a pregnant woman who was no longer pregnant when her case reached the Court. Roe v. Wade, 410 U.S. 113, 93 S.Ct. 705, 35 L.Ed.2d 147 (1973). Are the cases distinguishable?

Chapter Six

ADJUDICATORY AUTHORITY: BASES AND MEANS OF EXERCISE

SECTION 2. ADJUDICATORY AUTHORITY OVER THE SUBJECT MATTER

B. CONSTITUTIONAL AND STATUTORY RULES

1. DIVERSITY

[Insert at page 187, at the end of Note (6):]

In Rosa v. Allstate Insurance Co., 981 F.2d 669 (2d Cir.1992), the Second Circuit construed the provision in § 1332(c)(1), dealing with the insurance company's citizenship for diversity purposes in a "direct action" against an insurance company. The court declared that the provision applies only to cases in which state law permits a claimant to sue the derivatively liable insurance company directly, without first obtaining a recovery from the party at fault. The court held that the provision does not apply to claims under no-fault policies, which are in the nature of claims by the insured (or those standing in her shoes) to enforce a "first party" contractual obligation rather than a "third party" liability coverage.

[Insert at page 189, after Note (13):]

ADJUDICATORY AUTHORITY OVER FAMILY LAW DISPUTES: A SPECIAL CASE

ANKENBRANDT v. RICHARDS

Supreme Court of the United States, 1992.
504 U.S. 689, 112 S.Ct. 2206, 119 L.Ed.2d 468.

JUSTICE WHITE delivered the opinion of the Court.*

This case presents the issue whether the federal courts have jurisdiction or should abstain in a case involving alleged torts committed by the former husband of petitioner and his female companion against petitioner's children, when the sole basis for federal jurisdiction is the diversity-of-citizenship provision of 28 U.S.C. § 1332.

* Footnotes omitted.

I

Petitioner Carol Ankenbrandt, a citizen of Missouri, brought this lawsuit on September 26, 1989, on behalf of her daughters L.R. and S.R. against respondents Jon A. Richards and Debra Kesler, citizens of Louisiana, in the United States District Court for the Eastern District of Louisiana. Alleging federal jurisdiction based on the diversity of citizenship provision of § 1332, Ankenbrandt's complaint sought monetary damages for alleged sexual and physical abuse of the children committed by Richards and Kesler. Richards is the divorced father of the children and Kesler his female companion. On December 10, 1990, the District Court granted respondents' motion to dismiss this lawsuit. Citing In re Burrus, 136 U.S. 586, 593–594, 10 S.Ct. 850, 853, 34 L.Ed. 500 (1890), for the proposition that "[t]he whole subject of the domestic relations of husband and wife, parent and child, belongs to the laws of the States and not to the laws of the United States," the court concluded that this case fell within what has become known as the "domestic relations" exception to diversity jurisdiction, and that it lacked jurisdiction over the case.... The Court of Appeals affirmed....

We granted certiorari limited to the following questions: (1) Is there a domestic relations exception to federal jurisdiction? (2) If so, does it permit a district court to abstain from exercising diversity jurisdiction over a tort action for damages? ...

II

The domestic relations exception upon which the courts below relied to decline jurisdiction has been invoked often by the lower federal courts. The seeming authority for doing so originally stemmed from the announcement in Barber v. Barber, 21 How. 582, 16 L.Ed. 226 (1859), that the federal courts have no jurisdiction over suits for divorce or the allowance of alimony.

... Because we are unwilling to cast aside an understood rule that has been recognized for nearly a century and a half, we feel compelled to explain why we will continue to recognize this limitation on federal jurisdiction.

A

* * *

Article III, § 2, of the Constitution ... delineates the absolute limits on the federal courts' jurisdiction. But in articulating three different terms to define jurisdiction—"Cases, in Law and Equity," "Cases," and "Controversies"—this provision contains no limitation on subjects of a domestic relations nature. Nor did *Barber* purport to ground the domestic relations exception in those constitutional limits on federal jurisdiction....

* * *

Moreover, even while citing with approval the *Barber* language purporting to limit the jurisdiction of the federal courts over domestic relations matters, the Court has heard appeals from territorial courts involving divorce, see, e.g., ... Simms v. Simms, 175 U.S. 162, 20 S.Ct. 58, 44 L.Ed. 115 (1899), and has upheld the exercise of original jurisdiction by federal courts in the District of Columbia to decide divorce actions, see, e.g., Glidden Co. v. Zdanok, 370 U.S. 530, 581, n. 54, 82 S.Ct. 1459, 1489, n. 54, 8 L.Ed.2d 671 (1962)....

B

That Article III, § 2, does not mandate the exclusion of domestic relations cases from federal-court jurisdiction, however, does not mean that such courts necessarily must retain and exercise jurisdiction over such cases. Other constitutional provisions explain why this is so. Article I, § 8, cl. 9, for example, authorizes Congress "[t]o constitute Tribunals inferior to the supreme Court" and Article III, § 1, states that "[t]he judicial Power of the United States, shall be vested in one supreme Court, and in such inferior Courts as the Congress may from time to time ordain and establish." The Court's cases state the rule that "if inferior federal courts were created, [Congress was not] required to invest them with all the jurisdiction it was authorized to bestow under Art. III." Palmore v. United States, 411 U.S. 389, 401, 93 S.Ct. 1670, 1678, 36 L.Ed.2d 342 (1973).

* * *

The Judiciary Act of 1789 provided that "the circuit courts shall have original cognizance, concurrent with the courts of the several States, of all suits of a civil nature at common law or in equity, where the matter in dispute exceeds, exclusive of costs, the sum or value of five hundred dollars, and ... an alien is a party, or the suit is between a citizen of the State where the suit is brought, and a citizen of another State." Act of Sept. 24, 1789, § 11, 1 Stat. 73, 78. The defining phrase, "all suits of a civil nature at common law or in equity," remained a key element of statutory provisions demarcating the terms of diversity jurisdiction until 1948, when Congress amended the diversity jurisdiction provision to eliminate this phrase and replace in its stead the term "all civil actions." 1948 Judicial Code and Judiciary Act, 62 Stat. 930, 28 U.S.C. § 1332.

The *Barber* majority itself did not expressly refer to the diversity statute's use of the limitation on "suits of a civil nature at common law or in equity." The dissenters in *Barber,* however, implicitly made such a reference, for they suggested that the federal courts had no power over certain domestic relations actions because the court of chancery lacked authority to issue divorce and alimony decrees....

We have no occasion here to join the historical debate over whether the English court of chancery had jurisdiction to handle certain domestic relations matters, though we note that commentators have found some support for the *Barber* majority's interpretation.... Whatever Article III may or may not permit, we ... accept the *Barber* dictum as a correct interpretation of the Congressional grant. Considerations of stare decisis have particular strength in this context, where "the legislative power is implicated, and Congress remains free to alter what we have done." Patterson v. McLean Credit Union, 491 U.S. 164, 172–173, 109 S.Ct. 2363, 2370, 105 L.Ed.2d 132 (1989).

III

In the more than 100 years since this Court laid the seeds for the development of the domestic relations exception, the lower federal courts have applied it in a variety of circumstances....

Subsequently, this Court expanded the domestic relations exception to include decrees in child custody cases. In a child custody case brought pursuant to a writ of habeas corpus, for instance, the Court held void a writ issued by a Federal District Court to restore a child to the custody of the father. "As to the right to the control and possession of this child, as it is contested by its father and its grandfather, it is one in regard to which neither the Congress of the United States nor any authority of the United States has any special jurisdiction." In re Burrus, 136 U.S. 586, 594, 10 S.Ct. 850, 853, 34 L.Ed. 500 (1890).

* * *

Not only is our conclusion rooted in respect for this long-held understanding, it is also supported by sound policy considerations. Issuance of decrees of this type not infrequently involves retention of jurisdiction by the court and deployment of social workers to monitor compliance. As a matter of judicial economy, state courts are more eminently suited to work of this type than are federal courts, which lack the close association with state and local government organizations dedicated to handling issues that arise out of conflicts over divorce, alimony, and child custody decrees. Moreover, as a matter of judicial expertise, it makes far more sense to retain the rule that federal courts lack power to issue these types of decrees because of the special proficiency developed by state tribunals over the past century and a half in handling issues that arise in the granting of such decrees.

By concluding, as we do, that the domestic relations exception encompasses only cases involving the issuance of a divorce, alimony, or child custody decree, we necessarily find that the Court of Appeals erred by affirming the District Court's invocation of this exception. This lawsuit in no way seeks such a decree; rather, it alleges that respondents Richards and Kesler committed torts against L.R. and S.R., Ankenbrandt's children by Richards. Federal subject-matter jurisdiction pursuant to § 1332 thus is proper in this case....

* * *

V

* * *

Accordingly, we reverse the decision of the Court of Appeals and remand the case for further proceedings consistent with this opinion.

It is so ordered.

JUSTICE BLACKMUN, concurring:

* * *

I agree with the Court that the District Court had jurisdiction over petitioner's claims in tort. Moreover, I agree that the federal courts should not entertain claims for divorce, alimony, and child custody. I am unable to agree, however, that the diversity statute contains any "exception" for domestic relations matters. The Court goes to remarkable lengths to craft an exception that is simply not in the statute and is not supported by the case law. In my view, the longstanding, unbroken practice of the federal courts in refusing to hear domestic relations cases is precedent at most for continued discretionary abstention rather than mandatory limits on federal jurisdiction. For these reasons I concur only in the Court's judgment.

* * *

JUSTICES STEVENS and THOMAS, concurring [omitted].

NOTES

(1) At common law, wives were subordinated to husbands, and thus could not establish their own domicile, even when residing apart, see, e.g., Anderson v. Watt, 138 U.S. 694, 11 S.Ct. 449, 34 L.Ed. 1078 (1891). As divorce became common place, and the fiction of identity of person of husband and wife vanished, this rule changed. The "better" rule is now regarded as one in which even a married woman may have a domicile different from that of her husband, although courts tend to treat such claims, when a marriage is on-going, sceptically, Wright, Miller, & Cooper, Federal Practice and Procedure § 3614.

(2) The principal case's treatment of women's citizenship and the consequential non-involvement of the national courts in family law matters has been criticized by feminist theorists on the ground that women and their concerns are marginalized, Resnick, "Naturally" Without Gender: Women, Jurisdiction, and the Federal Courts, 66 N.Y.U.L.Rev. 1682 (1991).

(3) In Strate, Associate Tribal Judge v. A-1 Contractors, ___ U.S. ___, 117 S.Ct. 1404, 137 L.Ed.2d 661 (1997), the Supreme Court ruled that an Indian tribal court had no adjudicatory authority to entertain a claim by a non-member of the tribe against another non-member arising from an accident on a state highway maintained by North Dakota under a right-of-way granted on land held in trust for the tribe. Should the result be different when either the plaintiff or the defendant or both are members of the tribe?

---

2. FEDERAL QUESTION

[Insert on page 189 before *Franchise Tax Board:*]

LOUISVILLE & NASHVILLE R.R. CO. v. MOTTLEY

Supreme Court of the United States, 1908.
211 U.S. 149, 29 S.Ct. 42, 53 L.Ed. 126.

The appellees (husband and wife), being residents and citizens of Kentucky, brought this suit in equity in the Circuit Court of the United States for the Western District of Kentucky against the appellant, a railroad company and a citizen of the same State. The object of the suit was to compel the specific performance of the following contract:

"Louisville, Ky., Oct. 2nd, 1871.

"The Louisville & Nashville Railroad Company in consideration that E.L. Mottley and wife, Annie E. Mottley, have this day released Company from all damages or claims for damages for injuries received by them on the 7th day of September, 1871, in consequence of a collision of trains on the railroad of said Company at Randolph's Station, Jefferson County, Ky., hereby agrees to issue free passes on said Railroad and branches now existing or to exist, to said E.L. & Annie E. Mottley for the remainder of the present year, and thereafter, to renew said passes annually during the lives of said Mottley and wife or either of them."

The bill alleged that in September, 1871, plaintiffs, while passengers upon the defendant railroad, were injured by the defendant's negligence, and released their respective claims for damages in consideration of the agreement for transportation during their lives, expressed in the contract. It is alleged that the contract was performed by the defendant up to January 1, 1907, when the defendant declined to renew the passes. The bill then alleges that the refusal to comply with the contract was based solely upon that part of the act of Congress of June 29, 1906, 34 Stat. 584, which forbids the giving of free passes or free transportation. The bill further alleges: First, that the act of Congress referred to does not prohibit the giving of passes under the circumstances of this case; and, second, that if the law is to be construed as prohibiting such passes, it is in conflict with the Fifth Amendment of the Constitution, because it deprives the plaintiffs of their property without due process of law. The defendant demurred to the bill. The judge of the Circuit Court overruled the demurrer, entered a decree for the relief prayed for, and the defendant appealed directly to this court.

* * *

MR. JUSTICE MOODY, after making the foregoing statement, delivered the opinion of the court.

Two questions of law were raised by the demurrer to the bill, were brought here by appeal, and have been argued before us. They are, first, whether that part of the act of Congress of June 29, 1906 (34 Stat. 584), which forbids the giving of free passes or the collection of any different compensation for transportation of passengers than that specified in the tariff filed, makes it unlawful to perform a contract for transportation of persons, who in good faith, before the passage of the act, had accepted such contract in satisfaction of a valid cause of action against the railroad; and, second, whether the statute, if it should be construed to render such a contract unlawful, is in violation of the Fifth Amendment of the Constitution of the United States. We do not deem it necessary, however, to consider either of these questions, because, in our opinion, the court below was without jurisdiction of the cause. Neither party has questioned that jurisdiction, but it is the duty of this court to see to it that the jurisdiction of the Circuit Court, which is defined and limited by statute, is not exceeded. This duty we have frequently performed of our own motion. [Citations omitted.]

There was no diversity of citizenship and it is not and cannot be suggested that there was any ground of jurisdiction, except that the case was a "suit ... arising under the Constitution and laws of the United States." Act of August 13, 1888, c. 866, 25 Stat. 433, 434. It is the settled interpretation of these words, as used in this statute, conferring jurisdiction, that a suit arises under the Constitution and laws of the United States only when the plaintiff's statement of his own cause of action shows that it is based upon those laws or that Constitution. It is not enough that the plaintiff alleges some anticipated defense to his cause of action and asserts that the defense is invalidated by some provision of the Constitution of the United States. Although such allegations show that very likely, in the course of the litigation, a question under the Constitution would arise, they do not show that the suit, that is, the plaintiff's original cause of action, arises under the Constitution. In Tennessee v. Union & Planters' Bank, 152 U.S. 454, 38 L.Ed. 511, 14 S.Ct. 654, the plaintiff, the State of Tennessee, brought suit in the Circuit Court of the United States to recover from the defendant certain taxes alleged to be due under the laws of the State. The plaintiff alleged that the defendant claimed an immunity from the taxation by virtue of its charter, and that therefore the tax was void, because in violation of the provision of the Constitution of the United States, which forbids any State from passing a law impairing the obligation of contracts. The cause was held to be beyond the jurisdiction of the Circuit Court, the court saying, by Mr. Justice Gray (p. 464), "a suggestion of one party, that the other will or may set up a claim under the Constitution or laws of the United States, does not make the suit one arising under that Constitution or those laws." Again, in Boston & Montana Consolidated Copper & Silver Mining Company v. Montana Ore Purchasing Company, 188 U.S. 632, 47 L.Ed. 626, 23 S.Ct. 434, the plaintiff brought suit in the Circuit Court of the United States for the conversion of copper ore and for an injunction against its continuance.

The plaintiff then alleged, for the purpose of showing jurisdiction, in substance, that the defendant would set up in defense certain laws of the United States. The cause was held to be beyond the jurisdiction of the Circuit Court, the court saying, by Mr. Justice Peckham (pp. 638, 639).

"It would be wholly unnecessary and improper in order to prove complainant's cause of action to go into any matters of defence which the defendants might possibly set up and then attempt to reply to such defence, and thus, if possible, to show that a Federal question might or probably would arise in the course of the trial of the case. To allege such defence and then make an answer to it before the defendant has the opportunity to itself plead or prove its own defence is inconsistent with any known rule of pleading so far as we are aware, and is improper.

"The rule is a reasonable and just one that the complainant in the first instance shall be confined to a statement of its cause of action, leaving to the defendant to set up in his answer what his defense is and, if anything more than a denial of complainant's cause of action, imposing upon the defendant the burden of proving such defence.

"Conforming itself to that rule the complainant would not, in the assertion or proof of its cause of action, bring up a single Federal question. The presentation of its cause of action would not show that it was one arising under the Constitution or laws of the United States.

"The only way in which it might be claimed that a Federal question was presented would be in the complainant's statement of what the defence of defendants would be and complainant's answer to such defence. Under these circumstances the case is brought within the rule laid down in *Tennessee v. Union & Planters' Bank,* supra. That case has been cited and approved many times since, . . ."

The interpretation of the act which we have stated was first announced in Metcalf v. Watertown, 128 U.S. 586, 32 L.Ed. 543, 9 S.Ct. 173, and has since been repeated and applied [many times, citations omitted]. The application of this rule to the case at bar is decisive against the jurisdiction of the Circuit Court.

It is ordered that the

Judgment be reversed and the case remitted to the Circuit Court with instructions to dismiss the suit for want of jurisdiction.

3.   AMOUNT IN CONTROVERSY

[Insert at page 205, as Note (7) & (8):]

(7) May a federal district court, in a diversity case, in which claims under $50,000.00 are aggregated to meet the amount in controversy requirement of Section 1332(a) of Title 28 of the United States Code and one of the aggregated

claims is dismissed, thus reducing the amount in controversy below that requirement, retain the remaining claims for adjudication? Must this determination be made under Section 1332(a) or Section 1367 of Title 28 of the United States Code? In Shanaghan v. Cahill, 58 F.3d 106 (4th Cir.1995), the court, reading both sections together, ruled that the district court should use its "discretion" in determining whether to keep the case.

(8) At what stage of the proceedings must the requirements of subject matter competence be met? In Caterpillar Inc. v. Lewis, ___ U.S. ___, 117 S.Ct. 467, 136 L.Ed.2d 437 (1996), Justice Ginsburg ruled as follows (117 S.Ct. at 470-71):

CATERPILLAR INC. v. LEWIS

Supreme Court of the United States, 1996.
___ U.S. ___, 117 S.Ct. 467, 136 L.Ed.2d 437.

JUSTICE GINSBURG delivered the opinion of the Court.

This case, commenced in a state court, involves personal injury claims arising under state law. The case was removed to a federal court at a time when, the Court of Appeals concluded, complete diversity of citizenship did not exist among the parties. Promptly after the removal, the plaintiff moved to remand the case to the state court, but the District Court denied that motion. Before trial of the case, however, all claims involving the nondiverse defendant were settled, and that defendant was dismissed as a party to the action. Complete diversity thereafter existed. The case proceeded to trial, jury verdict, and judgment for the removing defendant. The Court of Appeals vacated the judgment, concluding that, absent complete diversity at the time of removal, the District Court lacked subject-matter jurisdiction.

The question presented is whether the absence of complete diversity at the time of removal is fatal to federal court adjudication. We hold that a district court's error in failing to remand a case improperly removed is not fatal to the ensuing adjudication if federal jurisdictional requirements are met at the time judgment is entered. . . .

4.   PENDENT, ANCILLARY, AND PROTECTIVE ADJUDICATORY AUTHORITY

[Insert on page 206, before *Finley:*]

UNITED MINE WORKERS OF AMERICA v. GIBBS

Supreme Court of the United States, 1966.
383 U.S. 715, 86 S.Ct. 1130, 16 L.Ed.2d 218.

MR. JUSTICE BRENNAN delivered the opinion of the Court.*

[Gibbs brought an action against the UMW in a federal district court in Tennessee seeking recovery under both the federal Labor Management Relations Act of 1947 and Tennessee law. Grundy, a mining

* Footnotes omitted.

company, had employed plaintiff as mine superintendent and had given him a contract to haul coal. Gibbs alleged that UMW had violated Section 303 of the federal Act by pressuring Grundy to discharge him as supervisor and hauler of its coal and by pressuring other companies to cease doing business with him. His claim based on Tennessee law asserted "an unlawful conspiracy and an unlawful boycott aimed at him and [Grundy] to maliciously, wantonly and wilfully interfere with his contract of employment and with his contract of haulage."]

* * *

The trial judge refused to submit to the jury the claims of pressure intended to cause mining firms other than Grundy to cease doing business with Gibbs; he found those claims unsupported by the evidence. The jury's verdict was that the UMW had violated both § 303 and state law. Gibbs was awarded $60,000 as damages under the employment contract and $14,500 under the haulage contract; he was also awarded $100,000 punitive damages. On motion, the trial court set aside the award of damages with respect to the haulage contract on the ground that damage was unproved. It also held that union pressure on Grundy to discharge respondent as supervisor would constitute only a primary dispute with Grundy, as respondent's employer, and hence was not cognizable as a claim under § 303. Interference with the employment relationship was cognizable as a state claim, however, and a remitted award was sustained on the state law claim. 220 F.Supp. 871. The Court of Appeals for the Sixth Circuit affirmed. 343 F.2d 609. We granted certiorari. 382 U.S. 809, 86 S.Ct. 59, 15 L.Ed.2d 58. We reverse.

I.

ISSUE

A threshold question is whether the District Court properly entertained jurisdiction of the claim based on Tennessee law.... The Court held in Hurn v. Oursler, 289 U.S. 238, 53 S.Ct. 586, 77 L.Ed. 1148, that state law claims are appropriate for federal court determination if they form a separate but parallel ground for relief also sought in a substantial claim based on federal law. The Court distinguished permissible from nonpermissible exercises of federal judicial power over state law claims by contrasting "a case where two distinct grounds in support of a single cause of action are alleged, one only of which presents a federal question, and a case where two separate and distinct causes of action are alleged, one only of which is federal in character. In the former, where the federal question averred is not plainly wanting in substance, the federal court, even though the federal ground be not established, may nevertheless retain and dispose of the case upon the nonfederal *ground;* in the latter it may not do so upon the nonfederal *cause of action.*" 289 U.S., at 246, 53 S.Ct., at 589. The question is into which category the present action fell.

2 categories

Hurn was decided in 1933, before the unification of law and equity by the Federal Rules of civil procedure. At the time, the meaning of "cause of action" was a subject of serious dispute; the phrase might "mean one thing for one purpose and something different for another." United States v. Memphis Cotton Oil Co., 288 U.S. 62, 67–68, 53 S.Ct. 278, 280, 77 L.Ed. 619. The Court in *Hurn* identified what it meant by the term by citation of Baltimore S.S. Co. v. Phillips, 274 U.S. 316, 47 S.Ct. 600, 71 L.Ed. 1069, a case in which "cause of action" had been used to identify the operative scope of the doctrine of *res judicata*. In that case the Court had noted that "the whole tendency of our decisions is to require a plaintiff to try his whole cause of action and his whole case at one time." 274 U.S., at 320, 47 S.Ct., at 602. . . . Had the Court found a jurisdictional bar to reaching the state claim in *Hurn,* we assume that the doctrine of *res judicata* would not have been applicable in any subsequent state suit. But the citation of *Baltimore S.S. Co.* shows that the Court found that the weighty policies of judicial economy and fairness to parties reflected in *res judicata* doctrine were in themselves strong counsel for the adoption of a rule which would permit federal courts to dispose of the state as well as the federal claims.

With the adoption of the Federal Rules of Civil Procedure and the unified form of action, Fed.Rule Civ.Proc. 2, much of the controversy over "cause of action" abated. The phrase remained as the keystone of the *Hurn* test, however, and, as commentators have noted, has been the source of considerable confusion. Under the Rules, the impulse is toward entertaining the broadest possible scope of action consistent with fairness to the parties; joinder of claims, parties and remedies is strongly encouraged. Yet because the *Hurn* question involves issues of jurisdiction as well as convenience, there has been some tendency to limit its application to cases in which the state and federal claims are, as in *Hurn,* "little more than the equivalent of different epithets to characterize the same group of circumstances." 289 U.S., at 246, 53 S.Ct., at 590.

This limited approach is unnecessarily grudging. Pendent jurisdiction, in the sense of judicial *power,* exists whenever there is a claim "arising under [the] Constitution, the Laws of the United States, and Treaties made, or which shall be made, under their Authority . . . ," U.S. Const., Art. III, § 2, and the relationship between that claim and the state claim permits the conclusion that the entire action before the court comprises but one constitutional "case." The federal claim must have substance sufficient to confer subject matter jurisdiction on the court. Levering & Garrigues Co. v. Morrin, 289 U.S. 103, 53 S.Ct. 549, 77 L.Ed. 1062. The state and federal claims must derive from a common nucleus of operative fact. But if, considered without regard to their federal or state character, a plaintiff's claims are such that he would ordinarily be expected to try them all in one judicial proceeding, then, assuming substantiality of the federal issues, there is *power* in federal courts to hear the whole.

That power need not be exercised in every case in which it is found to exist. It has consistently been recognized that pendent jurisdiction is a doctrine of discretion, not of plaintiff's right. Its justification lies in considerations of judicial economy, convenience and fairness to litigants; if these are not present a federal court should hesitate to exercise jurisdiction over state claims, even though bound to apply state law to them, Erie R. Co. v. Tompkins, 304 U.S. 64, 58 S.Ct. 817, 82 L.Ed. 1188. Needless decisions of state law should be avoided both as a matter of comity and to promote justice between the parties, by procuring for them a surer-footed reading of applicable law. Certainly, if the federal claims are dismissed before trial, even though not insubstantial in a jurisdictional sense, the state claims should be dismissed as well. Similarly, if it appears that the state issues substantially predominate, whether in terms of proof, of the scope of the issues raised, or of the comprehensiveness of the remedy sought, the state claims may be dismissed without prejudice and left for resolution to state tribunals. There may, on the other hand, be situations in which the state claim is so closely tied to questions of federal policy that the argument for exercise of pendent jurisdiction is particularly strong. In the present case, for example, the allowable scope of the state claim implicates the federal doctrine of preemption; while this interrelationship does not create statutory federal question jurisdiction, Louisville & N.R. Co. v. Mottley, 211 U.S. 149, 29 S.Ct. 42, 53 L.Ed. 126, its existence is relevant to the exercise of discretion. Finally, there may be reasons independent of jurisdictional considerations, such as the likelihood of jury confusion in treating divergent legal theories of relief, that would justify separating state and federal claims for trial, Fed.Rule Civ.Proc. 42(b). If so, jurisdiction should ordinarily be refused.

The question of power will ordinarily be resolved on the pleadings. But the issue whether pendent jurisdiction has been properly assumed is one which remains open throughout the litigation. Pretrial procedures or even the trial itself may reveal a substantial hegemony of state law claims, or likelihood of jury confusion, which could not have been anticipated at the pleading stage. Although it will of course be appropriate to take account in this circumstance of the already completed course of the litigation, dismissal of the state claim might even then be merited. For example, it may appear that the plaintiff was well aware of the nature of his proofs and the relative importance of his claims; recognition of a federal court's wide latitude to decide ancillary questions of state law does not imply that it must tolerate a litigant's effort to impose upon it what is in effect only a state law case. Once it appears that a state claim constitutes the real body of a case, to which the federal claim is only an appendage, the state claim may fairly be dismissed.

We are not prepared to say that in the present case the District Court exceeded its discretion in proceeding to judgment on the state claim. We may assume for purposes of decision that the District Court was correct in its holding that the claim of pressure on Grundy to terminate the employment contract was outside the purview of § 303. Even so, the § 303 claims based on secondary pressures on Grundy relative to the haulage contract and on other coal operators generally were substantial. Although § 303 limited recovery to compensatory damages based on secondary pressures, Teamsters Union v. Morton, supra, and state law allowed both compensatory and punitive damages, and allowed such damages as to both secondary and primary activity, the state and federal claims arose from the same nucleus of operative fact and reflected alternative remedies. Indeed, the verdict sheet sent into the jury authorized only one award of damages, so that recovery could not be given separately on the federal and state claims.

It is true that the § 303 claims ultimately failed and that the only recovery allowed respondent was on the state claim. We cannot confidently say, however, that the federal issues were so remote or played such a minor role at the trial that in effect the state claim only was tried. Although the District Court dismissed as unproved the § 303 claims that petitioner's secondary activities included attempts to induce coal operators other than Grundy to cease doing business with respondent, the court submitted the § 303 claims relating to Grundy to the jury. The jury returned verdicts against petitioner on those § 303 claims, and it was only on petitioner's motion for a directed verdict and a judgment n.o.v. that the verdicts on those claims were set aside. The District Judge considered the claim as to the haulage contract proved as to liability, and held it failed only for lack of proof of damages. Although there was some risk of confusing the jury in joining the state and federal claims—especially since, as will be developed, differing standards of proof of UMW involvement applied—the possibility of confusion could be lessened by employing a special verdict form, as the District Court did. Moreover, the question whether the permissible scope of the state claim was limited by the doctrine of preemption afforded a special reason for the exercise of pendent jurisdiction; the federal courts are particularly appropriate bodies for the application of preemption principles. We thus conclude that although it may be that the District Court might, in its sound discretion, have dismissed the state claim, the circumstances show no error in refusing to do so.

* * *

[Insert on page 210, after the Note:]

By the Judicial Improvements Act of 1990, 104 Stat. 5089 (Dec. 1, 1990), Congress legislatively overruled the Finley decision. It did so by adding a new section, § 1367, to Title 28 of the U.S.C.A.

NOTES

(1) Is this new section an example of felicitous draftsmanship? In subdivision (a), what is meant by the words "in any civil action of which the courts have

original jurisdiction?" If read literally to require that the court have original jurisdiction in the action, why is it necessary to provide for "supplemental jurisdiction?" No doubt the Congressional intention would have been more clearly expressed if the words "with respect to any claim" had been added to further define the court's original competence. Is the intent of subdivision (a) to extend subject matter competence to all claims that can properly be regarded as constituting one case or controversy in the constitutional sense? If so, would it have been preferable to provide that the district court shall have original competence with respect to all claims that constitute one case or controversy within the meaning of Article III of the Constitution? Would it have been necessary to add that the competence exists regardless of whether any of the claims are introduced by the plaintiff or the defendant or by or against any third party?

Section 1367 has generated considerable academic debate, beginning with a piece by its drafters. Mengler, Burbank, and Rowe, Congress Accepts Supreme Court's Invitation to Codify Supplemental Jurisdiction, 74 Judicature 213 (1991). This was followed by Freer, Compounding Confusion and Hampering Diversity: Life after Finley and the Supplemental Jurisdiction Statute, 40 Emory L.J. 445 (1991); Rowe, Mengler, & Burbank: Compounding or Creating Confusion About Supplemental Jurisdiction, A Reply to Professor Freer, 40 Emory L.J. 943 (1991); Freer & Arthur, Grasping at Burnt Straws: The Disaster of the Supplemental Jurisdiction Statute, 40 Emory L.J. 963 (1991); Rowe, Burbank & Mengler, A Coda on Supplemental Jurisdiction, 40 Emory L.J. 993 (1991); Arthur & Freer: Close Enough for Government to Work: What Happens When Congress Doesn't Do Its Job, 40 Emory L.J. 1007 (1991); as well as the first issue of 41 Emory L.J., which includes Dreyfuss, The Debate Over § 1367: Defining the Power to Define Federal Judicial Power, 41 Emory L.J. 13 (1992). See also McLaughlin, The Federal Supplemental Jurisdiction Statute, 24 Ariz.St.L.J. 849 (1992).

(2) Why was subdivision (b) added? Does it make sense not to authorize the exercise of supplemental competence merely because the introduction of an additional party would defeat the requirements of diversity or amount in controversy of § 1332? If diversity competence is not to be expanded, why permit supplemental competence in regard to compulsory counterclaims that could not be entertained independently under either § 1332 or § 1331? Could not subdivisions (a) and (b) have been formulated more simply to provide that the district courts have original competence in regard to all claims that constitute one case or controversy within the meaning of Article III other than claims that do not meet the diversity requirements of § 1332 and that are added to claims over which there is competence only by virtue of § 1332? Such a provision would carry forward consistently the notion that diversity competence should not be expanded beyond the confines set by § 1332. However, if the legislature is prepared to go beyond these confines in the case of compulsory counterclaims, why stop there? In any event, subdivision (b) does not provide a clear answer to when the exercise of competence over such claims is "inconsistent with the jurisdictional requirements of § 1332." This language begs, rather than resolves, the question of whether the court should interpret § 1332 sufficiently broadly to encompass such claims.

(3) Subdivision (c) appears to specify the circumstance in which the court, in the exercise of its "discretion", under the *Gibbs* case, could decline to exercise supplemental competence. Could you improve upon this subdivision's enumer-

ation? Does it state anywhere what overall consideration the court should take into account other than the circumstances mentioned? What is the use of paragraph (4) of subdivision (c)? Would it have been better to provide generally that the court may decline to exercise supplemental competence when the disadvantages of joint adjudication outweigh its advantages, and that, in making that determination, the court may consider the circumstances specified in paragraphs (1)–(3)?

(4) Is subdivision (d) constitutional under *Erie* as interpreted in Guaranty Trust Co. v. York, casebook at page 362? How artful is the draftsmanship of this subdivision? Does it seek to provide no more than that, if a claim as to which supplemental competence is asserted, is dismissed for want of such competence, the statute of limitations is tolled for the prescribed period? Or does it also apply when such a claim is dismissed for any other reason?

(5) One of the questions raised by the defective draftsmanship of Section 1367 is whether it overrules the *Zahn* case (p. 205 of casebook). In In re Abbott Laboratories, 51 F.3d 524 (5th Cir.1995), the court ruled that it did. Noting that it was unlikely that Congress intended this result and that the drafters of Section 1367 opposed it, the court nevertheless ruled the statute to be clear and unambiguous. This ruling was cited with approval by the Seventh Circuit in Stromberg Metal Works, Inc. v. Press Mechanical, Inc., 77 F.3d 928 (7th Cir.1996), in which the court found competence under Section 1367 in a multi-party diversity action, although the claim by one of the parties did not meet the jurisdictional amount. The court remarked that whether Section 1367 was a "model drafting exercise may be doubted" (at p. 932).

––––––––

SINCLAIR v. SONIFORM, INC.

United States Court of Appeals, Third Circuit, 1991.
935 F.2d 599.

COWEN, CIRCUIT JUDGE.*

The issue before us is whether an action arising from injuries sustained during a scuba diving excursion in navigable waters falls within federal admiralty jurisdiction. Plaintiff Terry Lee Sinclair alleges that he contracted and continues to suffer from the effects of decompression sickness due to a defect in the buoyancy compensator vest he wore while diving, as well as the failure by the crew of the vessel that transported him to the dive site to detect his symptoms and administer proper care. Alleging subject matter jurisdiction in admiralty pursuant to 28 U.S.C. § 1333(1) (1988), Sinclair filed this action in district court against the ship's crew and the manufacturers of the vest. The district court dismissed the action for lack of subject matter jurisdiction.

We hold that Sinclair's claims against the crew fall within federal admiralty jurisdiction since the crew was engaged in a quintessential maritime activity affecting commerce—the transport and care of paying

* Some footnotes omitted.

passengers. Because the claims against the manufacturers of the vest arise from the same common nucleus of operative fact as do his claims against the crew, they fall within the district court's supplemental jurisdiction.

I.

On August 16, 1987, Sinclair and three other passengers chartered the *Destitute* to transport them to a dive site approximately nine miles off the coast of New Jersey. The crew consisted of its owner and captain, David S. Madden, Jr., and a dive master employed by Madden to supervise the dive, Glen Hicks.

After being transported to the dive site, Sinclair and a partner dove to a depth of approximately 75 feet, where they remained for about twenty-seven minutes. As he began to ascend, Sinclair initially used the "finger dump valve" on his buoyancy compensator vest to control the rate of his ascent. Noticing that he was rising faster than his partner, Sinclair pulled the "shoulder dump/rapid exhaust valve" to expel the air from his vest to slow his ascent. The rapid exhaust valve failed, and Sinclair continued to rise at an increasing rate.

Upon reaching the water surface, Sinclair needed assistance to reboard the *Destitute*. Once aboard, he began to exhibit the symptoms of decompression sickness. Commonly referred to as "the bends," decompression sickness is a disorder caused by the release of nitrogen bubbles in the tissues and blood after returning from high pressure to atmospheric pressure too rapidly. His symptoms included nausea, vomiting, dizziness, and shortness of breath. The crew administered no medical care to Sinclair, continued the dive, and did not transport Sinclair back to shore until two and one-half hours after he surfaced.

Sinclair alleges that he developed and continues to suffer from painful, disfiguring, and disabling injuries attributable to decompression sickness as a result of the defect in his buoyancy compensator vest valve and the failure of the crew to detect his symptoms and administer the appropriate care. He filed actions against the crew of the *Destitute* and the manufacturers/distributors of the vest in federal district court and the Pennsylvania Court of Common Pleas.

The federal action was filed pursuant to the admiralty jurisdiction of the district court under 28 U.S.C. § 1333(1). The district court initially stayed the federal action pending resolution of the state actions, in accordance with a stipulation of the parties. Upon motion by one of the defendants, the district court lifted the stay. Sinclair thereafter moved for dismissal on three grounds: (1) lack of admiralty jurisdiction, (2) voluntary dismissal under Fed.R.Civ.P. 41(a), and (3) his right to pursue a concurrent state remedy under the "saving to suitors" provision of 28 U.S.C. § 1333.[1] The district court granted Sinclair's motion to dismiss

---

1. Sinclair moved to dismiss the federal action which he had initiated in order to have the action tried in state court before a jury. He contends that he always intended

on the grounds that it lacked admiralty jurisdiction over the action, finding that an isolated recreational scuba diving excursion was unrelated to traditional maritime activity. The district court did not reach Sinclair's two other grounds for dismissal. This appeal followed. We have jurisdiction under 28 U.S.C. § 1291 (1988). Our review of the district court's determination regarding subject matter jurisdiction is plenary. York Bank and Trust Co. v. Federal Sav. and Loan Ins. Corp., 851 F.2d 637, 638 (3d Cir.1988).

II.

[The Court of Appeals first determined that admiralty jurisdiction was proper under 28 U.S.C. § 1333.]

* * *

III.

* * *

B.

We look next at Sinclair's claims against the manufacturers of the buoyancy compensator vest. The manufacturers argue that the district court had direct admiralty jurisdiction with respect to the claims arising from the purported defects in the scuba diving equipment.... However, we need not decide that issue today because Sinclair's claims against the manufacturers fall within the district court's supplemental jurisdiction. We therefore express no opinion as to whether the district court had direct jurisdiction under 28 U.S.C. § 1333. Recently, Congress codified the existence of supplemental jurisdiction in 28 U.S.C. § 1367(a) (West Supp.1991): "[I]n any civil action of which the district courts have original jurisdiction, the district courts shall have supplemental jurisdiction over all other claims that are so related to claims in the action within such original jurisdiction that they form part of the same case or controversy under Article III of the United States Constitution. Such supplemental jurisdiction shall include claims that involve the joinder ... of additional parties." Claims are part of the same constitutional case if they "derive from a common nucleus of operative fact," and "are such that [the plaintiff] would ordinarily be expected to try them all in one judicial proceeding...." United Mine Workers v. Gibbs, 383 U.S. 715, 725, 86 S.Ct. 1130, 1138 (1966).

Sinclair's claims against the crew and his claims against the manufacturers did arise from a common nucleus of operative fact. Both sets of claims are based on the same purported injuries stemming from the

to have the action tried in state court, but feared that court might rule that his claims fell within exclusive federal admiralty jurisdiction. Sinclair contends that he filed in federal court right before the federal statute of limitations ran merely to maintain his ability to sue in federal court if the state court had refused to hear his claims.

same scuba diving incident. Those injuries were allegedly caused by the negligence of both the crew and the manufacturer. Accordingly, we find that Sinclair's claims against the manufacturers fall within the district court's supplemental jurisdiction.

　　* * *

V.

We hold that this action arising from a scuba diving incident in navigable waters falls within federal admiralty jurisdiction based on our findings that the alleged activities of the crew of the vessel transporting the diver create a potential impact on maritime commerce and bear a substantial relationship to traditional maritime activity. We further hold that the claims against the manufacturer of the buoyancy compensator vest arose from a common nucleus of operative fact as the claims against the crew so as to bring the former claims within the court's supplemental jurisdiction. The district court, therefore, erred in dismissing this action for lack of subject matter jurisdiction. We cannot affirm the dismissal on the alternative grounds raised in the district court because they fall within the sound discretion of the district court and that court did not actually exercise its discretion. We will reverse the dismissal of this action and remand for further proceedings consistent with this opinion. Each party to bear its own costs.

[On page 215, change "Note" into "Notes", insert (1) before the existing Note, and add the following Note:]

(2) Under § 1367, can the third party defendant assert a claim against the original plaintiff for which there is no independent basis of competence and invoke supplemental competence for such claim? If so, could the original plaintiff, under this Section, then assert a claim against the third party defendant and rely on supplemental competence?

[Insert on page 216, at the end of the Note:]

Section § 1367 avoids use of the terms "pendent" and "ancillary" competence and uses the comprehensive term "supplemental" to cover both concepts.

———

PEACOCK v. THOMAS

Supreme Court of the United States, 1996.
___ U.S. ___, 116 S.Ct. 862, 133 L.Ed.2d 817.

JUSTICE THOMAS delivered the opinion of the Court.*

This case presents the issue whether federal courts possess ancillary jurisdiction over new actions in which a federal judgment creditor seeks to impose liability for a money judgment on a person not otherwise liable for the judgment. We hold that they do not.

---

* Some footnotes omitted; others renumbered.

I

Respondent Jack L. Thomas is a former employee of Tru–Tech, Inc. In 1987, Thomas filed an ERISA class action in federal court against Tru–Tech and petitioner D. Grant Peacock, an officer and shareholder of Tru–Tech, for benefits due under the corporation's pension benefits plan. Thomas alleged primarily that Tru–Tech and Peacock breached their fiduciary duties to the class in administering the plan. The District Court found that Tru–Tech had breached its fiduciary duties, but ruled that Peacock was not a fiduciary. On November 28, 1988, the District Court entered judgment in the amount of $187,628.93 against Tru–Tech only. Thomas v. Tru–Tech, Inc., No. 87–2243–3 (D.S.C.). On April 3, 1990, the Court of Appeals for the Fourth Circuit affirmed. Judgt. order reported at, 900 F.2d 256. Thomas did not execute the judgment while the case was on appeal and, during that time, Peacock settled many of Tru–Tech's accounts with favored creditors, including himself.

After the Court of Appeals affirmed the judgment, Thomas unsuccessfully attempted to collect the judgment from Tru–Tech. Thomas then sued Peacock in federal court, claiming that Peacock had entered into a civil conspiracy to siphon assets from Tru–Tech to prevent satisfaction of the ERISA judgment. Thomas also claimed that Peacock fraudulently conveyed Tru–Tech's assets in violation of South Carolina and Pennsylvania law. Thomas later amended his complaint to assert a claim for "Piercing the Corporate Veil Under ERISA and Applicable Federal Law." App. 49. The District Court ultimately agreed to pierce the corporate veil and entered judgment against Peacock in the amount of $187,628.93—the precise amount of the judgment against Tru–Tech— plus interest and fees, notwithstanding the fact that Peacock's alleged fraudulent transfers totalled no more than $80,000. The Court of Appeals affirmed, holding that the District Court properly exercised ancillary jurisdiction over Thomas' suit. 39 F.3d 493 (1994). We granted certiorari to determine whether the District Court had subject-matter jurisdiction and to resolve a conflict among the Courts of Appeals. 514 U.S. ___ (1995). We now reverse.

II

Thomas relies on the Employee Retirement Income Security Act of 1974 (ERISA), 88 Stat. 832, as amended, 29 U.S.C. § 1001 et seq., as the source of federal jurisdiction for this suit. The District Court did not expressly rule on subject matter jurisdiction, but found that Thomas had properly stated a claim under ERISA for piercing the corporate veil. We disagree. We are not aware of, and Thomas does not point to, any provision of ERISA that provides for imposing liability for an extant ERISA judgment against a third party. See Mackey v. Lanier Collection Agency & Service, Inc., 486 U.S. 825, 833, 100 L.Ed.2d 836, 108 S.Ct. 2182 (1988) ("ERISA does not provide an enforcement mechanism for collecting judgments . . .").

We reject Thomas' suggestion, not made in the District Court, that this subsequent suit arose under § 502(a)(3) of ERISA, which authorizes civil actions for "appropriate equitable relief" to redress violations of ERISA or the terms of an ERISA plan. 29 U.S.C. § 1132(a)(3). Thomas' complaint in this lawsuit alleged no violation of ERISA or of the plan. The wrongdoing alleged in the complaint occurred in 1989 and 1990, some four to five years after Tru–Tech's ERISA plan was terminated, and Thomas did not—indeed, could not—allege that Peacock was a fiduciary to the terminated plan. Thomas further concedes that Peacock's alleged wrongdoing "did not occur with respect to the administration or operation of the plan." Under the circumstances, we think Thomas failed to allege a claim under § 502(a)(3) for equitable relief. Section 502(a)(3) "does not, after all, authorize 'appropriate equitable relief' at large, but only 'appropriate equitable relief' for the purpose of 'redress[ing any] violations or . . . enforcing any provisions' of ERISA or an ERISA plan." Mertens v. Hewitt Associates, 508 U.S. 248, ___, 113 S.Ct. 2063, 124 L.Ed.2d 161 (1993) (slip op., at 5) (emphasis and modifications in original).

Moreover, Thomas' veil-piercing claim does not state a cause of action under ERISA and cannot independently support federal jurisdiction. Even if ERISA permits a plaintiff to pierce the corporate veil to reach a defendant not otherwise subject to suit under ERISA, Thomas could invoke the jurisdiction of the federal courts only by independently alleging a violation of an ERISA provision or term of the plan. Piercing the corporate veil is not itself an independent ERISA cause of action, "but rather is a means of imposing liability on an underlying cause of action." 1 C. Keating & G. O'Gradney, Fletcher Cyclopedia of Law of Private Corporations § 41, p. 603 (perm. ed. 1990). Because Thomas alleged no "underlying" violation of any provision of ERISA or an ERISA plan, neither ERISA's jurisdictional provision, 29 U.S.C. § 1132(e)(1), nor 28 U.S.C. § 1331 supplied the District Court with subject matter jurisdiction over this suit.

III

Thomas also contends that this lawsuit is ancillary to the original ERISA suit.[1] We have recognized that a federal court may exercise ancillary jurisdiction "(1) to permit disposition by a single court of claims that are, in varying respects and degrees, factually interdependent; and (2) to enable a court to function successfully, that is, to manage its proceedings, vindicate its authority, and effectuate its decrees." Kokkonen v. Guardian Life Ins. Co., 511 U.S. ___, ___, 114 S.Ct. 1673, 128 L.Ed.2d 391 (1994) (slip op., at 4–5) (citations omitted). Thomas has not carried his burden of demonstrating that this suit falls

---

1. Congress codified much of the common-law doctrine of ancillary jurisdiction as part of "supplemental jurisdiction" in 28 U.S.C. § 1367.

within either category. See id., at (slip op., at 2) (burden rests on party asserting jurisdiction).

A

"Ancillary jurisdiction typically involves claims by a defending party haled into court against his will, or by another person whose rights might be irretrievably lost unless he could assert them in an ongoing action in a federal court." Owen Equipment & Erection Co. v. Kroger, 437 U.S. 365, 376, 57 L.Ed.2d 274, 98 S.Ct. 2396 (1978). Ancillary jurisdiction may extend to claims having a factual and logical dependence on "the primary lawsuit," ibid., but that primary lawsuit must contain an independent basis for federal jurisdiction. The court must have jurisdiction over a case or controversy before it may assert jurisdiction over ancillary claims. See Mine Workers v. Gibbs, 383 U.S. 715, 725, 16 L.Ed.2d 218, 86 S.Ct. 1130 (1966). In a subsequent lawsuit involving claims with no independent basis for jurisdiction, a federal court lacks the threshold jurisdictional power that exists when ancillary claims are asserted in the same proceeding as the claims conferring federal jurisdiction. See Kokkonen, supra, at (slip op., at 6); H.C. Cook Co. v. Beecher, 217 U.S. 497, 498–499, 54 L.Ed. 855, 30 S.Ct. 601 (1910). Consequently, claims alleged to be factually interdependent with and, hence, ancillary to claims brought in an earlier federal lawsuit will not support federal jurisdiction over a subsequent lawsuit. The basis of the doctrine of ancillary jurisdiction is the practical need "to protect legal rights or effectively to resolve an entire, logically entwined lawsuit." Kroger, 437 U.S. at 377. But once judgment was entered in the original ERISA suit, the ability to resolve simultaneously factually intertwined issues vanished. As in Kroger, "neither the convenience of litigants nor considerations of judicial economy" can justify the extension of ancillary jurisdiction over Thomas' claims in this subsequent proceeding. Ibid.

In any event, there is insufficient factual dependence between the claims raised in Thomas' first and second suits to justify the extension of ancillary jurisdiction. Thomas' factual allegations in this suit are independent from those asserted in the ERISA suit, which involved Peacock's and Tru–Tech's status as plan fiduciaries and their alleged wrongdoing in the administration of the plan. The facts relevant to this complaint are limited to allegations that Peacock shielded Tru–Tech's assets from the ERISA judgment long after Tru–Tech's plan had been terminated. The claims in these cases have little or no factual or logical interdependence, and, under these circumstances, no greater efficiencies would be created by the exercise of federal jurisdiction over them. See Kokkonen, supra, at (slip op., at 5).

B

The focus of Thomas' argument is that his suit to extend liability for payment of the ERISA judgment from Tru–Tech to Peacock fell under the District Court's ancillary enforcement jurisdiction. We have reserved

the use of ancillary jurisdiction in subsequent proceedings for the exercise of a federal court's inherent power to enforce its judgments. Without
jurisdiction to enforce a judgment entered by a federal court, "the
judicial power would be incomplete and entirely inadequate to the
purposes for which it was conferred by the Constitution." Riggs v.
Johnson County, 73 U.S. 166, 6 Wall. 166, 187, 18 L.Ed. 768 (1868). In
defining that power, we have approved the exercise of ancillary jurisdiction over a broad range of supplementary proceedings involving third
parties to assist in the protection and enforcement of federal judgments—including attachment, mandamus, garnishment, and the prejudgment avoidance of fraudulent conveyances. See, e.g., Mackey v.
Lanier Collection Agency & Service, Inc., 486 U.S. 825, 834, n. 10, 100
L.Ed.2d 836, 108 S.Ct. 2182 (1988) (garnishment); Swift & Co. Packers
v. Compania Colombiana Del Caribe, S. A., 339 U.S. 684, 690–692, 94
L.Ed. 1206, 70 S.Ct. 861 (1950) (prejudgment attachment of property);
Dewey v. West Fairmont Gas Coal Co., 123 U.S. 329, 332–333, 31 L.Ed.
179, 8 S.Ct. 148 (1887) (prejudgment voidance of fraudulent transfers);
Labette County Comm'rs v. United States ex rel. Moulton, 112 U.S. 217,
221–225, 28 L.Ed. 698, 5 S.Ct. 108 (1884) (mandamus to compel public
officials in their official capacity to levy tax to enforce judgment against
township); Krippendorf v. Hyde, 110 U.S. 276, 282–285, 28 L.Ed. 145, 4
S.Ct. 27 (1884) (prejudgment dispute over attached property); Riggs,
supra, at 187–188 (mandamus to compel public officials in their official
capacity to levy tax to enforce judgment against county).

Our recognition of these supplementary proceedings has not, however, extended beyond attempts to execute, or to guarantee eventual
executability of, a federal judgment. We have never authorized the
exercise of ancillary jurisdiction in a subsequent lawsuit to impose an
obligation to pay an existing federal judgment on a person not already
liable for that judgment. Indeed, we rejected an attempt to do so in H.C.
Cook Co. v. Beecher, 217 U.S. 497, 54 L.Ed. 855, 30 S.Ct. 601 (1910)....

In determining the reach of the federal courts' ancillary jurisdiction,
we have cautioned against the exercise of jurisdiction over proceedings
that are "entirely new and original," Krippendorf v. Hyde, supra, at 285
(quoting Minnesota Co. v. St. Paul Co., 69 U.S. 609, 2 Wall. 609, 633, 17
L.Ed. 886 (1865)), or where "the relief [sought is] of a different kind or
on a different principle" than that of the prior decree. Dugas v. American Surety Co., 300 U.S. 414, 428, 81 L.Ed. 720, 57 S.Ct. 515 (1937).
These principles suggest that ancillary jurisdiction could not properly be
exercised in this case. This action is founded not only upon different
facts than the ERISA suit, but also upon entirely new theories of
liability. In this suit, Thomas alleged civil conspiracy and fraudulent
transfer of Tru–Tech's assets, but, as we have noted, no substantive
ERISA violation. The alleged wrongdoing in this case occurred after the
ERISA judgment was entered, and Thomas' claims—civil conspiracy,
fraudulent conveyance, and "veil-piercing"—all involved new theories of

liability not asserted in the ERISA suit. Other than the existence of the
ERISA judgment itself, this suit has little connection to the ERISA case.
This is a new action based on theories of relief that did not exist, and
could not have existed, at the time the court entered judgment in the
ERISA case.

Ancillary enforcement jurisdiction is, at its core, a creature of
necessity. See Kokkonen, 511 U.S. at (slip op., at 5–6); Riggs, 6 Wall. at
187. When a party has obtained a valid federal judgment, only extraordinary circumstances, if any, can justify ancillary jurisdiction over a
subsequent suit like this. To protect and aid the collection of a federal
judgment, the Federal Rules of Civil Procedure provide fast and effective
mechanisms for execution. In the event a stay is entered pending appeal,
the Rules require the district court to ensure that the judgment creditor's position is secured, ordinarily by a supersedeas bond. The Rules
cannot guarantee payment of every federal judgment. But as long as they
protect a judgment creditor's ability to execute on a judgment, the
district court's authority is adequately preserved, and ancillary jurisdiction is not justified over a new lawsuit to impose liability for a judgment
on a third party. Contrary to Thomas' suggestion otherwise, we think
these procedural safeguards are sufficient to prevent wholesale fraud
upon the district courts of the United States.

IV

For these reasons, we hold that the District Court lacked jurisdiction
over Thomas' subsequent suit. Accordingly, the judgment of the Court of
Appeals is

Reversed.

JUSTICE STEVENS, dissenting. . . .

NOTES

(1) In the light of the motivating rationale for the concept of supplemental
jurisdiction, was the principal case decided correctly?

(2) Does 28 U.S.C. § 1367 deal exhaustively with supplemental jurisdiction?

5. REMOVAL

[Insert at page 219, at the end of "Note on Protective Jurisdiction":]

Suits involving protective jurisdiction can raise difficult issues of statutory
interpretation. In American National Red Cross v. S.G. and A.E., 505 U.S. 247,
112 S.Ct. 2465, 120 L.Ed.2d 201 (1992), the question was whether Congress,
when enacting the Red Cross charter empowering the Red Cross "to sue and be
sued in courts of law and equity within the jurisdiction of the United States,"
intended to confer subject matter competence on the federal courts in all cases in
which the Red Cross is a litigant. While the Court acknowledged that the phrase
"sue and be sued" is often used merely to describe capacity [see Fed.R.Civ.P.
17(b) for example], it held that, if Congress couples this language with a phrase
mentioning the federal courts, the intent is to create adjudicatory authority. In

addition, the Court held that the "arising under" provision of Art. III "is broad enough to authorize Congress to confer federal court jurisdiction over actions involving federally chartered corporations," 505 U.S. at 264, 112 S.Ct. at 2476.

[Insert on page 219, after 28 U.S.C.A. § 1441:]

The Judicial Improvement Act of 1990 amended § 1441(c). Prior to this amendment, removal was more generally available, for the amendment substituted the words "within the jurisdiction conferred by § 1331 of this title" for the words "which would be removable if sued upon alone". On the other hand, the amendment limits remand by substituting the words "may remand all matters in which State law predominates" for the words "remand all matters not otherwise within its original jurisdiction". Apart from the obvious error which resulted in duplication of the word "may", are the amendments desirable? Would it have been better to provide that, when removable claims are joined with non-removable claims as to which there would be supplemental competence under § 1367(a), the entire case may be removed, but that the district court may remand in the circumstances specified in § 1367(c)?

[Insert at page 220, after Note (5):]

(6) By separate legislation, Congress has provided federal officers with a right to remove state cases to federal court, 28 U.S.C.A. § 1442. In International Primate Protection League v. Administrators of Tulane Educ. Fund, 500 U.S. 72, 111 S.Ct. 1700, 114 L.Ed.2d 134 (1991), the Supreme Court interpreted this provision narrowly to prevent removal by federal agencies.

SECTION 3. ADJUDICATORY AUTHORITY OVER PERSONS

D. CONSENT

[Insert on page 235, after the Note:]

Carnival Cruise Lines, Inc. v. Shute, 499 U.S. 585, 111 S.Ct. 1522, 113 L.Ed.2d 622 (1991). The plaintiffs brought an action in a federal district court in Washington against Carnival Cruise for injuries suffered on board the defendant's ship in international waters off the coast of Mexico. The defendant sought dismissal on the ground that a forum selection clause in the tickets issued to plaintiffs rendered the courts in Florida exclusively competent. The plaintiffs had purchased their tickets through a Washington Travel agent. The district court held that the defendant's contacts with Washington were insufficient to justify the exercise of personal jurisdiction. The Court of Appeals reversed this ruling. It also ruled the forum selection clause unenforceable because it was not freely bargained for. It stated that there was evidence in the record to indicate that the plaintiffs were physically and financially incapable of pursuing this litigation in Florida.

The Supreme Court reversed and ruled the exclusive forum clause enforceable. It rejected the Court of Appeals' ruling that a non-negotiated forum clause in a form contract is not enforceable because it is not the subject of bargaining. Accepting that "forum-selection clauses contained in form passage contracts are subject to judicial scrutiny for fundamental fairness," the Court found the clause enforceable. It noted that the clause had various advantages to the defendant and that "it stands to reason that passengers who purchase tickets containing a forum clause like that at issue in this case benefit in the form of reduced fares relating to the savings that the cruise line enjoys by limiting the forum in which it may be sued." The Court rejected the appellate court's "independent justification" for its conclusions that the clause should not be enforced because "there is evidence in the record to indicate that the Shutes were physically and financially incapable of pursuing this litigation in Florida." It noted that the District Court had made no findings in that regard. Finding that plaintiffs were "given notice of the forum provisions and, therefore, presumably retained the option of rejecting the contract with impunity", and that there was no evidence of fraud or overreaching, the Court ruled that plaintiffs had failed to satisfy the "heavy burden of proof" required to set aside the clause on grounds of inconvenience. The Court also concluded that the clause did not violate 46 U.S.C.A. § 183c, which provides that the owner of a ship transporting passengers to or from a port in the United States may not contract "to lessen, weaken, or avoid the right of any claimant to a trial by court of competent jurisdiction."

Justice Stevens and Marshall dissented. They noted that passengers will not normally have the opportunity to read the clause until they have already purchased their tickets, that these clauses are typically the product of disparate bargaining power, and that admiralty courts have traditionally looked with disfavor upon clauses seeking to alleviate a shipowner's liability for negligent conduct. They also found the clause covered by 46 U.S.C.A. § 183(c).

NOTE

Do you side with the majority or the dissent? Would the Florida courts have in personam power over the Shutes in the absence of the forum selection clause? Cf. Burger King Corp. v. Rudzewicz, casebook at page 267. On the *Carnival Cruise* case, see Borchers, Forum Selection Agreements in the Federal Courts After Carnival Cruise: A Proposal for Congressional Reform, 67 Wash.L.Rev. 55 (1992); Mullenix, Another Easy Case, Some More Bad Law: Carnival Cruise Lines and Contractual Personal Jurisdiction, 27 Tex Int'l L.J. 323 (1992).

F.   CLAIMS ARISING FROM LOCAL ACTS OR CONSEQUENCES

[Insert at page 248 after Note (3):]

(4) Note that there were two issues in the principal case: in the part reproduced, the issue was whether Washington had judicial jurisdiction over International Shoe—that is, power to hale it before a Washington court. In another section of the opinion, the question was whether Washington had legislative jurisdiction over the shoe company, and the Court answered in the affirmative. But these two forms of jurisdiction do not necessarily go hand-in-hand. Thus, in Quill Corp. v. North Dakota, 504 U.S. 298, 112 S.Ct. 1904, 119 L.Ed.2d 91 (1992), the issue was whether North Dakota could impose a sales tax on the in-state sales of an out-of-state mail-order house. The Court found that, in so far as due process was concerned, the contacts between Quill Corp. and North Dakota were extremely similar to those involved in *International Shoe*:

> "In 'modern commercial life' it matters little that such solicitation is accomplished by a deluge of catalogs rather than a phalanx of drummers; the requirements of due process are met irrespective of a corporations lack of physical presence in the taxing state. . . .
>
> In this case, there is no question that Quill has purposely directed its activities at North Dakota residents, that the magnitude of those contacts is more than sufficient for due process purposes. . . .

504 U.S. at 308, 112 S.Ct. at 1911, 119 L.Ed.2d at 98. However, the Court went on to hold that the Commerce Clause is also a relevant consideration in determining legislative jurisdiction to tax, and that it is for Congress to decide that the imposition of an in-state tax would not disrupt Commerce Clause interests. Thus, Quill was found to be outside North Dakota's taxing jurisdiction. For a discussion of the *Quill* case, see Buntrock, Quill Corporation v. North Dakota: Spawning the Physical Presence "Nexus" Requirement Under the Commerce Clause, 38 S.D.L.Rev. 130 (1993).

[Insert on page 255, after the Notes:]

Gray v. American Radiator & Standard Sanitary Corporation, 22 Ill.2d 432, 176 N.E.2d 761 (1961). Gray was injured in Illinois when her water heater exploded. She sued the Titan Valve Manufacturing Company, alleging that Titan had negligently manufactured the safety valve on the heater. Titan had manufactured the valve in Ohio and had sold it to American Radiator which had incorporated the valve into the heater in Pennsylvania. Titan had done no business in Illinois, either directly or indirectly. Gray sought to base competence over Titan on the section in the Illinois long-arm statute which provides for competence over a defendant who commits a tortious act within the State. Titan moved to dismiss on the ground that it had not committed a tortious act within the State within the meaning of the Illinois Act and that, in any event, the exercise of competence over it would be unconstitutional. The lower court granted the motion, but the Illinois Supreme Court reversed. It ruled that the tortious act had occurred in Illinois. It drew in support of this ruling upon both the then prevailing conflict of laws rule that the law of the place where a wrong occurred determines the applicable law and that the place of a wrong is where the last event takes place necessary to render the wrongdoer liable, and upon the rule that, for the purpose of applying the statute of limitations, the limitations period commences when the injury is done.

Are these analogies apt? Regardless of whether the Illinois statute purported to create competence, could Illinois constitutionality create competence over Titan? Cf. Asahi Metal Industry Co., Ltd. v. Superior Court of California, Solano County, casebook at page 277.

————

SECTION 4. ADJUDICATORY AUTHORITY OVER THINGS

[Insert at page 306, at the end of Note (6):]

For an interesting discussion of that case, see Silberman, Reflections on *Burnham v. Superior Court:* Toward Presumptive Rules of Jurisdiction and Implications for Choice of Law, 22 Rutgers L.Rev. 569 (1991).

————

SECTION 5. FEDERAL BASES

[Insert on page 329, in lieu of the Note on the 1989 proposed amendments to the federal rules:]

NOTE ON 1993 AMENDMENTS TO THE FEDERAL RULES

[Insert on page 329, after the Heading and in lieu of the material on pp. 325–329:]

The preceding materials on adjudicatory authority over persons and things dealt with *state* courts. How should the adjudicatory authority of *federal* courts be determined? On the one hand, it could be argued that federal courts should have the same power over people and things found in federal territory, or related to federal territory, that states have over that which is found or related to state territory. After all, presence or relationship with the United States indicates it is not inconvenient to defend there; the United States should be allowed to use its own courts to further national policy in the same way that states use state courts to further state policy.

Given this analysis, it may seem curious that prior to the passage of a new version of Federal Rule of Civil Procedure 4 in December 1993, Congress had never enacted a generally-applicable statute that spelled out when federal courts had power over people and things. (There were, however, competence provisions for some specific situations). Many authorities, notably the Second Circuit's Chief Judge Tom Clark, thought that the prior version of Rule 4 impliedly created a federal basis of competence, even though the provision was entitled "Service and Filings of Pleadings and Other Papers" and lacked much of the material currently found in Rule 4(k). Jaftex Corporation v. Randolph Mills, Inc.,

282 F.2d 508 (2d Cir.1960). Under this view, if a case was filed in federal court and the defendant was served in accordance with one of the methods set out in Rule 4, the federal court acquired competence over her. Jurisdiction was, presumably, judged through a federal analogy to *International Shoe* by asking whether the defendant had sufficient contacts with the United States.

Others—notably the Second Circuit's Henry Friendly—argued Rule 4 did not create adjudicatory authority. Instead, proponents of this view thought that the federal court's power over a defendant depended on whether the state in which the court sat had adjudicatory authority, Arrowsmith v. United Press International, 320 F.2d 219 (2d Cir.1963), or—in some instances—on whether the state in which Congress authorized service of process had adjudicatory authority, Coleman v. American Export Isbrandtsen Lines, Inc., 405 F.2d 250 (2d Cir.1968) [at p. 326 of the casebook].

Weighty arguments support the Friendly view. As to competence, the lack of an express provision on such an important matter is, at best, curious. As a constitutional matter, nationwide jurisdiction has several problems. Defending far from home is inconvenient irrespective of whether the suit is in a distant state or federal court. For example, to a non-New Yorker, being haled into the N.Y. State Supreme Court on the north side of Foley Square in Manhattan is not much different from being haled into the United States Court on the south side of Foley Square. Moreover, reading Rule 4 as a competence provision creates a curious result in diversity cases. States like New York that have carefully limited their own competence to pursue important state goals may find that a party it did not want to force to appear could nonetheless be made to defend in its territory—albeit in federal court. The federal courts could, in other words, be used to frustrate state objectives. *Erie prob* As will be elucidated in Chapter Seven, under Erie Railroad Co. v. Tompkins, 304 U.S. 64, 58 S.Ct. 817, 82 L.Ed. 1188, 114 A.L.R. 1487 (1938), the structure of the Constitution is read to prevent the federal government from trumping valid state policies in the absence of a significant federal interest. This so-called *Erie* problem is another facet of the federalism issue Justice White discussed in *World–Wide Volkswagen.*

There was also a third view on the question of federal adjudicatory authority. It was that Rule 4 should be read to create competence in federal question and other non-diversity cases, and that state competence rules should apply in diversity cases. By the same token, a federal due process analysis should apply in non-diversity cases while *International Shoe* should apply on its own terms to diversity cases. That view had considerable appeal because it accorded to the United States the ability to act as any other sovereign to enforce its laws in its own courts, while avoiding the *Erie* problem perceived by Judge Friendly. The only problem with this interpretation was that it was rejected by the Supreme

Court in Omni Capital International v. Rudolf Wolff & Co., 484 U.S. 97, 108 S.Ct. 404, 98 L.Ed.2d 415 (1987) [cited in the casebook at p. 328].

Omni involved a claim brought in Louisiana federal court under the federal Commodity Exchange Act. The defendants moved to dismiss for lack of adjudicatory authority. The District Court initially took the view that in the absence of a specific provision in the controlling federal act, the court could and should fashion an appropriate basis of competence. However, in response to a Fifth Circuit decision in an unrelated case, the court withdrew this opinion and relied instead on Louisiana state law. Louisiana's statute was modeled on the Uniform Interstate and International Procedure Act, Art. 1, p. 253 of the casebook, and did not reach the defendants. Accordingly, the court dismissed the action. The Supreme Court affirmed. It ruled that federal courts should not fashion a rule of nationwide competence in the absence of congressional authorization. The Federal Rules of Civil Procedure did not create such authorization.

Omni led many commentators to argue for revision of Rule 4. It seemed wrong that Louisiana's parochial views on what was good for Louisiana should be allowed to create an obstacle to the enforcement of federal law. An initial draft of Rule 4 would have dealt with the problem by providing that service of a summons would establish competence over any defendant against whom is asserted a claim arising under federal law, unless the Constitution or an applicable federal statute required otherwise, Preliminary Draft of Proposed Amendments to the Federal Rules of Appellate Procedure and the Federal Rules of Civil Procedure (September 1989). That rule would have also provided for competence based on service of process abroad so long as asserting jurisdiction met with constitutional requirements—a limitation that many commentators argued should be judged by looking at the alien's contacts with the United States and not, as *Asahi* and *Helicol* seem to require, with an individual state, see, e.g., Gary B. Born, Reflections on Judicial Jurisdiction in International Cases, 17 Ga.J.Int'l & Comp.L. 1 (1987).

This proposal met with considerable resistance, both as to the competence and jurisdictional questions. In addition, there was a question as to how the new rule would operate when a supplemental claim was asserted under what is now § 1367. Since supplemental claims sound in state law, the *Erie* concerns are fully applicable.

The version of Rule 4 that Congress in fact enacted in 1993 takes a more modest approach. It ends the debate on *whether* it is about competence, by stating when service is "effective"—that is, creates adjudicatory authority, 4(k). For most cases, it explicitly adopts the

Friendly view that competence in federal court depends on competence in state courts, 4(k)(1)(A). If Congress wishes to rely more heavily on federal courts, it must, therefore, enact special competence legislation, 4(k)(1)(D). The Act does, however, create special federal competence rules in three specific situations:

1. Federal interpleader. Prior to the revision, 28 U.S.C.A. § 2361, which provides for nationwide service of process, was read as creating competence in interpleader cases. 4(k)(1)(C) makes this explicit.

2. The bulge rule. 4(k)(1)(B) creates competence over certain parties who are served within 100 miles of the federal courthouse, even if they lack contacts with the state in which the federal court is situated. In federal question cases, this rule is noncontroversial: there is no federalism problem since state law is not an issue and there is no due process problem because the bulge extends only for 100 miles from the courthouse. In diversity cases, however, 4(k)(1)(B) does raise something of an *Erie* question. If there were no federal interest at stake, it may even be unconstitutional. However, 4(k)(1)(B) is limited to asserting power over Rule 14 and Rule 19 parties. In both cases, the presence of the party in question is critical to reaching a just result. Since the United States has an independent interest in providing a forum for adjudicating cases that necessarily involve parties from several states, it is probably constitutional for a federal court to "bulge," even if it means that it will assert power over a party the state would prefer not to reach.

3. Competence over aliens. 4(k)(2) responds to those concerned that *Omni, Asahi,* and *Helicol* combine to frustrate enforcement of federal law against aliens. Under this provision, service under Rule 4 establishes jurisdiction over any defendant who is *not* subject to the adjudicatory authority of any state. The assertion of jurisdiction must, however, be consistent with the Constitution and U.S. law. Because the attempt here is to broaden the reach of federal courts, presumably the constitutional question will be resolved by looking at the defendant's contacts with the United States, and not with any particular state.

NOTE

Does 4(k)(2) do more than overrule *Omni* in federal question cases? Does it create competence in all federal question cases when it is constitutional to reach a party beyond the borders of the United States? Could it be applied to reach indispensable parties, claimants in interpleader actions, and members of a class that cannot be reached under other rules of in personam competence? If so, should the benefits of this provision also be made available in diversity cases and supplemental competence be created in such cases? For a discussion of amended Rule 4, see Symposium: Turbulence in the Federal Rules of Civil Procedure: The 1993 Amendments and Beyond, 14 Rev.Litig. 159 (1994).

SECTION 6. ADEQUATE NOTICE AND OPPORTUNITY TO BE HEARD

[Insert on page 330 before the Note:]

HENDERSON v. UNITED STATES

Supreme Court of the United States, 1996.
___ U.S. ___, 116 S.Ct. 1638, 134 L.Ed.2d 880.

JUSTICE GINSBURG delivered the opinion of the Court.*

This case concerns the period allowed for service of process in a civil action commenced by a seaman injured aboard a vessel owned by the United States. Recovery in such cases is governed by the Suits in Admiralty Act, 46 U.S.C.App. § 741 et seq., which broadly waives the Government's sovereign immunity. See § 742 (money judgments); § 743 (costs and interest). Rule 4 of the Federal Rules of Civil Procedure allows 120 days to effect service of the summons and timely filed complaint, a period extendable by the court. The Suits in Admiralty Act, however, instructs that service shall be made "forthwith." § 742. The question presented is whether the Act's "forthwith" instruction for service of process has been superseded by the Federal Rule.

In the Rules Enabling Act, 28 U.S.C. § 2071 et seq., Congress ordered that, in matters of "practice and procedure," § 2072(a), the Federal Rules shall govern, and "all laws in conflict with such rules shall be of no further force or effect," § 2072(b). We hold that, in actions arising under federal law, commenced in compliance with the governing statute of limitations, the manner and timing of serving process are generally nonjurisdictional matters of "procedure" controlled by the Federal Rules.

I

On August 27, 1991, petitioner Lloyd Henderson, a merchant mariner, was injured while working aboard a vessel owned and operated by the United States. On April 8, 1993, after exhausting administrative remedies, Henderson filed a seaman's personal injury action against the United States, pursuant to the Suits in Admiralty Act, 41 Stat. 525, as amended, 46 U.S.C.App. § 741 et seq. Under that Act, suits of the kind Henderson commenced "may be brought ... within two years after the cause of action arises." § 745. Henderson brought his action well within that time period. He commenced suit, as Federal Rule of Civil Procedure 3 instructs, simply "by filing a complaint with the court."[1]

---

* Some footnotes omitted; others renumbered.

1. In a suit on a right created by federal law, filing a complaint suffices to satisfy the statute of limitations. See West v. Conrail, 481 U.S. 35, 39, 95 L.Ed.2d 32, 107 S.Ct. 1538 (1987): In a federal-court suit on a state-created right, however, a plaintiff must serve process before the statute of limitations has run, if state law so requires for a similar state-court suit. See Walker v. Armco Steel Corp., 446 U.S. 740, 752–753, 64 L.Ed.2d 659, 100 S.Ct. 1978 (1980) (reaffirming Ragan v. Merchants Transfer & Warehouse Co., 337 U.S. 530, 93 L.Ed. 1520, 69 S.Ct. 1233 (1949)). But cf. Hanna v. Plumer, 380 U.S. 460, 14 L.Ed.2d 8, 85 S.Ct. 1136 (1965) (method of service, as

Having timely filed his complaint, Henderson attempted to follow the Federal Rules on service. It is undisputed that the following Rules, and nothing in the Suits in Admiralty Act, furnished the immediately relevant instructions. Federal Rule of Civil Procedure 4(a) (1988) provided: "Upon the filing of the complaint the clerk shall forthwith issue a summons and deliver the summons to the plaintiff or the plaintiff's attorney, who shall be responsible for prompt service of the summons and a copy of the complaint." Rule 4(b) provided: "The summons shall be signed by the clerk, [and] be under the seal of the court." Rule 4(d) stated: "The summons and complaint shall be served together."

A series of slips occurred in obtaining the summons required by Rule 4. . . .

Thus, the Attorney General received the complaint 47 days after Henderson filed suit, and the United States Attorney was personally served 148 days after Henderson commenced the action by filing his complaint with the court. On November 17, 1993, the United States moved to dismiss the action. The grounds for, and disposition of, that motion led to Henderson's petition for certiorari.

The United States has never maintained that it lacked notice of Henderson's complaint within the 2–year limitation period prescribed for Suits in Admiralty Act claims. See 46 U.S.C.App. § 745; Tr. of Oral Arg. 38–39 (counsel for United States acknowledged that service on Attorney General gave Government actual notice three months before 2–year limitation period ended). Nor has the Government asserted any prejudice to the presentation of its defense stemming from the delayed service of the summons and complaint. And the manner and timing of service, it appears beyond debate, satisfied the requirements of Federal Rule of Civil Procedure 4 (titled "Summons" and detailing prescriptions on service of process).

In support of its motion to dismiss, the United States relied exclusively on § 2 of the Suits in Admiralty Act, 46 U.S.C.App. § 742, which provides in part:

"The libelant [plaintiff] shall forthwith serve a copy of his libel [complaint] on the United States attorney for [the] district [where suit is brought] and mail a copy hereof by registered mail to the Attorney General of the United States."

This provision has remained unchanged since its enactment in 1920, 18 years before the Federal Rules of Civil Procedure became effective, and 46 years before admiralty cases were brought within the realm of the Civil Rules. The Government argued that Henderson's failure to serve process "forthwith," as required by § 742, deprived the District Court of subject-matter jurisdiction because § 742 describes the conditions of the United States' waiver of sovereign immunity. . . .

distinguished from time period for commencement of civil action, is governed by   Federal Rules in all actions, including suits based on state-created rights).

The Federal Rules thus convey a clear message: Complaints are not to be dismissed if served within 120 days, or within such additional time as the court may allow. Furthermore, the United States acknowledges that, § 2 of the Suits in Admiralty Act aside, Rule 4's extendable 120–day time prescription applies to the full range of civil litigation, including cases brought against the United States under the Federal Tort Claims Act, 28 U.S.C. § 2675, and the Tucker Act, ch. 359, 24 Stat. 505 (1887) (current version 28 U.S.C. §§ 1346, 1491 and other scattered sections of 28 U.S.C.). See Tr. of Oral Arg. 33. We are therefore satisfied that Rule 4's regime conflicts irreconcilably with Suits in Admiralty Act § 2's service "forthwith" instruction, and we turn to the dispositive question: Does the Rule supersede the inconsistent statutory direction? . . . .

Returning to the dispositive question, we need not linger over the answer. What we have so far said, and the further elaboration below, lead securely to this response: Rule 4 governs summons and service in this case in whole and not in part.

For the reasons stated, the judgment of the Court of Appeals affirming the dismissal of Henderson's complaint is reversed, and the case is remanded for proceedings consistent with this opinion.

It is so ordered.

JUSTICE SCALIA, with whom JUSTICE KENNEDY joins, concurring. . . .

JUSTICE THOMAS, with whom the CHIEF JUSTICE and JUSTICE O'CONNOR join, dissenting. . . .

A.   SERVICE IN A FOREIGN COUNTRY

[Insert on p. 335 in lieu of Note on Proposed 1989 Amendments:]

NOTE ON 1993 AMENDMENTS ON FOREIGN SERVICE

The 1993 Amendments also make substantial changes in the rules regulating service in a foreign country. They provide that such service must be made pursuant to any applicable international agreement, that it be reasonably calculated to lead to actual notice, and that service by personal delivery or by mail, return receipt requested, or by diplomatic or consular officer not be prohibited by foreign law. Are these limitations desirable? For a negative answer, see Smit, H., Recent Developments in International Litigation, 35 South Texas L.Rev. 201, 205–212 (1994); Smit, International Control of International Litigation: Who benefits? 57 Law & Contemp. PP. 25, 36–41 (1994).

SECTION 7.   VENUE AND FORUM NON CONVENIENS

[Insert on page 335, after 28 U.S.C.A. §§ 1391–1392:]

These provisions reflect changes made by the Judicial Improvement Act of 1990. Prior to this amendment, § 1391 lay venue in diversity cases in the district in which all the plaintiffs or all the defendants resided or in which the cause of action arose. Aliens could be sued in any district, and special provisions dealt with actions against corporations and officers, employees, and agents of the United States.

The purpose of the amendment was to eliminate problems that had arisen when there was doubt as to whether a cause of action arose within the district and when not all defendants resided within the same district. Under the amendment, only one of the defendants need reside in the district as long as the others reside in the same state. Even if no defendant resides in the district, venue lies in the district in which the defendants are subject to personal jurisdiction. The reference to the place where the cause of action arose was eliminated and a reference to the place "in which a substantial part of the events or omissions giving rise to the claim occurred" was substituted. Is this substitution likely to eliminate the difficulties that arose under the eliminated criterion?

The 1990 Amendment appears to render considerably more flexible the venue rules based on the defendant's residence. However, it eliminates venue based on the plaintiff's residence within the district. The venue rules in federal question cases are also made more flexible by the amendments introduced into subdivision (b), which parallel, but are not identical to, those made in subdivision (a). Are there good reasons for the differences?

All these changes have not simplified venue rules. What are the purposes venue rules serve? Once the court has the requisite subject matter and personal or in rem adjudicatory authority, does it make a great deal of difference in which district venue is laid? Would a simple rule laying venue in any district in which any plaintiff resides or in which any defendant resides or is subject to in personam competence or in which property which is the subject of the action is located, be adequate? If not, why not?

[Insert at page 336, at the end of Note (2):]

In Burlington Northern R.R. Co. v. Ford, 504 U.S. 648, 112 S.Ct. 2184, 119 L.Ed.2d 432 (1992), the Supreme Court rejected a challenge to a state venue law on the ground that the distinction it made between suits against domestic businesses and out-of-state businesses violated the Equal Protection Clause of the Fourteenth Amendment. The Court held that, since the venue rule rationally furthered a legitimate state interest, it was constitutional.

[Insert at page 350, at the end of Note (3):]

Could section 1406 be used to transfer a case from a court that lacked personal adjudicatory authority over the defendant to a state that had personal power when venue in the transferor court was *not* improper? See Carteret Savings Bank, FA v. Shushan, 954 F.2d 141 (3d Cir.1992) (no).

Chapter Seven

AT THE INTERSECTION OF STATE AND FEDERAL LAW

SECTION 2.   THE ERIE DECISION

[Insert on page 354 at the end of Section 1:]

SWIFT v. TYSON

Supreme Court of the United States, 1842.
41 U.S. (16 Pet.) 1, 10 L.Ed. 865.

MR. JUSTICE STORY delivered the opinion of the Court.

This cause comes before us from the Circuit Court of the southern district of New York, upon a certificate of division of the judges of that Court.

The action was brought by the plaintiff, Swift, as endorsee, against the defendant, Tyson, as acceptor, upon a bill of exchange dated at Portland, Maine, on the first day of May, 1836, for the sum of one thousand five hundred and forty dollars, thirty cents, payable six months after date and grace, drawn by one Nathaniel Norton and one Jairus S. Keith upon and accepted by Tyson, at the city of New York, in favour of the order of Nathaniel Norton, and by Norton endorsed to the plaintiff. The bill was dishonoured at maturity.

At the trial the acceptance and endorsement of the bill were admitted, and the plaintiff there rested his case. The defendant then introduced in evidence the answer of Swift to a bill of discovery, by which it appeared that Swift took the bill before it became due, in payment of a promissory note due to him by Norton and Keith; that he understood that the bill was accepted in part payment of some lands sold by Norton to a company in New York; that Swift was a bona fide holder of the bill, not having any notice of any thing in the sale or title to the lands, or otherwise, impeaching the transaction, and with the full belief that the bill was justly due. The particular circumstances are fully set forth in the answer in the record; but it does not seem necessary farther to state them. The defendant then offered to prove, that the bill was accepted by the defendant as part consideration for the purchase of certain lands in the state of Maine, which Norton and Keith represented themselves to be the owners of, and also represented to be of great value, and contracted to convey a good title thereto; and that the representations were in every respect fraudulent and false, and Norton and Keith had no title to the lands, and that the same were of little or no value. The plaintiff objected to the admission of such testimony, or of any testimony, as against him, impeaching or showing a failure of the consideration, on which the bill was accepted, under the facts admitted by the defendant, and those proved by him, by reading the answer of the plaintiff to the bill of discovery. The judges of the Circuit Court thereupon divided in opinion upon the following point or question of law; Whether, under the facts last mentioned, the defendant was entitled to the same defence to the action as if the suit was between the original parties to the bill, that is to say, Norton, or Norton and Keith, and the defendant; and whether the evidence so offered was admissible as against the plaintiff in the action. And this is the question certified to us for our decision.

There is no doubt, that a bona fide holder of a negotiable instrument for a valuable consideration, without any notice of facts which impeach its validity as between the antecedent parties, if he takes it under an endorsement made before the same becomes due, holds the title unaffected by these facts, and may recover thereon, although as between the antecedent parties the transaction may be without any legal validity. This is a doctrine so long and so well established, and so essential to the security of negotiable paper, that it is laid up among the fundamentals of the law, and requires no authority or reasoning to be now brought in its support. As little doubt is there, that the holder of any negotiable paper, before it is due, is not bound to prove that he is a bona fide holder for a valuable consideration, without notice; for the law will presume that, in the absence of all rebutting proofs, and therefore it is incumbent upon the defendant to establish by way of defence satisfactory proofs of the contrary, and thus to overcome the prima facie title of the plaintiff.

In the present case, the plaintiff is a bona fide holder without notice for what the law deems a good and valid consideration, that is, for a pre-existing debt; and the only real question in the cause is, whether, under the circumstances of the present case, such a pre-existing debt constitutes a valuable consideration in the sense of the general rule applicable to negotiable instruments. We say, under the circumstances of the present case, for the acceptance having been made in New York, the argument on behalf of the defendant is, that the contract is to be treated as a New York contract, and therefore to be governed by the laws of New York, as expounded by its Courts, as well upon general principles, as by the express provisions of the thirty-fourth section of the judiciary act of 1789, ch. 20. And then it is further contended, that by the law of New York, as thus expounded by its Courts, a pre-existing debt does not constitute, in the sense of the general rule, a valuable consideration applicable to negotiable instruments.

* * *

[A]dmitting the doctrine to be fully settled in New York, it remains to be considered, whether it is obligatory upon this Court, if it differs from the principles established in the general commercial law. It is observable that the Courts of New York do not found their decisions upon this point upon any local statute, or positive, fixed, or ancient local usage: but they deduce the doctrine from the general principles of commercial law. It is, however, contended, that the thirty-fourth section of the judiciary act of 1789, ch. 20, furnishes a rule obligatory upon this Court to follow the decisions of the state tribunals in all cases to which they apply. That section provides "that the laws of the several states, except where the Constitution, treaties, or statutes of the United States shall otherwise require or provide, shall be regarded as rules of decision in trials at common law in the Courts of the United States, in cases where they apply." In order to maintain the argument, it is essential, therefore, to hold, that the word "laws," in this section, includes within the scope of its meaning the decisions of the local tribunals. In the ordinary use of language it will hardly be contended that the decisions of Courts constitute laws. They are, at most, only evidence of what the laws are; and are not of themselves laws. They are often reexamined, reversed, and qualified by the Courts themselves, whenever they are found to be either defective, or ill-founded, or otherwise incorrect. The laws of a state are more usually understood to mean the rules and enactments promulgated by the legislative authority thereof, or long established local customs having the force of laws. In all the various cases which have hitherto come before us for decision, this Court have uniformly supposed, that the true interpretation of the thirty-fourth section limited its application to state laws strictly local, that is to say, to the positive statutes of the state, and the construction thereof adopted by the local tribunals, and to rights and titles to things having a permanent locality, such as the rights and titles to real estate, and other matters immovable and intraterritorial in their nature and character. It never has been supposed by us, that the section did apply, or was designed to apply, to questions of a more general nature, not at all dependent upon local statutes or local usages of a fixed and permanent operation, as, for example, to the construction of ordinary contracts or other written instruments, and especially to questions of general commercial law, where the state tribunals are called upon to perform the like functions as ourselves, that is, to ascertain upon general reasoning and legal analogies, what is the true exposition of the contract or instrument, or what is the just rule furnished by the principles of commercial law to govern the case. And we have not now the slightest difficulty in holding, that this section, upon its true intendment and construction, is strictly limited to local statutes and local usages of the character before stated, and does not extend to contracts and other instruments of a commercial nature, the true interpretation and effect whereof are to be sought, not in the decisions of the local tribunals, but in the general principles and doctrines of commercial jurisprudence. Undoubtedly, the decisions of the local tribunals upon such subjects are entitled to, and will receive, the most deliberate attention and respect of this Court; but they cannot furnish positive rules, or conclusive authority, by which our own judgments are to be bound up and governed. The law respecting negotiable instruments may be truly declared in the language of Cicero, adopted by Lord Mansfield in Luke v. Lyde, 2 Burr.R. 883, 887, to be in a great measure, not the law of a single country only, but of the commercial world. Non erit alia lex Romae, alia Athenis, alia nunc, alia posthac, sed et apud omnes gentes, et omni tempore, una eademque lex obtenebit.

    * * *

We are all, therefore, of opinion, that the question on this point, propounded by the Circuit Court for our consideration, ought to be answered in the negative; and we shall accordingly direct it so to be certified to the Circuit Court.

[Insert at page 359, at the end of Note (5):]

See also Deweerth v. Baldinger, 804 F.Supp. 539 (S.D.N.Y.1992), reversed 38 F.3d 1266 (2d Cir.1994), granting a plaintiff relief from judgment under Fed. R.Civ.P. 60(b)(6) when, four years after judgment was rendered, the state court, in an unrelated controversy, specifically rejected the interpretation of state law utilized by the federal appeals court. *Deweerth* involved the return of a painting stolen during World War II and later sold to a good faith purchaser. The Second Circuit had held that New York law required a demonstration of a level of diligence in attempting to locate the painting that the plaintiff could not show. Subsequently, in an unrelated case, Solomon R. Guggenheim Foundation v. Lubell, 77 N.Y.2d 311, 567 N.Y.S.2d 623, 569 N.E.2d 426 (1991), the New York Court of Appeals stated "the Second Circuit should not have imposed a duty of reasonable diligence." Should the district court have granted relief from the judgment in *Deweerth?* The Second Circuit did not think so: it reversed on the ground that the district court had abused its discretion in ordering relief from judgment, 24 F.3d 416 (2d Cir.1994).

Note that *Deweerth* involved a painting transported over national borders: does it make sense to apply state law to such a case? Would it not be better for a federal court to formulate a *federal* rule applicable to international art markets?

(6) In a diversity case should the court of appeals defer to the district court's interpretation of the law of the state in which the district court sits? The argument advanced for doing so is that the district court judge is more familiar with the local law than a court of appeals judge, particularly one hailing from a different state. But in Salve Regina College v. Russell, 501 U.S. 1203, 111 S.Ct. 2794, 115 L.Ed.2d 969 (1991), the Supreme Court held that appellate review of state law determinations is plenary. *Erie* was not intended to alter the "functional components of decisionmaking." Moreover, the "very essence of the *Erie* doctrine is that the bases of state law are presumed to be communicable by the parties to a federal judge no less than to a state judge."

[Insert at page 380, at the end of Note (3):]

At various times, Justices Douglas and Black dissented from the Supreme Court's approval of federal rules on precisely these grounds, see, e.g., 374 U.S. 865, 870 (1963):

The present rules produced under 28 U.S.C. § 2072 are not prepared by us but by Committees of the Judicial Conference designated by the Chief Justice. . . . It is they . . . who do the work, not we, and the rules have only our imprimatur. . . . If the rule-making for the Federal District Courts is to continue under the present plan, we believe that the Supreme Court should not have any part in this task; rather the statute should be amended to substitute the Judicial Conference. . . . Transfer of the function to the Judicial Conference would relieve us of the embarrassment of having to sit in judgment on the constitutionality of rules which we have approved. . . .

Approval of the 1993 amendments to the civil rules provided an occasion for Justice White to join in this sentiment, see 146 F.R.D. 501, 503 (1993).

[Insert at page 380, at the end of Note (4):]

See also Maltz, Choice of Forum and Choice of Law in the Federal Courts: A Reconsideration of *Erie* Principles, 79 Ky.L.J. 231 (1990); Stein, *Erie* and Court Access, 100 Yale L.J.1935 (1991).

SECTION 4. THE AFTERMATH OF HANNA

A. WHEN THERE IS A FEDERAL RULE DIRECTLY IN POINT

---

2. THE FEDERAL RULES OF EVIDENCE

[Insert on page 382, after the final paragraph:]

It should be noted that although the Rules of Evidence were originally promulgated pursuant to the Supreme Court's rule making authority, they were ultimately enacted by Congress as law, Pub.L. No. 93–595, 88 Stat. 1929 (1975), thereby resolving any residual problems as to the authority provided by the Rules Enabling Act.

B. THE "RELATIVELY UNGUIDED ERIE CHOICE"

[Insert on page 383, after the first paragraph:]

See also Gasperini v. Center for Humanities, Inc., ___ U.S. ___, 116 S.Ct. 2211, 135 L.Ed.2d 659 (1996), reprinted at p. 228, infra (state law requiring trial court review of jury verdicts applies in diversity, but appellate power is limited by Seventh Amendment); Chambers v. NAS-CO, infra, p. 172 (federal diversity court possesses inherent powers to sanction for abuse of process).

[Insert on page 383, after the final paragraph:]

Consider Rule 15(c). Under this provision, the timeliness of an amended pleading that changes the name of the party against whom the suit is brought is judged, in part, according to whether the proper party was notified within the time period provided by Rule 4. Will reliance on this provision in diversity cases conflict with the Court's resolution of *Walker?*

[Insert on page 386, after Note (2):]

See also Kamen v. Kemper Financial Services, Inc., 500 U.S. 90, 111 S.Ct. 1711, 114 L.Ed.2d 152 (1991), which reaffirmed the conclusion in Cohen v. Beneficial Industrial Loan Corp., casebook page 365, that state law has a role in determining whether a shareholder can maintain a derivative action under Rule 23.1.

[Insert on page 389, after Note (4):]

THE CONSEQUENCES OF *ERIE*

FERENS v. JOHN DEERE CO.

Supreme Court of the United States, 1990.
494 U.S. 516, 110 S.Ct. 1274, 108 L.Ed.2d 443.

JUSTICE KENNEDY delivered the opinion of the Court.

Section 1404(a) of Title 28 states: "For the convenience of parties and witnesses, in the interest of justice, a district court may transfer any civil action to any other district or division where it might have been brought." 28 U.S.C. § 1404(a) (1982 ed.). In Van Dusen v. Barrack, 376 U.S. 612, 84 S.Ct. 805, 11 L.Ed.2d 945 (1964), we held that, following a transfer under 1404(a) initiated by a defendant, the transferee court must follow the choice of law rules that prevailed in the transferor court. We now decide that, when a plaintiff moves for the transfer, the same rule applies.

I.

Albert Ferens lost his right hand when, the allegation is, it became caught in his combine harvester, manufactured by Deere & Company. The accident occurred while Ferens was working with the combine on his farm in Pennsylvania. For reasons not explained in the record, Ferens delayed filing a tort suit and Pennsylvania's 2–year limitations period expired. In the third year, he and his wife sued Deere in the United States District Court for the Western District of Pennsylvania, raising contract and warranty claims as to which the Pennsylvania limitations period had not yet run. The District Court had diversity jurisdiction, as Ferens and his wife are Pennsylvania residents, and Deere is incorporated in Delaware with its principal place of business in Illinois.

Not to be deprived of a tort action, the Ferenses in the same year filed a second diversity suit against Deere in the United States District Court for the Southern District of Mississippi, alleging negligence and products liability. Diversity jurisdiction and venue were proper. The

Ferenses sued Deere in the District Court in Mississippi because they knew that, under Klaxon Co. v. Stentor Electric Mfg. Co., 313 U.S. 487, 496, 61 S.Ct. 1020, 1021, 85 L.Ed. 1477 (1941), the federal court in the exercise of diversity jurisdiction must apply the same choice of law rules that Mississippi state courts would apply if they were deciding the case. A Mississippi court would rule that Pennsylvania substantive law controls the personal injury claim but that Mississippi's own law governs the limitation period.

* * *

The issue now before us arose when the Ferenses took their forum shopping a step further: having chosen the federal court in Mississippi to take advantage of the State's limitations period, they next moved, under § 1404(a), to transfer the action to the federal court in Pennsylvania on the ground that Pennsylvania was a more convenient forum. The Ferenses acted on the assumption that, after the transfer, the choice of law rules in the Mississippi forum, including a rule requiring application of the Mississippi statute of limitations, would continue to govern the suit.

[The Ferens' § 1404(a) motion was granted and the tort action consolidated with the pending warranty action. However, the Pennsylvania district court refused to honor Mississippi's statute of limitations on the theory that *Van Dusen* was inapplicable to transfers by plaintiff.] Invoking the 2–year limitations period set by Pennsylvania law, the District Court dismissed their tort action. Ferens v. Deere & Co., 639 F.Supp. 1484 (W.D.Pa.1986).

The Court of Appeals for the Third Circuit affirmed. . . .

II

Section 1404(a) states only that a district court may transfer venue for the convenience of the parties and witnesses when in the interest of justice. It says nothing about choice of law, and nothing about affording plaintiffs different treatment from defendants. We touched upon these issues in *Van Dusen* [where the Court held that "the law applicable to a diversity case does not change upon a transfer initiated by a defendant"], but left open the question presented in this case [involving a plaintiff-initiated transfer.]   . . .

* * *

III

. . . *Van Dusen* reveals three independent reasons for our decision. First, § 1404(a) should not deprive parties of state law advantages that exist absent diversity jurisdiction. Second, § 1404(a) should not create or multiply opportunities for forum shopping. Third, the decision to transfer venue under § 1404(a) should turn on considerations of convenience and the interest of justice rather than on the possible prejudice resulting from a change of law. Although commentators have questioned whether the scant legislative history of § 1404(a) compels reliance on these three policies, see Note, Choice of Law after Transfer of Venue, 75 Yale L.J. 90, 123 (1965), we find it prudent to consider them in deciding whether the rule in *Van Dusen* applies to transfers initiated by plaintiffs. We decide that, in addition to other considerations, these policies require a transferee forum to apply the law of the transferor court, regardless of who initiates the transfer. A transfer under § 1404(a), in other words, does not change the law applicable to a diversity case.

A

The policy that § 1404(a) should not deprive parties of state law advantages, although perhaps discernible in the legislative history, has its real foundation in Erie R. Co. v. Tompkins, 304 U.S. 64, 58 S.Ct. 817, 82 L.Ed. 1188 (1938). See *Van Dusen,* 376 U.S., at 637, 84 S.Ct., at 819. The *Erie* rule remains a vital expression of the federal system and the concomitant integrity of the separate States. We explained *Erie* in Guaranty Trust Co. v. York, 326 U.S. 99, 109, 65 S.Ct. 1464, 1470, 89 L.Ed. 2079 (1945), as follows:

> "In essence, the intent of [the *Erie*] decision was to insure that, in all cases where a federal court is exercising jurisdiction solely because of the diversity of citizenship of the parties, the outcome of the litigation in the federal court should be substantially the same, so far as legal rules determine the outcome of a litigation, as it would be if tried in a State court. The nub of the policy that underlies Erie R. Co. v. Tompkins is that for the same transaction the accident of a suit by a non-resident litigant in a federal court instead of in a State court a block away should not lead to a substantially different result."

In Hanna v. Plumer, 380 U.S. 460, 473, 85 S.Ct. 1136, 1145, 14 L.Ed.2d 8 (1965), we held that Congress has the power to prescribe procedural rules that differ from state law rules even at the expense of altering the outcome of litigation. This case does not involve a conflict. As in *Van Dusen,* our interpretation of § 1404(a) is in full accord with the *Erie* rule. The *Erie* policy had a clear implication for *Van Dusen.* The existence of diversity jurisdiction gave the defendants the opportunity to make a motion to transfer venue under § 1404(a), and if the applicable law were to change after transfer, the plaintiff's venue privilege and resulting state-law advantages could be defeated at the defendant's option. 376 U.S., at 638, 84 S.Ct., at 820. To allow the transfer and at the same time preserve the plaintiff's state-law advantages, we held that the choice of law rules should not change following a transfer initiated by a defendant. Id., at 639, 84 S.Ct., at 821.

Transfers initiated by a plaintiff involve some different considerations, but lead to the same result. Applying the transferor law, of course, will not deprive the plaintiff of any state law advantages. A defendant, in one sense, also will lose no legal advantage if the transferor law controls after a transfer initiated by the plaintiff; the same law, after all, would have applied if the plaintiff had not made the motion. In another sense, however, a defendant may lose a nonlegal advantage. Deere, for example, would lose whatever advantage inheres in not having to litigate in Pennsylvania, or, put another way, in forcing the Ferenses to litigate in Mississippi or not at all.

We, nonetheless, find the advantage that the defendant loses slight. A plaintiff always can sue in the favorable state court or sue in diversity and not seek a transfer. By asking for application of the Mississippi statute of limitations following a transfer to Pennsylvania on grounds of convenience, the Ferenses are seeking to deprive Deere only of the advantage of using against them the inconvenience of litigating in Mississippi. The text of § 1404(a) may not say anything about choice of law, but we think it not the purpose of the section to protect a party's ability to use inconvenience as a shield to discourage or hinder litigation otherwise proper.... By creating an opportunity to have venue transferred between courts in different States on the basis of convenience, an option that does not exist absent federal jurisdiction, Congress, with respect to diversity, retained the *Erie* policy while diminishing the incidents of inconvenience.

Applying the transferee law, by contrast, would undermine the *Erie* rule in a serious way. It would mean that initiating a transfer under § 1404(a) changes the state law applicable to a diversity case. We have held, in an isolated circumstance, that § 1404(a) may pre-empt state law. See Stewart Organization, Inc. v. Ricoh Corp., 487 U.S. 22, 108 S.Ct. 2239, 101 L.Ed.2d 22 (1988) (holding that federal law determines the validity of a forum selection clause). In general, however, we have seen § 1404(a) as a housekeeping measure that should not alter the state law governing a case under Erie. See *Van Dusen,* supra, 376 U.S., at 636–637, 84 S.Ct., at 819–20; see also *Stewart Organization,* supra, 487 U.S., at 37, 108 S.Ct., at 2247 (Scalia, J., dissenting) (finding the language of § 1404(a) "plainly insufficient" to work a change in the applicable state law through pre-emption). The Mississippi statute of limitations, which everyone agrees would have applied if the Ferenses had not moved for a transfer, should continue to apply in this case.

In any event, defendants in the position of Deere would not fare much better if we required application of the transferee law instead of the transferor law. True, if the transferee law were to apply, some plaintiffs would not sue these defendants for fear that they would have no choice but to litigate in an inconvenient forum. But applying the transferee law would not discourage all plaintiffs from suing....

B

Van Dusen also sought to fashion a rule that would not create opportunities for forum shopping. Some commentators have seen this policy as the most important rationale of *Van Dusen,* see, e.g., 19 C. Wright, A. Miller, & E. Cooper, Federal Practice and Procedure § 4506, p. 79 (1982), but few attempt to explain the harm of forum shopping when the plaintiff initiates a transfer. An opportunity for forum shopping exists whenever a party has a choice of forums that will apply different laws. The *Van Dusen* policy against forum shopping simply requires us to interpret § 1404(a) in a way that does not create an opportunity for obtaining a more favorable law by selecting a forum through a transfer of venue. In the *Van Dusen* case itself, this meant that we could not allow defendants to use a transfer to change the law. 376 U.S., at 636, 84 S.Ct., at 819.

No interpretation of § 1404(a), however, will create comparable opportunities for forum shopping by a plaintiff because, even without § 1404(a), a plaintiff already has the option of shopping for a forum with the most favorable law. The Ferenses, for example, had an opportunity for forum shopping in the state courts because both the Mississippi and Pennsylvania courts had jurisdiction and because they each would have applied a different statute of limitations. Diversity jurisdiction did not eliminate these forum shopping opportunities; instead, under *Erie,* the federal courts had to replicate them. See Klaxon Co. v. Stentor Electric Mfg. Co., Inc., 313 U.S., at 496, 61 S.Ct., at 1021 ("Whatever lack of uniformity *[Erie]* may produce between federal courts in different states is attributable to our federal system, which leaves to a state, within the limits permitted by the Constitution, the right to pursue local policies diverging from those of its neighbors") . . . .

* * *

C

Van Dusen also made clear that the decision to transfer venue under § 1404(a) should turn on considerations of convenience rather than on the possibility of prejudice resulting from a change in the applicable law. See 376 U.S., at 636, 84 S.Ct., at 819; Piper Aircraft Co. v. Reyno, 454 U.S. 235, 253–254, and n. 20, 102 S.Ct. 252, 264–65, and n. 20, 70 L.Ed.2d 419 (1981). We reasoned in *Van Dusen* that, if the law changed following a transfer initiated by the defendant, a district court "would at least be reluctant to grant transfers, despite considerations of convenience, if to do so might conceivably prejudice the claim of a plaintiff." 376 U.S., at 636, 84 S.Ct., at 819. The court, to determine the prejudice, might have to make an elaborate survey of the law, including statutes of limitations, burdens of proof, presumptions, and the like. This would turn what is supposed to be a statute for convenience of the courts into one expending extensive judicial time and resources. Because this difficult task is contrary to the purpose of the statute, in *Van Dusen* we made it unnecessary by ruling that a transfer of venue by the defendant does not result in a change of law. This same policy requires application of the transferor law when a plaintiff initiates a transfer.

* * *

Some might think that a plaintiff should pay the price for choosing an inconvenient forum by being put to a choice of law versus forum. But this assumes that § 1404(a) is for the benefit only of the moving party. By the statute's own terms, it is not. Section 1404(a) also exists for the benefit of the witnesses and the interest of justice, which must include the convenience of the court. . . .

D

This case involves some considerations to which we perhaps did not give sufficient attention in *Van Dusen*. Foresight and judicial economy now seem to favor the simple rule that the law does not change following a transfer of venue under § 1404(a). Affording transfers initiated by plaintiffs different treatment from transfers initiated by defendants may seem quite workable in this case, but the simplicity is an illusion. If we were to hold that the transferee law applies following a § 1404(a) motion by a plaintiff, cases such as this would not arise in the future. Although applying the transferee law, no doubt, would catch the Ferenses by surprise, in the future no plaintiffs in their position would move for a change of venue.

Other cases, however, would produce undesirable complications. The rule would leave unclear which law should apply when both a defendant and a plaintiff move for a transfer of venue or when the court transfers venue on its own motion. . . . The rule also might require variation in certain situations, such as when the plaintiff moves for a transfer following a removal from state court by the defendant, or when only one of several plaintiffs requests the transfer, or when circumstances change through no fault of the plaintiff making a once convenient forum inconvenient. True, we could reserve any consideration of these questions for a later day. But we have a duty, in deciding this case, to consider whether our decision will create litigation and uncertainty. On the basis of these considerations, we again conclude that the transferor law should apply regardless of who makes the § 1404(a) motion.

IV

Some may object that a district court in Pennsylvania should not have to apply a Mississippi statute of limitations to a Pennsylvania cause of action. This point, although understandable, should have little to do with the outcome of this case. Congress gave the Ferenses the power to seek a transfer in § 1404(a) and our decision in *Van Dusen* already could require a district court in Pennsylvania to apply the Mississippi statute of limitations to Pennsylvania claims. Our rule may seem too generous because it allows the Ferenses to have both their choice of law and their choice of forum, or even to reward the Ferenses for conduct that seems manipulative. We nonetheless see no alternative rule that would produce a more acceptable result. Deciding that the transferee law should apply, in effect, would tell the Ferenses that they should have continued to litigate their warranty action in Pennsylvania and their tort action in Mississippi. Some might find this preferable, but we do not. We have made quite clear that "[t]o permit a situation in which two cases involving precisely the same issues are simultaneously pending in different District Courts leads to the wastefulness of time, energy and money that § 1404(a) was designed to prevent." Continental Grain Co. v. The Barge FBL-585, 364 U.S. 19, 26, 80 S.Ct. 1470, 1474.

From a substantive standpoint, two further objections give us pause but do not persuade us to change our rule. First, one might ask why we require the Ferenses to file in the District Court in Mississippi at all. Efficiency might seem to dictate a rule allowing plaintiffs in the Ferenses' position not to file in an inconvenient forum and then to return to a convenient forum though a transfer of venue, but instead simply to file in the convenient forum and ask for the law of the inconvenient forum to apply. Although our rule may invoke certain formality, one must remember that § 1404(a) does not provide for an automatic transfer of venue. The section, instead, permits a transfer only when convenient and "in the interest of justice." Plaintiffs in the position of the Ferenses must go to the distant forum because they have no guarantee, until the court there examines the facts, that they may obtain a transfer. No one has contested the justice of transferring this particular case, but the option remains open to defendants in future cases. Although a court cannot ignore the systemic costs of inconvenience, it may consider the course that the litigation already has taken in determining the interest of justice.

Second, one might contend that, because no per se rule requiring a court to apply either the transferor law or the transferee law will seem appropriate in all circumstances, we should develop more sophisticated federal choice of law rules for diversity actions involving transfers. See Note, 75 Yale L.J., at 130–135. To a large extent, however, state conflicts of law rules already ensure that appropriate laws will apply to diversity cases. Federal law, as a general matter, does not interfere with these rules. Sun Oil Co. v. Wortman, 486 U.S. 717, 727–729, 108 S.Ct. 2117, 2124, 100 L.Ed.2d 743 (1988). In addition, even if more elaborate federal choice of law rules would not run afoul of Klaxon and Erie, we believe that applying the law of the transferor forum effects the appropriate balance between fairness and simplicity. Cf. R. Leflar, American Conflicts Law § 143, p. 293 (3d ed. 1977) (arguing against a federal common law of conflicts). For the foregoing reasons, we conclude that Mississippi's statute of limitations should govern the Ferenses' action. We reverse and remand for proceedings consistent with this opinion.

It is so ordered.

JUSTICE SCALIA, with whom JUSTICE BRENNAN, JUSTICE MARSHALL, and JUSTICE BLACKMUN join, dissenting.   [omitted]

NOTES

(1) Would Justice Brandeis have approved the result in *Ferens?*   On three separate occasions, the opinion invokes *Erie:* 1) to apply Mississippi's statute of limitations to a diversity action in Mississippi federal court; 2) to apply the law that would be used in the transferor court after a § 1404 transfer; and 3) to apply Mississippi's choice of law rule to a cause of action arising in Pennsylvania. Yet the bottom line seems to be exactly wrong: a case is litigated in Pennsylvania federal court that would have been dismissed from Pennsylvania state court; the accident of diversity enables the plaintiff to achieve a result that could not be reached in a wholly-Pennsylvania case.

(2) What went wrong?   Is this Mississippi's "fault" for applying its own statute of limitations to a cause of action that would be decided under Pennsylvania substantive law?   Should the Supreme Court step in to prevent a state from using this choice-of-law rule?   Review Sun Oil Co. v. Wortman, supra p. 361.

Is the problem attributable to *Klaxon:* should the Supreme Court revisit the question whether to use state choice of law rules in diversity actions now that the Court has been more willing to take federal interests seriously?   Review the material at pp. 359–360, supra.

Was the Court on the right track in *World–Wide Volkswagen:* that is, should the courts use personal jurisdiction rules to restrain adjudication of disputes in states whose law would achieve undesirable results?   Review the material at pp. 261–277, supra.

(3) Should a transferee forum apply the transferor forum's law if the transferor forum lacked in personam adjudicatory authority over the defendant? See Henninger, The Plaintiff's Forum Shopping Gold Card: Choice of Laws in the Federal Courts After Transfer of Venue Under § 1404(A)—Ferens v. John Deere Co., 26 Wake Forest L.Rev. 809 (1991); Rodden, Is 28 U.S.C.A. § 1404(A) A Federal Forum Shopping Statute?   66 Wash.L.Rev. 851 (1991); Norwood, Shopping For A Venue: The Need For More Limits on Choice, 50 U.Miami L.Rev. 267 (1996).

SECTION 5.   FEDERAL COMMON LAW

[Insert on page 395, after Note (2):]

(3) Kamen v. Kemper Financial Services, Inc., 500 U.S. 90, 111 S.Ct. 1711, 114 L.Ed.2d 152 (1991).   This case involved a shareholders' derivative action dismissed by the United States District Court for Maryland for failure to demand action from the corporation's directors before instituting a derivative proceeding. The district court ruled, as a matter of federal common law, that stockholders were required to make such a "universal demand," contradicting state law, which excused shareholders where a demand was deemed "futile."   The Supreme Court reversed:

This case calls upon us to determine whether we should fashion a federal common law rule obliging the representative shareholder in a derivative action founded on the Investment Company Act of 1940, 54 Stat. 789, 15 U.S.C. § 80a–1(a) et seq., to make a demand on the board of directors even when such a demand would be excused as futile under state law. Because the scope of the demand requirement embodies the incorporating State's allocation of governing powers within the corporation, and because a futility exception to demand does not impede the purposes of the Investment Company Act, we decline to displace state law with a uniform rule abolishing the futility exception in federal derivative actions.

While the Supreme Court deferred to state law in *Kamen,* it recognized that federal law might be created when "a distinct need for nationwide legal standards is shown."

[Insert on page 395, after the Notes:]

YAMAHA MOTOR CORPORATION, U.S.A. v. CALHOUN

Supreme Court of the United States, 1996.
___ U.S. ___, 116 S.Ct. 619; 133 L.Ed.2d 578.

JUSTICE GINSBURG delivered the opinion of the Court.*

Twelve-year-old Natalie Calhoun was killed in a jet ski accident on July 6, 1989. At the time of her death, she was vacationing with family friends at a beach-front resort in Puerto Rico. Alleging that the jet ski was defectively designed or made, Natalie's parents sought to recover from the manufacturer pursuant to state survival and wrongful death statutes. The manufacturer contended that state remedies could not be applied because Natalie died on navigable waters; federal, judge declared maritime law, the manufacturer urged, controlled to the exclusion of state law.

Traditionally, state remedies have been applied in accident cases of this order—maritime wrongful death cases in which no federal statute specifies the appropriate relief and the decedent was not a seaman, longshore worker, or person otherwise engaged in a maritime trade. We hold, in accord with the United States Court of Appeals for the Third Circuit, that state remedies remain applicable in such cases and have not been displaced by the federal maritime wrongful death action recognized in Moragne v. States Marine Lines, Inc., 398 U.S. 375, 26 L.Ed.2d 339, 90 S.Ct. 1772 (1970).

I

Natalie Calhoun, the twelve-year-old daughter of respondents Lucien and Robin Calhoun, died in a tragic accident on July 6, 1989. On

* Footnotes omitted.

vacation with family friends at a resort hotel in Puerto Rico, Natalie had rented a "WaveJammer" jet ski manufactured by Yamaha Motor Company, Ltd., and distributed by Yamaha Motor Corporation, U.S.A. (collectively, "Yamaha"), the petitioners in this case. While riding the Wave-Jammer, Natalie slammed into a vessel anchored in the waters off the hotel frontage, and was killed.

The Calhouns, individually and in their capacities as administrators of their daughter's estate, sued Yamaha in the United States District Court for the Eastern District of Pennsylvania. Invoking Pennsylvania's wrongful death and survival statutes, 42 Pa. Cons. Stat. §§ 8301–8302 (1982 and Supp. 1995), the Calhouns asserted several bases for recovery (including negligence, strict liability, and breach of implied warranties), and sought damages for lost future earnings, loss of society, loss of support and services, and funeral expenses, as well as punitive damages. They grounded federal jurisdiction on both diversity of citizenship, 28 U.S.C. § 1332, and admiralty, 28 U.S.C. § 1333.

Yamaha moved for partial summary judgment, arguing that the federal maritime wrongful death action this Court recognized in Moragne v. States Marine Lines, Inc., 398 U.S. 375, 26 L.Ed.2d 339, 90 S.Ct. 1772 (1970), provided the exclusive basis for recovery, displacing all remedies afforded by state law. Under Moragne, Yamaha contended, the Calhouns could recover as damages only Natalie's funeral expenses. The District Court agreed with Yamaha that Moragne's maritime death action displaced state remedies; the court held, however, that loss of society and loss of support and services were compensable under Moragne.

Both sides asked the District Court to present questions for immediate interlocutory appeal pursuant to 28 U.S.C. § 1292(b). The District Court granted the parties' requests. . . .

Although the Court of Appeals granted the interlocutory review petition, the panel to which the appeal was assigned did not reach the questions presented in the certified order, for it determined that an anterior issue was pivotal. The District Court, as just recounted, had concluded that any damages the Calhouns might recover from Yamaha would be governed exclusively by federal maritime law. But the Third Circuit panel questioned that conclusion and inquired whether state wrongful death and survival statutes supplied the remedial prescriptions for the Calhouns' complaint. The appellate panel asked whether the state remedies endured or were "displaced by a federal maritime rule of decision." 40 F.3d 622, 624 (1994). Ultimately, the Court of Appeals ruled that state law remedies apply in this case. Id., at 644.

II

In our order granting certiorari, we asked the parties to brief a preliminary question: "Under 28 U.S.C. § 1292(b), can the courts of appeals exercise jurisdiction over any question that is included within the order that contains the controlling question of law identified by the district court?" 514 U.S. ___ (1995). The answer to that question, we are satisfied, is yes.

Section 1292(b) provides, in pertinent part:

"When a district judge, in making in a civil action an order not otherwise appealable under this section, shall be of the opinion that such order involves a controlling question of law as to which there is substantial ground for difference of opinion and that an immediate appeal from the order may materially advance the ultimate termination of the litigation, he shall so state in writing in such order. The Court of Appeals ... may thereupon, in its discretion, permit an appeal to be taken from such order, if application is made to it within ten days after the entry of the order."

As the text of § 1292(b) indicates, appellate jurisdiction applies to the order certified to the court of appeals, and is not tied to the particular question formulated by the district court. The court of appeals may not reach beyond the certified order to address other orders made in the case. United States v. Stanley, 483 U.S. 669, 677, 97 L.Ed.2d 550, 107 S.Ct. 3054 (1987). But the appellate court may address any issue fairly included within the certified order because "it is the order that is appealable, and not the controlling question identified by the district court." 9 J. Moore & B. Ward, Moore's Federal Practice P110.25[1], p. 300 (2d ed. 1995). See also 16 C. Wright, A. Miller, E. Cooper, & E. Gressman, Federal Practice and Procedure § 3929, pp. 144–145 (1977) ("The court of appeals may review the entire order, either to consider a question different than the one certified as controlling or to decide the case despite the lack of any identified controlling question."); Note, Interlocutory Appeals in the Federal Courts Under 28 U.S.C. § 1292(b), 88 Harv.L.Rev. 607, 628–629 (1975) ("scope of review [includes] all issues material to the order in question").

We therefore proceed to the issue on which certiorari was granted: Does the federal maritime claim for wrongful death recognized in Moragne supply the exclusive remedy in cases involving the deaths of nonseafarers in territorial waters?

III

Because this case involves a watercraft collision on navigable waters, it falls within admiralty's domain. See Sisson v. Ruby, 497 U.S. 358, 361–367, 111 L.Ed.2d 292, 110 S.Ct. 2892 (1990); Foremost Ins. Co. v. Richardson, 457 U.S. 668, 677, 73 L.Ed.2d 300, 102 S.Ct. 2654 (1982). "With admiralty jurisdiction," we have often said, "comes the application of substantive admiralty law." East River S.S. Corp. v. Transamerica Delaval Inc., 476 U S. 858, 864, 90 L.Ed.2d 865, 106 S.Ct. 2295 (1986). The exercise of admiralty jurisdiction, however, "does not result in automatic displacement of state law." Jerome B. Grubart, Inc. v. Great Lakes Dredge & Dock Co., 513 U.S. ___, ___ (1995) (slip op., at 18). Indeed, prior to Moragne, federal admiralty courts routinely applied state wrongful death and survival statutes in maritime accident cases. The question before us is whether Moragne should be read to stop that practice.

When Congress has prescribed a comprehensive tort recovery regime to be uniformly applied, there is, we have generally recognized, no cause for enlargement of the damages statutorily provided. See Miles, 498 U.S. at 30–36 (Jones Act, rather than general maritime law, determines damages recoverable in action for wrongful death of seamen).... But Congress has not prescribed remedies for the wrongful deaths of nonseafarers in territorial waters. See Miles, 498 U.S. at 31. There is, however, a relevant congressional disposition. Section 7 of DOHSA states: "The provisions of any State statute giving or regulating rights of action or remedies for death shall not be affected by this chapter." 46 U.S.C.App. § 767. This statement, by its terms, simply stops DOHSA from displacing state law in territorial waters. See Miles, 498 U.S. at 25; Tallentire, 477 U.S. at 224–225; Moragne, 398 U.S. at 397–398. Taking into account what Congress sought to achieve, we preserve the application of state statutes to deaths within territorial waters.

* * *

...., [W]e hold that the damages available for the jet ski death of Natalie Calhoun are properly governed by state law. The judgment of the Court of Appeals for the Third Circuit is accordingly [a]ffirmed.

NOTE

Under which state law are the damages to be determined? Under Puerto Rican or Pennsylvania law? Should the Court look to internal state law or state conflict of law rules?

SECTION 6. "REVERSE" ERIE

[Insert on page 398, after the text:]

In Johnson v. Fankell, ___ U.S. ___, 117 S.Ct. 1800, 138 L.Ed.2d 108 (1997), the Supreme Court held a state trial court's rejection, in a case brought under 28 U.S.C. § 1983, of a defense of qualified immunity based on federal law, not appealable interlocutorily, even though that ruling, if made in a federal court, would have been immediately appealable. To what extent, must state courts, in federal question cases, follow federal rules of procedure, or, in other words, which federal rules of procedure are substantive for reverse–Erie purposes?

Chapter Eight

THE SCOPE OF THE LAWSUIT

SECTION 1. REAL PARTY IN INTEREST

[Page 403: delete the paragraph in the Notes that precedes *Tyler*.]
[Insert on page 405 at Note (2):]

Under the 1991 Amendments to the Federal Rules of Civil Procedure, the text of Fed.R.Civ.P. 15(c)(2) has been relocated, unchanged, to Fed.R.Civ.P. 15(c)(3)(B).

SECTION 4. COUNTERCLAIMS

[Insert on page 424 at Note (2):]

Note that 28 U.S.C.A. § 1367 replaces the terms "ancillary jurisdiction" and "pendent jurisdiction" with the phrase "supplemental jurisdiction."

SECTION 5. PERMISSIVE JOINDER OF PARTIES

[Insert on page 431 in lieu of Note (5):]

(5) If the principal case had been brought in a federal court, what would have been the requirements of (a) diversity of citizenship and (b) amount in controversy? Could the court's competence have been sustained by reliance on supplemental jurisdiction, 28 U.S.C.A. § 1367? Could the various claims have been aggregated to reach the requisite amount in controversy? See Phillips Petroleum v. Taylor, 115 F.2d 726 (5th Cir.1940), cert. denied 313 U.S. 565, 61 S.Ct. 941, 85 L.Ed. 1524 (1941). Cf. Snyder v. Harris, 394 U.S. 332, 89 S.Ct. 1053, 22 L.Ed.2d 319 (1969); Zahn v. International Paper Co., 414 U.S. 291, 94 S.Ct. 505, 38 L.Ed.2d 511 (1973); In re Abbott Laboratories, 51 F.3d 524 (5th Cir.1995), supra p. 63.

SECTION 6. CROSS–CLAIMS

[Insert on page 436 in lieu of first three sentences on page:]

Because cross claims can be asserted only if they are transactionally related to the main claim, they will generally support supplemental jurisdiction under the "same case or controversy" requirement of 28 U.S.C.A. § 1367.

119

Note that 28 U.S.C.A. § 1367 replaces the terms "ancillary jurisdiction" and "pendent jurisdiction" with the phrase "supplemental jurisdiction."

[Insert on page 437 in lieu of Note (1):]

(1) Are cases like *Fairview,* which permit the court to entertain crossclaims between nondiverse defendants, still good law after the passage of § 1367? Note that the statute does not deal with this issue explicitly (since, for most joinder rules, it discusses only claims by *plaintiffs;* it takes up *defendants* only in connection with Rule 19 and 24 parties). The drafters of the provision acknowledge that there are open questions like these, but they claim that they arise "more often on law school exams than in reported decisions." According to the drafters, "the final clause of section 1367(b) provides a basis for treating such situations," Rowe, Mengler, & Burbank: Compounding or Creating Confusion About Supplemental Jurisdiction, A Reply to Professor Freer, 40 Emory L.J. 943, 959 (1991). Perhaps the intent is to preserve prior case law in situations not covered by the statute.

SECTION 7.   COMPULSORY JOINDER OF PARTIES

[Insert on page 451 at Note (2):]

Note that 28 U.S.C.A. § 1367 codifies the proposition that indispensability is not a ground for expanding federal adjudicatory authority.

SECTION 8.   IMPLEADER

[Insert on page 456 in lieu of Note (3):]

(3) Third-party practice raises several subject matter jurisdiction problems. 28 U.S.C.A. § 1367 seems to confer supplemental jurisdiction over impleader claims asserted by third-party plaintiffs against third-party defendants and over claims asserted by third-party defendants against the original plaintiffs. Owen Equipment & Erection Co. v. Kroger, casebook page 210, however, required an independent basis for jurisdiction over claims asserted by original plaintiffs against third-party defendants. Allowing supplemental jurisdiction in such a case might permit plaintiffs to evade the maximum diversity requirement by intentionally failing to name a party who would destroy diversity, with the expectation the party would be impleaded by the defendant. 28 U.S.C.A. § 1367 specifically retains the rule in *Owen Equipment.* After the third-party defendant has asserted claims against the original plaintiff using supplemental jurisdiction, should the original plaintiff be allowed to assert permissive counterclaims? Should the original plaintiff be required to assert compulsory counterclaims? See Revere Copper & Brass, Inc. v. Aetna Casualty & Surety Co., 426 F.2d 709 (5th Cir.1970) (decided prior to *Owen Equipment* and before 28 U.S.C.A. § 1367 was enacted). The drafters of § 1367 apparently intended to preserve prior law for situations not directly covered by the terms of the statute. In addition, they give as an example of a situation in which supplemental jurisdiction exists: a

diversity plaintiff's compulsory counterclaim against a third-party defendant. Rowe, Mengler, & Burbank: Compounding or Creating Confusion About Supplemental Jurisdiction, A Reply to Professor Freer, 40 Emory L.J. 943, 959 (1991).

SECTION 9. INTERVENTION

[Insert on pages 467–68 in lieu of Notes (4) and (5):]

(4) In federal court, 28 U.S.C.A. § 1367 confers supplemental subject matter competence over intervenors in federal question cases, but not, apparently, in diversity cases.

SECTION 10. INTERPLEADER

[At page 476: Note that the cross cite to the facts of the *State Farm* case should be to page 183.]

SECTION 11. CLASS ACTIONS

B. REQUIREMENTS FOR CLASS ACTIONS

1. NOTICE

[Insert on page 505, before "2. OPPORTUNITY TO BE HEARD":]

IN THE MATTER OF RHONE–POULENC RORER INCORPORATED.

United States Court of Appeals, Seventh Circuit, 1995.
51 F.3d 1293.

POSNER, CHIEF JUDGE.*

Drug companies that manufacture blood solids are the defendants in a nationwide class action brought on behalf of hemophiliacs infected by the AIDS virus as a consequence of using the defendants' products. The defendants have filed with us a petition for mandamus, asking us to direct the district judge to rescind his order certifying the case as a class action. We have no appellate jurisdiction over that order. An order certifying a class is not a final decision within the meaning of 28 U.S.C. § 1291; it does not wind up the litigation in the district court. And, in

---

* Footnotes omitted.

part because it is reviewable (at least in principle—the importance of this qualification will appear shortly) on appeal from the final decision in the case, it has been held not to fit any of the exceptions to the rule that confines federal appellate jurisdiction to final decisions. In short, as the Supreme Court made clear in Coopers & Lybrand v. Livesay, 437 U.S. 463, 98 S.Ct. 2454, 57 L.Ed.2d 351 (1978), and Gardner v. Westinghouse Broadcasting Co., 437 U.S. 478, 480–82, 98 S.Ct. 2451, 2453–54, 57 L.Ed.2d 364 (1978), it is not an appealable order. Those decisions involved the denial rather than the grant of motions for class certification, but the grant is no more final than the denial and no more within any of the exceptions to the final-decision rule. Hoxworth v. Blinder, Robinson & Co., 903 F.2d 186, 208 (3d Cir.1990); 7B Charles Alan Wright, Arthur R. Miller & Mary Kay Kane, Federal Practice and Procedure § 1802, pp. 484–86 (2d ed. 1986). Still, even nonappealable orders can be challenged by asking the court of appeals to mandamus the district court. Indeed, as a practical matter only such orders can be challenged by filing a petition for mandamus; an appealable order can be challenged only by appealing from it; the possibility of appealing would be a compelling reason for denying mandamus. For obvious reasons, however, mandamus is issued only in extraordinary cases. Otherwise, interlocutory orders would be appealable routinely, but with "appeal" renamed "mandamus." Kerr v. United States District Court, 426 U.S. 394, 403, 96 S.Ct. 2119, 2124, 48 L.Ed.2d 725 (1976); Eisenberg v. United States District Court, 910 F.2d 374, 375 (7th Cir.1990).

How to cabin this too-powerful writ which if uncabined threatens to unravel the final-decision rule? By taking seriously the two conditions for the grant of a writ of mandamus. The first is that the challenged order not be effectively reviewable at the end of the case—in other words, that it inflict irreparable harm. Kerr v. United States, supra, 426 U.S. at 403, 96 S.Ct. at 2124; In re Sandahl, 980 F.2d 1118, 1119 (7th Cir.1992); Eisenberg v. United States District Court, supra, 910 F.2d at 375. The petitioner "must ordinarily demonstrate that something about the order, or its circumstances, would make an end-of-case appeal ineffectual or leave legitimate interests unduly at risk." In re Recticel Foam Corp., 859 F.2d 1000, 1005–06 (1st Cir.1988). Second, the order must so far exceed the proper bounds of judicial discretion as to be legitimately considered usurpative in character, or in violation of a clear and indisputable legal right, or, at the very least, patently erroneous. Gulfstream Aerospace Corp. v. Mayacamas Corp., 485 U.S. 271, 289, 108 S.Ct. 1133, 1143–44, 99 L.Ed.2d 296 (1988); Allied Chemical Corp. v. Daiflon, Inc., 449 U.S. 33, 35, 101 S.Ct. 188, 190, 66 L.Ed.2d 193 (1980) (per curiam); United States v. Spilotro, 884 F.2d 1003, 1006–07 (7th Cir.1989); In re Sandahl, supra, 980 F.2d at 1121; Maloney v. Plunkett, 854 F.2d 152 (7th Cir.1988). We shall not have to explore these gradations; it will be enough to consider whether the district judge's order can fairly be characterized as usurpative.

The set of orders in which both conditions are satisfied is small. It certainly is not coterminous with the set of orders certifying suits as class actions. For even though such orders often, perhaps typically, inflict irreparable injury on the defendants (just as orders denying class certification often, perhaps typically, inflict irreparable injury on the members of the class), irreparable injury is not sufficient for mandamus; there must also be an abuse of discretion that can fairly be characterized as gross, very clear, or unusually serious. But it is not an empty set. The point of cases like Coopers & Lybrand is that irreparable harm is not enough to make class certification orders automatically appealable under 28 U.S.C. § 1291, not that mandamus is never appropriate in a class certification setting. There is a big difference between saying that all class certification rulings are appealable as of right because they are final within the meaning of section 1291 (the position rejected in Coopers & Lybrand) and saying that a handful are—the handful in which the district judge committed a clear abuse of discretion. Mandamus has occasionally been granted to undue class certifications, see, e.g., In re Fibreboard Corp., 893 F.2d 706 (5th Cir.1990), and we are not aware that any case has held that mandamus will never be granted in such cases. See In re Catawba Indian Tribe, 973 F.2d 1133, 1137 (4th Cir.1992); DeMasi v. Weiss, 669 F.2d 114, 117–19 and n. 6 (3d Cir.1982). The present case, as we shall see, is quite extraordinary when all its dimensions are apprehended. We shall also see that when mandamus is sought to protect the Seventh Amendment's right to a jury trial in federal civil cases, as in this case, the requirement of proving irreparable harm is relaxed.

The suit to which the petition for mandamus relates, Wadleigh v. Rhone–Poulenc Rorer Inc., 157 F.R.D. 410 arises out of the infection of a substantial fraction of the hemophiliac population of this country by the AIDS virus because the blood supply was contaminated by the virus before the nature of the disease was well understood or adequate methods of screening the blood supply existed. The AIDS virus (HIV— human immunodeficiency virus) is transmitted by the exchange of bodily fluids, primarily semen and blood. Hemophiliacs depend on blood solids that contain the clotting factors whose absence defines their disease. These blood solids are concentrated from blood obtained from many donors. If just one of the donors is infected with the AIDS virus the probability that the blood solids manufactured in part from his blood will be infected is very high unless the blood is treated with heat to kill the virus. For general background, see Margaret W. Hilgartner, "AIDS and Hemophilia," 317 New England Journal of Medicine 1153 (1987); Leon W. Hoyer, "Hemophilia A," 330 New England Journal of Medicine 38 (1994); "U.S. CDC: HIV Cutting Lives Short in Hemophilia, Study Says," AIDS Weekly, Feb. 14, 1994.

First identified in 1981, AIDS was diagnosed in hemophiliacs beginning in 1982, and by 1984 the medical community agreed that the virus was transmitted by blood as well as by semen. That year it was demonstrated that treatment with heat could kill the virus in the blood supply and in the following year a reliable test for the presence of the virus in blood was developed. By this time, however, a large number of hemophiliacs had become infected. Since 1984 physicians have been advised to place hemophiliacs on heat-treated blood solids, and since 1985 all blood donated for the manufacture of blood solids has been screened and supplies discovered to be HIV-positive have been discarded. Supplies that test negative still are heat-treated, because the test is not infallible and in particular may fail to detect the virus in persons who became infected within six months before taking the test.

The plaintiffs have presented evidence that 2,000 hemophiliacs have died of AIDS and that half or more of the remaining U.S. hemophiliac population of 20,000 may be HIV-positive. Unless there are dramatic breakthroughs in the treatment of HIV or AIDS, all infected persons will die from the disease. The reason so many are infected even though the supply of blood for the manufacture of blood solids (as for transfusions) has been safe since the mid–80s is that the disease has a very long incubation period; the median period for hemophiliacs may be as long as 11 years. Probably most of the hemophiliacs who are now HIV-positive, or have AIDS, or have died of AIDS were infected in the early 1980s, when the blood supply was contaminated.

Some 300 lawsuits, involving some 400 plaintiffs, have been filed, 60 percent of them in state courts, 40 percent in federal district courts under the diversity jurisdiction, seeking to impose tort liability on the defendants for the transmission of HIV to hemophiliacs in blood solids manufactured by the defendants. Obviously these 400 plaintiffs represent only a small fraction of the hemophiliacs (or their next of kin, in cases in which the hemophiliac has died) who are infected by HIV or have died of AIDS. One of the 300 cases is Wadleigh, filed in September 1993, the case that the district judge certified as a class action. Thirteen other cases have been tried already in various courts around the country, and the defendants have won twelve of them. All the cases brought in federal court (like Wadleigh)—cases brought under the diversity jurisdiction—have been consolidated for pretrial discovery in the Northern District of Illinois by the panel on multidistrict litigation.

The plaintiffs advance two principal theories of liability. The first is that before anyone had heard of AIDS or HIV, it was known that Hepatitis B, a lethal disease though less so than HIV–AIDS, could be transmitted either through blood transfusions or through injection of blood solids. The plaintiffs argue that due care with respect to the risk of infection with Hepatitis B required the defendants to take measures to purge that virus from their blood solids, whether by treating the blood they bought or by screening the donors—perhaps by refusing to deal with paid donors, known to be a class at high risk of being infected with Hepatitis B. The defendants' failure to take effective measures was, the plaintiffs claim, negligent. Had the defendants not been negligent, the plaintiffs further argue, hemophiliacs would have been protected not only against Hepatitis B but also, albeit fortuitously or as the plaintiffs put it "serendipitously," against HIV.

The plaintiffs' second theory of liability is more conventional. It is that the defendants, again negligently, dragged their heels in screening donors and taking other measures to prevent contamination of blood solids by HIV when they learned about the disease in the early 1980s. The plaintiffs have other theories of liability as well, including strict products liability, but it is not necessary for us to get into them.

The district judge did not think it feasible to certify Wadleigh as a class action for the adjudication of the entire controversy between the plaintiffs and the defendants. Fed.R.Civ.P. 23(b)(3). The differences in the date of infection alone of the thousands of potential class members would make such a procedure infeasible. Hemophiliacs infected before anyone knew about the contamination of blood solids by HIV could not rely on the second theory of liability, while hemophiliacs infected after the blood supply became safe (not perfectly safe, but nearly so) probably were not infected by any of the defendants' products. Instead the judge certified the suit "as a class action with respect to particular issues" only. Fed.R.Civ.P. 23(c)(4)(A). He explained this decision in an opinion which implied that he did not envisage the entry of a final judgment but rather the rendition by a jury of a special verdict that would answer a number of questions bearing, perhaps decisively, on whether the defendants are negligent under either of the theories sketched above. If the special verdict found no negligence under either theory, that presumably would be the end of all the cases unless other theories of liability proved viable. If the special verdict found negligence, individual members of the class would then file individual tort suits in state and federal district courts around the nation and would use the special verdict, in conjunction with the doctrine of collateral estoppel, to block relitigation of the issue of negligence.

With all due respect for the district judge's commendable desire to experiment with an innovative procedure for streamlining the adjudication of this "mass tort," we believe that his plan so far exceeds the permissible bounds of discretion in the management of federal litigation as to compel us to intervene and order decertification. The plaintiffs' able counsel argues that we need not intervene now, that it will be time enough to intervene if and when a special verdict adverse to the defendants is entered and an appeal taken to us. But of course a verdict as such is not an appealable order. Only when a final judgment is entered, determining liability and assessing damages, will the case, including interim rulings such as the certification of certain issues in the case for determination in a class action, be appealable to us. Since without a final judgment the special verdict would not (with an exception noted later in this opinion) even have collateral estoppel effect,

Amcast Industrial Corp. v. Detrex Corp., 45 F.3d 155, 158 (7th Cir.1995), the district judge may have intended that the special verdict would be followed by a trial on any remaining liability issues, and on damages, limited to Wadleigh and the other named plaintiffs in the Wadleigh case. That trial would culminate in a final judgment, which would both be appealable to us and impart collateral estoppel effect to the special verdict. The members of the class, other than the named plaintiffs, would take the special verdict back to their home districts and use it to limit the scope of the individual trials that would be necessary—for remember that the district judge has refused to certify the case as a class action for a final adjudication of the controversy between the class and the defendants—to determine each class member's actual entitlement to damages and in what amount.

We asked at argument whether the district judge indeed planned to enter a final judgment at least with respect to the named plaintiffs, so that the ruling on class certification could eventually be appealed. The plaintiffs' counsel relayed the question to the judge, who wrote them that he does envisage the eventual entry of a final judgment with regard to the named plaintiffs. This procedure for eliciting the judge's views was irregular. A judge against whom mandamus is sought is authorized to file a brief, Fed.R.App.P. 21(b), and Judge Grady had not done so. In effect the letter was his brief, but because it was filed out of time the petitioners had no chance to respond to it.

Nevertheless we shall assume in accordance with the judge's letter that eventually there will be a final judgment to review. Only it will come too late to provide effective relief to the defendants; and this is an important consideration in relation to the first condition for mandamus, that the challenged ruling of the district court have inflicted irreparable harm, which is to say harm that cannot be rectified by an appeal from the final judgment in the lawsuit. The reason that an appeal will come too late to provide effective relief for these defendants is the sheer magnitude of the risk to which the class action, in contrast to the individual actions pending or likely, exposes them. Consider the situation that would obtain if the class had not been certified. The defendants would be facing 300 suits. More might be filed, but probably only a few more, because the statutes of limitations in the various states are rapidly expiring for potential plaintiffs. The blood supply has been safe since 1985. That is ten years ago. The risk to hemophiliacs of having become infected with HIV has been widely publicized; it is unlikely that many hemophiliacs are unaware of it. Under the usual discovery statute of limitations, they would have to have taken steps years ago to determine their infection status, and having found out file suit within the limitations period running from the date of discovery, in order to preserve their rights.

Three hundred is not a trivial number of lawsuits. The potential damages in each one are great. But the defendants have won twelve of the first thirteen, and, if this is a representative sample, they are likely to win most of the remaining ones as well. Perhaps in the end, if class-action treatment is denied (it has been denied in all the other hemophiliac HIV suits in which class certification has been sought), they will be compelled to pay damages in only 25 cases, involving a potential liability of perhaps no more than $125 million altogether. These are guesses, of course, but they are at once conservative and usable for the limited purpose of comparing the situation that will face the defendants if the class certification stands. All of a sudden they will face thousands of plaintiffs. Many may already be barred by the statute of limitations, as we have suggested, though its further running was tolled by the filing of Wadleigh as a class action. American Pipe & Construction Co. v. Utah, 414 U.S. 538, 554, 94 S.Ct. 756, 766, 38 L.Ed.2d 713 (1974). (If the class is decertified, the statute of limitations will start running again. Glidden v. Chromalloy American Corp., 808 F.2d 621, 627 (7th Cir.1986); Barrett v. U.S. Civil Service Comm'n, 439 F.Supp. 216, 218–19 (D.D.C. 1977); cf. American Pipe & Construction Co. v. Utah, supra, 414 U.S. at 552, 561, 94 S.Ct. at 765, 770; Crown, Cork & Seal Co. v. Parker, 462 U.S. 345, 354, 103 S.Ct. 2392, 2398, 76 L.Ed.2d 628 (1983)).

Suppose that 5,000 of the potential class members are not yet barred by the statute of limitations. And suppose the named plaintiffs in Wadleigh win the class portion of this case to the extent of establishing the defendants' liability under either of the two negligence theories. It is true that this would only be prima facie liability, that the defendants would have various defenses. But they could not be confident that the defenses would prevail. They might, therefore, easily be facing $25 billion in potential liability (conceivably more), and with it bankruptcy. They may not wish to roll these dice. That is putting it mildly. They will be under intense pressure to settle. Milton Handler, "The Shift from Substantive to Procedural Innovations in Antitrust Suits," 71 Column.L.Rev. 1, 8–9 (1971); William Simon, "Class Actions—Useful Tool or Engine of Destruction," 55 F.R.D. 375 (1972); Marc Galanter, "Why the 'Haves' Come Out Ahead: Speculations on the Limits of Legal Change," 9 Law & Soc'y Rev. 95, 143 and n. 121 (1974); Charles D. Schoor, "Class Actions: The Right to Solicit," 16 Santa Clara L.Rev. 215, 239–40 and n. 82 (1976); Joseph Grundfest, "Disimplying Private Rights of Action under the Federal Securities Laws: The Commission's Authority," 107 Harv.L.Rev. 963, 973 n. 38 (1994); Lester Brickman, "On the Relevance of the Admissibility of Scientific Evidence: Tort System Outcomes Are Principally Determined by Lawyer's Rates of Return," 15 Cardozo L.Rev. 1755, 1780–82 (1994); Note, "Conflicts in Class Actions and Protection of Absent Class Members," 91 Yale L.J. 590, 605 n. 67 (1982). If they settle, the class certification—the ruling that will have forced them to settle—will never be reviewed. General Motors Corp. v. City of New York, 501 F.2d 639, 657–58 (2d Cir.1974) (concurring opinion); cf. Mars Steel Corp. v. Continental Illinois National Bank & Trust Co., 834 F.2d 677, 682–83 (7th Cir.1987). Judge Friendly, who was not given to hyperbole, called settlements induced by a small probability of an immense judgment in a class action "blackmail settlements." Henry J. Friendly, Federal Jurisdiction: A General View 120 (1973). Judicial concern about them is legitimate, not "sociological," as it was derisively termed in In re Sugar Antitrust Litigation, 559 F.2d 481, 483 n. 1 (9th Cir.1977).

The defendants did not mention their concern about settlement pressures until the oral argument of this appeal, so we should consider whether the argument is waived and we therefore cannot consider it. If a party fails to present a ground for reversal, the appeals court will not supply it; this is the doctrine of waiver. Hartmann v. Prudential Ins. Co., 9 F.3d 1207, 1214 (7th Cir.1993); United States v. Rodriguez, 888 F.2d 519, 524 (7th Cir.1989); Bonds v. Coca–Cola Co., 806 F.2d 1324, 1328 (7th Cir.1986). The doctrine is not that if the party fails to offer a particular reason for its position, the court cannot consider that reason. Transcraft, Inc. v. Galvin, Stalmack, Kirschner & Clark, 39 F.3d 812, 820 (7th Cir.1994). Were that the rule, the role of an appellate court would be confined to weighing the reasons, pro and con a particular ground, that the parties happened to proffer. Appellate consideration so truncated could not produce durable rules to guide decision in future cases; judicial opinions would be impoverished if all they did were call balls and strikes. The defendants here properly asserted as the basis for mandamus the two necessary conditions: irreparable harm and clear violation of right. For obvious reasons they did not point out in support of the first condition that if mandamus is denied they will be forced to settle—for such an acknowledgment would greatly weaken them in any settlement negotiations. We should be realistic about what is feasible to put in a public brief.

We do not want to be misunderstood as saying that class actions are bad because they place pressure on defendants to settle. That pressure is a reality, but it must be balanced against the undoubted benefits of the class action that have made it an authorized procedure for employment by federal courts. We have yet to consider the balance. All that our discussion to this point has shown is that the first condition for the grant of mandamus—that the challenged ruling not be effectively reviewable at the end of the case—is fulfilled. The ruling will inflict irreparable harm; the next question is whether the ruling can fairly be described as usurpative. We have formulated this second condition as narrowly, as stringently, as can be, but even so formulated we think it is fulfilled. We do not mean to suggest that the district judge is engaged in a deliberate power-grab. We have no reason to suppose that he wants to preside over an unwieldy class action. We believe that he was responding imaginatively and in the best of faith to the challenge that mass torts, graphically illustrated by the avalanche of asbestos litigation, pose for the federal courts. But the plan that he has devised for the HIV-hemophilia litigation exceeds the bounds of allowable judicial discretion. Three concerns, none of them necessarily sufficient in itself but cumulatively compelling, persuade us to this conclusion.

The first is a concern with forcing these defendants to stake their companies on the outcome of a single jury trial, or be forced by fear of the risk of bankruptcy to settle even if they have no legal liability, when it is entirely feasible to allow a final, authoritative determination of their liability for the colossal misfortune that has befallen the hemophiliac population to emerge from a decentralized process of multiple trials, involving different juries, and different standards of liability, in different jurisdictions; and when, in addition, the preliminary indications are that the defendants are not liable for the grievous harm that has befallen the members of the class. These qualifications are important. In most class actions—and those [are] the ones in which the rationale for the procedure is most compelling—individual suits are infeasible because the claim of each class member is tiny relative to the expense of litigation. That plainly is not the situation here. A notable feature of this case, and one that has not been remarked upon or encountered, so far as we are aware, in previous cases, is the demonstrated great likelihood that the plaintiffs' claims, despite their human appeal, lack legal merit. This is the inference from the defendants' having won 92.3 percent (12/13) of the cases to have gone to judgment. Granted, thirteen is a small sample and further trials, if they are held, may alter the pattern that the sample reveals. But whether they do or not, the result will be robust if these further trials are permitted to go forward, because the pattern that results will reflect a consensus, or at least a pooling of judgment, of many different tribunals.

For this consensus or maturing of judgment the district judge proposes to substitute a single trial before a single jury instructed in accordance with no actual law of any jurisdiction—a jury that will receive a kind of Esperanto instruction, merging the negligence standards of the 50 states and the District of Columbia. One jury, consisting of six persons (the standard federal civil jury nowadays consists of six regular jurors and two alternates), will hold the fate of an industry in the palm of its hand. This jury, jury number fourteen, may disagree with twelve of the previous thirteen juries—and hurl the industry into bankruptcy. That kind of thing can happen in our system of civil justice (it is not likely to happen, because the industry is likely to settle— whether or not it really is liable) without violating anyone's legal rights. But it need not be tolerated when the alternative exists of submitting an issue to multiple juries constituting in the aggregate a much larger and more diverse sample of decision-makers. That would not be a feasible option if the stakes to each class member were too slight to repay the cost of suit, even though the aggregate stakes were very large and would repay the costs of a consolidated proceeding. But this is not the case with regard to the HIV-hemophilia litigation. Each plaintiff if successful is apt to receive a judgment in the millions. With the aggregate stakes in the tens or hundreds of millions of dollars, or even in the billions, it is not a waste of judicial resources to conduct more than one trial, before more than six jurors, to determine whether a major segment of the international pharmaceutical industry is to follow the asbestos manufacturers into Chapter 11.

We have hinted at the second reason for concern that the district judge exceeded the bounds of permissible judicial discretion. He proposes to have a jury determine the negligence of the defendants under a legal standard that does not actually exist anywhere in the world. One is put in mind of the concept of "general" common law that prevailed in the era of Swift v. Tyson. The assumption is that the common law of the 50 states and the District of Columbia, at least so far as bears on a claim of negligence against drug companies, is basically uniform and can be abstracted in a single instruction. It is no doubt true that at some level of generality the law of negligence is one, not only nationwide but worldwide. Negligence is a failure to take due care, and due care a function of the probability and magnitude of an accident and the costs of avoiding it. A jury can be asked whether the defendants took due care. And in many cases such differences as there are among the tort rules of the different states would not affect the outcome. The Second Circuit was willing to assume dubitante that this was true of the issues certified for class determination in the Agent Orange litigation. In re Diamond Shamrock Chemicals Co., 725 F.2d 858, 861 (2d Cir.1984).

We doubt that it is true in general, and we greatly doubt that it is true in a case such as this in which one of the theories pressed by the plaintiffs, the "serendipity" theory, is novel. If one instruction on negligence will serve to instruct the jury on the legal standard of every state of the United States applicable to a novel claim, implying that the claim despite its controversiality would be decided identically in all 50 states and the District of Columbia, one wonders what the Supreme Court thought it was doing in the Erie case when it held that it was unconstitutional for federal courts in diversity cases to apply general common law rather than the common law of the state whose law would apply if the case were being tried in state rather than federal court. Erie R.R. v. Tompkins, 304 U.S. 64, 78–80, 58 S.Ct. 817, 822, 82 L.Ed. 1188 (1938). The law of negligence, including subsidiary concepts such as duty of care, foreseeability, and proximate cause, may as the plaintiffs have argued forcefully to us differ among the states only in nuance, though we think not, for a reason discussed later. But nuance can be important, and its significance is suggested by a comparison of differing state pattern instructions on negligence and differing judicial formulations of the meaning of negligence and the subordinate concepts. ...
The voices of the quasi-sovereigns that are the states of the United States sing negligence with a different pitch.

The "serendipity" theory advanced by the plaintiffs in Wadleigh is that if the defendants did not do enough to protect hemophiliacs from the risk of Hepatitis B, they are liable to hemophiliacs for any consequences—including infection by the more dangerous and at the time completely unknown AIDS virus—that proper measures against Hepatitis B would, all unexpectedly, have averted. This theory of liability, which draws support from Judge Friendly's opinion in Petition of Kinsman Transit Co., supra, 338 F.2d at 725, dispenses, rightly or wrongly from the standpoint of the Platonic Form of negligence, with proof of foreseeability, even though a number of states, in formulating their tests for negligence, incorporate the foreseeability of the risk into the test. See, e.g., Fawley v. Martin's Supermarkets, Inc., 618 N.E.2d 10, 13 (Ind.App.1993); Comment Note, "Foreseeability as an Element of Negligence and Proximate Cause," 100 A.L.R.2d 942 (1994). These states follow Judge Cardozo's famous opinion in Palsgraf v. Long Island R.R., 248 N.Y. 339, 162 N.E. 99 (1928), under which the HIV plaintiffs might (we do not say would—we express no view on the substantive issues in this litigation) be barred from recovery on the ground that they were unforeseeable victims of the alleged failure of the defendants to take adequate precautions against infecting hemophiliacs with Hepatitis B and that therefore the drug companies had not violated any duty of care to them.

The plaintiffs' second theory focuses on the questions when the defendants should have learned about the danger of HIV in the blood supply and when, having learned about it, they should have taken steps to eliminate the danger or at least warn hemophiliacs or their physicians of it. These questions also may be sensitive to the precise way in which a state formulates its standard of negligence. If not, one begins to wonder why this country bothers with different state legal systems.

Both theories, incidentally, may be affected by differing state views on the role of industry practice or custom in determining the existence of negligence. In some states, the standard of care for a physician, hospital, or other provider of medical services, including blood banks, is a professional standard, that is, the standard fixed by the relevant profession. In others, it is the standard of ordinary care, which may, depending on judge or jury, exceed the professional standard. Joseph Kelly, "The Liability of Blood Banks and Manufacturers of Clotting Products to Recipients of HIV–Infected Blood: A Comparison of the Law and Reaction in the United States, Canada, Great Britain, Ireland, and Australia," 27 John Marshall Law Review 465, 472–74 (1994); United Blood Services v. Quintana, 827 P.2d 509, 525–26 (Colo.1992). Which approach a state follows, and whether in those states that follow the professional-standard approach manufacturers of blood solids would be assimilated to blood banks as providers of medical services entitled to shelter under the professional standard, could make a big difference in the liability of these manufacturers. We note that persons infected by

HIV through blood transfusions appear to have had little better luck suing blood banks than HIV-positive hemophiliacs have had suing the manufacturers of blood solids. ....

The diversity jurisdiction of the federal courts is, after Erie, designed merely to provide an alternative forum for the litigation of state-law claims, not an alternative system of substantive law for diversity cases. But under the district judge's plan the thousands of members of the plaintiff class will have their rights determined, and the four defendant manufacturers will have their duties determined, under a law that is merely an amalgam, an averaging, of the nonidentical negligence laws of 51 jurisdictions. No one doubts that Congress could constitutionally prescribe a uniform standard of liability for manufacturers of blood solids. It might we suppose promulgate pertinent provisions of the Restatement (Second) of Torts. The point of Erie is that Article III of the Constitution does not empower the federal courts to create such a regime for diversity cases.

If in the course of individual litigations by HIV-positive hemophiliacs, juries render special verdicts that contain findings which do not depend on the differing state standards of negligence—for example a finding concerning the date at which one or more of the defendants learned of the danger of HIV contamination of the blood supply—these findings may be given collateral estoppel effect in other lawsuits, at least in states that allow "offensive" use of collateral estoppel. In that way the essential purpose of the class action crafted by Judge Grady will be accomplished. If there are relevant differences in state law, findings in one suit will not be given collateral estoppel effect in others, Commissioner v. Sunnen, 333 U.S. 591, 599–600, 68 S.Ct. 715, 720–21, 92 L.Ed. 898 (1948); Goodson v. McDonough Power Equipment, Inc., 2 Ohio St.3d 193, 2 OBR 732, 443 N.E.2d 978, 987–88 (1983)—and that is as it should be.

The plaintiffs argue that an equally important purpose of the class certification is to overcome the shyness or shame that many people feel at acknowledging that they have AIDS or are HIV-positive even when the source of infection is not a stigmatized act. That, the plaintiffs tell us, is why so few HIV-positive hemophiliacs have sued. We do not see how a class action limited to a handful of supposedly common issues can alleviate that problem. Any class member who wants a share in any judgment for damages or in any settlement will have to step forward at some point and identify himself as having AIDS or being HIV-positive. He will have to offer jury findings as collateral estoppel, overcome the defendants' defenses to liability (including possible efforts to show that the class member became infected with HIV through a source other than the defendants' product), and establish his damages. If the privacy of these class members in these follow-on proceedings to the class action is sought to be protected by denominating them "John Does," that is something that can equally well be done in individual lawsuits. The

"John Doe" device—and with it the issue of privacy—is independent of class certification.

The third respect in which we believe that the district judge has exceeded his authority concerns the point at which his plan of action proposes to divide the trial of the issues that he has certified for class-action treatment from the other issues involved in the thousands of actual and potential claims of the representatives and members of the class.   Bifurcation and even finer divisions of lawsuits into separate trials are authorized in federal district courts.   Fed.R.Civ.P. 42(b); Sellers v. Baisier, 792 F.2d 690, 694 (7th Cir.1986).   And a decision to employ the procedure is reviewed deferentially.   Berry v. Deloney, 28 F.3d 604, 610 (7th Cir.1994); De Witt, Porter, Huggett, Schumacher & Morgan, S.C. v. Kovalic, 991 F.2d 1243, 1245 (7th Cir.1993); Barr Laboratories, Inc. v. Abbott Laboratories, 978 F.2d 98, 105 (3d Cir.1992). However, as we have been at pains to stress recently, the district judge must carve at the joint.   Hydrite Chemical Co. v. Calumet Lubricants Co., 47 F.3d 887, 890–91 (7th Cir.1995); cf. McLaughlin v. State Farm Mutual Automobile Ins. Co., 30 F.3d 861, 870–71 (7th Cir.1994).   Of particular relevance here, the judge must not divide issues between separate trials in such a way that the same issue is reexamined by different juries.   The problem is not inherent in bifurcation.   It does not arise when the same jury is to try the successive phases of the litigation. But most of the separate "cases" that compose this class action will be tried, after the initial trial in the Northern District of Illinois, in different courts, scattered throughout the country.   The right to a jury trial in federal civil cases, conferred by the Seventh Amendment, is a right to have juriable issues determined by the first jury impaneled to hear them (provided there are no errors warranting a new trial), and not reexamined by another finder of fact.   This would be obvious if the second finder of fact were a judge.   Byrd v. Blue Ridge Rural Electric Cooperative, Inc., 356 U.S. 525, 537–38, 78 S.Ct. 893, 900–01, 2 L.Ed.2d 953 (1958); Davenport v. DeRobertis, 844 F.2d 1310, 1313–14 (7th Cir.1988); Hunter v. Allis–Chalmers Corp., 797 F.2d 1417, 1421 (7th Cir.1986).   But it is equally true if it is another jury.   Gasoline Products Co. v. Champlin Refining Co., 283 U.S. 494, 500, 51 S.Ct. 513, 515, 75 L.Ed. 1188 (1931); McDaniel v. Anheuser–Busch, Inc., 987 F.2d 298, 305 (5th Cir.1993); Alabama v. Blue Bird Body Co., 573 F.2d 309, 318 (5th Cir.1978).   In this limited sense, a jury verdict can have collateral estoppel effect.   Davenport v. DeRobertis, supra, 844 F.2d at 1313–14; Hudson Ins. Co. v. City of Chicago Heights, 48 F.3d 234, 237–38 (7th Cir.1995).

The plan of the district judge in this case is inconsistent with the principle that the findings of one jury are not to be reexamined by a second, or third, or nth jury.   The first jury will not determine liability. It will determine merely whether one or more of the defendants was

negligent under one of the two theories. The first jury may go on to
decide the additional issues with regard to the named plaintiffs. But it
will not decide them with regard to the other class members. Unless the
defendants settle, a second (and third, and fourth, and hundredth, and
conceivably thousandth) jury will have to decide, in individual follow-on
litigation by class members not named as plaintiffs in the Wadleigh case,
such issues as comparative negligence—did any class members knowingly continue to use unsafe blood solids after they learned or should have
learned of the risk of contamination with HIV?—and proximate causation. Both issues overlap the issue of the defendants' negligence.
Comparative negligence entails, as the name implies, a comparison of the
degree of negligence of plaintiff and defendant. See, e.g., Alaska Stat.
§ 09.17.080; ILCS 735 5/2–1116; N.J.Stat. § 2A:15–5.1; Ohio Rev.Code
§ 2315.19; Utah Code § 78–27–38. Proximate causation is found by
determining whether the harm to the plaintiff followed in some sense
naturally, uninterruptedly, and with reasonable probability from the
negligent act of the defendant. It overlaps the issue of the defendants'
negligence even when the state's law does not (as many states do) make
the foreseeability of the risk to which the defendant subjected the
plaintiff an explicit ingredient of negligence. See, e.g., Powell v. Drum-
heller, ___ Pa. ___, 653 A.2d 619 (1995); Whittaker v. Saraceno, 418
Mass. 196, 635 N.E.2d 1185 (1994); Vincent v. Fairbanks Memorial
Hospital, 862 P.2d 847, 851–52 (Alaska 1993); Flight Line, Inc. v.
Tanksley, supra, 608 So.2d at 1158–59; Wasfi v. Chaddha, 218 Conn.
200, 588 A.2d 204 (1991). A second or subsequent jury might find that
the defendants' failure to take precautions against infection with Hepatitis B could not be thought the proximate cause of the plaintiffs' infection
with HIV, a different and unknown blood-borne virus. How the resulting inconsistency between juries could be prevented escapes us.

The protection of the right conferred by the Seventh Amendment to
trial by jury in federal civil cases is a traditional office of the writ of
mandamus. Beacon Theatres v. Westover, 359 U.S. 500, 510–11, 79
S.Ct. 948, 956–57, 3 L.Ed.2d 988 (1959); Dairy Queen, Inc. v. Wood, 369
U.S. 469, 472, 82 S.Ct. 894, 897, 8 L.Ed.2d 44 (1962); Maloney v.
Plunkett, supra; First National Bank v. Warren, 796 F.2d 999 (7th
Cir.1986). When the writ is used for that purpose, strict compliance
with the stringent conditions on the availability of the writ (including
the requirement of proving irreparable harm) is excused. In Beacon, for
example, if the judge had gone ahead and tried the equitable claims first
and made his decision collateral estoppel in the subsequent jury trial, the
losing party would have been entitled to a new trial, wiping out the
judge's decision. There was no irreparable harm, yet mandamus was
granted—which is one reason why in cases like Maloney and Sandahl we
have said that the use of the writ cannot be reduced to formula. But the
looming infringement of Seventh Amendment rights is only one of our

grounds for believing this to be a case in which the issuance of a writ of mandamus is warranted. The others as we have said are the undue and unnecessary risk of a monumental industry-busting error in entrusting the determination of potential multi-billion dollar liabilities to a single jury when the results of the previous cases indicate that the defendants' liability is doubtful at best and the questionable constitutionality of trying a diversity case under a legal standard in force in no state. We need not consider whether any of these grounds standing by itself would warrant mandamus in this case. Together they make a compelling case.

We know that an approach similar to that proposed by Judge Grady has been approved for asbestos litigation. See in particular Jenkins v. Raymark Industries, Inc., 782 F.2d 468 (5th Cir.1986); In re School Asbestos Litigation, 789 F.2d 996 (3d Cir.1986). Most federal courts, however, refuse to permit the use of the class-action device in mass-tort cases, even asbestos cases. Thomas E. Willging, Trends in Asbestos Litigation 93–98 (Federal Judicial Center 1987); cf. In re Fibreboard Corp., supra; In re Joint Eastern & Southern District Asbestos Litigation, 982 F.2d 721 (2d Cir.1992). Those courts that have permitted it have been criticized, and alternatives have been suggested which recognize that a sample of trials makes more sense than entrusting the fate of an industry to a single jury. See, e.g., Michael J. Saks & Peter David Blanck, "Justice Improved: The Unrecognized Benefits of Aggregation and Sampling in the Trial of Mass Torts," 44 Stan.L.Rev. 815 (1992). The number of asbestos cases was so great as to exert a well-nigh irresistible pressure to bend the normal rules. No comparable pressure is exerted by the HIV-hemophilia litigation. That litigation can be handled in the normal way without undue inconvenience to the parties or to the state or federal courts.

The defendants have pointed out other serious problems with the district judge's plan, but it is unnecessary to discuss them. The petition for a writ of mandamus is granted, and the district judge is directed to decertify the plaintiff class.

ROVNER, CIRCUIT JUDGE, dissenting.

The majority today takes the extraordinary step of granting defendants' petition for a writ of mandamus and directing the district court to rescind its order certifying the plaintiff class. Although certification orders like this one are not immediately appealable (see Coopers & Lybrand v. Livesay, 437 U.S. 463, 98 S.Ct. 2454, 57 L.Ed.2d 351 (1978)), the majority seizes upon our mandamus powers to effectively circumvent that rule. Because, in my view, our consideration of Judge Grady's decision to certify an issue class under Fed.R.Civ.P. 23(c)(4) should await an appeal from the final judgment in Wadleigh, I would deny the writ.

* * *

AMCHEM PRODUCTS, INC. v. WINDSOR
Supreme Court of the United States, 1997.
___ U.S. ___, 117 S.Ct. 2231, ___ L.Ed.2d ___.*

JUSTICE GINSBURG delivered the opinion of the Court.

This case concerns the legitimacy under Rule 23 of the Federal Rules of Civil Procedure of a class-action certification sought to achieve global settlement of current and future asbestos-related claims. The class proposed for certification potentially encompasses hundreds of thousands, perhaps millions, of individuals tied together by this commonality: each was, or some day may be, adversely affected by past exposure to asbestos products manufactured by one or more of 20 companies. Those companies, defendants in the lower courts, are petitioners here.

The United States District Court for the Eastern District of Pennsylvania certified the class for settlement only, finding that the proposed settlement was fair and that representation and notice had been adequate. That court enjoined class members from separately pursuing asbestos-related personal-injury suits in any court, federal or state, pending the issuance of a final order. The Court of Appeals for the Third Circuit vacated the District Court's orders, holding that the class certification failed to satisfy Rule 23's requirements in several critical respects. We affirm the Court of Appeals' judgment.

I

A

The settlement-class certification we confront evolved in response to an asbestos-litigation crisis. See Georgine v. Amchem Products, Inc., 83 F.3d 610, 618, and n. 2 (C.A.3 1996) (citing commentary). A United States Judicial Conference Ad Hoc Committee on Asbestos Litigation, appointed by the Chief Justice in September 1990, described facets of the problem in a 1991 report:

"[This] is a tale of danger known in the 1930s, exposure inflicted upon millions of Americans in the 1940s and 1950s, injuries that began to take their toll in the 1960s, and a flood of lawsuits beginning in the 1970s. On the basis of past and current filing data, and because of a latency period that may last as long as 40 years for some asbestos related diseases, a continuing stream of claims can be expected. The final toll of asbestos related injuries is unknown. Predictions have been made of 200,000 asbestos disease deaths before the year 2000 and as many as 265,000 by the year 2015.

"The most objectionable aspects of asbestos litigation can be briefly summarized: dockets in both federal and state courts continue to grow; long delays are routine; trials are too long; the same issues are litigated over and over; transaction costs exceed the victims' recovery by nearly two to one; exhaustion of assets threatens and distorts the process; and

* Some footnotes omitted; others renumbered.

future claimants may lose altogether." Report of The Judicial Conference Ad Hoc Committee on Asbestos Litigation 2–3 (Mar. 1991).

Real reform, the report concluded, required federal legislation creating a national asbestos dispute-resolution scheme. See id., at 3, 27–35; see also id., at 42 (dissenting statement of Hogan, J.) (agreeing that "a national solution is the only answer" and suggesting "passage by Congress of an administrative claims procedure similar to the Black Lung legislation"). As recommended by the Ad Hoc Committee, the Judicial Conference of the United States urged Congress to act. See Report of the Proceedings of the Judicial Conference of the United States 33 (Mar. 12, 1991). To this date, no congressional response has emerged.

In the face of legislative inaction, the federal courts—lacking authority to replace state tort systems with a national toxic tort compensation regime—endeavored to work with the procedural tools available to improve management of federal asbestos litigation. Eight federal judges, experienced in the superintendence of asbestos cases, urged the Judicial Panel on Multidistrict Litigation (MDL Panel), to consolidate in a single district all asbestos complaints then pending in federal courts. Accepting the recommendation, the MDL Panel transferred all asbestos cases then filed, but not yet on trial in federal courts to a single district, the United States District Court for the Eastern District of Pennsylvania; pursuant to the transfer order, the collected cases were consolidated for pretrial proceedings before Judge Weiner. See In re Asbestos Products Liability Litigation (No. VI), 771 F.Supp. 415, 422–424 (JPML 1991). The order aggregated pending cases only; no authority resides in the MDL Panel to license for consolidated proceedings claims not yet filed.

B

After the consolidation, attorneys for plaintiffs and defendants formed separate steering committees and began settlement negotiations.... Counsel for the Center for Claims Resolution (CCR), the consortium of 20 former asbestos manufacturers now before us as petitioners, participated in the Defendants' Steering Committee. Although the MDL order collected, transferred, and consolidated only cases already commenced in federal courts, settlement negotiations included efforts to find a "means of resolving . . . future cases." Record, Doc. 3, p. 2 (Memorandum in Support of Joint Motion for Conditional Class Certification); see also Georgine v. Amchem Products, Inc., 157 F.R.D. 246, 266 (E.D.Pa.1994) ("primary purpose of the settlement talks in the consolidated MDL litigation was to craft a national settlement that would provide an alternative resolution mechanism for asbestos claims," including claims that might be filed in the future).

In November 1991, the Defendants' Steering Committee made an offer designed to settle all pending and future asbestos cases by providing a fund for distribution by plaintiffs' counsel among asbestos-exposed individuals. The Plaintiffs' Steering Committee rejected this offer, and negotiations fell apart. CCR, however, continued to pursue "a workable administrative system for the handling of future claims." Id., at 270.

To that end, CCR counsel approached the lawyers who had headed the Plaintiffs' Steering Committee in the unsuccessful negotiations, and a new round of negotiations began; that round yielded the mass settlement agreement now in controversy. At the time, the former heads of the Plaintiffs' Steering Committee represented thousands of plaintiffs with then-pending asbestos-related claims—claimants the parties to this suit call "inventory" plaintiffs. CCR indicated in these discussions that it would resist settlement of inventory cases absent "some kind of protection for the future." Id., at 294; see also id., at 295 (CCR communicated to the inventory plaintiffs' attorneys that once the CCR defendants saw a rational way to deal with claims expected to be filed in the future, those defendants would be prepared to address the settlement of pending cases).

Settlement talks thus concentrated on devising an administrative scheme for disposition of asbestos claims not yet in litigation. In these negotiations, counsel for masses of inventory plaintiffs endeavored to represent the interests of the anticipated future claimants, although those lawyers then had no attorney-client relationship with such claimants.

Once negotiations seemed likely to produce an agreement purporting to bind potential plaintiffs, CCR agreed to settle, through separate agreements, the claims of plaintiffs who had already filed asbestos-related lawsuits. In one such agreement, CCR defendants promised to pay more than $200 million to gain release of the claims of numerous inventory plaintiffs. After settling the inventory claims, CCR, together with the plaintiffs' lawyers CCR had approached, launched this case, exclusively involving persons outside the MDL Panel's province—plaintiffs without already pending lawsuits.[1]

C

The class action thus instituted was not intended to be litigated. Rather, within the space of a single day, January 15, 1993, the settling parties—CCR defendants and the representatives of the plaintiff class described below—presented to the District Court a complaint, an answer, a proposed settlement agreement, and a joint motion for conditional class certification.[2]

---

1. It is basic to comprehension of this proceeding to notice that no transferred case is included in the settlement at issue, and no case covered by the settlement existed as a civil action at the time of the MDL Panel transfer.

2. Also on the same day, the CCR defendants filed a third-party action against their insurers, seeking a declaratory judgment holding the insurers liable for the costs of the settlement. The insurance litigation, upon which implementation of the settlement is conditioned, is still pending in the District Court. See, e.g., Georgine v. Amchem Prods., Inc., No. 930215, 1994 WL 502475 (E.D.Pa., Sept.2, 1994) (denying motion of insurers to compel discovery).

The complaint identified nine lead plaintiffs, designating them and members of their families as representatives of a class comprising all persons who had not filed an asbestos-related lawsuit against a CCR defendant as of the date the class action commenced, but who (1) had been exposed—occupationally or through the occupational exposure of a spouse or household member—to asbestos or products containing asbestos attributable to a CCR defendant, or (2) whose spouse or family member had been so exposed. Untold numbers of individuals may fall within this description. All named plaintiffs alleged that they or a member of their family had been exposed to asbestos-containing products of CCR defendants. More than half of the named plaintiffs alleged that they or their family members had already suffered various physical injuries as a result of the exposure. The others alleged that they had not yet manifested any asbestos-related condition. The complaint delineated no subclasses; all named plaintiffs were designated as representatives of the class as a whole.

The complaint invoked the District Court's diversity jurisdiction and asserted various state-law claims for relief, including (1) negligent failure to warn, (2) strict liability, (3) breach of express and implied warranty, (4) negligent infliction of emotional distress, (5) enhanced risk of disease, (6) medical monitoring, and (7) civil conspiracy. Each plaintiff requested unspecified damages in excess of $100,000. CCR defendants' answer denied the principal allegations of the complaint and asserted 11 affirmative defenses.

A stipulation of settlement accompanied the pleadings; it proposed to settle, and to preclude nearly all class members from litigating against CCR companies, all claims not filed before January 15, 1993, involving compensation for present and future asbestos-related personal injury or death. An exhaustive document exceeding 100 pages, the stipulation presents in detail an administrative mechanism and a schedule of payments to compensate class members who meet defined asbestos-exposure and medical requirements. The stipulation describes four categories of compensable disease: mesothelioma; lung cancer; certain "other cancers" (colon-rectal, laryngeal, esophageal, and stomach cancer); and "non-malignant conditions" (asbestosis and bilateral pleural thickening). Persons with "exceptional" medical claims—claims that do not fall within the four described diagnostic categories—may in some instances qualify for compensation, but the settlement caps the number of "exceptional" claims CCR must cover.

For each qualifying disease category, the stipulation specifies the range of damages CCR will pay to qualifying claimants. Payments under the settlement are not adjustable for inflation. Mesothelioma claimants—the most highly compensated category—are scheduled to receive between $20,000 and $200,000. The stipulation provides that CCR is to propose the level of compensation within the prescribed ranges; it also establishes procedures to resolve disputes over medical diagnoses and levels of compensation.

Compensation above the fixed ranges may be obtained for "extraordinary" claims. But the settlement places both numerical caps and dollar limits on such claims. The settlement also imposes "case flow maximums," which cap the number of claims payable for each disease in a given year.

Class members are to receive no compensation for certain kinds of claims, even if otherwise applicable state law recognizes such claims. Claims that garner no compensation under the settlement include claims by family members of asbestos-exposed individuals for loss of consortium, and claims by so-called "exposure-only" plaintiffs for increased risk of cancer, fear of future asbestos-related injury, and medical monitoring. "Pleural" claims, which might be asserted by persons with asbestos-related plaques on their lungs but no accompanying physical impairment, are also excluded. Although not entitled to present compensation, exposure-only claimants and pleural claimants may qualify for benefits when and if they develop a compensable disease and meet the relevant exposure and medical criteria. Defendants forgo defenses to liability, including statute of limitations pleas.

Class members, in the main, are bound by the settlement in perpetuity, while CCR defendants may choose to withdraw from the settlement after ten years. A small number of class members—only a few per year—may reject the settlement and pursue their claims in court. Those permitted to exercise this option, however, may not assert any punitive damages claim or any claim for increased risk of cancer. Aspects of the administration of the settlement are to be monitored by the AFL–CIO and class counsel. Class counsel are to receive attorneys' fees in an amount to be approved by the District Court.

D

On January 29, 1993, as requested by the settling parties, the District Court conditionally certified, under Federal Rule of Civil Procedure 23(b)(3), an encompassing opt-out class. The certified class included persons occupationally exposed to defendants' asbestos products, and members of their families, who had not filed suit as of January 15. Judge Weiner appointed Locks, Motley, and Rice [formerly co-chairs of the Plaintiff's Steering Committee,] as class counsel, noting that "the Court may in the future appoint additional counsel if it is deemed necessary and advisable." Record, Doc. 11, p. 3 (Class Certification Order). At no stage of the proceedings, however, were additional counsel in fact appointed. Nor was the class ever divided into subclasses. In a separate order, Judge Weiner assigned to Judge Reed, also of the Eastern District of Pennsylvania, "the task of conducting fairness proceedings and of determining whether the proposed settlement is fair to the class." See

157 F.R.D., at 258. Various class members raised objections to the settlement stipulation, and Judge Weiner granted the objectors full rights to participate in the subsequent proceedings. Ibid. [3]

In preliminary rulings, Judge Reed held that the District Court had subject-matter jurisdiction, see Carlough v. Amchem Products, Inc., 834 F.Supp. 1437, 1467–1468 (E.D.Pa.1993), and he approved the settling parties' elaborate plan for giving notice to the class, see Carlough v. Amchem Products, Inc., 158 F.R.D. 314, 336 (E.D.Pa.1993). The court-approved notice informed recipients that they could exclude themselves from the class, if they so chose, within a three-month opt-out period.

Objectors raised numerous challenges to the settlement. They urged that the settlement unfairly disadvantaged those without currently compensable conditions in that it failed to adjust for inflation or to account for changes, over time, in medical understanding. They maintained that compensation levels were intolerably low in comparison to awards available in tort litigation or payments received by the inventory plaintiffs. And they objected to the absence of any compensation for certain claims, for example, medical monitoring, compensable under the tort law of several States. Rejecting these and all other objections, Judge Reed concluded that the settlement terms were fair and had been negotiated without collusion. See 157 F. R. D., at 325, 331–332. He also found that adequate notice had been given to class members, see id., at 332–334, and that final class certification under Rule 23(b)(3) was appropriate, see id., at 315.

As to the specific prerequisites to certification, the District Court observed that the class satisfied Rule 23(a)(1)'s numerosity requirement, ..., a matter no one debates. The Rule 23(a)(2) and (b)(3) requirements of commonality and preponderance were also satisfied, the District Court held, in that "the members of the class have all been exposed to asbestos products supplied by the defendants and all share an interest in receiving prompt and fair compensation for their claims, while minimizing the risks and transaction costs inherent in the asbestos litigation process as it occurs presently in the tort system. Whether the proposed settlement satisfies this interest and is otherwise a fair, reasonable and adequate compromise of the claims of the class is a predominant issue for purposes of Rule 23(b)(3)." Id., at 316.

The District Court held next that the claims of the class representatives were "typical" of the class as a whole, a requirement of Rule

---

3. These objectors, now respondents before this Court, include three groups of individuals with overlapping interests, designated as the "Windsor Group," the New Jersey "White Lung Group," and the "Cargile Group." Margaret Balonis, an individual objector, is also a respondent before this Court. Balonis states that her husband, Casimir, was exposed to asbestos in the late 1940s and was diagnosed with mesothelioma in May 1994, after expiration of the opt-out period, see infra, at 11, 13. The Balonises sued CCR members in Maryland state court, but were charged with civil contempt for violating the federal District Court's anti-suit injunction. Casimir Balonis died in October 1996. See Brief for Balonis Respondents 9–11.

23(a)(3), and that, as Rule 23(b)(3) demands, the class settlement was "superior" to other methods of adjudication. See ibid.

Strenuous objections had been asserted regarding the adequacy of representation, a Rule 23(a)(4) requirement. Objectors maintained that class counsel and class representatives had disqualifying conflicts of interests. In particular, objectors urged, claimants whose injuries had become manifest and claimants without manifest injuries should not have common counsel and should not be aggregated in a single class. Furthermore, objectors argued, lawyers representing inventory plaintiffs should not represent the newly-formed class.

Satisfied that class counsel had ably negotiated the settlement in the best interests of all concerned, and that the named parties served as adequate representatives, the District Court rejected these objections. See id., at 317–319, 326–332. Subclasses were unnecessary, the District Court held, bearing in mind the added cost and confusion they would entail and the ability of class members to exclude themselves from the class during the three-month opt-out period. See id., at 318–319. Reasoning that the representative plaintiffs "have a strong interest that recovery for all of the medical categories be maximized because they may have claims in any, or several categories," the District Court found "no antagonism of interest between class members with various medical conditions, or between persons with and without currently manifest asbestos impairment." Id., at 318. Declaring class certification appropriate and the settlement fair, the District Court preliminarily enjoined all class members from commencing any asbestos-related suit against the CCR defendants in any state or federal court. See Georgine v. Amchem Products, Inc., 878 F.Supp. 716, 726–727 (E.D.Pa.1994).

The objectors appealed. The United States Court of Appeals for the Third Circuit vacated the certification, holding that the requirements of Rule 23 had not been satisfied. See Georgine v. Amchem Products, Inc., 83 F.3d 610 (1996).

E

The Court of Appeals, in a long, heavily detailed opinion by Judge Becker, first noted several challenges by objectors to justiciability, subject-matter jurisdiction, and adequacy of notice. These challenges, the court said, raised "serious concerns." Id., at 623. However, the court observed, "the jurisdictional issues in this case would not exist but for the [class action] certification." Ibid. Turning to the class-certification issues and finding them dispositive, the Third Circuit declined to decide other questions.

On class-action prerequisites, the Court of Appeals referred to an earlier Third Circuit decision, In re General Motors Corp. Pick–Up Truck Fuel Tank Products Liability Litigation, 55 F.3d 768 (C.A.3), cert. denied, 516 U.S. ___ (1995) (hereinafter GM Trucks), which held that although a class action may be certified for settlement purposes only,

Rule 23(a)'s requirements must be satisfied as if the case were going to be litigated. 55 F.3d, at 799–800. The same rule should apply, the Third Circuit said, to class certification under Rule 23(b)(3). See 83 F.3d, at 625. But cf. In re Asbestos Litigation, 90 F.3d 963, 975–976, and n. 8 (C.A.5 1996), cert. pending, Nos. 96–1379, 96–1394. While stating that the requirements of Rule 23(a) and (b)(3) must be met "without taking into account the settlement," 83 F.3d, at 626, the Court of Appeals in fact closely considered the terms of the settlement as it examined aspects of the case under Rule 23 criteria. See id., at 630–634.

The Third Circuit recognized that Rule 23(a)(2)'s "commonality" requirement is subsumed under, or superseded by, the more stringent Rule 23(b)(3) requirement that questions common to the class "predominate over" other questions. The court therefore trained its attention on the "predominance" inquiry. See id., at 627. The harmfulness of asbestos exposure was indeed a prime factor common to the class, the Third Circuit observed. See id., at 626, 630. But uncommon questions abounded.

In contrast to mass torts involving a single accident, class members in this case were exposed to different asbestos-containing products, in different ways, over different periods, and for different amounts of time; some suffered no physical injury, others suffered disabling or deadly diseases. See id., at 626, 628. "These factual differences," the Third Circuit explained, "translated into significant legal differences." Id., at 627. State law governed and varied widely on such critical issues as "viability of [exposure-only] claims [and] availability of causes of action for medical monitoring, increased risk of cancer, and fear of future injury." Ibid.[4] "The number of uncommon issues in this humongous class action," the Third Circuit concluded, ibid., barred a determination, under existing tort law, that common questions predominated, see id., at 630.

The Court of Appeals next found that "serious intraclass conflicts precluded the class from meeting the adequacy of representation requirement" of Rule 23(a)(4). Ibid. Adverting to, but not resolving charges of attorney conflict of interests, the Third Circuit addressed the question whether the named plaintiffs could adequately advance the interests of all class members. The Court of Appeals acknowledged that the District Court was certainly correct to this extent: " 'The members of the class are united in seeking the maximum possible recovery for their asbestos-related claims.' " Ibid. (quoting 157 F.R.D., at 317). "But the settlement does more than simply provide a general recovery fund," the Court of

---

4. Recoveries under the laws of different States spanned a wide range. Objectors assert, for example, that 15% of current mesothelioma claims arise in California, where the statewide average recovery is $419,-674—or more than 209% above the $200,- 000 maximum specified in the settlement for mesothelioma claims not typed "extraordinary." See Brief for Respondents George Windsor et al. 5–6, n. 5 (citing 2 App. 461).

Appeals immediately added; "rather, it makes important judgments on how recovery is to be allocated among different kinds of plaintiffs, decisions that necessarily favor some claimants over others." 83 F.3d, at 630.

In the Third Circuit's view, the "most salient" divergence of interests separated plaintiffs already afflicted with an asbestos-related disease from plaintiffs without manifest injury (exposure-only plaintiffs). The latter would rationally want protection against inflation for distant recoveries. See ibid. They would also seek sturdy back-end opt-out rights and "causation provisions that can keep pace with changing science and medicine, rather than freezing in place the science of 1993." Id., at 630–631. Already injured parties, in contrast, would care little about such provisions and would rationally trade them for higher current payouts. See id., at 631. These and other adverse interests, the Court of Appeals carefully explained, strongly suggested that an undivided set of representatives could not adequately protect the discrete interests of both currently afflicted and exposure-only claimants.

The Third Circuit next rejected the District Court's determination that the named plaintiffs were "typical" of the class, noting that this Rule 23(a)(3) inquiry overlaps the adequacy of representation question: "both look to the potential for conflicts in the class." Id., at 632. Evident conflict problems, the court said, led it to hold that "no set of representatives can be 'typical' of this class." Ibid.

The Court of Appeals similarly rejected the District Court's assessment of the superiority of the class action. The Third Circuit initially noted that a class action so large and complex "could not be tried." Ibid. The court elaborated most particularly, however, on the unfairness of binding exposure-only plaintiffs who might be unaware of the class action or lack sufficient information about their exposure to make a reasoned decision whether to stay in or opt out. See id., at 633. "A series of statewide or more narrowly defined adjudications, either through consolidation under Rule 42(a) or as class actions under Rule 23, would seem preferable," the Court of Appeals said. Id., at 634.

The Third Circuit, after intensive review, ultimately ordered decertification of the class and vacation of the District Court's anti-suit injunction. Id., at 635. Judge Wellford concurred, "fully subscribing to the decision of Judge Becker that the plaintiffs in this case had not met the requirements of Rule 23." Ibid. He added that in his view, named exposure-only plaintiffs had no standing to pursue the suit in federal court, for their depositions showed that "they claimed no damages and no present injury." Id., at 638.

We granted certiorari, 519 U.S. ___ (1996), and now affirm.

II

Objectors assert in this Court, as they did in the District Court and Court of Appeals, an array of jurisdictional barriers. Most fundamentally, they maintain that the settlement proceeding instituted by class counsel and CCR is not a justiciable case or controversy within the confines of Article III of the Federal Constitution. In the main, they say, the proceeding is a nonadversarial endeavor to impose on countless individuals without currently ripe claims an administrative compensation regime binding on those individuals if and when they manifest injuries.

Furthermore, objectors urge that exposure-only claimants lack standing to sue: Either they have not yet sustained any cognizable injury or, to the extent the complaint states claims and demands relief for emotional distress, enhanced risk of disease, and medical monitoring, the settlement provides no redress. Objectors also argue that exposure-only claimants did not meet the then current amount-in-controversy requirement (in excess of $50,000) specified for federal-court jurisdiction based upon diversity of citizenship. See 28 U.S.C. § 1332(a).

As earlier recounted, the Third Circuit declined to reach these issues because they "would not exist but for the [class action] certification." 83 F.3d, at 623. We agree that "the class certification issues are dispositive," ibid.; because their resolution here is logically antecedent to the existence of any Article III issues, it is appropriate to reach them first, cf. Arizonans for Official English v. Arizona, 520 U.S. __, __ (1997) (slip op., at 21) (declining to resolve definitively question whether petitioners had standing because mootness issue was dispositive of the case). We therefore follow the path taken by the Court of Appeals, mindful that Rule 23's requirements must be interpreted in keeping with Article III constraints, and with the Rules Enabling Act, which instructs that rules of procedure "shall not abridge, enlarge or modify any substantive right," 28 U.S.C. § 2072(b). See also Fed. Rule Civ. Proc. 82 ("rules shall not be construed to extend ... the [subject matter] jurisdiction of the United States district courts").

III

To place this controversy in context, we briefly describe the characteristics of class actions for which the Federal Rules provide. Rule 23, governing federal-court class actions, stems from equity practice and gained its current shape in an innovative 1966 revision. See generally Kaplan, Continuing Work of the Civil Committee: 1966 Amendments of the Federal Rules of Civil Procedure (I), 81 Harv. L. Rev. 356, 375–400 (1967) (hereinafter Kaplan, Continuing Work). Rule 23(a) states four threshold requirements applicable to all class actions: (1) numerosity (a "class [so large] that joinder of all members is impracticable"); (2) commonality ("questions of law or fact common to the class"); (3) typicality (named parties' claims or defenses "are typical ... of the class"); and (4) adequacy of representation (representatives "will fairly and adequately protect the interests of the class").

In addition to satisfying Rule 23(a)'s prerequisites, parties seeking class certification must show that the action is maintainable under Rule 23(b)(1), (2), or (3). Rule 23(b)(1) covers cases in which separate actions by or against individual class members would risk establishing "incompatible standards of conduct for the party opposing the class," Fed. Rule Civ. Proc. 23(b)(1)(A), or would "as a practical matter be dispositive of the interests" of nonparty class members "or substantially impair or impede their ability to protect their interests," Fed. Rule Civ. Proc. 23(b)(1)(B). Rule 23(b)(1)(A) "takes in cases where the party is obliged by law to treat the members of the class alike (a utility acting toward customers; a government imposing a tax), or where the party must treat all alike as a matter of practical necessity (a riparian owner using water as against downriver owners)." Kaplan, Continuing Work 388 (footnotes omitted). Rule 23(b)(1)(B) includes, for example, "limited fund" cases, instances in which numerous persons make claims against a fund insufficient to satisfy all claims. See Advisory Committee's Notes on Fed. Rule Civ. Proc. 23, 28 U.S.C. App., pp. 696–697 (hereinafter Adv. Comm. Notes).

Rule 23(b)(2) permits class actions for declaratory or injunctive relief where "the party opposing the class has acted or refused to act on grounds generally applicable to the class." Civil rights cases against parties charged with unlawful, class-based discrimination are prime examples. Adv. Comm. Notes, 28 U.S.C. App., p. 697; see Kaplan, Continuing Work 389 (subdivision (b)(2) "builds on experience mainly, but not exclusively, in the civil rights field").

In the 1966 class-action amendments, Rule 23(b)(3), the category at issue here, was "the most adventuresome" innovation. See Kaplan, A Prefatory Note, 10 B. C. Ind. & Com. L. Rev. 497, 497 (1969) (hereinafter Kaplan, Prefatory Note). Rule 23(b)(3) added to the complex-litigation arsenal class actions for damages designed to secure judgments binding all class members save those who affirmatively elected to be excluded. See 7A C. Wright, A. Miller, & M. Kane, Federal Practice and Procedure § 1777, p. 517 (2d ed. 1986) (hereinafter Wright, Miller, & Kane); see generally Kaplan, Continuing Work 379–400. Rule 23(b)(3) "opt out" class actions superseded the former "spurious" class action, so characterized because it generally functioned as a permissive joinder ("opt in") device. See 7A Wright, Miller, & Kane § 1753, at 28–31, 42–44; see also Adv. Comm. Notes, 28 U.S.C. App., p. 695.

Framed for situations in which "class-action treatment is not as clearly called for" as it is in Rule 23(b)(1) and (b)(2) situations, Rule 23(b)(3) permits certification where class suit "may nevertheless be convenient and desirable." Adv. Comm. Notes, 28 U.S.C. App., p. 697. To qualify for certification under Rule 23(b)(3), a class must meet two requirements beyond the Rule 23(a) prerequisites: Common questions must "predominate over any questions affecting only individual members"; and class resolution must be "superior to other available methods for the fair and efficient adjudication of the controversy." In adding "predominance" and "superiority" to the qualification-for-certification list, the Advisory Committee sought to cover cases "in which a class action would achieve economies of time, effort, and expense, and promote ... uniformity of decision as to persons similarly situated, without sacrificing procedural fairness or bringing about other undesirable results." Ibid. Sensitive to the competing tugs of individual autonomy for those who might prefer to go it alone or in a smaller unit, on the one hand, and systemic efficiency on the other, the Reporter for the 1966 amendments cautioned: "The new provision invites a close look at the case before it is accepted as a class action...." Kaplan, Continuing Work 390.

Rule 23(b)(3) includes a nonexhaustive list of factors pertinent to a court's "close look" at the predominance and superiority criteria:

"(A) the interest of members of the class in individually controlling the prosecution or defense of separate actions; (B) the extent and nature of any litigation concerning the controversy already commenced by or against members of the class; (C) the desirability or undesirability of concentrating the litigation of the claims in the particular forum; (D) the difficulties likely to be encountered in the management of a class action."

In setting out these factors, the Advisory Committee for the 1966 reform anticipated that in each case, courts would "consider the interests of individual members of the class in controlling their own litigations and carrying them on as they see fit." Adv. Comm. Notes, 28 U.S.C. App., p. 698. They elaborated:

"The interests of individuals in conducting separate lawsuits may be so strong as to call for denial of a class action. On the other hand, these interests may be theoretic rather than practical; the class may have a high degree of cohesion and prosecution of the action through representatives would be quite unobjectionable, or the amounts at stake for individuals may be so small that separate suits would be impracticable." Ibid.

See also Kaplan, Continuing Work 391 ("The interest [in individual control] can be high where the stake of each member bulks large and his will and ability to take care of himself are strong; the interest may be no more than theoretic where the individual stake is so small as to make a separate action impracticable.") (footnote omitted). As the Third Circuit observed in the instant case: "Each plaintiff [in an action involving claims for personal injury and death] has a significant interest in individually controlling the prosecution of [his case]"; each "has a substantial stake in making individual decisions on whether and when to settle." 83 F.3d, at 633.

While the text of Rule 23(b)(3) does not exclude from certification cases in which individual damages run high, the Advisory Committee had dominantly in mind vindication of "the rights of groups of people who individually would be without effective strength to bring their opponents into court at all." Kaplan, Prefatory Note 497. As concisely recalled in a recent Seventh Circuit opinion:

"The policy at the very core of the class action mechanism is to overcome the problem that small recoveries do not provide the incentive for any individual to bring a solo action prosecuting his or her rights. A class action solves this problem by aggregating the relatively paltry potential recoveries into something worth someone's (usually an attorney's) labor." Mace v. Van Ru Credit Corp., 109 F.3d 338, 344 (1997).

To alert class members to their right to "opt out" of a (b)(3) class, Rule 23 instructs the court to "direct to the members of the class the best notice practicable under the circumstances, including individual notice to all members who can be identified through reasonable effort." Fed. Rule Civ. Proc. 23(c)(2); see Eisen v. Carlisle & Jacquelin, 417 U.S. 156, 173–177 (1974) (individual notice to class members identifiable through reasonable effort is mandatory in (b)(3) actions; requirement may not be relaxed based on high cost).

No class action may be "dismissed or compromised without [court] approval," preceded by notice to class members. Fed. Rule Civ. Proc. 23(e). The Advisory Committee's sole comment on this terse final provision of Rule 23 restates the rule's instruction without elaboration: "Subdivision (e) requires approval of the court, after notice, for the dismissal or compromise of any class action." Adv. Comm. Notes, 28 U.S.C. App., p. 699.

In the decades since the 1966 revision of Rule 23, class action practice has become ever more "adventuresome" as a means of coping with claims too numerous to secure their "just, speedy, and inexpensive determination" one by one. See Fed. Rule Civ. Proc. 1. The development reflects concerns about the efficient use of court resources and the conservation of funds to compensate claimants who do not line up early in a litigation queue. See generally J. Weinstein, Individual Justice in Mass Tort Litigation: The Effect of Class Actions, Consolidations, and Other Multiparty Devices (1995); Schwarzer, Settlement of Mass Tort Class Actions: Order Out of Chaos, 80 Cornell L. Rev. 837 (1995).

Among current applications of Rule 23(b)(3), the "settlement only" class has become a stock device. See, e.g., T. Willging, L. Hooper, & R. Niemic, Empirical Study of Class Actions in Four Federal District Courts: Final Report to the Advisory Committee on Civil Rules 61–62 (1996) (noting large number of such cases in districts studied). Although all Federal Circuits recognize the utility of Rule 23(b)(3) settlement classes, courts have divided on the extent to which a proffered settlement affects court surveillance under Rule 23's certification criteria.

In GM Trucks, 55 F.3d, at 799–800, and in the instant case, 83 F.3d, at 624–626, the Third Circuit held that a class cannot be certified for settlement when certification for trial would be unwarranted. Other courts have held that settlement obviates or reduces the need to measure a proposed class against the enumerated Rule 23 requirements. See, e.g., In re Asbestos Litigation, 90 F.3d, at 975 (C.A.5) ("in settlement class context, common issues arise from the settlement itself") (citing H. Newberg & A. Conte, 2 Newberg on Class Actions § 11.28, at 11–58 (3d ed. 1992)); White v. National Football League, 41 F.3d 402, 408 (C.A.8 1994) ("adequacy of class representation ... is ultimately determined by the settlement itself"), cert. denied, 515 U.S. 1137 (1995); In re A. H. Robins Co., 880 F.2d 709, 740 (C.A.4) ("if not a ground for certification per se, certainly settlement should be a factor, and an important factor, to be considered when determining certification"), cert. denied sub nom. Anderson v. Aetna Casualty & Surety Co., 493 U.S. 959 (1989); Malchman v. Davis, 761 F.2d 893, 900 (C.A.2 1985) (certification appropriate, in part, because "the interests of the members of the broadened class in the settlement agreement were commonly held"), cert. denied, 475 U.S. 1143 (1986).

A proposed amendment to Rule 23 would expressly authorize settlement class certification, in conjunction with a motion by the settling parties for Rule 23(b)(3) certification, "even though the requirements of subdivision (b)(3) might not be met for purposes of trial." Proposed Amendment to Fed. Rule Civ. Proc. 23(b), 117 S.Ct. No. I CXIX, CLIV to CLV (Aug. 1996) (Request for Comment). In response to the publication of this proposal, voluminous public comments—many of them opposed to, or skeptical of, the amendment—were received by the Judicial Conference Standing Committee on Rules of Practice and Procedure. See, e.g., Letter from Steering Committee to Oppose Proposed Rule 23, signed by 129 law professors (May 28, 1996); Letter from Paul D. Carrington (May 21, 1996). The Committee has not yet acted on the matter. We consider the certification at issue under the rule as it is currently framed.

IV

We granted review to decide the role settlement may play, under existing Rule 23, in determining the propriety of class certification. The Third Circuit's opinion stated that each of the requirements of Rule 23(a) and (b)(3) "must be satisfied without taking into account the settlement." 83 F.3d, at 626 (quoting GM Trucks, 55 F.3d, at 799). That statement, petitioners urge, is incorrect.

We agree with petitioners to this limited extent: settlement is relevant to a class certification. The Third Circuit's opinion bears modification in that respect. But, as we earlier observed, ... the Court of Appeals in fact did not ignore the settlement; instead, that court homed in on settlement terms in explaining why it found the absentees' interests inadequately represented. See 83 F.3d, at 630–631. The Third Circuit's close inspection of the settlement in that regard was altogether proper.

Confronted with a request for settlement-only class certification, a district court need not inquire whether the case, if tried, would present intractable management problems, see Fed. Rule Civ. Proc. 23(b)(3)(D), for the proposal is that there be no trial. But other specifications of the rule—those designed to protect absentees by blocking unwarranted or overbroad class definitions—demand undiluted, even heightened, attention in the settlement context. Such attention is of vital importance, for a court asked to certify a settlement class will lack the opportunity, present when a case is litigated, to adjust the class, informed by the proceedings as they unfold. See Fed. Rule Civ. Proc. 23(c), (d).

And, of overriding importance, courts must be mindful that the rule as now composed sets the requirements they are bound to enforce. Federal Rules take effect after an extensive deliberative process involving many reviewers: a Rules Advisory Committee, public commenters, the Judicial Conference, this Court, the Congress. See 28 U.S.C. §§ 2073, 2074. The text of a rule thus proposed and reviewed limits judicial inventiveness. Courts are not free to amend a rule outside the process Congress ordered, a process properly tuned to the instruction that rules of procedure "shall not abridge . . . any substantive right." § 2072(b).

Rule 23(e), on settlement of class actions, reads in its entirety: "A class action shall not be dismissed or compromised without the approval of the court, and notice of the proposed dismissal or compromise shall be given to all members of the class in such manner as the court directs." This prescription was designed to function as an additional requirement, not a superseding direction, for the "class action" to which Rule 23(e) refers is one qualified for certification under Rule 23(a) and (b). Cf. Eisen, 417 U.S., at 176–177 (adequate representation does not eliminate additional requirement to provide notice). Subdivisions (a) and (b) focus court attention on whether a proposed class has sufficient unity so that absent members can fairly be bound by decisions of class representatives. That dominant concern persists when settlement, rather than trial, is proposed.

The safeguards provided by the Rule 23(a) and (b) class-qualifying criteria, we emphasize, are not impractical impediments—checks shorn of utility—in the settlement class context. First, the standards set for the protection of absent class members serve to inhibit appraisals of the chancellor's foot kind—class certifications dependent upon the court's gestalt judgment or overarching impression of the settlement's fairness.

Second, if a fairness inquiry under Rule 23(e) controlled certification, eclipsing Rule 23(a) and (b), and permitting class designation despite the impossibility of litigation, both class counsel and court would be disarmed. Class counsel confined to settlement negotiations could not use the threat of litigation to press for a better offer, see Coffee, Class Wars: The Dilemma of the Mass Tort Class Action, 95 Colum. L. Rev. 1343, 1379–1380 (1995), and the court would face a bargain proffered for its approval without benefit of adversarial investigation, see, e.g., Kamilewicz v. Bank of Boston Corp., 100 F.3d 1348, 1352 (C.A.7 1996) (Easterbrook, J., dissenting from denial of rehearing en banc) (parties "may even put one over on the court, in a staged performance"), cert. denied, 520 U.S. ___ (1997).

Federal courts, in any case, lack authority to substitute for Rule 23's certification criteria a standard never adopted—that if a settlement is "fair," then certification is proper. Applying to this case criteria the rulemakers set, we conclude that the Third Circuit's appraisal is essentially correct. Although that court should have acknowledged that settlement is a factor in the calculus, a remand is not warranted on that account. The Court of Appeals' opinion amply demonstrates why—with or without a settlement on the table—the sprawling class the District Court certified does not satisfy Rule 23's requirements.

A

We address first the requirement of Rule 23(b)(3) that "[common] questions of law or fact ... predominate over any questions affecting only individual members." The District Court concluded that predominance was satisfied based on two factors: class members' shared experience of asbestos exposure and their common "interest in receiving prompt and fair compensation for their claims, while minimizing the risks and transaction costs inherent in the asbestos litigation process as it occurs presently in the tort system." 157 F.R.D., at 316. The settling parties also contend that the settlement's fairness is a common question, predominating over disparate legal issues that might be pivotal in litigation but become irrelevant under the settlement.

The predominance requirement stated in Rule 23(b)(3), we hold, is not met by the factors on which the District Court relied. The benefits asbestos-exposed persons might gain from the establishment of a grand-scale compensation scheme is a matter fit for legislative consideration, ... but it is not pertinent to the predominance inquiry. That inquiry trains on the legal or factual questions that qualify each class member's case as a genuine controversy, questions that preexist any settlement.[5]

The Rule 23(b)(3) predominance inquiry tests whether proposed classes are sufficiently cohesive to warrant adjudication by representation. See 7A Wright, Miller, & Kane 518–519. The inquiry appropriate under Rule 23(e), on the other hand, protects unnamed class members "from unjust or unfair settlements affecting their rights when the

---

5. In this respect, the predominance requirement of Rule 23(b)(3) is similar to the requirement of Rule 23(a)(3) that "claims or defenses" of the named representatives must be "typical of the claims or defenses of the class." The words "claims or defenses" in this context—just as in the context of Rule 24(b)(2) governing permissive intervention—"manifestly refer to the kinds of claims or defenses that can be raised in courts of law as part of an actual or impending law suit." Diamond v. Charles, 476 U.S. 54, 76–77 (1986) (O'CONNOR, J., concurring in part and concurring in judgment).

representatives become fainthearted before the action is adjudicated or are able to secure satisfaction of their individual claims by a compromise." See 7B Wright, Miller, & Kane § 1797, at 340–341. But it is not the mission of Rule 23(e) to assure the class cohesion that legitimizes representative action in the first place. If a common interest in a fair compromise could satisfy the predominance requirement of Rule 23(b)(3), that vital prescription would be stripped of any meaning in the settlement context.

The District Court also relied upon this commonality: "The members of the class have all been exposed to asbestos products supplied by the defendants. . . ." 157 F.R.D., at 316. Even if Rule 23(a)'s commonality requirement may be satisfied by that shared experience, the predominance criterion is far more demanding. See 83 F.3d, at 626–627. Given the greater number of questions peculiar to the several categories of class members, and to individuals within each category, and the significance of those uncommon questions, any overarching dispute about the health consequences of asbestos exposure cannot satisfy the Rule 23(b)(3) predominance standard.

The Third Circuit highlighted the disparate questions undermining class cohesion in this case:

"Class members were exposed to different asbestos-containing products, for different amounts of time, in different ways, and over different periods. Some class members suffer no physical injury or have only asymptomatic pleural changes, while others suffer from lung cancer, disabling asbestosis, or from mesothelioma. . . . Each has a different history of cigarette smoking, a factor that complicates the causation inquiry.

"The [exposure-only] plaintiffs especially share little in common, either with each other or with the presently injured class members. It is unclear whether they will contract asbestos-related disease and, if so, what disease each will suffer. They will also incur different medical expenses because their monitoring and treatment will depend on singular circumstances and individual medical histories." Id., at 626.

Differences in state law, the Court of Appeals observed, compound these disparities. See id., at 627 (citing Phillips Petroleum Co. v. Shutts, 472 U.S. 797, 823 (1985)).

No settlement class called to our attention is as sprawling as this one. Cf. In re Asbestos Litigation, 90 F.3d, at 976, n. 8 ("We would likely agree with the Third Circuit that a class action requesting individual damages for members of a global class of asbestos claimants would not satisfy [Rule 23] requirements due to the huge number of individuals and their varying medical expenses, smoking histories, and family situations."). Predominance is a test readily met in certain cases alleging consumer or securities fraud or violations of the antitrust laws. See Adv. Comm. Notes, 28 U.S.C. App., p. 697; . . . . Even mass tort cases arising from a common cause or disaster may, depending upon the circumstances, satisfy the predominance requirement. The Advisory Committee for the 1966 revision of Rule 23, it is true, noted that "mass accident" cases are likely to present "significant questions, not only of damages but of liability and defenses of liability, ... affecting the individuals in different ways." Ibid. And the Committee advised that such cases are "ordinarily not appropriate" for class treatment. Ibid. But the text of the rule does not categorically exclude mass tort cases from class certification, and district courts, since the late 1970s, have been certifying such cases in increasing number. See Resnik, From "Cases" to "Litigation," 54 Law & Contemp. Prob. 5, 17–19 (Summer 1991) (describing trend). The Committee's warning, however, continues to call for caution when individual stakes are high and disparities among class members great. As the Third Circuit's opinion makes plain, the certification in this case does not follow the counsel of caution. That certification cannot be upheld, for it rests on a conception of Rule 23(b)(3)'s predominance requirement irreconcilable with the rule's design.

B

Nor can the class approved by the District Court satisfy Rule 23(a)(4)'s requirement that the named parties "will fairly and adequately protect the interests of the class." The adequacy inquiry under Rule 23(a)(4) serves to uncover conflicts of interest between named parties and the class they seek to represent. See General Telephone Co. of Southwest v. Falcon, 457 U.S. 147, 157–158, n. 13 (1982). "[A] class representative must be part of the class and 'possess the same interest and suffer the same injury' as the class members." East Tex. Motor Freight System, Inc. v. Rodriguez, 431 U.S. 395, 403 (1977) (quoting Schlesinger v. Reservists Comm. to Stop the War, 418 US. 208, 216 (1974)).[6]

As the Third Circuit pointed out, named parties with diverse medical conditions sought to act on behalf of a single giant class rather than on behalf of discrete subclasses. In significant respects, the interests of those within the single class are not aligned. Most saliently, for the currently injured, the critical goal is generous immediate payments. That goal tugs against the interest of exposure-only plaintiffs in ensuring an ample, inflation-protected fund for the future. Cf. General Telephone Co. of Northwest v. EEOC, 446 U.S. 318, 331 (1980) ("In employment discrimination litigation, conflicts might arise, for example, between

---

6. The adequacy-of-representation requirement "tends to merge" with the commonality and typicality criteria of Rule 23(a), which "serve as guideposts for determining whether ... maintenance of a class action is economical and whether the named plaintiff's claim and the class claims are so interrelated that the interests of the class members will be fairly and adequately protected in their absence." General Telephone Co. of Southwest v. Falcon, 457 U.S. 147, 157, n. 13 (1982). The adequacy heading also factors in competency and conflicts of class counsel. See id., at 157–158, n. 13. Like the Third Circuit, we decline to address adequacy-of-counsel issues discretely in light of our conclusions that common questions of law or fact do not predominate and that the named plaintiffs cannot adequately represent the interests of this enormous class.

employees and applicants who were denied employment and who will, if granted relief, compete with employees for fringe benefits or seniority. Under Rule 23, the same plaintiff could not represent these classes.").

The disparity between the currently injured and exposure-only categories of plaintiffs, and the diversity within each category are not made insignificant by the District Court's finding that petitioners' assets suffice to pay claims under the settlement. See 157 F.R.D., at 291. Although this is not a "limited fund" case certified under Rule 23(b)(1)(B), the terms of the settlement reflect essential allocation decisions designed to confine compensation and to limit defendants' liability. For example, as earlier described, . . . the settlement includes no adjustment for inflation; only a few claimants per year can opt out at the back end; and loss-of-consortium claims are extinguished with no compensation.

The settling parties, in sum, achieved a global compromise with no structural assurance of fair and adequate representation for the diverse groups and individuals affected. Although the named parties alleged a range of complaints, each served generally as representative for the whole, not for a separate constituency. In another asbestos class action, the Second Circuit spoke precisely to this point:

"Where differences among members of a class are such that subclasses must be established, we know of no authority that permits a court to approve a settlement without creating subclasses on the basis of consents by members of a unitary class, some of whom happen to be members of the distinct subgroups. The class representatives may well have thought that the Settlement serves the aggregate interests of the entire class. But the adversity among subgroups requires that the members of each subgroup cannot be bound to a settlement except by consents given by those who understand that their role is to represent solely the members of their respective subgroups." In re Joint Eastern and Southern Dist. Asbestos Litigation, 982 F.2d 721, 742–743 (C.A.2 1992), modified on reh'g sub nom. In re Findley, 993 F.2d 7 (C.A.2 1993).

The Third Circuit found no assurance here—either in the terms of the settlement or in the structure of the negotiations—that the named plaintiffs operated under a proper understanding of their representational responsibilities. See 83 F.3d, at 630–631. That assessment, we conclude, is on the mark.

C

Impediments to the provision of adequate notice, the Third Circuit emphasized, rendered highly problematic any endeavor to tie to a settlement class persons with no perceptible asbestos-related disease at the time of the settlement. Id., at 633; cf. In re Asbestos Litigation, 90 F.3d, at 999–1000 (Smith, J., dissenting). Many persons in the exposure-only category, the Court of Appeals stressed, may not even know of their exposure, or realize the extent of the harm they may incur. Even of they fully appreciate the significance of class notice, those without current afflictions may not have the information or foresight needed to decide, intelligently, whether to stay in or opt out.

Family members of asbestos-exposed individuals may themselves fall prey to disease or may ultimately have ripe claims for loss of consortium. Yet large numbers of people in this category—future spouses and children of asbestos victims—could not be alerted to their class membership. And current spouses and children of the occupationally exposed may know nothing of that exposure.

Because we have concluded that the class in this case cannot satisfy the requirements of common issue predominance and adequacy of representation, we need not rule, definitively, on the notice given here. In accord with the Third Circuit, however, see 83 F.3d, at 633–634, we recognize the gravity of the question whether class action notice sufficient under the Constitution and Rule 23 could ever be given to legions so unselfconscious and amorphous.

V

The argument is sensibly made that a nationwide administrative claims processing regime would provide the most secure, fair, and efficient means of compensating victims of asbestos exposure. Congress, however, has not adopted such a solution. And Rule 23, which must be interpreted with fidelity to the Rules Enabling Act and applied with the interests of absent class members in close view, cannot carry the large load CCR, class counsel, and the District Court heaped upon it. As this case exemplifies, the rulemakers' prescriptions for class actions may be endangered by "those who embrace [Rule 23] too enthusiastically just as [they are by] those who approach [the rule] with distaste." C. Wright, Law of Federal Courts 508 (5th ed. 1994); cf. 83 F.3d, at 634 (suggesting resort to less bold aggregation techniques, including more narrowly defined class certifications).

* * *

For the reasons stated, the judgment of the Court of Appeals for the Third Circuit is

Affirmed.

JUSTICE O'CONNOR took no part in the consideration or decision of this case.

JUSTICE BREYER, with whom JUSTICE STEVENS joins, concurring in part and dissenting in part.

Although I agree with the Court's basic holding that "settlement is relevant to a class certification," ..., I find several problems in its approach that lead me to a different conclusion. First, I believe that the need for settlement in this mass tort case, with hundreds of thousands of lawsuits, is greater than the Court's opinion suggests. Second, I would give more weight than would the majority to settlement-related issues for purposes of determining whether common issues predominate. Third, I am uncertain about the Court's determination of adequacy of representation, and do not believe it appropriate for this Court to second-guess the District Court on the matter without first having the Court of Appeals consider it. Fourth, I am uncertain about the tenor of an opinion that seems to suggest the settlement is unfair. And fifth, in the absence of further review by the Court of Appeals, I cannot accept the majority's suggestions that "notice" is inadequate.

* * * * *

NOTES

1. Should the judgment as to whether actions of the kind involved in the principal case can be maintained as class actions be made by the legislature or by the courts' creative manipulation of Federal Rule 23, which, according to its principal draftsman, never contemplated its use in this context? Can society devise more effective and less costly ways of affording relief to the victims? But what if the legislative or administrative branch do not afford such relief?

2. Note that in the principal case the prospective defendants encouraged the prospective plaintiffs to bring a class action in order to obtain a settlement that would bind all members of the class. Is that permissible under the law and the Code of Ethics?

3. A great advantage of permitting a class action is that a settlement approved by the court binds all members of the class who did not properly opt out. This may even move prospective defendants to encourage the bringing of a class action and to agree to a settlement. In Georgine v. Amchem Products, Inc., 878 F.Supp. 716 (E.D.Pa.1994), discontented members of the class who had not opted out nevertheless brought their own class actions seeking a declaration that a settlement thus obtained was not binding upon them. The court that had approved the settlement granted an injunction under the All–Writs Act (28 U.S.C.A. § 1651 (1988)) against the bringing of such class action. However, the Court of Appeals, reversed.

4. In the Tobacco cases, the parties reached a settlement that cannot become effective unless approved legislatively. See Time, vol. 149, no.16, p.25–30 (June 30, 1997). Among the plaintiffs in these actions were a number of States, whose attorney-generals had retained plaintiff-class-action lawyers on a contingency fee basis. The plaintiffs' lawyers stand to receive billions of dollars in fees. Part of the recovery will be used for such varied purposes as the provision of health case coverage for uninsured children and anti-tobacco advertising. Does the class action displace both the executive and the legislative branch of government? Note that the bar and the courts have transformed the original spurious class action from a joinder device into a regulatory scheme that is in large measure the product of their creative efforts rather than that of deliberate legislative and executive action. Does the Proposal Amendment to Rule 23 (b), set forth below, provide the answer? Or should we limit the class action to the cases in which it was developed historically?

———————

On April 18 and 19, 1996, The Civil Rules Advisory Committee approved for publication and comment the following proposed revision of Rule 23:

PROPOSED AMENDMENTS TO THE FEDERAL
RULES OF CIVIL PROCEDURE*
Rule 23.   Class Actions

* * * * *

(b) CLASS ACTIONS MAINTAINABLE. An action may be maintained as a class action if the prerequisites of subdivision (a) are satisfied, and in addition:

* * * * *

(3) the court finds that the questions of law or fact common to the members of the class predominate over any questions affecting only individual members, and that a class action is superior to other available methods for the fair and efficient adjudication of the controversy. The matters pertinent to the findings include:

(A) the practical ability of individual class members to pursue their claims without class certification;

(AB) ~~the interest of members of the class in individually controlling the prosecution or defense of~~ class members' interests in maintaining or defending separate actions;

(BC) the extent, ~~and~~ nature, and maturity of any related litigation ~~concerning the controversy already commenced by or against~~ involving class members ~~of the class~~;

(CD) the desirability or undesirability of concentrating the litigation of the claims in the particular forum;

(DE) the difficulties likely to be encountered in the management of a class action; and

(F) whether the probable relief to individual class members justifies the costs and burdens of class litigation; or

(4) the parties to a settlement request certification under subdivision (b)(3) for purposes of settlement, even though the requirements of subdivision (b)(3) might not be met for purposes of trial.

(c) DETERMINATION BY ORDER WHETHER CLASS ACTION TO BE MAINTAINED; NOTICE; JUDGMENT; ACTIONS CONDUCTED PARTIALLY AS CLASS ACTIONS.

(1) ~~As soon as~~ When practicable after the commencement of an action brought as a class action, the court shall determine by order whether it is to be so maintained. An order under this subdivision may be conditional, and may be altered or amended before the decision on the merits.

* * * * *

* New material is underlined. Superseded material is struck out.

(e) DISMISSAL OR COMPROMISE. A class action shall not be dismissed or compromised without <u>hearing and</u> the approval of the court, ~~and~~ <u>after</u> notice of the proposed dismissal or compromise ~~shall be~~ <u>has been</u> given to all members of the class in such manner as the court directs.

(f) APPEALS. <u>A court of appeals may in its discretion permit an appeal from an order of a district court granting or denying class action certification under this rule if application is made to it within ten days after entry of the order. An appeal does not stay proceedings in the district court unless the district judge or the court of appeals so orders.</u>

3.   SUBJECT MATTER COMPETENCE

[Insert on page 512 in lieu of the first full paragraph and Note (1):]

The decision in Snyder v. Harris, which seriously limits use of class actions in federal courts, did not seem to preclude the possibility of entertaining claims under the requisite amount, as long as one or more of the representative members of the class alleged claims that did satisfy the amount in controversy requirement.   However, in Zahn v. International Paper Co., 414 U.S. 291, 94 S.Ct. 505, 38 L.Ed.2d 511 (1973), the Supreme Court ruled this avenue foreclosed.   Interestingly, 28 U.S.C.A. § 1367 omits mention of Rule 23 cases.   Whether this omission modifies *Zahn* awaits decision of the courts.

[Insert at p. 521, after note (3):]

4.   PERSONAL JURISDICTION

IN RE "AGENT ORANGE" PRODUCT LIABILITY LITIGATION
United States Court of Appeals, Second Circuit, 1993.
996 F.2d 1425.

VAN GRAAFEILAND, CIRCUIT JUDGE:

Two groups of veterans and their family members, who sue both individually and on behalf of others similarly situated, appeal from a judgment of the United States District Court for the Eastern District of New York (Weinstein, J.) dismissing their tort claims against seven chemical companies which manufactured the defoliant Agent Orange. Ryan v. Dow Chemical Co., 781 F.Supp. 902 (E.D.N.Y.1991)....

These actions are an attempted revival of the massive tort litigation (collectively "Agent Orange I"), which arose from the United States Armed Services' use of Agent Orange during the Vietnam War.   [The history of the litigation is omitted.]

* * *

In 1989 and 1990, two overlapping class actions, Ivy v. Diamond Shamrock Chemicals Co. and Hartman v. Diamond Shamrock Chemicals Co., were brought in Texas courts.   Both alleged that the named plaintiffs or their family members suffered injury as a result of Agent Orange exposure and that the injuries sustained by these plaintiffs did not manifest themselves or were not discovered until after May 7, 1984, the Agent Orange I settlement date. Both complaints sounded exclusively in state law and explicitly abjured reliance on federal law. Defendants removed the cases to the United States District Courts for the Eastern and Southern Districts of Texas, alleging "artful pleading" of a federal claim or, alternatively, complete federal preemption. The Judicial Panel on Multidistrict Litigation transferred the cases to the Eastern District of New York.

On January 31, 1990, the Ivy plaintiffs petitioned this court for a writ of mandamus directing remand. On March 28, we denied the motion, ruling that the question of subject matter jurisdiction should be decided in the first instance by the district court. In re Ivy, 901 F.2d 7, 10 (2d Cir.1990). Plaintiffs then moved in the district court for remand of both cases. The district court heard oral argument on March 6, 1991, and scheduled an additional hearing on the motion to remand and other motions for May 6, 1991, to allow for further briefing. In the interim, defendants moved to dismiss and to amend their notice of removal to assert federal officer removal pursuant to 28 U.S.C. § 1442(a)(1).

The district court remanded the claims of two civilian plaintiffs alleging injury, holding that they were not within the Agent Orange I class and that federal officer removal was inapplicable. Ryan v. Dow Chemical Co., 781 F.Supp. 934 (E.D.N.Y.1992). The court denied the motion to remand of the veteran plaintiffs and their family members and dismissed their claims as barred by the Agent Orange I settlement and the court's order enjoining future suits by class members. 781 F.Supp. 902, 918–20. Plaintiffs moved for reconsideration of the latter decision and for disqualification of Judge Weinstein pursuant to 28 U.S.C. § 455. The court, in an unpublished order, denied both motions and kept its original decision substantially intact.

FEDERAL JURISDICTION

[In this part of the opinion, the court sustains Judge Weinstein's holding that the case is removable, stating in part:

A district court, in exceptional circumstances, may use its All Writs authority to remove an otherwise unremovable state court case in order to "effectuate and prevent the frustration of orders it has previously issued in its exercise of jurisdiction otherwise obtained." United States v. New York Tel. Co., 434 U.S. 159, 172, 98 S.Ct. 364, 372, 54 L.Ed.2d 376 (1977).

If Agent Orange victims were allowed to maintain separate actions in state court, the deleterious effect on the Agent Orange I settlement mechanism would be substantial. The parties to the settlement implicitly recognized this when they agreed that all future suits by class members would be permanently barred. It is difficult to conceive of any state court properly addressing a victim's tort claim without first deciding the scope of the Agent Orange I class action and settlement. The court best situated to make this determination is the court that approved the settlement and entered the judgment enforcing it. Removal in the instant case was an appropriate use of federal judicial power under 28 U.S.C. § 1651.]

CLASS MEMBERSHIP

Having resolved the preliminary jurisdictional questions, we turn to the central question of appellants' membership vel non in the Agent Orange I class. The answer to this question lies in the meaning of the phrase "who were injured while in or near Vietnam from exposure to Agent Orange." Appellants contend that persons are not "injured" until medical symptoms become manifest. Appellees argue in response that injury occurs when a deleterious substance enters a person's body, even though its adverse effects are not immediately apparent. In the instant case, appellees' definition is correct.

The words "injury" and "injured" appear to have received the attention of courts and legislatures most often where limitation periods for suit are involved. For example, some authorities hold that the prescribed limitation period begins to run when one's personal physical rights are invaded; others hold that the limitation period does not begin to run until the hurt or damage resulting from the invasion is discovered. Absent a specific statutory mandate to the contrary, the definition of "injury" and "injured" generally remains the same regardless of which limitation period is applied; i.e., the limitation runs either from the time the "injury" occurs or the time the damage resulting from the "injury" is discovered. In the strict legal sense " '[i]njury' means a wrongful invasion of legal rights, and is not concerned with the hurt or damage resulting from such invasion...." 43A C.J.S. Injury at 767; see also Restatement (Second) of Torts § 7.

* * *

Appellants next contend that they are not bound by the Agent Orange I class action and settlement because the court did not have personal jurisdiction over them. We rejected this argument on the appeal in Agent Orange I, 818 F.2d at 163. We there quoted the Judicial Panel on Multidistrict Litigation to the effect that transfers under 28 U.S.C. § 1407, the multidistrict litigation statute, "are simply not encumbered by considerations of in personam jurisdiction and venue" and that the transferee judge has all the pretrial jurisdiction the transferor judge would have had if the transfer had not occurred. We then proceeded in that opinion to discuss the adequacy of notice of the class action and proposed settlement, id. at 167–70, and held that the notices were adequate. Our view has not changed.

Appellants contend, as did appellants in Agent Orange I, that all class members did not receive adequate notice of their membership in the Agent Orange I action and the opportunity to exclude themselves therefrom. This, appellants allege, was a due process violation under the standards of Phillips Petroleum Co. v. Shutts, 472 U.S. 797, 105 S.Ct. 2965, 86 L.Ed.2d 628 (1985). Appellants misapprehend the reach of Shutts. The Court's decision in that case "is limited to those class actions which seek to bind known plaintiffs concerning claims wholly or predominantly for money judgments," and "intimate [s] no view concerning other types of class actions." Id. at 811 n. 3, 105 S.Ct. at 2974 n. 3. As such, "Shutts does not apply directly to classes of unknown plaintiffs." See 1 Newberg on Class Actions § 1.23, at 1–54 (3d ed. 1992). We distinguished Shutts in Agent Orange I, pointing out that here "there was no easily accessible list of veterans, as there must have been of royalty holders in [Shutts]." 818 F.2d at 169.

We again decline to extend the Shutts holding into situations such as this. "Due process, the courts have often declared, 'is a flexible concept,' intended to ensure 'fundamental fairness.'" In re A.H. Robins Co., 880 F.2d 709, 745 (4th Cir.) (quoting Walters v. National Ass'n of Radiation Survivors, 473 U.S. 305, 320, 105 S.Ct. 3180, 3189, 87 L.Ed.2d 220 (1985) and Mathews v. Eldridge, 424 U.S. 319, 334, 96 S.Ct. 893, 902, 47 L.Ed.2d 18 (1976)), cert. denied, 493 U.S. 959, 110 S.Ct. 377, 107 L.Ed.2d 362 (1989). What process is due in a given instance requires the balancing of a variety of interests. In some cases, "the marginal gains from affording an additional procedural safeguard ... may be outweighed by the societal cost of providing such a safeguard." Walters, supra, 473 U.S. at 320–21, 105 S.Ct. at 3189.

In the instant case, society's interest in the efficient and fair resolution of large-scale litigation outweighs the gains from individual notice and opt-out rights, whose benefits here are conjectural at best. As appellants correctly note, providing individual notice and opt-out rights to persons who are unaware of an injury would probably do little good. Their rights are better served, we think, by requiring that "fair and just recovery procedures be [ ] made available to these claimants," 1 Newberg, supra, § 1.23, at 1–56, and by ensuring that they receive vigorous and faithful vicarious representation.

It is axiomatic that a class action binds absent members only so long as they were adequately represented therein. See generally Hansberry v. Lee, 311 U.S. 32, 41, 61 S.Ct. 115, 118, 85 L.Ed. 22 (1940). Our decision in Eisen v. Carlisle & Jacquelin, 391 F.2d 555 (2d Cir.1968), describes the requisites of adequate representation as follows: [A]n essential concomitant of adequate representation is that the party's attorney be qualified, experienced and generally able to conduct the proposed litigation. Additionally, it is necessary to eliminate so far as possible the likelihood that the litigants are involved in a collusive suit or that plaintiff has interests antagonistic to those of the remainder of the class. Id. at 562. Appellants do not challenge the qualifications of the Agent Orange I class counsel. Moreover, their conflict-of-interest claims are unpersuasive. Although, as the district court noted, "[o]ne can imagine many genuine conflicts of interest" in a situation such as this, the court concluded that any potential conflicts that might have infected Agent Orange I never materialized: In many cases the conflict between the interests of present and future claimants is more imagined than real. In the instant case, for example, the injustice wrought upon the plaintiffs is nonexistent. These plaintiffs, like all class members who suffer death or disability before the end of 1994, are eligible for compensation from the Agent Orange Payment Fund. The relevant latency periods and the age of the veterans ensure that almost all valid claims will be revealed before that time. 781 F.Supp. at 919.

        * * *

Indeed, we note that, despite some intervening changes in the law, serious obstacles to recovery remain. Thus, although the scope of the government contract defense has been somewhat limited by the Supreme Court's decision in Boyle v. United Technologies Corp., 487 U.S. 500, 512, 108 S.Ct. 2510, 2518, 101 L.Ed.2d 442 (1988), under proper circumstances the defense is still available to government contractors. See Lewis v. Babcock Indus., Inc., 985 F.2d 83 (2d Cir.1993); Stout v. Borg–Warner Corp., 933 F.2d 331 (5th Cir.), cert. denied, 502 U.S. 981, 112 S.Ct. 584, 116 L.Ed.2d 609 (1991); Maguire v. Hughes Aircraft Corp., 912 F.2d 67 (3d Cir.1990). There is more than a mere possibility that such circumstances exist in the instant case. It is clear from the chemical companies' contracts with the Government that the Government specified Agent Orange's ingredients in great detail. There also is documentary evidence tending to show that the Government strictly prescribed the markings on Agent Orange barrels, and prohibited all extraneous label information, including warnings. Finally, there is evidence that the Government's knowledge of the hazards of Agent Orange and dioxin was at least as great as that of the chemical companies, making it unlikely that there were "dangers ... that were known to the supplier but not to the United States," of which the suppliers should have warned. Boyle, supra, 487 U.S. at 512, 108 S.Ct. at 2518. In sum, although the availability of the government contract defense might not be a foregone conclusion, there is a reasonable probability that it would apply, barring any recovery by the plaintiffs.

In addition, despite continuing research, the crucial issue of "general causation," i.e., whether any injuries are attributable to Agent Orange, remains unsettled. As one 1992 commentator noted, reviewing the scientific literature: "To date, there has been no conclusive evidence that exposure to Agent Orange is carcinogenic, mutagenic or teratogenic in humans. Furthermore, no deaths attributable solely to exposure to Agent Orange and its dioxin contaminant have been reported." 13B

Arthur L. Frank, Courtroom Medicine: Cancer, § 25A.00, at 25A–4 (1992).

Indeed, it remains as difficult as ever to prove individual levels of exposure to Agent Orange. For instance, a 1990 study conducted under the auspices of the Environmental Protection Agency and the Veterans Administration compared Vietnam veterans to veterans not serving in Vietnam and civilian men, all of like age, and concluded that: with or without adjustment for several demographic variables, the mean level of [dioxin] in the adipose tissue of the 36 Vietnam veterans was not significantly different from that of the 79 non-Vietnam veterans or the 80 civilian men.... Furthermore, the results showed no association between [dioxin] levels and any estimate of Agent Orange exposure opportunity based on military records.... The study results suggest that heavy exposure to [dioxin] for most Vietnam veterans was unlikely and that available military unit records used in the study were inadequate in assessing exposure to Agent Orange for those Vietnam veterans. Han K. Kang et al., Dioxins and Dibenzofurans in Adipose Tissue of U.S. Vietnam Veterans and Controls, at x (1990).

Even if appellants were to surmount the military contractor defense, provide satisfactory epidemiological evidence on the issue of general causation, and demonstrate with sufficient accuracy their levels of personal exposure to Agent Orange, they still would face the difficult task of demonstrating individual causation, i.e., that Agent Orange exposure caused the particular illnesses upon which they base their claims. Unlike asbestos, dioxin has not been recognized as the source of a distinctive medical illness.

The lesson to be drawn from this discussion is that the fundamental fairness of the Agent Orange I settlement remains unshaken. Notwithstanding the legal and scientific developments of the past nine years, the chances of recovery are nearly as speculative today as they were at the time of settlement. Appellants' challenges to the adequacy of their representation therefore must be rejected.

* * *

[Insert on page 542, before "6 DERIVATIVE ACTIONS" and renumber Numbers 6 and 7 as 7 and 8:]

6. PRECLUSIVE EFFECT

MATSUSHITA ELECTRIC INDUSTRIAL CO., LTD. v. EPSTEIN

Supreme Court of the United States, 1996.
___ U.S. ___, 116 S.Ct. 873, 134 L.Ed.2d 6.

JUSTICE THOMAS delivered the opinion of the Court.*

This case presents the question whether a federal court may withhold full faith and credit from a state-court judgment approving a class-

* Footnotes omitted.

action settlement simply because the settlement releases claims within the exclusive jurisdiction of the federal courts. The answer is no. Absent a partial repeal of the Full Faith and Credit Act, 28 U.S.C. § 1738, by another federal statute, a federal court must give the judgment the same effect that it would have in the courts of the State in which it was rendered.

I

In 1990, petitioner Matsushita Electric Industrial Co. made a tender offer for the common stock of MCA, Inc., a Delaware corporation. The tender offer not only resulted in Matsushita's acquisition of MCA, but also precipitated two lawsuits on behalf of the holders of MCA's common stock. First, a class action was filed in the Delaware Court of Chancery against MCA and its directors for breach of fiduciary duty in failing to maximize shareholder value. The complaint was later amended to state additional claims against MCA's directors for, inter alia, waste of corporate assets by exposing MCA to liability under the federal securities laws. In addition, Matsushita was added as a defendant and was accused of conspiring with MCA's directors to violate Delaware law. The Delaware suit was based purely on state-law claims.

While the state class action was pending, the instant suit was filed in Federal District Court in California. The complaint named Matsushita as a defendant and alleged that Matsushita's tender offer violated Securities Exchange Commission (SEC) Rules 10b–3 and 14d–10. These Rules were created by the SEC pursuant to the 1968 Williams Act Amendments to the Securities Exchange Act of 1934 (Exchange Act), 48 Stat. 881, as amended, 15 U.S.C. § 78a et seq. Section 27 of the Exchange Act confers exclusive jurisdiction upon the federal courts for suits brought to enforce the Act or rules and regulations promulgated thereunder. See 15 U.S.C. § 78aa. The District Court declined to certify the class, entered summary judgment for Matsushita, and dismissed the case. The plaintiffs appealed to the Court of Appeals for the Ninth Circuit.

After the federal plaintiffs filed their notice of appeal but before the Ninth Circuit handed down a decision, the parties to the Delaware suit negotiated a settlement. In exchange for a global release of all claims arising out of the Matsushita–MCA acquisition, the defendants would deposit $2 million into a settlement fund to be distributed pro rata to the members of the class. As required by Delaware Chancery Rule 23, which is modeled on Federal Rule of Civil Procedure 23, the Chancery Court certified the class for purposes of settlement and approved a notice of the proposed settlement. The notice informed the class members of their right to request exclusion from the settlement class and to appear and present argument at a scheduled hearing to determine the fairness of the settlement. In particular, the notice stated that "[b]y filing a valid Request for Exclusion, a member of the Settlement Class will not be precluded by the Settlement from individually seeking to pursue the claims alleged in the ... California Federal Actions, ... or any other claim relating to the events at issue in the Delaware Actions." App. to Pet. for Cert. 96a. Two such notices were mailed to the class members and the notice was also published in the national edition of the Wall Street Journal. The Chancery Court then held a hearing. After argument from several objectors, the Court found the class representation adequate and the settlement fair.

The order and final judgment of the Chancery Court incorporated the terms of the settlement agreement, providing:

"All claims, rights and causes of action (state or federal, including but not limited to claims arising under the federal securities law, any rules or regulations promulgated thereunder, or otherwise), whether known or unknown that are, could have been or might in the future be asserted by any of the plaintiffs or any member of the Settlement Class (other than those who have validly requested exclusion therefrom), ... in connection with or that arise now or hereafter out of the Merger Agreement, the Tender Offer, the Distribution Agreement, the Capital Contribution Agreement, the employee compensation arrangements, the Tender Agreements, the Initial Proposed Settlement, this Settlement ... and including without limitation the claims asserted in the California Federal Actions ... are hereby compromised, settled, released and discharged with prejudice by virtue of the proceedings herein and this Order and Final Judgment.' In re MCA, Inc. Shareholders Litigation, C.A. No. 11740 (Feb. 22, 1993), reprinted in App. to Pet. for Cert. 74a–75a (emphasis added)."

The judgment also stated that the notice met all the requirements of due process. The Delaware Supreme Court affirmed. In re MCA, Inc., Shareholders Litigation, 633 A.2d 370 (1993) (judgment order).

Respondents were members of both the state and federal plaintiff classes. Following issuance of the notice of proposed settlement of the Delaware litigation, respondents neither opted out of the settlement class nor appeared at the hearing to contest the settlement or the representation of the class. On appeal in the Ninth Circuit, petitioner Matsushita invoked the Delaware judgment as a bar to further prosecution of that action under the Full Faith and Credit Act, 28 U.S.C. § 1738.

The Ninth Circuit rejected petitioner's argument, ruling that § 1738 did not apply. Epstein v. MCA, Inc., 50 F.3d 644, 661–666 (1995). Instead, the Court of Appeals fashioned a test under which the preclusive force of a state court settlement judgment is limited to those claims that "could ... have been extinguished by the issue preclusive effect of an adjudication of the state claims." Id., at 665. The lower courts have taken varying approaches to determining the preclusive effect of a state court judgment, entered in a class or derivative action, that provides for the release of exclusively federal claims. We granted certiorari to clarify this important area of federal law. 515 U.S. ___ (1995).

II

The Full Faith and Credit Act mandates that the "judicial proceedings" of any State "shall have the same full faith and credit in every court within the United States ... as they have by law or usage in the courts of such State ... from which they are taken." 28 U.S.C. § 1738. The Act thus directs all courts to treat a state court judgment with the same respect that it would receive in the courts of the rendering state. Federal courts may not "employ their own rules ... in determining the effect of state judgments," but must "accept the rules chosen by the State from which the judgment is taken." Kremer v. Chemical Constr. Corp., 456 U.S. 461, 481–482 (1982). Because the Court of Appeals failed to follow the dictates of the Act, we reverse.

A

The state court judgment in this case differs in two respects from the judgments that we have previously considered in our cases under the Full Faith and Credit Act. As respondents and the Court of Appeals stressed, the judgment was the product of a class action and incorporated a settlement agreement releasing claims within the exclusive jurisdiction of the federal courts. Though respondents urge "the irrelevance of section 1738 to this litigation," Brief for Respondents 25, we do not think that either of these features exempts the judgment from the operation of § 1738.

That the judgment at issue is the result of a class action, rather than a suit brought by an individual, does not undermine the initial applicability of § 1738. The judgment of a state court in a class action is plainly the product of a "judicial proceeding" within the meaning of § 1738. Cf. McDonald v. West Branch, 466 U.S. 284, 287–288 (1984) (holding that § 1738 does not apply to arbitration awards because arbitration is not a "judicial proceeding"). Therefore, a judgment entered in a class action, like any other judgment entered in a state judicial proceeding, is presumptively entitled to full faith and credit under the express terms of the Act.

Further, § 1738 is not irrelevant simply because the judgment in question might work to bar the litigation of exclusively federal claims. Our decision in Marrese v. American Academy of Orthopaedic Surgeons, 470 U.S. 373 (1985), made clear that where § 1738 is raised as a defense in a subsequent suit, the fact that an allegedly precluded "claim is within the exclusive jurisdiction of the federal courts does not necessarily make § 1738 inapplicable." Id., at 380 (emphasis added). In so holding, we relied primarily on Kremer v. Chemical Constr. Corp., supra, which held, without deciding whether Title VII claims are exclusively federal, that state court proceedings may be issue preclusive in Title VII suits in federal court. Kremer, we said, "implies that absent an exception to § 1738, state law determines at least the . . . preclusive effect of a prior state judgment in a subsequent action involving a claim within the exclusive jurisdiction of the federal courts." Marrese, 470 U.S., at 381. Accordingly, we decided that "a state court judgment may in some circumstances have preclusive effect in a subsequent action within the exclusive jurisdiction of the federal courts." Id., at 380.

In Marrese, we discussed Nash County Board of Education v. Biltmore Co., 640 F.2d 484 (CA4), cert. denied, 454 U.S. 878 (1981), a case that concerned a state court settlement judgment. In Nash, the question was whether the judgment, which approved the settlement of state antitrust claims, prevented the litigation of exclusively federal antitrust claims. See 470 U.S., at 382, n. 2. We suggested that the approach outlined in Marrese would also apply in cases like Nash that involve judgments upon settlement: that is, § 1738 would control at the outset. See ibid. In accord with these precedents, we conclude that § 1738 is generally applicable in cases in which the state court judgment at issue incorporates a class action settlement releasing claims solely within the jurisdiction of the federal courts.

B

Marrese provides the analytical framework for deciding whether the Delaware court's judgment precludes this exclusively federal action. When faced with a state court judgment relating to an exclusively federal claim, a federal court must first look to the law of the rendering State to ascertain the effect of the judgment. See id., at 381–382. If state law indicates that the particular claim or issue would be barred from litigation in a court of that state, then the federal court must next decide whether, "as an exception to § 1738," it "should refuse to give preclusive effect to [the] state court judgment." Id., at 383. See also Migra v. Warren City School Dist. Bd. of Ed., 465 U.S. 75, 80 (1984) ("[I]n the absence of federal law modifying the operation of § 1738, the preclusive effect in federal court of [a] state-court judgment is determined by [state] law").

1

We observed in Marrese that the inquiry into state law would not always yield a direct answer. Usually, "a state court will not have occasion to address the specific question whether a state judgment has issue or claim preclusive effect in a later action that can be brought only in federal court." 470 U.S., at 381–382. Where a judicially approved settlement is under consideration, a federal court may consequently find guidance from general state law on the preclusive force of settlement judgments. See, e.g., id., at 382–383, n. 2 (observing in connection with Nash that "[North Carolina] law gives preclusive effect to consent judgment[s]"). Here, in addition to providing rules regarding the preclusive force of class-action settlement judgments in subsequent suits in state court, the Delaware courts have also spoken to the particular effect of such judgments in federal court.

Delaware has traditionally treated the impact of settlement judgments on subsequent litigation in state court as a question of claim preclusion. Early cases suggested that Delaware courts would not afford claim preclusive effect to a settlement releasing claims that could not have been presented in the trial court. See Ezzes v. Ackerman, 234 A.2d 444, 445–446 (Del.1967) ("[A] judgment entered either after trial on the merits or upon an approved settlement is res judicata and bars subsequent suit on the same claim. . . . [T]he defense of res judicata . . . is available if the pleadings framing the issues in the first action would have permitted the raising of the issue sought to be raised in the second action, and if the facts were known or could have been known to the plaintiff in the second action at the time of the first action"). As the Court of Chancery has perceived, however, "the Ezzes inquiry [was] modified in regard to class actions," In re Union Square Associates Securities Litigation, C.A. No. 11028, 1993 WL 220528, (June 16, 1993), by the Delaware Supreme Court's decision in Nottingham Partners v. Dana, 564 A.2d 1089 (1989).

In Nottingham, a class action, the Delaware Supreme Court approved a settlement that released claims then pending in federal court. In approving that settlement, the Nottingham Court appears to have eliminated the Ezzes requirement that the claims could have been raised in the suit that produced the settlement, at least with respect to class actions: " '[I]n order to achieve a comprehensive settlement that would prevent relitigation of settled questions at the core of a class action, a court may permit the release of a claim based on the identical factual predicate as that underlying the claims in the settled class action even though the claim was not presented and might not have been presentable in the class action.' " 564 A.2d, at 1106 (quoting TBK Partners, Ltd. v. Western Union Corp., 675 F.2d 456, 460 (C.A.2 1982)). See Union Square, C.A. No. 11028, 1993 WL 220528, ___ (relying directly on Nottingham to hold that a Delaware court judgment settling a class action was res judicata and barred arbitration of duplicative claims that could not have been brought in the first suit). These cases indicate that even if, as here, a claim could not have been raised in the court that rendered the settlement judgment in a class action, a Delaware court would still find that the judgment bars subsequent pursuit of the claim.

The Delaware Supreme Court has further manifested its understanding that when the Court of Chancery approves a global release of claims, its settlement judgment should preclude on-going or future federal court litigation of any released claims. In Nottingham, the Court stated that "[t]he validity of executing a general release in conjunction with the termination of litigation has long been recognized by the Delaware courts. More specifically, the Court of Chancery has a history of approving settlements that have implicitly or explicitly included a general release, which would also release federal claims." 564 A.2d, at 1105 (citation omitted). Though the Delaware Supreme Court correctly recognized in Nottingham that it lacked actual authority to order the dismissal of any case pending in federal court, it asserted that state-court approval of the settlement would have the collateral effect of preventing class members from prosecuting their claims in federal court. Perhaps the clearest statement of the Delaware Chancery Court's view on this matter was articulated in the suit preceding this one: "When a state court settlement of a class action releases all claims which arise out of the challenged transaction and is determined to be fair and to have met all due process requirements, the class members are bound by the release or the doctrine of issue preclusion. Class members cannot subsequently relitigate the claims barred by the settlement in a federal court." In re MCA, Inc. Shareholders Litigation, 598 A.2d 687, 691 (1991). We are aware of no Delaware case that suggests otherwise.

Given these statements of Delaware law, we think that a Delaware court would afford preclusive effect to the settlement judgment in this case, notwithstanding the fact that respondents could not have pressed their Exchange Act claims in the Court of Chancery. The claims are clearly within the scope of the release in the judgment, since the judgment specifically refers to this lawsuit. As required by Delaware Court of Chancery Rule 23, see Prezant v. De Angelis, 636 A.2d 915, 920 (1994), the Court of Chancery found, and the Delaware Supreme Court affirmed, that the settlement was "fair, reasonable and adequate and in the best interests of the ... Settlement class" and that notice to the class was "in full compliance with ... the requirements of due process." In re MCA, Inc. Shareholders Litigation, C.A. No. 11740 (Feb. 22, 1993), reprinted in App. to Pet. for Cert. 73a, 74a. Cf. Phillips Petroleum Co. v. Shutts, 472 U.S. 797, 812 (1985) (due process for class action plaintiffs requires "notice plus an opportunity to be heard and participate in the litigation"). The Court of Chancery "further determined that the plaintiffs[,] ... as representatives of the Settlement Class, have fairly and adequately protected the interests of the Settlement Class." In re MCA, Inc. Shareholders Litigation, supra, reprinted in App. to Pet. for Cert. 73a. Cf. Phillips Petroleum Co., supra, at 812 (due process requires "that the named plaintiff at all times adequately represent the interests of the absent class members"). Under Delaware Rule 23, as under Federal Rule of Civil Procedure 23, "[a]ll members of the class, whether of a plaintiff or a defendant class, are bound by the judgment entered in the action unless, in a Rule 23(b)(3) action, they make a timely election for exclusion." 2 H. Newberg, Class Actions § 2755, p. 1224 (1977). See also Cooper v. Federal Reserve Bank of Richmond, 467 U.S. 867, 874 (1984) ("There is of course no dispute that under elementary principles of prior adjudication of a judgment in a properly entertained class action is binding on class members in any subsequent litigation"). Respondents do not deny that, as shareholders of MCA's common stock, they were part of the plaintiff class and that they never opted out; they are bound, then, by the judgment.

2

Because it appears that the settlement judgment would be res judicata under Delaware law, we proceed to the second step of the Marrese analysis and ask whether § 27 of the Exchange Act, which confers exclusive jurisdiction upon the federal courts for suits arising under the Act, partially repealed § 1738. Section 27 contains no express language regarding its relationship with § 1738 or the preclusive effect of related state court proceedings. Thus, any modification of § 1738 by § 27 must be implied. In deciding whether § 27 impliedly created an exception to § 1738, the "general question is whether the concerns underlying a particular grant of exclusive jurisdiction justify a finding of an implied partial repeal of § 1738." Marrese, 470 U.S., at 386. "Resolution of this question will depend on the particular federal statute as well as the nature of the claim or issue involved in the subsequent federal action.... [T]he primary consideration must be the intent of Congress." Ibid.

As an historical matter, we have seldom, if ever, held that a federal statute impliedly repealed § 1738. See Parsons Steel, Inc. v. First Alabama Bank, 474 U.S. 518, 523–524 (1986) (Anti–Injunction Act does not limit § 1738); Migra v. Warren City School Dist. Bd. of Ed., 465 U.S. 75, 83–85 (1984) (§ 1983 does not limit claim preclusion under § 1738); Kremer v. Chemical Constr. Corp., 456 U.S. 461, 468–476 (1982) (Title VII of the Civil Rights Act of 1964 does not limit § 1738); Allen v. McCurry, 449 U.S. 90, 96–105 (1980) (§ 1983 does not limit issue preclusion under § 1738). But cf. Brown v. Felsen, 442 U.S. 127, 138–139 (1979) (declining to give claim preclusive effect to prior state court debt collection proceeding in federal bankruptcy suit, without discussing § 1738, state law or implied repeals). The rarity with which we have discovered implied repeals is due to the relatively stringent standard for such findings, namely, that there be an " 'irreconcilable conflict' " between the two federal statutes at issue. Kremer v. Chemical Constr. Corp., supra, at 468 (quoting Radzanower v. Touche Ross & Co., 426 U.S. 148, 154 (1976)).

Section 27 provides that "[t]he district courts of the United States ... shall have exclusive jurisdiction ... of all suits in equity and actions at law brought to enforce any liability or duty created by this chapter or the rules and regulations thereunder." 15 U.S.C. § 78aa. There is no suggestion in § 27 that Congress meant for plaintiffs with Exchange Act claims to have more than one day in court to challenge the legality of a securities transaction. Though the statute plainly mandates that suits alleging violations of the Exchange Act may be maintained only in federal court, nothing in the language of § 27 "remotely expresses any congressional intent to contravene the common-law rules of preclusion or to repeal the express statutory requirements of ... 28 U.S.C. § 1738." Allen v. McCurry, supra, at 97–98.

Nor does § 27 evince any intent to prevent litigants in state court—whether suing as individuals or as part of a class—from voluntarily releasing Exchange Act claims in judicially approved settlements. While § 27 prohibits state courts from adjudicating claims arising under the Exchange Act, it does not prohibit state courts from approving the release of Exchange Act claims in the settlement of suits over which they have properly exercised jurisdiction, i.e., suits arising under state law or under federal law for which there is concurrent jurisdiction. In this case, for example, the Delaware action was not "brought to enforce" any rights or obligations under the Act. The Delaware court asserted judicial power over a complaint asserting purely state law causes of action and, after the parties agreed to settle, certified the class and approved the settlement pursuant to the requirements of Delaware Rule of Chancery 23 and the Due Process Clause. Thus, the Delaware court never trespassed upon the exclusive territory of the federal courts, but merely approved the settlement of a common-law suit pursuant to state and nonexclusive federal law. See Abramson v. Pennwood Investment Corp., 392 F.2d 759, 762 (C.A.2 1968) ("Although the state court could not adjudicate the federal claim, it was within its powers over the corporation and the parties to approve the release of that claim as a condition of settlement of the state action"). While it is true that the state court assessed the general worth of the federal claims in determining the fairness of the settlement, such assessment does not amount to a judgment on the merits of the claims. See TBK Partners, Ltd. v. Western Union Corp., 675 F.2d 456, 461 (C.A.2 1982) (" 'Approval of a settlement does not call for findings of fact regarding the claims to be compromised. The court is concerned only with the likelihood of success or failure; the actual merits of the controversy are not to be determined' ") (quoting Haudek, The Settlement and Dismissal of Stockholders' Actions–Part II: The Settlement, 23 Sw.L.J. 765, 809 (1969) (footnotes omitted)). The Delaware court never purported to resolve the merits of the Exchange Act claims in the course of appraising the settlement; indeed, it expressly disavowed that purpose. See In re MCA, Inc. Shareholders Litigation, C.A. No. 11740 (Feb. 16, 1993), reprinted in App. to Pet. for Cert. 68a ("In determining whether a settlement should be approved, a court should not try the merits of the underlying claims. This principle would seem to be especially appropriate where the underlying claims, like the federal claims here, are outside the jurisdiction of this Court" (citation omitted)).

The legislative history of the Exchange Act elucidates no specific purpose on the part of Congress in enacting § 27. See Murphy v. Gallagher, 761 F.2d 878, 885 (C.A.2 1985) (noting that the legislative history of the Exchange Act provides no readily apparent explanation for the provision of exclusive jurisdiction in § 27) (citing 2 & 3 L. Loss,

Securities Regulation 997, 2005 (2d ed. 1961)). We may presume, however, that Congress intended § 27 to serve at least the general purposes underlying most grants of exclusive jurisdiction: "to achieve greater uniformity of construction and more effective and expert application of that law." Murphy v. Gallager, supra, at 885. When a state court upholds a settlement that releases claims under the Exchange Act, it threatens neither of these policies. There is no danger that state court judges who are not fully expert in federal securities law will say definitively what the Exchange Act means and enforce legal liabilities and duties thereunder. And the uniform construction of the Act is unaffected by a state court's approval of a proposed settlement because the state court does not adjudicate the Exchange Act claims but only evaluates the overall fairness of the settlement, generally by applying its own business judgment to the facts of the case. See, e.g., Polk v. Good, 507 A.2d 531, 535 (Del.1986).

Furthermore, other provisions of the Exchange Act suggest that Congress did not intend to create an exception to § 1738 for suits alleging violations of the Act. Congress plainly contemplated the possibility of dual litigation in state and federal courts relating to securities transactions. See 15 U.S.C. § 78bb(a) (preserving "all other rights and remedies that may exist at law or in equity"). And all that Congress chose to say about the consequences of such litigation is that plaintiffs ought not obtain double recovery. See ibid. Congress said nothing to modify the background rule that where a state court judgment precedes that of a federal court, the federal court must give full faith and credit to the state court judgment. ....

Finally, precedent supports the conclusion that the concerns underlying the grant of exclusive jurisdiction in § 27 are not undermined by state court approval of settlements releasing Exchange Act claims. We have held that state court proceedings may, in various ways, subsequently affect the litigation of exclusively federal claims without running afoul of the federal jurisdictional grant in question. In Becher v. Contoure Laboratories, Inc., 279 U.S. 388 (1929) (cited in Marrese, 470 U.S., at 381), we held that state court findings of fact were issue preclusive in federal patent suits. We did so with full recognition that "the logical conclusion from the establishing of [the state law] claim is that Becher's patent is void." 279 U.S., at 391. Becher reasoned that although "decrees validating or invalidating patents belong to the Courts of the United States," that "does not give sacrosanctity to facts that may be conclusive upon the question in issue." Ibid. Similarly, while binding legal determinations of rights and liabilities under the Exchange Act are for federal courts only, there is nothing sacred about the approval of settlements of suits arising under state law, even where the parties agree to release exclusively federal claims. See also Brown v. Felsen, 442 U.S., at 139, n. 10 (noting that "[i]f, in the course of adjudicating a state-law question, a state court should determine factual issues using standards identical to those of § 17, then collateral estoppel, in the absence of countervailing statutory policy, would bar relitigation of those issues in the bankruptcy court"); Pratt v. Paris Gaslight & Coke Co., 168 U.S. 255, 258 (1897) (when a state court has jurisdiction of the parties and the subject matter of the complaint, the state court may decide the validity of a patent when that issue is raised as a defense).

We have also held that Exchange Act claims may be resolved by arbitration rather than litigation in federal court. In Shearson/American Express Inc. v. McMahon, 482 U.S. 220 (1987), we found that parties to an arbitration agreement could waive the right to have their Exchange Act claims tried in federal court and agree to arbitrate the claims. Id., at 227–228. It follows that state court litigants ought also to be able to waive, or "release," the right to litigate Exchange Act claims in a federal forum as part of a settlement agreement. As Shearson/American Express Inc. demonstrates, a statute conferring exclusive federal jurisdiction for a certain class of claims does not necessarily require resolution of those claims in a federal court.

Taken together, these cases stand for the general proposition that even when exclusively federal claims are at stake, there is no "universal right to litigate a federal claim in a federal district court." Allen v. McCurry, 449 U.S., at 105. If class action plaintiffs wish to preserve absolutely their right to litigate exclusively federal claims in federal court, they should either opt out of the settlement class or object to the release of any exclusively federal claims. In fact, some of the plaintiffs in the Delaware class action requested exclusion from the settlement class. They are now proceeding in federal court with their federal claims, unimpeded by the Delaware judgment.

In the end, §§ 27 and 1738 "do not pose an either-or proposition." Connecticut Nat. Bank v. Germain, 503 U.S. 249, 253 (1992). They can be reconciled by reading s 1738 to mandate full faith and credit of state court judgments incorporating global settlements, provided the rendering court had jurisdiction over the underlying suit itself, and by reading § 27 to prohibit state courts from exercising jurisdiction over suits arising under the Exchange Act. Cf. C. Wright, A. Miller, & E. Cooper, Federal Practice and Procedure § 4470 pp. 688–689 (1981) ("[S]ettlement of state court litigation has been held to defeat a subsequent federal action if the settlement was intended to apply to claims in exclusive federal jurisdiction as well as other claims.... These rulings are surely correct"). Congress' intent to provide an exclusive federal forum for adjudication of suits to enforce the Exchange Act is clear enough. But we can find no suggestion in § 27 that Congress meant to override the "principles of comity and repose embodied in § 1738," Kremer v. Chemical Constr. Corp., 456 U.S., at 463, by allowing plaintiffs with Exchange Act claims to release those claims in state court and then litigate them in federal court. We conclude that the Delaware courts would give the settlement judgment preclusive effect in a subsequent proceeding and, further, that § 27 did not effect a partial repeal of § 1738.

C

The Court of Appeals did not engage in any analysis of Delaware law pursuant to § 1738. Rather, the Court of Appeals declined to apply § 1738 on the ground that where the rendering forum lacked jurisdiction over the subject matter or the parties, full faith and credit is not required. 50 F.3d, at 661, 666. See Underwriters Nat. Assurance Co. v. North Carolina Life & Accident & Health Ins. Guaranty Assn., 455 U.S. 691, 704–705 (1982) (" '[A] judgment of a court in one State is conclusive upon the merits in a court in another State only if the court in the first State had power to pass on the merits—had jurisdiction, that is, to render the judgment' ") (quoting Durfee v. Duke, 375 U.S. 106, 110 (1963)). The Court of Appeals decided that the subject-matter jurisdiction exception to full faith and credit applies to this case because the Delaware court acted outside the bounds of its own jurisdiction in approving the settlement, since the settlement released exclusively federal claims. See 50 F.3d, at 661–662, and n. 25.

As explained above, the state court in this case clearly possessed jurisdiction over the subject matter of the underlying suit and over the defendants. Only if this were not so—for instance, if the complaint alleged violations of the Exchange Act and the Delaware court rendered a judgment on the merits of those claims—would the exception to § 1738 for lack of subject-matter jurisdiction apply. Where, as here, the rendering court in fact had subject-matter jurisdiction, the subject-matter-jurisdiction exception to full faith and credit is simply inapposite. In such a case, the relevance of a federal statute that provides for exclusive federal jurisdiction is not to the state court's possession of jurisdiction per se, but to the existence of a partial repeal of § 1738.

The judgment of the Court of Appeals is reversed and remanded for proceedings consistent with this opinion.

It is so ordered.

Justice Stevens, concurring in part and dissenting in part.

While I join Parts I, II–A, and II–C of the Court's opinion, and while I also agree with the Court's reasons for concluding that § 27 of the Exchange Act does not create an implied partial repeal of the Full Faith and Credit Act, I join neither Part II–B nor the Court's judgment because I agree with Justice Ginsburg that the question of Delaware law should be addressed by the Court of Appeals in the first instance, and that the Ninth Circuit remains free to consider whether Delaware courts fully and fairly litigated the adequacy of class representation.

Justice Ginsburg, concurring in part, dissenting in part [omitted].

NOTES

(1) In the principal case, would the Delaware state court have had the authority to adjudicate an action brought by individual shareholders on a settlement agreement in which the shareholders compromised their claims under the federal securities laws? Would the circumstance that the claims under the securities laws could be adjudicated only by a federal court have deprived the Delaware court of adjudicatory authority?

(2) Did the named plaintiffs in the class action represent all shareholders who had not opted out in regard to all claims these shareholders might have or only in regard to the claims properly asserted by the named plaintiffs in the Delaware court? If the named plaintiffs represented the other shareholders only in regard to the latter claims, where did they obtain the authority to represent them in regard to claims under the securities laws? Is it still possible for the objecting shareholders to advance the argument that the named plaintiffs had no such authority? Could and should the Supreme Court have decided the principal case differently on the ground that the named plaintiffs had no such authority?

RICHARDS v. JEFFERSON COUNTY

Supreme Court of the United States, 1996.
___ U.S. ___, 116 S.Ct. 1761, 135 L.Ed.2d 76.

JUSTICE STEVENS delivered the opinion of the Court.*

In Hansberry v. Lee, 311 U.S. 32, 37, 85 L.Ed. 22, 61 S.Ct. 115 (1940), we held that it would violate the Due Process Clause of the Fourteenth Amendment to bind litigants to a judgment rendered in an earlier litigation to which they were not parties and in which they were not adequately represented. The decision of the Supreme Court of Alabama that we review today presents us with the same basic question in a somewhat different context.

I

Jason Richards and Fannie Hill (petitioners) are privately employed in Jefferson County, Alabama. In 1991 they filed a complaint in the Federal District Court challenging the validity of the occupation tax imposed by Jefferson County Ordinance 1120, which had been adopted in 1987. That action was dismissed as barred by the Tax Injunction Act, 28 U.S.C. § 1341. They then commenced this action in the Circuit Court of Jefferson County.

Petitioners represent a class of all nonfederal employees subject to the county's tax. Petitioners alleged that the tax, which contains a lengthy list of exemptions, violates the Due Process and Equal Protection Clauses of the Fourteenth Amendment and similar provisions of the Alabama Constitution. Because $10 million of the annual proceeds from the county tax have been pledged to the Birmingham–Jefferson Civic Center for a period of 20 years, the court permitted the Center to intervene and support Jefferson County's defense of its tax.

---

* Some footnotes omitted; others renumbered.

The county moved for summary judgment on the ground that petitioners' claims were barred by a prior adjudication of the tax in an earlier action brought by the acting director of finance for the city of Birmingham and the city itself. That earlier action had been consolidated for trial with a separate suit brought by three county taxpayers, and the Supreme Court of Alabama upheld the tax in the resulting appeal. See Bedingfield v. Jefferson County, 527 So.2d 1270 (1988). After examining the course of this prior litigation, the trial court granted the county's motion for summary judgment as to the state constitutional claims, but refused to do so as to the federal claims because they had not been decided by either the trial court or the Alabama Supreme Court in Bedingfield.

On appeal, the county argued that the federal claims as well as the state claims were barred by the adjudication in Bedingfield. The Alabama Supreme Court agreed. The majority opinion noted that in Alabama, as in most States, a prior judgment on the merits rendered by a court of competent jurisdiction precludes the relitigation of a claim if there is a "substantial identity of the parties" and if the "same cause of action" is presented in both suits. 662 So.2d 1127, 1128 (1995). Moreover, the explained, the prior judgment is generally " 'res judicata not only as to all matters litigated and decided by it, but as to all relevant issues which could have been but were not raised and litigated in the suit.' " Ibid. (quoting Heiser v. Woodruff, 327 U.S. 726, 735, 90 L. Ed. 970, 66 S.Ct. 853 (1946)).

The Alabama Supreme Court concluded that even though the opinion in Bedingfield did not mention any federal issue, the judgment in that case met these requirements. The court gave three reasons for this conclusion: (1) the complaints in the earlier case had alleged that the county tax violated the Equal Protection Clause of the Fourteenth Amendment and an equal protection issue had been argued in the appellate briefs, 662 So.2d at 1129; (2) the taxpayers in Bedingfield adequately represented petitioners because their respective interests were "essentially identical," 662 So.2d at 1130, and (3) in pledging tax revenues and issuing bonds in 1989, the county and the intervenor "could have lied on Bedingfield as authoritatively establishing that the county occupational tax was not unconstitutional for the reasons asserted by the Bedingfield plaintiffs." 662 So.2d, at 1130.

Justice Maddox dissented. He agreed with the trial judge that no federal constitutional claim had been adjudicated in Bedingfield, 662 So.2d at 1130–1131. Moreover, he concluded that the mere fact that the theory advanced by the petitioners in this case could have been asserted in Bedingfield constituted an insufficient reason for barring this action. 662 So.2d at 1131–1132.

We now conclude that the State Supreme Court's holding that petitioners are bound by the adjudication in Bedingfield deprived them of the due process of law guaranteed by the Fourteenth Amendment.

II

State courts are generally free to develop their own rules for protecting against the relitigation of common issues or the piecemeal resolution of disputes. Postal Telegraph Cable Co. v. Newport, 247 U.S. 464, 475, 62 L.Ed. 1215, 38 S.Ct. 566 (1918). We have long held, however, that extreme applications of the doctrine of res judicata may be inconsistent with a federal right that is fundamental in character. Id., at 476.

The limits on a state court's power to develop estoppel rules reflect the general consensus " 'in Anglo–American jurisprudence that one is not bound by a judgment in personam, in a litigation in which he is not designated as a party or to which he has not been made a party by service of process.' Hansberry v. Lee, 311 U.S. 32, 40, 85 L.Ed. 22, 61 S.Ct. 115 (1940).... This rule is part of our 'deep-rooted historic tradition that everyone should have his own day in court.' 18 C. Wright, A. Miller, & E. Cooper, Federal Practice and Procedure § 4449, p. 417 (1981)." Martin v. Wilks, 490 U.S. 755, 761–762, 104 L.Ed.2d 835, 109 S.Ct. 2180 (1989). As a consequence, "[a] judgment or decree among parties to a lawsuit resolves issues as among them, but it does not conclude the rights of strangers to those proceedings." Id., at 762; Blonder–Tongue Laboratories, Inc. v. University of Ill. Foundation, 402 U.S. 313, 329, 28 L.Ed.2d 788, 91 S.Ct. 1434 (1971).

Of course, these principles do not always require one to have been a party to a judgment in order to be bound by it. Most notably, there is an exception when it can be said that there is "privity" between a party to the second case and a party who is bound by an earlier judgment. For example, a judgment that is binding on a guardian or trustee may also bind the ward or the beneficiaries of a trust. Moreover, although there are clearly constitutional limits on the "privity" exception, the term "privity" is now used to describe various relationships between litigants that would not have come within the traditional definition of that term. See generally Restatement (Second) of Judgments, ch. 4 (1980) (Parties and Other Persons Affected by Judgments).

In addition, as we explained in Wilks:

"We have recognized an exception to the general rule when, in certain limited circumstances, a person, although not a party, has his interests adequately represented by someone with the same interests who is a party. See Hansberry v. Lee, 311 U.S. 32, 41–42, 85 L.Ed. 22, 61 S.Ct. 115 (1940) ('class' or 'representative' suits); Fed. Rule Civ. Proc. 23 (same); Montana v. United States, 440 U.S. 147, 154–155, 59 L.Ed.2d 210, 99 S.Ct. 970 (1979) (control of litigation on behalf of one of the parties in the litigation). Additionally, where a special remedial scheme exists expressly foreclosing successive litigation by nonlitigants, as for example in bankruptcy or probate, legal proceedings may terminate pre-existing rights if the scheme is otherwise consistent with due process.

See NLRB v. Bildisco & Bildisco, 465 U.S. 513, 529–530, n. 10, 79 L.Ed.2d 482, 104 S.Ct. 1188 (1984) ('Proof of claim must be presented to the Bankruptcy Court ... or be lost'); Tulsa Professional Collection Services, Inc. v. Pope, 485 U.S. 478, 99 L.Ed.2d 565, 108 S.Ct. 1340 (1988) (nonclaim, statute terminating unsubmitted claims against the estate)." 490 U.S. at 762, n. 2.

Here, the Alabama Supreme Court concluded that res judicata applied because petitioners were adequately represented in the Bedingfield action. 662 So.2d at 1130. We now consider the propriety of that determination.

III

We begin by noting that the parties to the Bedingfield case failed to provide petitioners with any notice that a suit was pending which would conclusively resolve their legal rights. That failure is troubling because, as we explained in Mullane v. Central Hanover Bank & Trust Co., 339 U.S. 306, 94 L.Ed. 865, 70 S.Ct. 652 (1950), the right to be heard ensured by the guarantee of due process "has little reality or worth unless one is informed that the matter is pending and can choose for himself whether to appear or default, acquiesce or contest." Id., at 314; Phillips Petroleum Co. v. Shutts, 472 U.S. 797, 812, 86 L.Ed.2d 628, 105 S.Ct. 2965 (1985); Schroeder v. City of New York, 371 U.S. 208, 212–213, 9 L.Ed.2d 255, 83 S.Ct. 279 (1962). Nevertheless, respondents ask us to excuse the lack of notice on the ground that petitioners, as the Alabama Supreme Court concluded, were adequately represented in Bedingfield.[1]

Our answer is informed by our decision in Hansberry v. Lee, 311 U.S. at 40–41. There, certain property owners brought suit to enforce a restrictive covenant that purported to forbid the sale or lease of any property within a defined area to "any person of the colored race." Id., at 37–38. By its terms the covenant was not effective unless signed by the owners of 95 percent of frontage in the area. At trial, the defendants proved that the signers of the covenant owned only about 54 percent of the frontage. Nevertheless, the trial court held that the covenant was enforceable because the issue had been resolved in a prior suit in which the parties had stipulated that the owners of 95 percent had signed. Id., at 38 (referring to Burke v. Kleiman, 277 Ill.App. 519 (1934)).

Despite the fact that the stipulation was untrue, the Illinois Supreme Court held that the second action was barred by res judicata. See Lee v. Hansberry, 372 Ill. 369, 24 N.E.2d 37 (1939). Because the plaintiff in the earlier case had alleged that she was proceeding "on behalf of

---

1. Of course, mere notice may not suffice to preserve one's right to be heard in a case such as the one before us. The general rule is that "the law does not impose upon any person absolutely entitled to a hearing the burden of voluntary intervention in a suit to which he is a stranger." Chase Nat. Bank v. Norwalk, 291 U.S. 431, 441, 78 L.Ed. 894, 54 S.Ct. 475 (1934); but cf. Penn-Central Merger and N & W Inclusion Cases, 389 U.S. 486, 505, n. 4, 19 L.Ed.2d 723, 88 S.Ct. 602 (1968) (noting that absent parties were invited to intervene by the court).

herself and on behalf of all other property owners in the district," id., at
372, 24 N.E.2d at 39, the Illinois Supreme Court concluded that all
members of that "class," including the defendants challenging the
stipulation in the present action, were bound by the decree. We reversed.

We recognized the "familiar doctrine ... that members of a class
not present as parties to the litigation may be bound by the judgment
where they are in fact adequately represented by parties who are
present, or ... the relationship between the parties present and those
who are absent is such as legally to entitle the former to stand in
judgment for the latter." Hansberry, 311 U.S. at 42–43. We concluded,
however, that because the interests of those class members who had
been a party to the prior litigation were in conflict with the absent
members who were the defendants in the subsequent action, the doctrine of representation of absent parties in a class suit could not support
the decree.

Even assuming that our opinion in Hansberry may be read to leave
open the possibility that in some class suits adequate representation
might cure a lack of notice, but cf., id., at 40; Eisen v. Carlisle &
Jacquelin, 417 U.S. 156, 177, 40 L.Ed.2d 732, 94 S.Ct. 2140 (1974);
Mullane v. Central Hanover Bank & Trust Co., 339 U.S. at 319, it may
not be read to permit the application of res judicata here. Our opinion
explained that a prior proceeding, to have binding effect on absent
parties, would at least have to be "so devised and applied as to insure
that those present are of the same class as those absent and that the
litigation is so conducted as to insure the full and fair consideration of
the common issue." 311 U.S. at 43; cf. Phillips Petroleum Co. v. Shutts,
472 U.S. at 811–812. It is plain that the Bedingfield action, like the prior
proceeding in Hansberry itself, does not fit such a description.

The Alabama Supreme Court concluded that the "taxpayers in the
Bedingfield action adequately represented the interests of the taxpayers
here," 662 So.2d at 1130 (emphasis added), but the three county taxpayers who were parties in Bedingfield did not sue on behalf of a class; their
pleadings did not purport to assert any claim against or on behalf of any
nonparties; and the judgment they received did not purport to bind any
county taxpayers who were nonparties. That the acting director of
finance for the city of Birmingham also sued in his capacity as both an
individual taxpayer and a public official does not change the analysis.
Even if we were to assume, as the Alabama Supreme Court did not, that
by suing in his official capacity, the finance director intended to represent the pecuniary interests of all city taxpayers, and not simply the
corporate interests of the city itself, he did not purport to represent the
pecuniary interests of county taxpayers like petitioners. As a result,
there is no reason to suppose that the Bedingfield court took care to
protect the interests of petitioners in the manner suggested in Hansberry. Nor is there any reason to suppose that the individual taxpayers in
Bedingfield understood their suit to be on behalf of absent county

taxpayers. Thus, to contend that the plaintiffs in Bedingfield somehow represented petitioners, let alone represented them in a constitutionally adequate manner, would be "to attribute to them a power that it cannot be said that they had assumed to exercise." Hansberry, 311 U.S. at 46.

Because petitioners and the Bedingfield litigants are best described as mere "strangers" to one another, Martin v. Wilks, 490 U.S. at 762, we are unable to conclude that the Bedingfield plaintiffs provided representation sufficient to make up for the fact that petitioners neither participated in, see Montana v. United States, 440 U.S. 147, 154, 59 L.Ed.2d 210, 99 S.Ct. 970 (1979), nor had the opportunity to participate in, the Bedingfield action. Accordingly, due process prevents the former from being bound by the latter's judgment.

IV

Respondents contend that, even if petitioners did not receive the kind of opportunity to make their case in court that due process would ordinarily ensure, the character of their action renders the usual constitutional protections inapplicable. They contend that invalidation of the occupation tax would have disastrous consequences on the county, which has made substantial commitments of tax revenues based on its understanding that Bedingfield determined the constitutionality of the tax. Respondents argue that in cases raising a public issue of this kind, the people may properly be regarded as the real party in interest and thus that petitioners received all the process they were due in the Bedingfield action.

Our answer requires us to distinguish between two types of actions brought by taxpayers. In one category are cases in which the taxpayer is using that status to entitle him to complain about an alleged misuse of public funds, see, e.g., Massachusetts v. Mellon, 262 U.S. 447, 486–489, 67 L.Ed. 1078, 43 S.Ct. 597 (1923), or about other public action that has only an indirect impact on his interests, e.g., Stromberg v. Board of Ed. of Bratenahl, 64 Ohio St.2d 98, 413 N.E.2d 1184 (1980); Tallassee v. State ex rel. Brunson, 206 Ala. 169, 89 So. 514 (1921). As to this category of cases, we may assume that the States have wide latitude to establish procedures not only to limit the number of judicial proceedings that may be entertained but also to determine whether to accord a taxpayer any standing at all.

Because the guarantee of due process is not a mere form, however, there obviously exists another category of taxpayer cases in which the State may not deprive individual litigants of their own day in court. By virtue of presenting a federal constitutional challenge to a State's attempt to levy personal funds, petitioners clearly bring an action of this latter type. Cf. ibid. (distinguishing between "public" and "private" actions). Indeed, we have previously struck down as a violation of due process a state court's decision denying an individual taxpayer any practicable opportunity to contest a tax on federal constitutional grounds. See Brinkerhoff–Faris Trust & Sav. Co. v. Hill, 281 U.S. 673, 74 L.Ed. 1107, 50 S.Ct. 451 (1930). There, we explained:

"We are not now concerned with the rights of the plaintiff on the merits, although it may be observed that the plaintiff's claim is one arising under the Federal Constitution and, consequently, one on which the opinion of the state court is not final. . . . Our present concern is solely with the question whether the plaintiff has been accorded due process in the primary sense,—whether it has had an opportunity to present its case and be heard in its support. . . . While it is for the state courts to determine the adjective as well as the substantive law of the State, they must, in so doing, accord the parties due process of law. Whether acting through its judiciary or through its legislature, a State may not deprive a person of all existing remedies for the enforcement of a right, which the State has no power to destroy, unless there is, or was, afforded to him some real opportunity to protect it." Id., at 681–682.

In any event, the Alabama Supreme Court did not hold here that petitioners' suit was of a kind that, under state law, could be brought only on behalf of the public at large. Cf. Corprew v. Tallapoosa County, 241 Ala. 492, 3 So.2d 53 (1941) (discussing state statutory quo warranto proceedings). To conclude that the suit may nevertheless be barred by the prior action in Bedingfield would thus be to deprive petitioners of their "chose in action," which we have held to be a protected property interest in its own right. See Logan v. Zimmerman Brush Co., 455 U.S. 422, 429–430, 71 L.Ed.2d 265, 102 S.Ct. 1148 (1982); Phillips Petroleum Co. v. Shutts, 472 US. at 812 (relying on Mullane v. Central Hanover Bank & Trust Co., 339 U.S. 306, 94 L.Ed. 865, 70 S.Ct. 652 (1950)); Hansberry v. Lee, 311 U.S. at 37. Thus, we are not persuaded that the nature of petitioners' action permits us to deviate from the traditional rule that an extreme application of state-law res judicata principles violates the Federal Constitution.

Of course, we are aware that governmental and private entities have substantial interests in the prompt and determinative resolution of challenges to important legislation. We do not agree with the Alabama Supreme Court, however, that, given the amount of money at stake, respondents were entitled to rely on the assumption that the Bedingfield action "authoritatively established" the constitutionality of the tax. 662 So.2d at 1130. A state court's freedom to rely on prior precedent in rejecting a litigant's claims does not afford it similar freedom to bind a litigant to a prior judgment to which he was not a party. That general rule clearly applies when a taxpayer seeks a hearing to prevent the State from subjecting him to a levy in violation of the Federal Constitution.

V

Because petitioners received neither notice of, nor sufficient representation in, the Bedingfield litigation, that adjudication, as a matter of federal due process, may not bind them and thus cannot bar them from challenging an allegedly unconstitutional deprivation of their property. Accordingly, the judgment of the Alabama Supreme Court is reversed, and the case is remanded to that court for further proceedings not inconsistent with this opinion.

It is so ordered.

NOTE

(1) Since, in the principal case, the first action was not a class action, how could the judgment in that case possibly bind the plaintiffs in the second case? Would the result have been different if the first action had been a class action?

(2) Does the Court's stress, in the principal case, on the circumstance that the plaintiffs in the second action had not received notice of the first action warrant the conclusion that they could have been held bound by the first judgment if such notice had been given? See Note (3) on p. 451 of the Casebook.

[On page 542, at the bottom of the page, add:]

9.   SPECIAL RULES FOR SPECIAL CLASS ACTION

On December 22, 1995, the U.S. Congress enacted a special treat for the securities industry, the Private Securities Litigation Reform Act of 1995, 104 P.L. 67, 109 Stat. 737.

The Act contains detailed provisions applicable to plaintiff class actions brought under the 1933 Securities Act. It regulates in great detail such questions as who might be appointed as lead plaintiff, what discovery may be had during the pendency of a motion to dismiss, what sanctions are to be applied for abusive litigation, what notices are to be given, how attorney's fees are to be determined, the maximum amount of damages that may be recovered, to what extent liability may attach for forward looking statements, what referrals and referral fees are proper, how coercive settlements are to be treated and how liability is to be proportioned. Is this a desirable way of dealing with perceived disadvantages of class actions? See generally, Kahan and Silberman, Matsushita and Beyond: The Role of State Courts in Class Actions Involving Exclusive Federal Claims, 1997 S.Ct.Rev. 219.

Part IV

PRELIMINARIES TO THE TRIAL

Chapter Nine

PLEADING

SECTION 4. HONESTY IN PLEADING

C. CERTIFICATION

[Insert on p. 566 in lieu of the material on pp. 566–572:]

Another way to motivate parties to plead accurately is through certification requirements, which deem the signature on pleadings and other documents as representing that some level of care was taken in formulating the allegations made. Usually, it is the attorney who signs the pleadings; unrepresented parties sign for themselves. Certification has had a checkered career within the federal system. As originally drafted, Rule 11 imposed a subjective standard of care that allowed attorneys with kind hearts but empty heads to file anything they wished. Moreover, although a failure to file with subjective good faith could lead to disciplinary action against the attorney, such actions were rarely brought. Similarly, pleadings that did not conform with the Rule could be struck, but rarely were. Courts were simply unwilling to destroy an attorney's livelihood for pleading irregularities. Nor were they eager to destroy or distort a litigant's case because of errors on the part of the attorney.

As dockets got more crowded and abuse of the adjudicatory system was perceived as more of a problem, the Advisory Committee decided to write a Rule with more bite. The 1983 version of Rule 11 imposed an objective standard that was meant to require attorneys to stop and think before they filed. "To the best of the signer's knowledge, information and belief formed after reasonable inquiry," the pleading was to be "well grounded in fact and ... warranted by existing law or a good faith argument for the extension, modification, or reversal of existing law, and ... not imposed for any improper purpose, such as to harass or to cause unnecessary delay or needlessly increase ... the cost of litigation." A new sanction was devised: the court was to order the attorney (or the party) that failed to meet the new standard to pay the expense that the failure imposed on the other side.

As the next case and the notes that follow it demonstrate, the new version created more problems than it solved. Following these cases, the 1993 version of Rule 11 will be discussed.

[Insert on page 567, in lieu of *Zaldivar* :]

COOTER & GELL v. HARTMARX CORPORATION

Supreme Court of the United States, 1990.
496 U.S. 384, 110 S.Ct. 2447, 110 L.Ed.2d 359.

JUSTICE O'CONNOR delivered the opinion of the Court.*

This case presents three issues related to the application of Rule 11 of the Federal Rules of Civil Procedure: whether a district court may impose Rule 11 sanctions on a plaintiff who has voluntarily dismissed his complaint pursuant to Rule 41(a)(1)(i) of the Federal Rules of Civil Procedure; what constitutes the appropriate standard of appellate review of a district court's imposition of Rule 11 sanctions; and whether Rule 11 authorizes awards of attorney's fees incurred on appeal of a Rule 11 sanction.

I

In 1983, Danik, Inc., owned and operated a number of discount men's clothing stores in the Washington, D.C., area. In June 1983, Intercontinental Apparel, a subsidiary of respondent Hartmarx Corp., brought a breach-of-contract action against Danik in the United States District Court for the District of Columbia. Danik, represented by the law firm of Cooter & Gell (petitioner), responded to the suit by filing a counterclaim against Intercontinental, alleging violations of the Robinson–Patman Act, 49 Stat. 1526, 15 U.S.C. § 13. In March 1984, the District Court granted summary judgment for Intercontinental in its suit against Danik, and, in February 1985, a jury returned a verdict for Intercontinental on Danik's counterclaim. Both judgments were affirmed on appeal. . . .

While this litigation was proceeding, petitioner prepared two additional antitrust complaints against Hartmarx and its two subsidiaries, respondents Hart, Schaffner & Marx and Hickey–Freeman Co. One of the complaints, the one giving rise to the Rule 11 sanction at issue in this case, alleged a nationwide conspiracy to fix prices and to eliminate competition through an exclusive retail agent policy and uniform pricing scheme, as well as other unfair competition practices such as resale price maintenance and territorial restrictions. . . .

---

* Footnotes omitted.

Petitioner filed the two complaints in November 1983. Respondents moved to dismiss the antitrust complaint at issue, alleging, among other things, that Danik's allegations had no basis in fact. Respondents also moved for sanctions under Rule 11. In opposition to the Rule 11 motion, petitioner filed three affidavits setting forth the prefiling research that supported the allegations in the complaint. . . .

In essence, petitioner's research consisted of telephone calls to salespersons in a number of men's clothing stores in New York City, Philadelphia, Baltimore, and Washington, D.C. Petitioner inferred from this research that only one store in each major metropolitan area nationwide sold Hart, Schaffner & Marx suits.

In April 1984, petitioner filed a notice of voluntary dismissal of the complaint, pursuant to Rule 41(a)(1)(i). The dismissal became effective in July 1984, when the District Court granted petitioner's motion to dispense with notice of dismissal to putative class members. In June 1984, before the dismissal became effective, the District Court heard oral argument on the Rule 11 motion. The District Court took the Rule 11 motion under advisement.

In December 1987, 3½ years after its hearing on the motion and after dismissal of the complaint, the District Court ordered respondents to submit a statement of costs and attorney's fees. Respondents filed a statement requesting $61,917.99 in attorney's fees. Two months later, the District Court granted respondent's motion for Rule 11 sanctions, holding that petitioner's prefiling inquiry was grossly inadequate. Specifically, the District Court found that the allegations in the complaint regarding exclusive retail agency arrangements for Hickey–Freeman clothing were completely baseless because petitioner researched only the availability of Hart, Schaffner & Marx menswear. In addition, the District Court found that petitioner's limited survey of only four Eastern cities did not support the allegation that respondents had exclusive retailer agreements in every major city in the United States. Accordingly, the District Court determined that petitioner violated Rule 11 and imposed a sanction of $21,452.52 against petitioner and $10,701.26 against Danik.

The Court of Appeals for the District of Columbia Circuit affirmed the imposition of Rule 11 sanctions [and, after affirming the district court's determination that petitioner had violated Rule 11] held that an appellant who successfully defends a Rule 11 award was entitled to recover its attorney's fees on appeal and remanded the case to the district court to determine the amount of reasonable attorney's fees and to enter an appropriate award.

II

* * *

An interpretation of the current Rule 11 must be guided, in part, by an understanding of the deficiencies in the original version of Rule 11 that led to its revision. The 1938 version of Rule 11 required an attorney to certify by signing the pleading "that to the best of his knowledge, information, and belief there is good ground to support [the pleading]; and that it is not interposed for delay ... or is signed with intent to defeat the purpose of this rule." 28 U.S.C., pp. 2616–2617 (1940 ed.) An attorney who willfully violated the rule could be "subjected to appropriate disciplinary action." Ibid. Moreover, the pleading could "be stricken as sham and false and the action [could] proceed as though the pleading had not been served." Ibid. In operation, the rule did not have the deterrent effect expected by its drafters. See Advisory Committee Note on Rule 11, 28 U.S.C.App., pp. 575–576. The Advisory Committee identified two problems with the old Rule. First, the Rule engendered confusion regarding when a pleading should be struck, what standard of conduct would make an attorney liable to sanctions, and what sanctions were available. Second, courts were reluctant to impose disciplinary measures on attorneys, see ibid., and attorneys were slow to invoke the rule. Vairo, Rule 11: A Critical Analysis, 118 F.R.D. 189, 191 (1988).

To ameliorate these problems, and in response to concerns that abusive litigation practices abounded in the federal courts, the rule was amended in 1983. See Schwarzer, Sanctions Under the New Federal Rule 11—A Closer Look, 104 F.R.D. 181 (1985). It is now clear that the central purpose of Rule 11 is to deter baseless filings in District Court and thus, consistent with the Rule Enabling Act's grant of authority, streamline the administration and procedure of the federal courts. See Advisory Committee Note on Rule 11, 28 U.S.C.App., p. 576. Rule 11 imposes a duty on attorneys to certify that they have conducted a reasonable inquiry and have determined that any papers filed with the court are well-grounded in fact, legally tenable, and "not interposed for any improper purpose." An attorney who signs the paper without such a substantiated belief "shall" be penalized by "an appropriate sanction." Such a sanction may, but need not, include payment of the other parties' expenses. See ibid. Although the rule must be read in light of concerns that it will spawn satellite litigation and chill vigorous advocacy, ibid., any interpretation must give effect to the rule's central goal of deterrence.

III

We first address the question whether petitioner's dismissal of its antitrust complaint pursuant to Rule 41(a)(1)(i) deprived the District Court of the jurisdiction to award attorney's fees....

Petitioner contends that filing a notice of voluntary dismissal pursuant to this rule automatically deprives a court of jurisdiction over the action, rendering the court powerless to impose sanctions thereafter. Of the Circuit Courts to consider this issue, only the Court of Appeals for the Second Circuit has held that a voluntary dismissal acts as a jurisdictional bar to further Rule 11 proceedings. See Johnson Chemical Co., Inc. v. Home Care Products, Inc., 823 F.2d 28, 31 (1987).

The view more consistent with Rule 11's language and purposes, and the one supported by the weight of Circuit authority, is that district courts may enforce Rule 11 even after the plaintiff has filed a notice of dismissal under Rule 41(a)(1). See Szabo Food Service, Inc. v. Canteen Corp., 823 F.2d 1073, 1076–1079 (C.A.7 1987), cert. dism'd, 485 U.S. 901, 108 S.Ct. 1101, 99 L.Ed.2d 229 (1988); Greenberg v. Sala, 822 F.2d 882, 885 (C.A.9 1987); Muthig v. Brant Point Nantucket, Inc., 838 F.2d 600, 603–604 (C.A.1 1988). The district court's jurisdiction, invoked by the filing of the underlying complaint, supports consideration of both the merits of the action and the motion for Rule 11 sanctions arising from that filing. As the "violation of Rule 11 is complete when the paper is filed," Szabo Food Service, Inc., 823 F.2d, at 1077, a voluntary dismissal does not expunge the Rule 11 violation. In order to comply with Rule 11's requirement that a court "shall" impose sanctions "[i]f a pleading, motion, or other paper is signed in violation of this rule," a court must have the authority to consider whether there has been a violation of the signing requirement regardless of the dismissal of the underlying action. In our view, nothing in the language of Rule 41(a)(1)(i), Rule 11, or other statute or Federal Rule terminates a district court's authority to impose sanctions after such a dismissal.

It is well established that a federal court may consider collateral issues after an action is no longer pending. For example, district courts may award costs after an action is dismissed for want of jurisdiction. See 28 U.S.C. § 1919. This Court has indicated that motions for costs or attorney's fees are "independent proceeding[s] supplemental to the original proceeding and not a request for a modification of the original decree." Sprague v. Ticonic National Bank, 307 U.S. 161, 170, 59 S.Ct. 777, 781, 83 L.Ed. 1184 (1939). Thus, even "years after the entry of a judgment on the merits" a federal court could consider an award of counsel fees. White v. New Hampshire Dept. of Employment Security, 455 U.S. 445, 451, n. 13, 102 S.Ct. 1162, 1166, n. 13, 71 L.Ed.2d 325 (1982). A criminal contempt charge is likewise " 'a separate and independent proceeding at law' " that is not part of the original action. Bray v. United States, 423 U.S. 73, 75, 96 S.Ct. 307, 309, 46 L.Ed.2d 215 (1975), quoting Gompers v. Bucks Stove & Range Co., 221 U.S. 418, 445, 31 S.Ct. 492, 499, 55 L.Ed. 797 (1911). A court may make an adjudication of contempt and impose a contempt sanction even after the action in which the contempt arose has been terminated. See United States v. Mine Workers, 330 U.S. 258, 294, 67 S.Ct. 677, 696, 91 L.Ed. 884 (1947) ("Violations of an order are punishable as criminal contempt even though ... the basic action has become moot"); Gompers v. Bucks Stove & Range Co., supra, 451, 31 S.Ct., at 502 (when main case was settled, action became moot, "of course without prejudice to the power and right of the court to punish for contempt by proper proceedings"). Like the imposition of costs, attorney's fees, and contempt sanctions, the imposition of a Rule 11 sanction is not a judgment on the merits of an action. Rather, it requires the determination of a collateral issue: whether the attorney has abused the judicial process, and, if so, what sanction would be appropriate. Such a determination may be made after the principal suit has been terminated.

Because a Rule 11 sanction does not signify a District Court's assessment of the legal merits of the complaint, the imposition of such a sanction after a voluntary dismissal does not deprive the plaintiff of his right under Rule 41(a) to dismiss an action without prejudice. "Dismissal without prejudice" is a dismissal that does not "operat[e] as an adjudication upon the merits," Rule 41(a)(1), and thus does not have a res judicata effect. Even if a district court indicated that a complaint was not legally tenable or factually well founded for Rule 11 purposes, the resulting Rule 11 sanction would nevertheless not preclude the refiling of a complaint. Indeed, even if the Rule 11 sanction imposed by the court were a prohibition against refiling the complaint (assuming that would be an "appropriate sanction" for Rule 11 purposes), the preclusion of refiling would be neither a consequence of the dismissal (which was without prejudice) nor a "term or condition" placed upon the dismissal (which was unconditional), see Rule 41(a)(2).

* * *

Both Rule 41(a)(1) and Rule 11 are aimed at curbing abuses of the judicial system, and thus their policies, like their language, are completely compatible. Rule 41(a)(1) limits a litigant's power to dismiss actions, but allows one dismissal without prejudice. Rule 41(a)(1) does not codify any policy that the plaintiff's right to one free dismissal also secures the right to file baseless papers. The filing of complaints, papers, or other motions without taking the necessary care in their preparation is a separate abuse of the judicial system, subject to separate sanction. . . .

IV

Petitioner further contends that the Court of Appeals did not apply a sufficiently rigorous standard in reviewing the District Court's imposition of Rule 11 sanctions. Determining whether an attorney has violated Rule 11 involves a consideration of three types of issues. The court must consider factual questions regarding the nature of the attorney's prefiling inquiry and the factual basis of the pleading or other paper. Legal issues are raised in considering whether a pleading is "warranted by existing law or a good faith argument" for changing the law and whether the attorney's conduct violated Rule 11. Finally, the district court must exercise its discretion to tailor an "appropriate sanction."

The Court of Appeals in this case did not specify the applicable standard of review. There is, however, precedent in the District of Columbia Circuit for applying an abuse of discretion standard to the determination whether a filing had an insufficient factual basis or was interposed for an improper purpose, but reviewing de novo the question whether a pleading or motion is legally sufficient. See, e.g., International Brotherhood of Teamsters, Chauffeurs, Warehousemen & Helpers of America (Airline Div.) v. Association of Flight Attendants, 274 U.S.App. D.C. 370, 373, 864 F.2d 173, 176 (1988); Westmoreland v. CBS, Inc., 248 U.S.App.D.C., at 261, 770 F.2d, at 1174–1175. Petitioner contends that the Court of Appeals for the Ninth Circuit has adopted the appropriate approach. That Circuit reviews findings of historical fact under the clearly erroneous standard, the determination that counsel violated Rule 11 under a de novo standard, and the choice of sanction under an abuse-of-discretion standard. See Zaldivar v. Los Angeles, 780 F.2d 823, 828 (C.A.9 1986). The majority of Circuits follow neither approach; rather, they apply a deferential standard to all issues raised by a Rule 11 violation. See Kale v. Combined Ins. Co. of America, 861 F.2d 746, 757–758 (C.A.1 1988); Teamsters Local Union No. 430 v. Cement Express, Inc., 841 F.2d 66, 68 (C.A.3 1988), cert. denied, 488 U.S. 848, 109 S.Ct. 128, 102 L.Ed.2d 101 (1988); Stevens v. Lawyers Mutual Liability Ins. Co. of North Carolina, 789 F.2d 1056, 1060 (C.A.4 1986); Thomas v. Capital Security Services, Inc., 836 F.2d 866, 872 (C.A.5 1988) (en banc); Century Products, Inc. v. Sutter, 837 F.2d 247, 250 (C.A.6 1988); Mars Steel Corp. v. Continental Bank N.A., 880 F.2d 928, 933 (C.A.7 1989); Adamson v. Bowen, 855 F.2d 668, 673 (C.A.10 1988).

Although the Courts of Appeal use different verbal formulas to characterize their standards of review, the scope of actual disagreement is narrow. No dispute exists that the appellate courts should review the district court's selection of a sanction under a deferential standard. In directing the district court to impose an "appropriate" sanction, Rule 11 itself indicates that the district court is empowered to exercise its discretion. See also Advisory Committee Note on Rule 11, 28 U.S.C.App., p. 576 (suggesting a district court "has discretion to tailor sanctions to the particular facts of the case, with which it should be well acquainted").

The Circuits also agree that, in the absence of any language to the contrary in Rule 11, courts should adhere to their usual practice of reviewing the district court's finding of facts under a deferential standard. See Fed.Rule Civ.Proc. 52(a) ("Findings of fact ... shall not be set aside unless clearly erroneous, and due regard shall be given to the opportunity of the trial court to judge of the credibility of the witnesses"). In practice, the "clearly erroneous" standard requires the appellate court to uphold any district court determination that falls within a broad range of permissible conclusions. See, e.g., Anderson v. Bessemer City, 470 U.S. 564, 573–574, 105 S.Ct. 1504, 1511–1512, 84

L.Ed.2d 518 (1985) ("If the district court's account of the evidence is plausible in light of the record viewed in its entirety, the court of appeals may not reverse it even though convinced that had it been sitting as the trier of fact, it would have weighed the evidence differently. Where there are two permissible views of the evidence, the factfinder's choice between them cannot be clearly erroneous"); Inwood Laboratories, Inc., v. Ives Laboratories, Inc., 456 U.S. 844, 857–858, 102 S.Ct. 2182, 2190–2191, 72 L.Ed.2d 606 (1982). When an appellate court reviews a district court's factual findings, the abuse of discretion and clearly erroneous standards are indistinguishable: A court of appeals would be justified in concluding that a district court had abused its discretion in making a factual finding only if the finding were clearly erroneous.

The scope of disagreement over the appropriate standard of review can thus be confined to a narrow issue: whether the court of appeals must defer to the district court's legal conclusions in Rule 11 proceedings. A number of factors have led the majority of Circuits, see supra, at, as well as a number of commentators, see, e.g., C. Shaffer & P. Sandler, Sanctions: Rule 11 and Other Powers 14–15 (2d ed. 1988) (hereinafter Shaffer & Sandler); American Judicature Society, Rule 11 in Transition, The Report of the Third Circuit Task Force on Federal Rule of Civil Procedure 11, 45–49 (Burbank, reporter 1989), to conclude that appellate courts should review all aspects of a district court's imposition of Rule 11 sanctions under a deferential standard.

The Court has long noted the difficulty of distinguishing between legal and factual issues. See Pullman–Standard v. Swint, 456 U.S. 273, 288, 102 S.Ct. 1781, 1789, 72 L.Ed.2d 66 (1982) ("Rule 52(a) does not furnish particular guidance with respect to distinguishing law from fact. Nor do we yet know of any other rule or principle that will unerringly distinguish a factual finding from a legal conclusion"). Making such distinctions is particularly difficult in the Rule 11 context. Rather than mandating an inquiry into purely legal questions, such as whether the attorney's legal argument was correct, the rule requires a court to consider issues rooted in factual determinations. For example, to determine whether an attorney's prefiling inquiry was reasonable, a court must consider all the circumstances of a case. An inquiry that is unreasonable when an attorney has months to prepare a complaint may be reasonable when he has only a few days before the statute of limitations runs. In considering whether a complaint was supported by fact and law "to the best of the signer's knowledge, information, and belief," a court must make some assessment of the signer's credibility. Issues involving credibility are normally considered factual matters. See Fed.Rule Civ.Proc. 52; see also United States v. Oregon Medical Society, 343 U.S. 326, 332, 72 S.Ct. 690, 695, 96 L.Ed. 978 (1952). The considerations involved in the Rule 11 context are similar to those involved in determining negligence, which is generally reviewed deferentially. See Mars Steel Corp. v. Continental Bank, N.A., supra, at 932;

see also 9 C. Wright & A. Miller, Federal Practice and Procedure § 2590 (1971); McAllister v. United States, 348 U.S. 19, 20–22, 75 S.Ct. 6, 7–9, 99 L.Ed. 20 (1954) (holding that the District Court's findings of negligence were not clearly erroneous). Familiar with the issues and litigants, the district court is better situated than the court of appeals to marshall the pertinent facts and apply the fact-dependent legal standard mandated by Rule 11. Of course, this standard would not preclude the appellate court's correction of a district court's legal errors, e.g., determining that Rule 11 sanctions could be imposed upon the signing attorney's law firm, see Pavelic & LeFlore v. Marvel Entertainment Group, 493 U.S. 120, 110 S.Ct. 456, 107 L.Ed.2d 438 (1989), or relying on a materially incorrect view of the relevant law in determining that a pleading was not "warranted by existing law or a good faith argument" for changing the law. An appellate court would be justified in concluding that, in making such errors, the district court abused its discretion. "[I]f a district court's findings rest on an erroneous view of the law, they may be set aside on that basis." Pullman–Standard v. Swint, 456 U.S., supra, at 287, 102 S.Ct. at 1789. See also Icicle Seafoods, Inc. v. Worthington, 475 U.S. 709, 714, 106 S.Ct. 1527, 1530, 89 L.Ed.2d 739 (1986) ("If [the Court of Appeals] believed that the District Court's factual findings were unassailable, but that the proper rule of law was misapplied to those findings, it could have reversed the District Court's judgment").

Pierce v. Underwood, 487 U.S. 552, 108 S.Ct. 2541, 101 L.Ed.2d 490 (1988), strongly, supports applying a unitary abuse of discretion standard to all aspects of a Rule 11 proceeding. In *Pierce*, the Court held a District Court's determination under the Equal Access to Justice Act (EAJA), 28 U.S.C. § 2412(d) (1982 ed.), that "the position of the United States was substantially justified" should be reviewed for an abuse of discretion. As a position is "substantially justified" if it "has a reasonable basis in law and fact," 487 U.S., at 566, n. 2, 108 S.Ct., at 2550, n. 2, EAJA requires an inquiry similar to the Rule 11 inquiry as to whether a pleading is "well grounded in fact" and legally tenable. Although the EAJA and Rule 11 are not completely analogous, the reasoning in Pierce is relevant for determining the Rule 11 standard of review.

Two factors the Court found significant in *Pierce* are equally pertinent here. First, the Court indicated that " 'as a matter of the sound administration of justice,' " deference was owed to the " 'judicial actor . . . better positioned than another to decide the issue in question.' " 487 U.S., at 559–560, 108 S.Ct., at 2547, quoting Miller v. Fenton, 474 U.S. 104, 114, 106 S.Ct. 445, 451, 88 L.Ed.2d 405 (1985). Because a determination whether a legal position is "substantially justified" depends greatly on factual determinations, the Court reasoned that the district court was "better positioned" to make such factual determinations. See 487 U.S., at 560, 108 S.Ct., at 2547. A district court's ruling that a litigant's position is factually well grounded and legally tenable for

Rule 11 purposes is similarly fact-specific. Pierce also concluded that district court's rulings on legal issues should be reviewed deferentially. See id., at 560–561, 108 S.Ct. at 2547–2548. According to the Court, review of legal issues under a de novo standard would require the courts of appeals to invest time and energy in the unproductive task of determining "not what the law now is, but what the Government was substantially justified in believing it to have been." Ibid. Likewise, an appellate court reviewing legal issues in the Rule 11 context would be required to determine whether, at the time the attorney filed the pleading or other paper, his legal argument would have appeared plausible. Such determinations "will either fail to produce the normal law-clarifying benefits that come from an appellate decision on a question of law, or else will strangely distort the appellate process" by establishing circuit law in "a most peculiar, secondhanded fashion." Id., at 561, 108 S.Ct., at 2548.

Second, *Pierce* noted that only deferential review gave the district court the necessary flexibility to resolve questions involving " 'multifarious, fleeting, special, narrow facts that utterly resist generalization.' " Id., at 561–562, 108 S.Ct., at 2548. The question whether the government has taken a "substantially justified" position under all the circumstances involves the consideration of unique factors that are "little susceptible … of useful generalization." Ibid. The issues involved in determining whether an attorney has violated Rule 11 likewise involve "fact-intensive, close calls." Shaffer & Sandler 15. Contrary to petitioner's contentions, Pierce v. Underwood is not distinguishable on the ground that sanctions under Rule 11 are mandatory: that sanctions "shall" be imposed when a violation is found does not have any bearing on how to review the question whether the attorney's conduct violated Rule 11.

Rule 11's policy goals also support adopting an abuse-of-discretion standard. The district court is best acquainted with the local bar's litigation practices and thus best situated to determine when a sanction is warranted to serve Rule 11's goal of specific and general deterrence. Deference to the determination of courts on the front lines of litigation will enhance these courts' ability to control the litigants before them. Such deference will streamline the litigation process by freeing appellate courts from the duty of reweighing evidence and reconsidering facts already weighed and considered by the district court; it will also discourage litigants from pursuing marginal appeals, thus reducing the amount of satellite litigation.

Although district court's identification of what conduct violates Rule 11 may vary, see Schwarzer, Rule 11 Revisited, 101 Harv.L.Rev. 1013, 1015–1017 (1988); Note, A Uniform Approach to Rule 11 Sanctions, 97 Yale L.J. 901 (1988), some variation in the application of a standard based on reasonableness is inevitable. "Fact-bound resolutions cannot be made uniform through appellate review, de novo or otherwise." Mars

Steel Corp. v. Continental Bank N.A., 880 F.2d, at 936; see also Shaffer & Sandler 14–15. An appellate court's review of whether a legal position was reasonable are plausible enough under the circumstances is unlikely to establish clear guidelines for lower courts; nor will it clarify the underlying principles of law. See *Pierce,* supra, at 560–561, 108 S.Ct., at 2547–2548.

In light of our consideration of the purposes and policies of Rule 11 and in accordance with our analysis of analogous EAJA provisions, we reject petitioner's contention that the Court of Appeals should have applied a three-tiered standard of review. Rather, an appellate court should apply an abuse-of-discretion standard in reviewing all aspects of a district court's Rule 11 determination. A district court would necessarily abuse its discretion if it based its ruling on an erroneous view of the law or on a clearly erroneous assessment of the evidence. Here, the Court of Appeals determined that the District Court "applied the correct legal standard and offered substantial justification for its finding of a Rule 11 violation." 277 U.S.App.D.C., at 339, 875 F.2d, at 896. Its affirmance of the District Court's liability determination is consistent with the deferential standard we adopt today.

V

    * * *

On its face, Rule 11 does not apply to appellate proceedings. Its provision allowing the court to include "an order to pay to the other party or parties the amount of the reasonable expenses, incurred because of the filing of the pleading, motion, or other paper, including a reasonable attorney's fee" must be interpreted in light of Federal Rule of Civil Procedure 1, which indicates that the rules only "govern the procedure in the United States district courts." Neither the language of Rule 11 nor the Advisory Committee Note suggests that the Rule could require payment for any activities outside the context of district court proceedings. . . .

The Federal Rules of Appellate Procedure place a natural limit on Rule 11's scope. On appeal, the litigants' conduct is governed by Federal Rule of Appellate Procedure 38, which provides: "If a court of appeals shall determine that an appeal is frivolous, it may award just damages and single or double costs to the appellee." If the appeal of a Rule 11 sanction is itself frivolous, Rule 38 gives appellate courts ample authority to award expenses. Indeed, because the district court has broad discretion to impose Rule 11 sanctions, appeals of such sanctions may frequently be frivolous. See 9 J. Moore, B. Ward, & J. Lucas, Moore's Federal Practice ¶ 238.03[2] pp. 38–13, 38–14 (2d ed. 1989) ("[W]here an appeal challenges actions or findings of the district court to which an appellate court gives deference by judging under an abuse of discretion or clearly erroneous standard, the court is more likely to find that the appellant's arguments are frivolous"). If the appeal is not frivolous under this standard, Rule 38 does not require the appellee to pay the appellant's attorney's fees. Respondent's interpretation of Rule 11 would give a district court the authority to award attorney's fees to the appellee even when the appeal would not be sanctioned under the appellate rules. To avoid this somewhat anomalous result, Rules 11 and 38 are better read together as allowing expenses incurred on appeal to be shifted onto appellants only when those expenses are caused by a frivolous appeal, and not merely because a Rule 11 sanction upheld on appeal can ultimately be traced to a baseless filing in district court.

* * *

We affirm the Court of Appeals' conclusion that a voluntary dismissal does not deprive a district court of jurisdiction over a Rule 11 motion and hold that an appellate court should review the district court's decision in a Rule 11 proceeding for an abuse of discretion. As Rule 11 does not authorize a district court to award attorneys' fees incurred on appeal, we reverse that portion of the Court of Appeals' judgment remanding the case to the district court for a determination of reasonable appellate expenses. For the foregoing reasons, the judgment of the court below is affirmed in part and reversed in part.

* * *

JUSTICE STEVENS, concurring in part and dissenting in part.

Rule 11 and Rule 41(a)(1) are both designed to facilitate the just, speedy and inexpensive determination of cases in federal court. Properly understood, the two Rules should work in conjunction to prevent the prosecution of needless or baseless lawsuits. Rule 11 requires the court to impose an "appropriate sanction" on a litigant who wastes judicial resources by filing a pleading that is not well grounded in fact and warranted by existing law or a good-faith argument for its extension, modification or reversal. Rule 41(a)(1) permits a plaintiff who decides not to continue a lawsuit to withdraw his complaint before an answer or motion for summary judgment has been filed and avoid further proceedings on the basis of that complaint. The Court today, however, refuses to read the two Rules together in light of their limited, but valuable, purposes. By focusing on the filing of baseless complaints, without any attention to whether those complaints will result in the waste of judicial resources, the Court vastly expands the contours of Rule 11, eviscerates Rule 41(a)(1), and creates a federal common law of malicious prosecution inconsistent with the limited mandate of the Rules Enabling Act.

* * *

In theory, Rule 11 and Rule 41(a)(1) should work in tandem. When a complaint is withdrawn under Rule 41(a)(1), the merits of that complaint are not an appropriate area of further inquiry for the federal court. The predicate for the imposition of sanctions, the complaint, has been eliminated under the express authorization of the Federal Rules before the court has been required to take any action on it, and the consideration of a Rule 11 motion on a dismissed complaint would necessarily result in an increase in the judicial workload. When a plaintiff persists in the prosecution of a meritless complaint, however, or the defendant joins issue by filing an answer or motion for summary judgment, Rule 11 has a proper rule to play. The prosecution of baseless lawsuits and the filing of frivolous papers are matters of legitimate concern to the federal courts and are abuses that Rule 11 was designed to deter.

The Court holds, however, that a voluntary dismissal does not eliminate the predicate for a Rule 11 violation because a frivolous complaint that is withdrawn burdens "courts and individuals alike with needless expense and delay." Ante, at 11. That assumption is manifestly incorrect with respect to courts. The filing of a frivolous complaint which is voluntarily withdrawn imposes a burden on the court only if the notation of an additional civil proceeding on the court's docket sheet can be said to constitute a burden. By definition, a voluntary dismissal under rule 41(a)(1) means that the court has not had to consider the factual allegations of the complaint or ruled on a motion to dismiss its legal claims.

The Court's observation that individuals are burdened, even if correct, is irrelevant. Rule 11 is designed to deter parties from abusing judicial resources, not from filing complaints.

[Insert on page 572, in lieu of Notes (1) and (2):]

NOTES

(1) Other cases decided by the Supreme Court subsequent to the change in Rule 11 emphasize the reach of the duties imposed. In Pavelic & LeFlore v. Marvel Entertainment Group, 493 U.S. 120, 110 S.Ct. 456, 107 L.Ed.2d 438 (1989), the Court reasoned that in order to "bring home to the individual signer his personal, nondelegable responsibility ... to validate the truth and legal reasonableness of the document [he signs]," sanctions are imposed on the individual attorney who signed the pleading, rather than on the law firm of which the attorney is a member. Business Guides, Inc. v. Chromatic Communications Enterprises, Inc., 498 U.S. 533, 111 S.Ct. 922, 112 L.Ed.2d 1140 (1991), held that the litigants themselves can be sanctioned if they signed the pleadings without complying with the requirements of the Rule, even when they are represented by counsel. However, the Court emphasized that in determining reasonableness, the experience and sophistication of the party sanctioned should be taken into account.

See also Chambers v. NASCO, 501 U.S. 32, 111 S.Ct. 2123, 115 L.Ed.2d 27 (1991), infra, page 90 holding that federal courts possess inherent powers to fashion sanctions for bad-faith conduct not within the scope of Rule 11.

(2) Willy v. Coastal Corp., 503 U.S. 131, 112 S.Ct. 1076, 117 L.Ed.2d 280 (1992), raised the question whether a federal district court could impose sanctions under Fed.R.Civ.P. 11 in a case in which it is later determined that the court lacked subject matter adjudicatory authority. The Supreme Court held

that it could do so. The Court reasoned that since *judgments* rendered without subject matter adjudicatory authority are nonetheless enforceable (citing Chicot County Drainage District v. Baxter State Bank, 308 U.S. 371, 60 S.Ct. 317, 84 L.Ed. 329 (1940)), an order in a collateral matter is also enforceable despite lack of adjudicatory authority, especially since the order furthered the important interest in having rules of procedure obeyed.

NOTE ON THE 1993 AMENDMENT TO RULE 11

The new version of Rule 11 attempts to find a middle ground between the overly lax standard of the 1938 Rule and the harsh results reached under the 1983 version. Its implications are best understood by examining how it will change the results in the cited cases. Consider *Cooter & Gell*. It has been criticized for two reasons. First, it was claimed, the decision failed to take into account the fact that the objectionable pleading was a counterclaim. Although four telephone calls do not a conspiracy make, answers are due 20 days after service of process, Rule 12(a). That does not leave much time to discover a secret agreement. The new Rule looks to what is "reasonable under the circumstances," 11(b). Four calls may be reasonable for a counterclaim even if they would be insufficient basis for a complaint. In addition, 11(b)(3) allows the pleader to flag allegations that lack evidentiary support. In the *Cooter & Gell* case, this would have allowed the defendant to make the conspiracy claim without risking sanctions by simply identifying it as one requiring more support. Note, however, that the Rule now applies to "advocating" positions that lack support, 11(b). This language may be interpreted to require the firm to continue its inquiries and withdraw the pleading as soon as it becomes clear the conspiracy could not be proved.

A second criticism of *Cooter & Gell* is the one discussed by Justice Stevens, who noted that sanctioning voluntarily dismissed claims has the perverse effect of discouraging pleaders from withdrawing allegations. Under new 11(c)(1)(A), a Rule 11 motion cannot be filed until 21 days after it is served. During this 21–day "safe harbor," the pleader can withdraw the offending paper and avoid sanction.

Similarly, the new Rule deals with the argument that *Pavelic* and *Business Guides* sanctioned the wrong party. *Pavelic* imposed costs on an individual attorney rather than his law firm; critics argued that the Rule should have been interpreted so that the entire firm is enlisted in the effort to curb abusive practices. Under the new Rule's 11(c)(1)(A), absent exceptional circumstances, it is now the firm that is sanctioned. *Business Guides* sanctioned a represented party; 11(c)(2)(A) now makes clear that a represented party is entitled to rely on his attorney's assessment of the reasonableness of legal positions. Under this provision, only the attorney will be sanctioned for frivolous legal contentions.

The new version of Rule 11 does not expressly treat the *Willy* situation of imposition of sanctions by a court that lacks subject matter adjudicatory authority. The new Rule does, however, make it somewhat less likely that this situation will arise. First, the safe harbor provision gives the pleader an opportunity to withdraw the frivolous pleading. Second, the Rule now gives the sanctionable party an opportunity to be heard, 11(c). The need to hold a hearing on a case outside the court's authority may discourage courts from imposing such sanctions. Most importantly, the new Rule moves from a compensatory vision of sanctions to a deterrent vision. The compensatory impulse had the negative effect of encouraging parties to make Rule 11 motions to recover the costs of the action. Under the deterrence view, the sanction may provide less than full compensation: It could even be nonmonetary or paid into court, 11(c)(2). Now that there is less likelihood of recovering meaningful amounts, the volume of Rule 11 motions should decrease.

———

Will these changes preserve the benefits that Rule 11 is thought to provide? Justice Scalia, joined by Justice Thomas, dissented from the Supreme Court's approval of these amendments to Rule 11, stating in part:

> The proposed revision would render the Rule toothless, by allowing judges to dispense with sanction, by disfavoring compensation for litigation expenses, and by providing a 21–day "safe harbor" within which, if the party accused of a frivolous filing withdraws the filing, he is entitled to escape with no sanction at all.

>   * * *

> Finally, the likelihood that frivolousness will even be *challenged* is diminished by the proposed rule, which restricts the award of compensation to "unusual circumstances," with monetary sanctions "ordinarily" to be payable to the court.

146 F.R.D. 501, 507–509 (1993).

———

SECTION 5. THE COMPLAINT

———

C. SUBSTANTIVE LEGAL SUFFICIENCY

———

1. IN GENERAL

[Insert on page 596, after Note (2):]

(3) Leatherman v. Tarrant County Narcotics Intelligence and Coordination Unit, 507 U.S. 163, 113 S.Ct. 1160, 122 L.Ed.2d 517 (1993), represents another attempt by a lower court to protect municipalities with a heightened pleading

standard.   The District Court ordered a complaint dismissed because the § 1983 claim asserted by the plaintiff was based on "nothing more than a bare allegation that the individual officers' conduct conformed to official policy, custom, or practice."   The Supreme Court reversed the Fifth Circuit's affirmance, arguing that Rule 8(a)(2) requires only a short and plain statement of the claim; and that while Rule 9(b) imposes a particularity requirement, it does so only in connection with fraud and mistake.   Noting that "expressio unius est exclusio alterius," the Court suggested that Congress could amend the Federal Rules if it desired the result the lower court sought to achieve.

SECTION 7.   AMENDMENT

E.   STATUTE OF LIMITATIONS AND "RELATION BACK"

[Insert on page 626 after *Schiavone* :]

Congress has purportedly solved the problem in *Schiavone* through an amendment to Rule 15, which considers an action timely so long as the intended defendant is notified of it within the period allowed by Rule 4 for service of a summons and complaint, and so long as she is not prejudiced in her ability to defend the suit and she knew or should have known that but for the mistake, she would have been the party sued.   If a case comes only within the court's diversity jurisdiction, and the applicable state statute of limitations does not provide for relation back, will this proposal give rise to an *Erie* problem?   What if the relevant state law deems an action commenced for statute of limitations purposes when the summons is served, rather than when the action is filed: will the practice in diversity cases under Rule 15 conflict with practice in diversity cases where no mistake has been made?   See Ragan v. Merchants Transfer and Warehouse Co., casebook page 365, and Walker v. Armco Steel Corp., casebook page 383.

Chapter Eleven

OBTAINING INFORMATION BEFORE TRIAL

SECTION 1. BACKGROUND AND PERSPECTIVES

[Insert on page 660, in lieu of the paragraph that precedes *Dodson* :]

A few years after the curative amendments of 1970 took effect, a sharp change in the profession's view of the discovery rules surfaced. By the late 1970's the perception that discovery was often abusive had gathered wide support. The Advisory Committee's response was the introduction into the rules of limits on the scope of discovery and restrictions on how lawyers were to practice discovery. In addition, the amendments that became effective in 1980 and 1983 encouraged judges to take a more active role in enforcing restrictions. Still, discovery abuse was perceived to be on the increase. In 1990, Congress enacted the Civil Justice Reform Act, 28 U.S.C.A. §§ 471–482, which shifted some authority over rulemaking to the federal districts and encouraged them to search for alternative methods for conducting discovery. While these experiments were underway, in 1993, Congress enacted a comprehensive revision of the discovery rules.

DREYFUSS, THE WHAT AND WHY OF
THE NEW DISCOVERY RULES
46 Univ.Fla.L.Rev. 9, 10–21 (1994).[1]

* * *

I. THE NEW RULES

The December 1993 Amendments to the Federal Rules consist of a fairly large package of revisions . . . the primary significance [of which] is likely to be considered the revisions made to Rules 16 and 26–37. Together, these rules fundamentally alter the pretrial discovery period by effecting, essentially, three major changes.

The first is external control. When the Federal Rules were initially promulgated, discovery was largely envisioned as a matter for the parties, not the court, to sort out. After an interval designed to ensure adequate representation of all parties, each side was permitted as much

---

1. Used with permission of the University of Florida Law Review. Most footnotes omitted; others renumbered.

discovery as it considered necessary, with little consideration given to issues such as duplicativeness or the relationship between the cost of responding and the value of the lawsuit. To be sure, discovery was not a free-for-all. Rules of privilege and evidence—and considerations of due process—provided some limits. However, in the original vision, even these limits were self-administered. The court could be called upon to settle discovery disputes, but fee shifting provisions discouraged routine resort to judicial umpiring. Judicial management, if it was considered at all, was viewed as a threat to impartial adjudication and an intrusion into the adversarial process.[2]

The new Rules stand in sharp contrast in that they impose a substantial degree of judicial management. Henceforth, parties are not permitted discovery until the contours of the process have been defined by a court. Under Rules 26(d) and (f), the parties are required to meet soon after the answer is filed to discuss their case and formulate a discovery plan. That plan becomes, under Rule 16(b), a topic of a mandatory pretrial conference with the court, a conference that must be held as soon as practicable or within 90 days of the defendant's appearance or 120 days of service of complaint. The final plan is then incorporated into a scheduling order, which can be changed only on a showing of good cause, Rule 16(b)(6).

The second major change is closely related to the first, for it too circumscribes party control. Along with judicial supervision, the 1993 revision interposes presumptive limits on the use of formal discovery devices. Thus, where discovery was once essentially endlessly available, under the current rules, absent agreement between the parties or action by the court, parties are now limited to 10 depositions, Rule 30(a)(2)(A), and 25 interrogatories, Rule 33(a). In addition, the court has power under Rule 26(b)(2) to limit the length of depositions and the number of requests to admit.

Despite the fundamental reorientation that these two modifications represent, the third change—disclosure—is the one that will surely make the most significant difference to practitioners. Whereas formerly, each side's access to information turned solely on its own investigative ability, including its ability to ask and draft clever questions, and request the right documents and admissions, the new rules require the automatic disclosure—without request—of entire categories of information. This is to occur in four stages:

> 1. Under Rule 26(a)(1), parties must provide, within 10 days of their initial conference, the names and addresses of people having discoverable information relevant to disputed facts alleged with particularity in the pleadings; copies or descriptions and location of all documents within their control relevant to disputed facts alleged with particularity in the

---

2. See, e.g., Resnick, Managerial Judges, 96 Harv.L.Rev. 374, 426–31 (1982).

pleadings; computations of damages claimed, including the material on which the calculations are based; and insurance agreements that may be called on to satisfy the judgment.

2. Under Rule 26(a)(2), parties must disclose in a time frame directed by the court, or at least 90 days before trial, the information each side needs to defend against the adversary's expert witnesses. For retained or specially employed experts who will testify, what is required here is entirely new: a report of the expert's opinions, including their bases, the data utilized in formulating these opinions, the exhibits prepared to explain and support them, as well as information on the expert's qualifications, compensation, and other testimony given in the last four years.

3. Under Rule 26(a)(3), each party must, at least 30 days before trial, provide to all other parties the names, addresses, and telephone numbers of each witness, categorized according to whether that witness will definitely testify, or will be used only if the need arises, and according to whether the testimony will be offered live or through deposition. Documentary evidence, including exhibits, must also be identified and categorized according to the likelihood of use.

4. Under Rule 26(e), parties must now, at appropriate intervals, supplement all disclosures as well as all responses to other forms of discovery in order to correct information that is found, in some material aspect, to be incomplete or incorrect.

Despite the mandatory nature of these disclosure requirements, the privilege rules remain intact, at least ostensibly, and the court retains the power to issue protective orders. But even here there is a sort of disclosure requirement. Under Rule 26(b)(5), a party asserting a privilege or in possession of information subject to protection must describe enough about the nature of the material to permit the other parties to assess whether the information is properly withheld.

And, to give all of this bite, there are new sanctions. Cost-shifting is provided by Rules 37(g) and 37(a)(4) for a party's failure to participate in the development and submission of a discovery plan and to compensate for motions to compel disclosure. Unjustified failure to disclose information can also be sanctioned using the standard procedures of 37(b)(2)(A), (B), and (C). In addition, Rule 37(c) prohibits parties from using as evidence at trial information that should have been disclosed.

II.   PERCEIVED PROBLEMS

Evaluated in the abstract, the discovery amendments appear to offer substantial benefits. In theory, they streamline litigation, automatically correct the initial asymmetry in the distribution of information, and reduce both cost and delay. The simple exchange of information envisioned by disclosure eliminates first-wave interrogatories and the hair-splitting disputation over meaning that often accompanies them. Experts need not make themselves available (or charge) for depositions because the expert witness reports will furnish the information opposing parties need to prepare for cross examination. Presumptive limits reverse the leave-no-stone-unturned and no-source-of-imposing-costs-unused mentality that has characterized discovery in recent years. Instead, the rules encourage cooperation and professionalism.

Given these obvious advantages, why then, did these changes face, in the words of Justice Scalia in his dissent to transmitting the discovery rules to Congress, "nearly universal criticism from every conceivable sector of our judicial system, including judges, practitioners, litigants, academics, public interest groups, and national, state and local bar and professional associations"? [3]

Before detailing the problems these groups perceive in the new rules, it is worth acknowledging that all procedural changes are subject to a certain amount of grumbling on the part of the bar—grumbling that does not always signify. After all, practicing lawyers know how the old rules work; learning new ones costs them and their clients money. Or to be cynical, lawyers know how to manipulate the old rules to their clients' advantage; that is what they are in the business of selling. At the same time, however, strong arguments can be made that there is more here than mere self-interest.

A. Expense. As noted above, one of the goals of the revision was to reduce the expense of the discovery phase. There is, however, considerable dispute as to the impact of disclosure on cost. As argued by both the defendant's bar and by Justice Scalia, disclosure may well lead to overproduction of information. Since sanctions are imposed only in the event too little information is produced, parties will protect themselves in the only way possible: by interpreting disclosure requirements very liberally. Defendants will compile material plaintiffs never use, on issues that quickly disappear from the case, and in lawsuits that may have settled in any event.

Even some plaintiff lawyers, who, as the people on the short end of the asymmetry problem, theoretically stand to gain from automatic disclosure, echo this concern. For them, cost increases in several ways. The amount of cheap discovery they can do is reduced by the limit on the number of interrogatories they can propound. Furthermore, disclosure imposes new expenses. In many kinds of litigation (civil rights is an example), defendants have not, traditionally, conducted much discovery. Hence, disclosure represents an entirely new cost. Similarly, litigants will now be required to bear the new expense of paying experts to draft

---

3. See 146 F.R.D. 501, 512 (1993) (Scalia, J. dissenting from the transmission of   the Revisions to Congress).

the reports required by Rule 26(a)(2). This cost will not, critics say, be offset by eliminating the need for depositions because written reports do not reveal how convincingly the witness testifies, or on how well the witness withstands cross-examination. Thus, depositions will be required in any event.

Plaintiffs' bar even anticipates new costs at the receiving end of disclosure. Under prior law, they drafted interrogatories in a manner designed to elicit only the material they wanted, and if things went well, that was all that they received. Of course, if the other side was recalcitrant, they might receive a key to a warehouse, Rule 33(c), but that would occur only if things went badly. Under the new disclosure regime, a warehouse of information may be produced in the ordinary course, and the expense of sifting through it could be high.

Of course, the Advisory Committee on the Civil Rules did foresee the overproduction problem. To correct it, the Committee considered a variety of formulations for the standard of relevance, moving from requiring disclosure of information "material to any claim or defense;" to "likely to bear significantly on any claim or defense;" to "relevant to those factual disputes that are reasonably identifiable." The standard finally adopted—mandating disclosure of all material "relevant to disputed facts alleged with particularity in the pleadings"—provides an interesting bonus in that it encourages parties who seek information to plead with more specificity than is strictly required by the notice pleading rules.

It is not, however, clear to those who oppose the new rules how this standard will solve the overproduction problem. "Particularity" is not defined by the Rule (although it has long been used in Rule 9). The Advisory Notes give one example in the product-liability area [4] and further suggest disclosure will be judged with a sliding scale: "[t]he greater the specificity and clarity of the allegations in the pleadings, the more complete should be the listing of potential witnesses and types of documentary evidence." Neither elaboration, it is claimed, is concrete enough to be of use in actual cases.

In this regard, it is important to remember that Rule 11 has also been modified. The new version now permits the assertion of claims that lack evidentiary support, so long as the claims are flagged and withdrawn when the inability to find evidence becomes clear, Rule 11(b)(4) and (c). If disclosure is required in response to every particularized allegation, even those that lack evidentiary support, then the Committee's standard, clever though it is, will not effectively reduce the amount of disclosure necessary or reduce expense significantly. Indeed,

---

4. "Broad, vague, and conclusory allegations, sometimes tolerated in notice pleading—for example the assertion that a product with many component parts is defective in some unspecified manner—should not impose upon responding parties the obligation at that point to search for and identify all persons possibly involved in, or all documents affecting, the design, manufacture, and assembly of the product."

the need to engage in costly compilation of information increases the nuisance value of baseless suits and could lead to more improvident settlements.

B. Interference with notice pleading. The second major perceived problem with discovery revision is, in a sense, the flip side of the first. It is the claim that in raising the level of specificity required to elicit disclosure, the Rules, in effect, undermine the principle of notice pleading.

To see why this argument is plausible, consider the result if disclosure is not required in response to particularized claims that are flagged as lacking evidentiary support. In those cases, and in cases where plaintiff is so lacking information, she must plead generally, mandatory disclosure will not yield much information. Plaintiff will therefore be forced to rely on formal discovery mechanisms. But use of these devices is now limited. If the necessary information is not revealed in the 10 depositions and 25 interrogatories allowable, the plaintiff will need to petition the court for leave to discover more. Rebutting statutory presumptions generally requires some information. Since, by definition, the plaintiff lacks information, it will be difficult to overcome the presumptive limit and avoid summary judgment.

To put this another way, the goal of a demonstrative (as opposed to inquisitorial) adjudicatory system is that at the end of the pretrial phase, the parties possess the information they need to try their case. If the pleading system does not require parties to reveal what they know, then discovery must take up the slack. The 1993 revision upsets the balance of the original federal rules because, to put it bluntly, it provides information only to those who already have it—to those plaintiffs who possess enough information to draft their complaints with specificity. The fact that disclosure is presumptively simultaneous compounds the problem. By forcing each side to turn over information at an early stage, disclosure increases the likelihood that one side will inadvertently freeze her story or legal theory.

Of course, the Advisory Committee considered this issue as well. In its view, however, these informational and timing problems will be resolved easily because they will be discussed in advance—at the parties' meet and confer session and in the first pretrial conference. There, the participants will at the very beginning see the need for, and arrange, additional formal discovery and multiphased discovery procedures. Indeed, the beauty of the new system is that it encourages the court and the parties to tailor discovery to the real needs of real cases.

* * *

D. Ethics. [Another problem, cited by] both plaintiff and defendant bars—as well as Justice Scalia—[is that the rules are in conflict with the culture and ethics of the bar.] Turning over information inimical to the client's case conflicts with the duty to represent zealously. That is, it is one thing to reveal material the other side has unambiguously requested, it is quite another to alert the adversary to a set of information whose existence was previously unknown. Moreover, disclosure requires each party to identify the other side's plausible theories, figure out the information best suited to prove a case on these theories, and then comb files to find that information. This, critics claim, is very close to what is currently protected by the work-product privilege. It allows the winner to perform its function "on wits borrowed from the adversary." [5]

E. Nonuniformity. Even if every issue mentioned above were easily resolved, two problems would remain. Both can be classified as impinging on uniformity issues. First, there is the question of nationwide uniformity, which is threatened by the fact that districts are permitted to opt out from most of the new discovery rules. The motivation here is easy to understand. The Civil Justice Reform Act had encouraged districts to adopt their own plans to curb discovery, and the opt-out permits these districts to continue their work. However, the result approaches chaos. As of the end of December 1993, approximately a third of the districts had opted out of some or all of the new Rules, somewhat less than a third of the districts had announced their adherence to the new rules, and the rest were undecided. The combined effect of the 1993 Revision and the Civil Justice Reform Act is that it will no longer be possible to walk into a federal court knowing how to practice there. In New York, for example, there are now different rules on different sides of the harbor.

The second problem is case-uniformity. The Federal Rules have long avoided unequal treatment and the perception of inequality by taking a trans-substantive approach; by using the same set of rules for all substantive areas of law within the federal docket. As a formal matter, the new Rules are also trans-substantive. However, it is quite clear that this is not what the Advisory Committee meant to achieve as a matter of practice. It is, for example, highly unlikely that any Committee member thought 10 depositions and 25 interrogatories were the right number for every kind of case. Rather, a part of the Committee's thinking appears to be that over time, courts will begin to get a feel for what particular classes of cases require, and evaluate discovery plans in accordance with this experience. The result will surely be substance-specific discovery. Although this change may represent progress, it is a departure from one of the bedrock principles of federal adjudication. According to the critics, this departure should have been more fully debated before it was instituted. At the very least, the Committee's justifications for departing from the trans-substantive ideal would be useful to future Advisory and Standing Committees, which may well consider making other substance-specific revisions.

---

5. Hickman v. Taylor, 329 U.S. 495   (Jackson, J., concurring).

In reading the material in the following Chapter, keep in mind that all the cases were decided under discovery rules that did not require automatic disclosure. In each case, ask whether the new Rules would change the way the parties acquired the information in issue or their ability to do so. Would such a case even need to be brought under the new Rules?

NOTE

Are the Rulemakers, in their efforts to exorcise undue delay and expense from the litigation process, focussing on the wrong institution? Should the pleading rules be changed to require provision of most of the information that is presently obtainable only through discovery? See Smit, H., Substance and Procedure in International Arbitration, 65 Tul.L.Rev. 1309, 1313–15 (1991).

On October 21, 1996, the Advisory Committee on Civil Rules approved the following amendment to Rule 26 for publication and comment.

Rule 26. General Provisions Governing Discovery; Duty of Disclosure

* * * * *

(c)(1) Protective Orders. ~~Upon~~ On motion by a party or by the person from whom discovery is sought, accompanied by a certification that the movant has in good faith conferred or attempted to confer with other affected parties in an effort to resolve the dispute without court action, ~~and for good cause shown,~~ the court ~~in which~~ where the action is pending ~~or~~—and ~~alternatively,~~ on matters relating to a deposition, also the court in the district where the deposition ~~is to~~ will be taken—may, for good cause shown or on stipulation of the parties, make any order ~~which~~ that justice requires to protect a party or person from annoyance, embarrassment, oppression, or undue burden or expense, including one or more of the following:

(~~1~~A) ~~that~~ precluding the disclosure or discovery ~~not be had~~;

(~~2~~B) ~~that~~ specifying conditions, including time and place, for the disclosure or discovery ~~may be had only on specified terms and conditions, including a designation of time or place~~;

(~~3~~C) ~~that the discovery may be had only by~~ prescribing a discovery method ~~of discovery~~ other than that selected by the party seeking discovery;

(~~4~~D) ~~that~~ excluding certain matters ~~not be inquired into~~, or ~~that~~ limiting the scope of ~~the~~ disclosure or discovery ~~be limited~~ to certain matters;

(~~5~~E) designating the persons who may be present while ~~that~~ the discovery is ~~be~~ conducted ~~with no one present except persons designated by the court~~;

(6F) ~~that a deposition, after being sealed,~~ directing that a sealed deposition be opened only ~~by order of the~~ upon court order;

(7G) ordering that a trade secret or other confidential research, development, or commercial information not be revealed or be revealed only in a designated way; or

(8H) directing that the parties simultaneously file specified documents or information enclosed in sealed envelopes, to be opened as ~~directed by~~ the court directs.

(2) If ~~the~~ a motion for a protective order is wholly or partly denied ~~in whole or in part~~, the court may, on ~~such~~ just terms ~~and conditions as are just~~, order that any party or ~~other~~ person provide or permit discovery or disclosure. ~~The provisions of~~ Rule 37(a)(4) ~~appl~~ies to the award of expenses incurred in relation to the motion.

(3)(A) The court may modify or dissolve a protective order on motion made by a party, a person bound by the order, or a person who has been allowed to intervene to seek modification or dissolution.

(B) In ruling on a motion to dissolve or modify a protective order, the court must consider, among other matters, the following:

(i) the extent of reliance on the order;

(ii) the public and private interests affected by the order, including any risk to public health or safety;

(iii) the movant's consent to submit to the terms of the order;

(iv) the reasons for entering the order, and any new information that bears on the order; and

(v) the burden that the order imposes on persons seeking information relevant to other litigation.

Chapter Twelve

THE RIGHT TO A JURY

SECTION 2.   RECEPTION IN THE UNITED STATES

[Insert on page 760, before Section 3:]

On October 21, 1994, the Advisory Committee on Civil Rules approved the following for publication and comment:

Rule 47.   Selecting ~~Selection of~~ Jurors

(a) ~~Examination of~~ Examining Jurors. The court ~~may~~ shall ~~permit the parties or their attorneys to~~ conduct the voir dire examination of prospective jurors ~~or may itself conduct the examination~~. But the court shall also permit the parties to orally examine the prospective jurors to supplement the court's examination within reasonable limits of time, manner, and subject matter, as the court determines in its discretion. The court may terminate examination by a person who violates those limits, or for other good cause. ~~In the latter event, the court shall permit the parties or their attorneys to supplement the examination by such further inquiry as it deems proper or shall itself submit to the prospective jurors such additional questions of the parties or their attorneys as it deems proper.~~

* * * * *

Rule 48.   Number of Jurors—Participation in Verdict

The court shall seat a jury of ~~not fewer than six and not more than~~ twelve members. ~~and a~~ All jurors shall participate in the verdict unless excused from service ~~by the court pursuant to~~ under Rule 47(c). Unless the parties ~~otherwise~~ stipulate otherwise, (1) the verdict shall be unanimous, and (2) no verdict ~~shall~~ may be taken from a jury ~~reduced in size to~~ of fewer than six members.

SECTION 4.   LIMITATIONS UPON THE RIGHT TO A JURY

[Insert on page 776 the following new subsection A and renumber subsequent subsections:]

A. PATENTS

MARKMAN v. WESTVIEW INSTRUMENTS, INC.

Supreme Court of the United States, 1996.
___ U.S. ___, 116 S.Ct. 1384, 134 L.Ed.2d 577.

JUSTICE SOUTER delivered the opinion of the Court.*

The question here is whether the interpretation of a so-called patent claim, the portion of the patent document that defines the scope of the patentee's rights, is a matter of law reserved entirely for the court, or subject to a Seventh Amendment guarantee that a jury will determine the meaning of any disputed term of art about which expert testimony is offered. We hold that the construction of a patent, including terms of art within its claim, is exclusively within the province of the court.

I

The Constitution empowers Congress "to promote the Progress of Science and useful Arts, by securing for limited Times to Authors and Inventors the exclusive Right to their respective Writings and Discoveries." U.S. Const., Art. I, § 8, cl. 8. Congress first exercised this authority in 1790, when it provided for the issuance of "letters patent," Act of Apr. 10, 1790, ch. 7, § 1, 1 Stat. 109, which, like their modern counterparts, granted inventors "the right to exclude others from making, using, offering for sale, selling, or importing the patented invention," in exchange for full disclosure of an invention, H. Schwartz, Patent Law and Practice 1, 33 (2d ed. 1995). It has long been understood that a patent must describe the exact scope of an invention and its manufacture to "secure to [the patentee] all to which he is entitled, [and] to apprise the public of what is still open to them." McClain v. Ortmayer, 141 U.S. 419, 424, 35 L.Ed. 800, 12 S.Ct. 76 (1891). Under the modern American system, these objectives are served by two distinct elements of a patent document. First, it contains a specification describing the invention "in such full, clear, concise, and exact terms as to enable any person skilled in the art ... to make and use the same." 35 U.S.C. § 112; see also 3 E. Lipscomb, Walker on Patents § 10:1, pp. 183–184 (3d ed. 1985) (Lipscomb) (listing the requirements for a specification). Second, a patent includes one or more "claims," which "particularly point out and distinctly claim the subject matter which the applicant regards as his invention." 35 U.S.C. § 112. "A claim covers and secures a process, a machine, a manufacture, a composition of matter, or a design, but never the function or result of either, nor the scientific explanation of their operation." 6 Lipscomb § 21:17, at 315–316. The claim "defines the scope of a patent grant," 3 id., § 11:1, at 280, and functions to forbid not only exact copies of an invention, but products that go to "the heart of the invention but avoid the literal language of

---

* Some footnotes omitted.

the claim by making a noncritical change," Schwartz, supra, at 82.[1] In this opinion, the word "claim" is used only in this sense peculiar to patent law.

Characteristically, patent lawsuits charge what is known as infringement, Schwartz, supra, at 75, and rest on allegations that the defendant "without authority made, used or [sold the] patented invention, within the United States during the term of the patent therefor...." 35 U.S.C. § 271(a). Victory in an infringement suit requires a finding that the patent claim "covers the alleged infringer's product or process," which in turn necessitates a determination of "what the words in the claim mean." Schwartz, supra, at 80; see also 3 Lipscomb, § 11:2, at 288–290.

Petitioner in this infringement suit, Markman, owns United States Reissue Patent No. 33,054 for his "Inventory Control and Reporting System for Drycleaning Stores." The patent describes a system that can monitor and report the status, location, and movement of clothing in a dry-cleaning establishment. The Markman system consists of a keyboard and data processor to generate written records for each transaction, including a bar code readable by optical detectors operated by employees, who log the progress of clothing through the dry-cleaning process. Respondent Westview's product also includes a keyboard and processor, and it lists charges for the dry-cleaning services on bar-coded tickets that can be read by portable optical detectors.

Markman brought an infringement suit against Westview and Althon Enterprises, an operator of dry-cleaning establishments using Westview's products (collectively, Westview). Westview responded that Markman's patent is not infringed by its system because the latter functions merely to record an inventory of receivables by tracking invoices and transaction totals, rather than to record and track an inventory of articles of clothing. Part of the dispute hinged upon the meaning of the word "inventory," a term found in Markman's independent claim 1, which states that Markman's product can "maintain an inventory total" and "detect and localize spurious additions to inventory." The case was tried before a jury, which heard, among others, a witness produced by Markman who testified about the meaning of the claim language.

After the jury compared the patent to Westview's device, it found an infringement of Markman's independent claim 1 and dependent claim 10. The District Court nevertheless granted Westview's deferred motion for judgment as a matter of law, one of its reasons being that the term "inventory" in Markman's patent encompasses "both cash inventory and the actual physical inventory of articles of clothing." 772 F.Supp.

1. Thus, for example, a claim for a ceiling fan with three blades attached to a solid rod connected to a motor would not only cover fans that take precisely this form, but would also cover a similar fan that includes some additional feature, e.g., such a fan with a cord or switch for turning it on and off, and may cover a product deviating from the core design in some noncritical way, e.g., a three-bladed ceiling fan with blades attached to a hollow rod connected to a motor. H. Schwartz, Patent Law and Practice 81–82 (2d ed. 1995).

1535, 1537–1538 (E.D.Pa.1991). Under the trial court's construction of the patent, the production, sale, or use of a tracking system for dry cleaners would not infringe Markman's patent unless the product was capable of tracking articles of clothing throughout the cleaning process and generating reports about their status and location. Since Westview's system cannot do these things, the District Court directed a verdict on the ground that Westview's device does not have the "means to maintain an inventory total" and thus cannot "detect and localize spurious additions to inventory as well as spurious deletions therefrom," as required by claim 1. Id., at 1537.

Markman appealed, arguing it was error for the District Court to substitute its construction of the disputed claim term "inventory" for the construction the jury had presumably given it. The United States Court of Appeals for the Federal Circuit affirmed, holding the interpretation of claim terms to be the exclusive province of the court and the Seventh Amendment to be consistent with that conclusion. 52 F.3d 967 (1995). Markman sought our review on each point, and we granted certiorari. 515 U.S. ___ (1995). We now affirm.

II

The Seventh Amendment provides that "in Suits at common law, where the value in controversy shall exceed twenty dollars, the right of trial by jury shall be preserved. . . ." U.S. Const., Amdt. 7. Since Justice Story's day, United States v. Wonson, I Gall. 5, 28 F.Cas. 745, 750 (No. 16,750) (C.C.Mass. 1812), we have understood that "the right of trial by jury thus preserved is the right which existed under the English common law when the Amendment was adopted." Baltimore & Carolina Line, Inc. v. Redman, 295 U.S. 654, 657, 79 L.Ed. 1636, 55 S.Ct. 890 (1935). In keeping with our long-standing adherence to this "historical test," Wolfram, The Constitutional History of the Seventh Amendment, 57 Minn. L. Rev. 639, 640–643 (1973), we ask, first, whether we are dealing with a cause of action that either was tried at law at the time of the Founding or is at least analogous to one that was, see, e.g., Tull v. United States, 481 U.S. 412, 417, 95 L.Ed.2d 365, 107 S.Ct. 1831 (1987). If the action in question belongs in the law category, we then ask whether the particular trial decision must fall to the jury in order to preserve the substance of the common-law right as it existed in 1791. See infra, at 6–9.[2]

A

As to the first issue, going to the character of the cause of action, "the form of our analysis is familiar. 'First we compare the statutory action to 18th century actions brought in the courts of England prior to

---

2. Our formulations of the historical test do not deal with the possibility of conflict between actual English common law practice and American assumptions about what that practice was, or between English and American practices at the relevant time. No such complications arise in this case.

the merger of the courts of law and equity.' " Granfinanciera, S. A. v. Nordberg, 492 U.S. 33, 42, 106 L.Ed.2d 26, 109 S.Ct. 2782 (1989) (citation omitted). Equally familiar is the descent of today's patent infringement action from the infringement actions tried at law in the 18th century, and there is no dispute that infringement cases today must be tried to a jury, as their predecessors were more than two centuries ago. See, e.g., Bramah v. Hardcastle, 1 Carp.P.C. 168 (K. B. 1789).

B

This conclusion raises the second question, whether a particular issue occurring within a jury trial (here the construction of a patent claim) is itself necessarily a jury issue, the guarantee being essential to preserve the right to a jury's resolution of the ultimate dispute. In some instances the answer to this second question may be easy because of clear historical evidence that the very subsidiary question was so regarded under the English practice of leaving the issue for a jury. But when, as here, the old practice provides no clear answer, ... we are forced to make a judgment about the scope of the Seventh Amendment guarantee without the benefit of any foolproof test.

The Court has repeatedly said that the answer to the second question "must depend on whether the jury must shoulder this responsibility as necessary to preserve the 'substance of the common-law right of trial by jury.' " Tull v. United States, supra, at 426 (emphasis added) (quoting Colgrove v. Battin, 413 U.S. 149, 157, 37 L.Ed.2d 522, 93 S.Ct. 2448 (1973)); see also Baltimore & Carolina Line, supra, at 657 " 'Only those incidents which are regarded as fundamental, as inherent in and of the essence of the system of trial by jury, are placed beyond the reach of the legislature.' " Tull v. United States, supra, at 426 (citations omitted); see also Galloway v. United States, 319 U.S. 372, 392, 87 L.Ed. 1458, 63 S.Ct. 1077 (1943).

The "substance of the common-law right" is, however, a pretty blunt instrument for drawing distinctions. We have tried to sharpen it, to be sure, by reference to the distinction between substance and procedure. See Baltimore & Carolina Line, supra, at 657; see also Galloway v. United States, supra, at 390–391; Ex parte Peterson, 253 U.S. 300, 309, 64 L.Ed. 919, 40 S.Ct. 543 (1920); Walker v. New Mexico & Southern Pacific R. Co., 165 U.S. 593, 596, 41 L.Ed. 837, 17 S.Ct. 421 (1897); but see Sun Oil Co. v. Wortman, 486 U.S. 717, 727, 100 L.Ed.2d 743, 108 S.Ct. 2117 (1988). We have also spoken of the line as one between issues of fact and law. See Baltimore & Carolina Line, supra, at 657; see also Ex parte Peterson, supra, at 310; Walker v. New Mexico & Southern Pacific R. Co., supra, at 597, but see Pullman–Standard v. Swint, 456 U.S. 273, 288, 72 L.Ed.2d 66, 102 S.Ct. 1781 (1982).

But the sounder course, when available, is to classify a mongrel practice (like construing a term of art following receipt of evidence) by using the historical method, much as we do in characterizing the suits and actions within which they arise. Where there is no exact antecedent, the best hope lies in comparing the modern practice to earlier ones whose allocation to court or jury we do know, cf. Baltimore & Carolina Line, supra, at 659, 660, Dimick v. Schiedt, 293 U.S. 474, 477, 482, 79 L.Ed. 603, 55 S.Ct. 296 (1935), seeking the best analogy we can draw between an old and the new, see Tull v. United States, supra, at 420–421 (we must search the English common law for "appropriate analogies" rather than a "precisely analogous common-law cause of action").

C

"Prior to 1790 nothing in the nature of a claim had appeared either in British patent practice or in that of the American states," Lutz, Evolution of the Claims of U.S. Patents, 20 J. Pat. Off. Soc. 134 (1938), and we have accordingly found no direct antecedent of modern claim construction in the historical sources. Claim practice did not achieve statutory recognition until the passage of the Act of 1836, Act of July 4, 1836, ch. 357, § 6, 5 Stat. 119, and inclusion of a claim did not become a statutory requirement until 1870, Act of July 8, 1870, ch. 230, § 26, 16 Stat. 201; see 1 A. Deller, Patent Claims § 4, p. 9 (2d ed. 1971). Although, as one historian has observed, as early as 1850 "judges were ... beginning to express more frequently the idea that in seeking to ascertain the invention 'claimed' in a patent the inquiry should be limited to interpreting the summary, or 'claim,'" Lutz, supra, at 145, "the idea that the claim is just as important if not more important than the description and drawings did not develop until the Act of 1870 or thereabouts." Deller, supra, § 4, at 9.

At the time relevant for Seventh Amendment analogies, in contrast, it was the specification, itself a relatively new development, H. Dutton, The Patent System and Inventive Activity During the Industrial Revolution, 1750–1852, pp. 75–76 (1984), that represented the key to the patent. Thus, patent litigation in that early period was typified by so-called novelty actions, testing whether "any essential part of [the patent had been] disclosed to the public before," Huddart v. Grimshaw, Dav. Pat. Cas. 265, 298 (K. B. 1803), and "enablement" cases, in which juries were asked to determine whether the specification described the invention well enough to allow members of the appropriate trade to reproduce it, see, e.g., Arkwright v. Nightingale, Dav. Pat. Cas. 37, 60 (C.P. 1785).

The closest 18th-century analogue of modern claim construction seems, then, to have been the construction of specifications, and as to that function the mere smattering of patent cases that we have from this period shows no established jury practice sufficient to support an argument by analogy that today's construction of a claim should be a guaranteed jury issue. Few of the case reports even touch upon the proper interpretation of disputed terms in the specifications at issue, see, e.g., Bramah v. Hardcastle, 1 Carp. P. C. 168 (K. B. 1789); King v. Else, 1 Carp. P. C. 103, Dav. Pat. Cas., 144 (K. B. 1785); Dollond's Case, 1 Carp.

P. C. 28 (C.P. 1758); Administrators of Calthorp v. Waymans, 3 Keb. 710, 84 Eng. Rep. 966 (K. B. 1676), and none demonstrates that the definition of such a term was determined by the jury. This absence of an established practice should not surprise us, given the primitive state of jury patent practice at the end of the 18th century, when juries were still new to the field. Although by 1791 more than a century had passed since the enactment of the Statute of Monopolies, which provided that the validity of any monopoly should be determined in accordance with the common law, patent litigation had remained within the jurisdiction of the Privy Council until 1752 and hence without the option of a jury trial. E. Walterscheid, Early Evolution of the United States Patent Law: Antecedents (Part 3), 77 J. Pat. & Tm. Off. Soc. 771, 771–776 (1995). Indeed, the state of patent law in the common-law courts before 1800 led one historian to observe that "the reported cases are destitute of any decision of importance.... At the end of the eighteenth century, therefore, the Common Law Judges were left to pick up the threads of the principles of law without the aid of recent and reliable precedents." Hulme, On the Consideration of the Patent Grant, Past and Present, 13 L. Q. Rev. 313, 318 (1897). Earlier writers expressed similar discouragement at patent law's amorphous character, and, as late as the 1830's, English commentators were irked by enduring confusion in the field. See Dutton, supra, at 69–70.

Markman seeks to supply what the early case reports lack in so many words by relying on decisions like Turner v. Winter, 1 T. R. 602, 99 Eng. Rep. 1274 (K. B. 1787). and Arkwright v. Nightingale, Dav. Pat. Cas. 37 (C. P. 1785), to argue that the 18th-century juries must have acted as definers of patent terms just to reach the verdicts we know they rendered in patent cases turning on enablement or novelty. But the conclusion simply does not follow. There is no more reason to infer that juries supplied plenary interpretation of written instruments in patent litigation than in other cases implicating the meaning of documentary terms, and we do know that in other kinds of cases during this period judges, not juries, ordinarily construed written documents. The probability that the judges were doing the same thing in the patent litigation of the time is confirmed by the fact that as soon as the English reports did begin to describe the construction of patent documents, they show the judges construing the terms of the specifications. See Bovill v. Moore, Dav. Pat. Cas. 361, 399, 404 (C. P. 1816) (judge submits question of novelty to the jury only after explaining some of the language and "stating in what terms the specification runs"); cf. Russell v. Cowley & Dixon, Webs. Pat. Cas. 457, 467–470 (Exch. 1834) (construing the terms of the specification in reviewing a verdict); Haworth v. Hardcastle, Webs. Pat. Cas. 480, 484–485 (1834) (same). This evidence is in fact buttressed by cases from this Court; when they first reveal actual practice, the practice revealed is of the judge construing the patent. See, eg. Winans v. New York & Erie R. Co., 62 U.S. 88, 21 How. 88, 100, 16 L.Ed. 68 (1859);

Winans v. Denmead, 56 U.S. 330, 15 How. 330, 338, 14 L.Ed. 717 (1854);
Hogg v. Emerson, 47 U.S. 437, 6 How. 437, 484, 12 L.Ed. 505 (1848); cf.
Parker v. Hulme, 1 Fish. Pat. Cas. 44, 18 F. Cas. 1138 (No. 10,740) (CC
ED Pa. 1849). These indications of our patent practice are the more
impressive for being all of a piece with what we know about the
analogous contemporary practice of interpreting terms within a land
patent, where it fell to the judge, not the jury, to construe the words.

D

Losing, then, on the contention that juries generally had interpretive responsibilities during the 18th century, Markman seeks a different
anchor for analogy in the more modest contention that even if judges
were charged with construing most terms in the patent, the art of
defining terms of art employed in a specification fell within the province
of the jury. Again, however, Markman has no authority from the period
in question, but relies instead on the later case of Neilson v. Harford,
Webs. Pat. Cas. 328 (Exch. 1841). There, an exchange between the judge
and the lawyers indicated that although the construction of a patent was
ordinarily for the court, id., at 349 (Alderson, B.), judges should "leave
the question of words of art to the jury," id., at 350 (Alderson, B.); see
also id., at 370 (judgment of the court); Hill v. Evans, 4 De. G. F. & J.
288, 293–294, 45 Eng. Rep. 1195, 1197 (Ch. 1862). Without, however, in
any way disparaging the weight to which Baron Alderson's view is
entitled, the most we can say is that an English report more than 70
years after the time that concerns us indicates an exception to what
probably had been occurring earlier. In place of Markman's inference
that this exceptional practice existed in 1791 there is at best only a
possibility that it did, and for anything more than a possibility we have
found no scholarly authority.

III

Since evidence of common law practice at the time of the Framing
does not entail application of the Seventh Amendment's jury guarantee
to the construction of the claim document, we must look elsewhere to
characterize this determination of meaning in order to allocate it as
between court or jury. We accordingly consult existing precedent and
consider both the relative interpretive skills of judges and juries and the
statutory policies that ought to be furthered by the allocation.

A

The two elements of a simple patent case, construing the patent and
determining whether infringement occurred, were characterized by the
former patent practitioner, Justice Curtis. "The first is a question of law,
to be determined by the court, construing the letters-patent, and the
description of the invention and specification of claim annexed to them.
The second is a question of fact, to be submitted to a jury." Winans v.
Denmead, 15 How., at 338; see Winans v. New York & Erie R. Co., 21

How., at 100; Hogg v. Emerson, supra, at 484; cf. Parker v. Hulme, supra, at 1140.

In arguing for a different allocation of responsibility for the first question, Markman relies primarily on two cases, Bischoff v. Wethered, 76 U.S. 812, 9 Wall. 812, 19 L.Ed. 829 (1870), and Tucker v. Spalding, 80 U.S. 453, 13 Wall. 453, 20 L.Ed. 515 (1872). These are said to show that evidence of the meaning of patent terms was offered to 19th-century juries, and thus to imply that the meaning of a documentary term was a jury issue whenever it was subject to evidentiary proof. That is not what Markman's cases show, however. . . .

* * * * *

In sum, neither Bischoff nor Tucker indicates that juries resolved the meaning of terms of art in construing a patent, and neither case undercuts Justice Curtis's authority.

B

Where history and precedent provide no clear answers, functional considerations also play their part in the choice between judge and jury to define terms of art. We said in Miller v. Fenton, 474 U.S. 104, 114, 88 L.Ed.2d 405, 106 S.Ct. 445 (1985), that when an issue "falls somewhere between a pristine legal standard and a simple historical fact, the fact/law distinction at times has turned on a determination that, as a matter of the sound administration of justice, one judicial actor is better positioned than another to decide the issue in question." So it turns out here, for judges, not juries, are the better suited to find the acquired meaning of patent terms.

The construction of written instruments is one of those things that judges often do and are likely to do better than jurors unburdened by training in exegesis. Patent construction in particular "is a special occupation, requiring, like all others, special training and practice. The judge, from his training and discipline, is more likely to give a proper interpretation to such instruments than a jury; and he is, therefore, more likely to be right, in performing such a duty, than a jury can be expected to be." Parker v Hulme, 18 F. Cas. at 1140. Such was the understanding nearly a century and a half ago, and there is no reason to weigh the respective strengths of judge and jury differently in relation to the modern claim; quite the contrary, for "the claims of patents have become highly technical in many respects as the result of special doctrines relating to the proper form and scope of claims that have been developed by the courts and the Patent Office." Woodward, Definiteness and Particularity in Patent Claims, 46 Mich. L. Rev. 755, 765 (1948).

Markman would trump these considerations with his argument that a jury should decide a question of meaning peculiar to a trade or profession simply because the question is a subject of testimony requiring credibility determinations, which are the jury's forte. It is, of course, true that credibility judgments have to be made about the experts who testify in patent cases, and in theory there could be a case in which a simple credibility judgment would suffice to choose between experts whose testimony was equally consistent with a patent's internal logic. But our own experience with document construction leaves us doubtful that trial courts will run into many cases like that. In the main, we expect, any credibility determinations will be subsumed within the necessarily sophisticated analysis of the whole document, required by the standard construction rule that a term can be defined only in a way that comports with the instrument as a whole. See Bates v. Coe, 98 U.S. 31, 38, 25 L.Ed. 68 (1878); 6 Lipscomb § 21:40, at 393; 2 Robinson, supra, § 734, at 484; Woodward, supra, at 765; cf. U.S. Industrial Chemicals, Inc. v. Carbide & Carbon Chemicals Corp., 315 U.S. 668, 678, 86 L.Ed. 1105, 62 S.Ct. 839 (1942); cf. 6 Lipscomb at § 21:40, at 393. Thus, in these cases a jury's capabilities to evaluate demeanor, cf. Miller, supra, at 114, 117, to sense the "mainsprings of human conduct," Commissioner v. Duberstein, 363 U.S. 278, 289, 4 L.Ed.2d 1218, 80 S.Ct. 1190 (1960), or to reflect community standards, United States v. McConney, 728 F.2d 1195, 1204 (C.A.9 1984) (en banc), are much less significant than a trained ability to evaluate the testimony in relation to the overall structure of the patent. The decisionmaker vested with the task of construing the patent is in the better position to ascertain whether an expert's proposed definition fully comports with the specification and claims and so will preserve the patent's internal coherence. We accordingly think there is sufficient reason to treat construction of terms of art like many other responsibilities that we cede to a judge in the normal course of trial, notwithstanding its evidentiary underpinnings.

C

Finally, we see the importance of uniformity in the treatment of a given patent as an independent reason to allocate all issues of construction to the court. As we noted in General Elec. Co. v. Wabash Appliance Corp., 304 U.S. 364, 369, 82 L.Ed. 1402, 58 S.Ct. 899 (1938), "the limits of a patent must be known for the protection of the patentee, the encouragement of the inventive genius of others and the assurance that the subject of the patent will be dedicated ultimately to the public." Otherwise, a "zone of uncertainty which enterprise and experimentation may enter only at the risk of infringement claims would discourage invention only a little less than unequivocal foreclosure of the field," United Carbon Co. v. Binney & Smith Co., 317 U.S. 228, 236, 87 L.Ed. 232, 63 S.Ct. 165 (1942), and "the public [would] be deprived of rights supposed to belong to it, without being clearly told what it is that limits these rights." Merrill v. Yeomans, 94 U.S. 568, 573, 24 L.Ed. 235 (1877). It was just for the sake of such desirable uniformity that Congress created the Court of Appeals for the Federal Circuit as an exclusive appellate court for patent cases, H. R. Rep. No. 97–312, pp. 20–23 (1981), observing that increased uniformity would "strengthen the United

States patent system in such a way as to foster technological growth and industrial innovation." Id., at 20.

Uniformity would, however, be ill served by submitting issues of document construction to juries. Making them jury issues would not, to be sure, necessarily leave evidentiary questions of meaning wide open in every new court in which a patent might be litigated, for principles of issue preclusion would ordinarily foster uniformity. Cf. Blonder–Tongue Laboratories, Inc. v. University of Ill. Foundation, 402 U.S. 313, 28 L.Ed.2d 788, 91 S.Ct. 1434 (1971). But whereas issue preclusion could not be asserted against new and independent infringement defendants even within a given jurisdiction, treating interpretive issues as purely legal will promote (though it will not guarantee) intrajurisdictional certainty through the application of stare decisis on those questions not yet subject to interjurisdictional uniformity under the authority of the single appeals court

　　　* * *

Accordingly, we hold that the interpretation of the word "inventory" in this case is an issue for the judge, not the jury, and affirm the decision of the Court of Appeals for the Federal Circuit.

It is so ordered.

Part V

THE RISING ART OF JUDICIAL ADMINISTRATION

Chapter Thirteen

JUDICIAL ADMINISTRATION IN CIVIL COURT

SECTION 1. EXORCISING COURT DELAY

[Insert on page 806 before Section 2:]

CHAMBERS v. NASCO

Supreme Court of the United States, 1991.
501 U.S. 32, 111 S.Ct. 2123, 115 L.Ed.2d 27.

JUSTICE WHITE delivered the opinion of the Court.*

This case requires us to explore the scope of the inherent power of a federal court to sanction a litigant for bad-faith conduct. Specifically, we are asked to determine whether the District Court, sitting in diversity, properly invoked its inherent power in assessing as a sanction for a party's bad-faith conduct attorney's fees and related expenses paid by the party's opponent to its attorneys. We hold that the District Court acted within its discretion, and we therefore affirm the judgment of the Court of Appeals.

I

This case began as a simple action for specific performance of a contract, but it did not remain so. Petitioner G. Russell Chambers was the sole shareholder and director of Calcasieu Television and Radio, Inc. (CTR), which operated television station KPLC–TV in Lake Charles, Louisiana. On August 9, 1983, Chambers, acting both in his individual capacity and on behalf of CTR, entered into a purchase agreement to sell the station's facilities and broadcast license to respondent NASCO, Inc., for a purchase price of $18 million. The agreement was not recorded in the parishes in which the two properties housing the station's facilities were located. Consummation of the agreement was subject to the approval of the Federal Communications Commission (FCC); both par-

* Some footnotes omitted; others ronum bered.

219

ties were obligated to file the necessary documents with the FCC no later than September 23, 1983. By late August, however, Chambers had changed his mind and tried to talk NASCO out of consummating the sale. NASCO refused. On September 23, Chambers, through counsel, informed NASCO that he would not file the necessary papers with the FCC.

NASCO decided to take legal action. On Friday, October 14, 1983, NASCO's counsel informed counsel for Chambers and CTR that NASCO would file suit the following Monday in the United States District Court for the Western District of Louisiana, seeking specific performance of the agreement, as well as a temporary restraining order (TRO) to prevent the alienation or encumbrance of the properties at issue. NASCO provided this notice in accordance with Federal Rule of Civil Procedure 65 and Rule 11 of the District Court's Local Rules (now Rule 10), both of which are designed to give a defendant in a TRO application notice of the hearing and an opportunity to be heard.

The reaction of Chambers and his attorney, A.J. Gray III, was later described by the District Court as having "emasculated and frustrated the purposes of these rules and the powers of [the District] Court by utilizing this notice to prevent NASCO's access to the remedy of specific performance." Nasco, Inc. v. Calcasieu Television & Radio, Inc., 623 F.Supp. 1372, 1383 (W.D.La.1985). On Sunday, October 16, 1983, the pair acted to place the properties at issue beyond the reach of the District Court by means of the Louisiana Public Records Doctrine. Because the purchase agreement had never been recorded, they determined that if the properties were sold to a third party, and if the deeds were recorded before the issuance of a TRO, the District Court would lack jurisdiction over the properties.

To this end, Chambers and Gray created a trust, with Chambers' sister as trustee and Chambers' three adult children as beneficiaries. The pair then directed the president of CTR, who later became Chambers' wife, to execute warranty deeds conveying the two tracts at issue to the trust for a recited consideration of $1.4 million. Early Monday morning, the deeds were recorded. The trustee, as purchaser, had not signed the deeds; none of the consideration had been paid; and CTR remained in possession of the properties. Later that morning, NASCO's counsel appeared in the District Court to file the complaint and seek the TRO. With NASCO's counsel present, the District Judge telephoned Gray. Despite the judge's queries concerning the possibility that CTR was negotiating to sell the properties to a third person, Gray made no mention of the recordation of the deeds earlier that morning. NASCO, Inc. v. Calcasieu Television & Radio, Inc., 124 F.R.D. 120, 126, n. 8 (W.D.La.1989). That afternoon, Chambers met with his sister and had her sign the trust documents and a $1.4 million note to CTR. The next morning, Gray informed the District Court by letter of the recordation of the deeds the day before, and admitted that he had intentionally withheld the information from the court. Within the next few days, Chambers' attorneys prepared a leaseback agreement from the trustee to CTR, so that CTR could remain in possession of the properties and continue to operate the station. The following week, the District Court granted a preliminary injunction against Chambers and CTR and entered a second TRO to prevent the trustee from alienating or encumbering the properties. At that hearing, the District Judge warned that Gray's and Chambers' conduct had been unethical.

Despite this early warning, Chambers, often acting through his attorneys, continued to abuse the judicial process. [The Court next summarizes Chambers' behavior in refusing to comply with discovery, proceeding with meritless motions, pleadings and delaying tactics before trial, delaying the trial and interfering with entry and execution of judgment. At intervals, NASCO sought contempt sanctions.]

* * *

Immediately following oral argument on Chambers' appeal from the District Court's judgment on the merits, the Court of Appeals, ruling from the bench, found the appeal frivolous. The court imposed appellate sanctions in the form of attorney's fees and double costs, pursuant to Federal Rule of Appellate Procedure 38, and remanded the case to the District Court with orders to fix the amount of appellate sanctions and to determine whether further sanctions should be imposed for the manner in which the litigation had been conducted. Nasco, Inc. v. Calcasieu Television & Radio, Inc., 797 F.2d 975 (CA5 1986) (per curiam) (unpublished order).

On remand, NASCO moved for sanctions, invoking the District Court's inherent power, Fed.Rule Civ.Proc. 11, and 28 U.S.C. § 1927. After full briefing and a hearing, see 124 F.R.D., at 141, n. 11, the District Court determined that sanctions were appropriate....

* * *

In imposing the sanctions, the District Court first considered Federal Rule of Civil Procedure 11. It noted that the alleged sanctionable conduct was that Chambers and the other defendants had "(1) attempted to deprive this Court of jurisdiction by acts of fraud, nearly all of which were performed outside the confines of this Court, (2) filed false and frivolous pleadings, and (3) attempted, by other tactics of delay, oppression, harassment and massive expense to reduce plaintiff to exhausted compliance." Id., at 138. The court recognized that the conduct in the first and third categories could not be reached by Rule 11, which governs only papers filed with a court. As for the second category, the court explained that the falsity of the pleadings at issue did not become apparent until after the trial on the merits, so that it would have been impossible to assess sanctions at the time the papers were filed. Id., at 138–139. Consequently, the District Court deemed Rule 11 "insufficient" for its purposes. Id., at 139. The court likewise declined to impose sanctions under § 1927,[1] both because the statute applies only to attorneys, and therefore would not reach Chambers, and because the statute was not broad enough to reach "acts which degrade the judicial system," including "attempts to deprive the Court of jurisdiction, fraud, misleading and lying to the Court." Ibid. The court therefore relied on its inherent power in imposing sanctions, stressing that "[t]he wielding of that inherent power is particularly appropriate when the offending parties have practiced a fraud upon the court." Ibid.

The Court of Appeals affirmed.... Because of the importance of these issues, we granted certiorari, 498 U.S. 807, 111 S.Ct. 38, 112 L.Ed.2d 15 (1990).

II

Chambers maintains that 28 U.S.C. § 1927 and the various sanctioning provisions in the Federal Rules of Civil Procedure reflect a legislative intent to displace the inherent power. At least, he argues that they obviate or foreclose resort to the inherent power in this case. We agree with the Court of Appeals that neither proposition is persuasive.

A

It has long been understood that "[c]ertain implied powers must necessarily result to our Courts of justice from the nature of their institution," powers "which cannot be dispensed with in a Court, because they are necessary to the exercise of all others." United States v. Hudson, 7 Cranch 32, 34, 3 L.Ed. 259 (1812); see also Roadway Express, Inc. v. Piper, 447 U.S. 752, 764, 100 S.Ct. 2455, 2463, 65 L.Ed.2d 488 (1980) (citing Hudson). For this reason, "Courts of justice are universally acknowledged to be vested, by their very creation, with power to impose silence, respect, and decorum, in their presence, and submission to their lawful mandates." Anderson v. Dunn, 6 Wheat. 204, 227, 5 L.Ed. 242 (1821); see also Ex parte Robinson, 19 Wall. 505, 510, 22 L.Ed. 205 (1874). These powers are "governed not by rule or statute but by the control necessarily vested in courts to manage their own affairs so as to achieve the orderly and expeditious disposition of cases." Link v. Wabash R. Co., 370 U.S. 626, 630–631, 82 S.Ct. 1386, 1388–1389, 8 L.Ed.2d 734 (1962).

Prior cases have outlined the scope of the inherent power of the federal courts. For example, the Court has held that a federal court has the power to control admission to its bar and to discipline attorneys who appear before it. See Ex parte Burr, 9 Wheat. 529, 531, 6 L.Ed. 152

1. That statute provides: "Any attorney ... who so multiplies the proceedings in any case unreasonably and vexatiously may be required by the court to satisfy personally the excess costs, expenses, and attorneys' fees reasonably incurred because of such conduct." 28 U.S.C. § 1927.

(1824). While this power "ought to be exercised with great caution," it is nevertheless "incidental to all Courts." Ibid.

In addition, it is firmly established that "[t]he power to punish for contempts is inherent in all courts." Robinson, supra, at 510. This power reaches both conduct before the court and that beyond the court's confines. . . .

Of particular relevance here, the inherent power also allows a federal court to vacate its own judgment upon proof that a fraud has been perpetrated upon the court. See Hazel–Atlas Glass Co. v. Hartford–Empire Co., 322 U.S. 238, 64 S.Ct. 997, 88 L.Ed. 1250 (1944); Universal Oil Products Co. v. Root Refining Co., 328 U.S. 575, 580, 66 S.Ct. 1176, 1179, 90 L.Ed. 1447 (1946). This "historic power of equity to set aside fraudulently begotten judgments," *Hazel–Atlas,* 322 U.S., at 245, 64 S.Ct., at 1001, is necessary to the integrity of the courts, for "tampering with the administration of justice in [this] manner . . . involves far more than an injury to a single litigant. It is a wrong against the institutions set up to protect and safeguard the public." Id., at 246, 64 S.Ct., at 1001. Moreover, a court has the power to conduct an independent investigation in order to determine whether it has been the victim of fraud. *Universal Oil,* supra, 328 U.S., at 580, 66 S.Ct., at 1179. There are other facets to a federal court's inherent power. The court may bar from the courtroom a criminal defendant who disrupts a trial. Illinois v. Allen, 397 U.S. 337, 90 S.Ct. 1057, 25 L.Ed.2d 353 (1970). It may dismiss an action on grounds of forum non conveniens, Gulf Oil Corp. v. Gilbert, 330 U.S. 501, 507–508, 67 S.Ct. 839, 842–843, 91 L.Ed. 1055 (1947); and it may act sua sponte to dismiss a suit for failure to prosecute, *Link,* supra, 370 U.S., at 630–631, 82 S.Ct., at 1388–1389.

Because of their very potency, inherent powers must be exercised with restraint and discretion. See *Roadway Express,* supra, 447 U.S., at 764, 100 S.Ct., at 2463. A primary aspect of that discretion is the ability to fashion an appropriate sanction for conduct which abuses the judicial process. As we recognize in *Roadway Express,* outright dismissal of a lawsuit, which we had upheld in *Link,* is a particularly severe sanction, yet is within the court's discretion. 447 U.S., at 765, 100 S.Ct., at 2463. Consequently, the "less severe sanction" of an assessment of attorney's fees is undoubtedly within a court's inherent power as well. Ibid. See also Hutto v. Finney, 437 U.S. 678, 689, n. 14, 98 S.Ct. 2565, 2573, n. 14, 57 L.Ed.2d 522 (1978).

Indeed, "[t]here are ample grounds for recognizing . . . that in narrowly defined circumstances federal courts have inherent power to assess attorney's fees against counsel," *Roadway Express,* supra, 447 U.S., at 765, 100 S.Ct., at 2463, even though the so-called "American Rule" prohibits fee-shifting in most cases. See Alyeska Pipeline Service Co. v. Wilderness Society, 421 U.S. 240, 259, 95 S.Ct. 1612, 1622, 44 L.Ed.2d 141 (1975). As we explained in *Alyeska,* these exceptions fall into three categories. The first, known as the "common fund exception," derives not from a court's power to control litigants, but from its historic equity jurisdiction, see Sprague v. Ticonic National Bank, 307 U.S. 161, 164, 59 S.Ct. 777, 778, 83 L.Ed. 1184 (1939), and allows a court to award attorney's fees to a party whose litigation efforts directly benefit others. *Alyeska,* 421 U.S., at 257–258, 95 S.Ct., at 1621–1622. Second, a court may assess attorney's fees as a sanction for the " 'willful disobedience of a court order.' " Id., at 258, 95 S.Ct., at 1622 (quoting Fleischmann Distilling Corp. v. Maier Brewing Co., 386 U.S. 714, 718, 87 S.Ct. 1404, 1407, 18 L.Ed.2d 475 (1967)). Thus, a court's discretion to determine "[t]he degree of punishment for contempt" permits the court to impose as part of the fine attorney's fees representing the entire cost of the litigation. Toledo Scale Co. v. Computing Scale Co., 261 U.S. 399, 428, 43 S.Ct. 458, 466, 67 L.Ed. 719 (1923).

Third, and most relevant here, a court may assess attorney's fees when a party has " 'acted in bad faith, vexatiously, wantonly, or for oppressive reasons.' " *Alyeska,* supra, 421 U.S., at 258–259, 95 S.Ct., at 1622–1623 (quoting F.D. Rich Co. v. United States ex rel. Industrial Lumber Co., 417 U.S. 116, 129, 94 S.Ct. 2157, 2165, 40 L.Ed.2d 703 (1974)).... In this regard, if a court finds "that fraud has been practiced upon it, or that the very temple of justice has been defiled," it may assess attorney's fees against the responsible party, *Universal Oil,* supra, 328 U.S., at 580, 66 S.Ct., at 1179, as it may when a party "shows bad faith by delaying or disrupting the litigation or by hampering enforcement of a court order," *Hutto,* 437 U.S., at 689, n. 14, 98 S.Ct., at 2573, n. 14. The imposition of sanctions in this instance transcends a court's equitable power concerning relations between the parties and reaches a court's inherent power to police itself, thus serving the dual purpose of "vindicat[ing] judicial authority without resort to the more drastic sanctions available for contempt of court and mak[ing] the prevailing party whole for expenses caused by his opponent's obstinacy." Ibid.

B

We discern no basis for holding that the sanctioning scheme of the statute and the rules displaces the inherent power to impose sanctions for the bad-faith conduct described above. These other mechanisms, taken alone or together, are not substitutes for the inherent power, for that power is both broader and narrower than other means of imposing sanctions. First, whereas each of the other mechanisms reaches only certain individuals or conduct, the inherent power extends to a full range of litigation abuses. At the very least, the inherent power must continue to exist to fill in the interstices.... Second, while the narrow exceptions to the American Rule effectively limit a court's inherent power to impose attorney's fees as a sanction to cases in which a litigant has engaged in bad-faith conduct or willful disobedience of a court's orders, many of the other mechanisms permit a court to impose attorney's fees as a sanction for conduct which merely fails to meet a reasonableness standard. Rule 11, for example, imposes an objective standard of reasonable inquiry which does not mandate a finding of bad faith. See Business Guides, Inc. v. Chromatic Communications Enterprises, Inc., 498 U.S. 533, ___, 111 S.Ct. 922, 932, 112 L.Ed.2d 1140 (1991).

It is true that the exercise of the inherent power of lower federal courts can be limited by statute and rule, for "[t]hese courts were created by act of Congress." *Robinson,* 19 Wall., at 511. Nevertheless, "we do not lightly assume that Congress has intended to depart from established principles" such as the scope of a court's inherent power. Weinberger v. Romero–Barcelo, 456 U.S. 305, 313, 102 S.Ct. 1798, 1803, 72 L.Ed.2d 91 (1982); see also *Link,* 370 U.S., at 631–632, 82 S.Ct., at 1389–1390....

* * *

The Court's prior cases have indicated that the inherent power of a court can be invoked even if procedural rules exist which sanction the same conduct. In *Link,* it was recognized that a federal district court has the inherent power to dismiss a case sua sponte for failure to prosecute, even though the language of Federal Rule of Civil Procedure 41(b) appeared to require a motion from a party:

"The authority of a court to dismiss sua sponte for lack of prosecution has generally been considered an 'inherent power,' governed not by rule or statute but by the control necessarily vested in courts to manage their own affairs so as to achieve the orderly and expeditious disposition of cases. That it has long gone unquestioned is apparent not only from the many state court decisions sustaining such dismissals, but even from language in this Court's opinion in Redfield v. Ystalyfera Iron Co., 110 U.S. 174, 176 [3 S.Ct. 570, 571, 28 L.Ed. 109 (1884)]. It also has the sanction of wide usage among the District Courts. It would require a much clearer expression of purpose than Rule 41(b) provides for us to assume that it was intended to abrogate so well-acknowledged a proposition." 370 U.S., at 630–632, 82 S.Ct., at 1388–1390 (footnotes omitted).

In *Roadway Express,* a party failed to comply with discovery orders and a court order concerning the schedule for filing briefs. 447 U.S., at 755, 100 S.Ct., at 2458. After determining that § 1927, as it then existed, would not allow for the assessment of attorney's fees, we remanded the case for a consideration of sanctions under both Federal Rule of Civil Procedure 37 and the court's inherent power, while recognizing that invocation of the inherent power would require a finding of bad faith. Id., at 767, 100 S.Ct., at 2464.

* * *

... Much of the bad-faith conduct by Chambers, however, was beyond the reach of the rules, his entire course of conduct throughout the lawsuit evidenced bad faith and an attempt to perpetrate a fraud on the court, and the conduct sanctionable under the rules was intertwined within conduct that only the inherent power could address. In circumstances such as these in which all of a litigant's conduct is deemed sanctionable, requiring a court first to apply rules and statutes containing sanctioning provisions to discrete occurrences before invoking inherent power to address remaining instances of sanctionable conduct would serve only to foster extensive and needless satellite litigation, which is contrary to the aim of the rules themselves. See, e.g., Advisory Committee Notes on the 1983 Amendment to Rule 11, 28 U.S.C.App., pp. 575–576....

III

Chambers asserts that even if federal courts can use their inherent power to assess attorney's fees as a sanction in some cases, they are not free to do so when they sit in diversity, unless the applicable state law recognizes the "bad-faith" exception to the general rule against fee shifting. He relies on footnote 31 in *Alyeska,* in which we stated with regard to the exceptions to the American Rule that "[a] very different situation is presented when a federal court sits in a diversity case. '[I]n an ordinary diversity case where the state law does not run counter to a valid federal statute or rule of court, and usually it will not, state law denying the right to attorney's fees or giving a right thereto, which reflects a substantial policy of the state, should be followed.' 6 J. Moore, Federal Practice ¶ 54.77[2], pp. 1712–1713 (2d ed. 1974) (footnotes omitted)." 421 U.S., at 259, n. 31, 95 S.Ct., at 1622, n. 31. We agree with NASCO that Chambers has misinterpreted footnote 31. The limitation on a court's inherent power described a statute which permits a prevailing party in certain classes of litigation to recover fees....

Only when there is a conflict between state and federal substantive law are the concerns of Erie R. Co. v. Tompkins, 304 U.S. 64, 58 S.Ct. 817, 82 L.Ed. 1188 (1938), at issue. As we explained in Hanna v. Plumer, 380 U.S. 460, 85 S.Ct. 1136, 14 L.Ed.2d 8 (1965), the "outcome determinative" test of *Erie* and Guaranty Trust Co. v. York, 326 U.S. 99, 65 S.Ct. 1464, 89 L.Ed. 2079 (1945), "cannot be read without reference to the twin aims of the *Erie* rule: discouragement of forum-shopping and avoidance of inequitable administration of the laws." 380 U.S., at 468, 85 S.Ct., at 1142. Despite Chambers' protestations to the contrary, neither of these twin aims is implicated by the assessment of attorney's fees as a sanction for bad-faith conduct before the court which involved disobedience of the court's orders and the attempt to defraud the court itself. In our recent decision in Business Guides, Inc. v. Chromatic Communications Enterprises, Inc., 498 U.S., at ___, 111 S.Ct., at 934, we stated, "Rule 11 sanctions do not constitute the kind of fee shifting at issue in *Alyeska* [because they] are not tied to the outcome of litigation; the relevant inquiry is whether a specific filing was, if not successful, at least well founded." Likewise, the imposition of sanctions under the bad-faith exception depends not on which party wins the lawsuit, but on how the parties conduct themselves during the litigation. Consequently, there is no risk that the exception will lead to forum-shopping. Nor is it inequitable to apply the exception to citizens and noncitizens alike, when the party, by controlling his or her conduct in litigation, has the power to determine whether sanctions will be assessed. As the Court of Appeals expressed it, "*Erie* guarantees a litigant that if he takes his state law cause of action to federal court, and abides by the rules of that court, the result in his case will be the same as if he had brought it in state court. It does not allow him to waste the court's time and resources with cantankerous conduct, even in the unlikely event a state court would allow him to do so." 894 F.2d, at 706.

* * *

[In Part IV, the Court finds that the district court acted within its discretion in sanctioning Chambers.]

[Dissenting opinions omitted.]

NOTE

How far does the court's inherent power extend? What is the relation of the decision in the principal case to that in *Alyeska,* casebook at page 116? On the *Chambers v. NASCO* case, see Christiansen, Inherent Sanctioning Power in the Federal Courts After Chambers v. Nasco, Inc., 1992 B.Y.U.L.Rev. 1209; Shuler, Chambers v. Nasco, Inc.: Moving Beyond Rule 11 into the Uncharted Territory of Courts Inherent Power to Sanction, 66 Tul.L.Rev. 591 (1991); Papachristos, Inherent Power Found, Rule 11 Lost: Taking a Shortcut to Impose Sanctions in Chambers v. Nasco, 59 Brook.L.Rev. 1225 (1993).

Part VI

ADJUDICATION AND ITS EFFECTS

Chapter Fourteen

TRIAL

SECTION 1.   STEPS IN A TRIAL

B.   THE VOIR DIRE

[Insert on page 836 at the end of Note (3):]

Batson's bar on the use of peremptory challenges to exclude potential jurors who share a criminal defendant's ethnic group membership was extended to civil litigants in Edmonson v. Leesville Concrete Co., 500 U.S. 614, 111 S.Ct. 2077, 114 L.Ed.2d 660 (1991); in Georgia v. McCollum, 505 U.S. 42, 112 S.Ct. 2348, 120 L.Ed.2d 33 (1992), the *Batson* principle was applied in a criminal prosecution to the defendant's use of peremptory challenges, and in J.E.B. v. Alabama ex rel. T.B., 511 U.S. 127, 114 S.Ct. 1419, 128 L.Ed.2d 89 (1994), the ban was extended to peremptory challenges based on gender.

SECTION 4.   ERRORS LEADING TO NEW TRIALS

C.   CONDITION NEW TRIAL—REMITTITUR AND ADDITUR

GASPERINI v. CENTER FOR HUMANITIES, INC.

Supreme Court of the United States, 1996.
__ U.S. __, 116 S.Ct. 2211, 135 L.Ed.2d 659.

JUSTICE GINSBURG delivered the opinion of the Court.*

Under the law of New York, appellate courts are empowered to review the size of jury verdicts and to order new trials when the jury's award "deviates materially from what would be reasonable compensation." N. Y. Civ. Prac. Law and Rules (CPLR) § 5501(c) (McKinney 1995). Under the Seventh Amendment, which governs proceedings in federal court, but not in state court, "the right of trial by jury shall be

---

* Some footnotes omitted; others renumbered.

228

preserved, and no fact tried by a jury, shall be otherwise re-examined in any Court of the United States, than according to the rules of the common law." U.S. Const., Amdt. 7. The compatibility of these provisions, in an action based on New York law but tried in federal court by reason of the parties' diverse citizenship, is the issue we confront in this case. We hold that New York's law controlling compensation awards for excessiveness or inadequacy can be given effect, without detriment to the Seventh Amendment, if the review standard set out in CPLR § 5501(c) is applied by the federal trial court judge, with appellate control of the trial court's ruling limited to review for "abuse of discretion." *Holding*

I

Petitioner William Gasperini, a journalist for CBS News and the Christian Science Monitor, began reporting on events in Central America in 1984. He earned his living primarily in radio and print media and only occasionally sold his photographic work. During the course of his seven-year stint in Central America, Gasperini took over 5,000 slide transparencies, depicting active war zones, political leaders, and scenes from daily life. In 1990, Gasperini agreed to supply his original color transparencies to The Center for Humanities, Inc. (Center) for use in an educational videotape, Conflict in Central America. Gasperini selected 300 of his slides for the Center; its videotape included 110 of them. The Center agreed to return the original transparencies, but upon the completion of the project, it could not find them.

Gasperini commenced suit in the United States District Court for the Southern District of New York, invoking the court's diversity jurisdiction pursuant to 28 U.S.C. § 1332[1] He alleged several state-law claims for relief, including breach of contract, conversion, and negligence. See App. 5–6. The Center conceded liability for the lost transparencies and the issue of damages was tried before a jury.

At trial, Gasperini's expert witness testified that the "industry standard" within the photographic publishing community valued a lost transparency at $1,500. See id., at 227. This industry standard, the expert explained, represented the average license fee a commercial photograph could earn over the full course of the photographer's copyright, i.e., in Gasperini's case, his lifetime plus 50 years. See id., at 228; see also 17 U.S.C. § 302(a). Gasperini estimated that his earnings from photography totaled just over $10,000 for the period from 1984 through 1993. He also testified that he intended to produce a book containing his best photographs from Central America. See App. 175.

After a three-day trial, the jury awarded Gasperini $450,000 in compensatory damages. This sum, the jury foreperson announced, "is [$]1500 each, for 300 slides." Id., at 313. Moving for a new trial under Federal Rule of Civil Procedure 59, the Center attacked the verdict on

---

1. Plaintiff Gasperini, petitioner here, is a citizen of California; defendant Center, respondent here, is incorporated, and has its principal place of business, in New York.

various grounds, including excessiveness. Without comment, the District Court denied the motion. See App. to Pet. for Cert. 12a.

The Court of Appeals for the Second Circuit vacated the judgment entered on the jury's verdict. 66 F.3d 427 (1995). Mindful that New York law governed the controversy, the Court of Appeals endeavored to apply CPLR § 5501(c), which instructs that, when a jury returns an itemized verdict, as the jury did in this case, the New York Appellate Division "shall determine that an award is excessive or inadequate if it deviates materially from what would be reasonable compensation." The Second Circuit's application of § 5501(c) as a check on the size of the jury's verdict followed Circuit precedent elaborated two weeks earlier in Consorti v. Armstrong World Industries, Inc., 64 F.3d 781, superseded, 72 F.3d 1003 (1995). Surveying Appellate Division decisions that reviewed damage awards for lost transparencies, the Second Circuit concluded that testimony on industry standard alone was insufficient to justify a verdict; prime among other factors warranting consideration were the uniqueness of the slides' subject matter and the photographer's earning level.[2]

Guided by Appellate Division rulings, the Second Circuit held that the $450,000 verdict "materially deviates from what is reasonable compensation." 66 F.3d at 431. Some of Gasperini's transparencies, the second Circuit recognized, were unique, notably those capturing combat situations in which Gasperini was the only photographer present. Id., at 429. But others "depicted either generic scenes or events at which other professional photojournalists were present." Id., at 431. No more than 50 slides merited a $1,500 award, the court concluded, after "giving Gasperini every benefit of the doubt." Ibid. Absent evidence showing significant earnings from photographic endeavors or concrete plans to publish a book, the court further determined, any damage award above $100 each for the remaining slides would be excessive. Remittiturs "present difficult problems for appellate courts," the Second Circuit acknowledged, for court of appeals judges review the evidence from "a cold paper record." Ibid. Nevertheless, the Second Circuit set aside the $450,000 verdict and ordered a new trial, unless Gasperini agreed to an award of $100,000.

---

2. See Nierenberg v. Wursteria, Inc., 189 A.D.2d 571, 571–572, 592 N.Y.S.2d 27, 27–28 (1st Dept.1993) (award reduced from $1,500 to $500 per slide because evidence showed photographer earned little from slide sales); Alen MacWeeney, Inc. v. Esquire Assocs., 176 A.D.2d 217, 218; 574 N.Y.S.2d 340, 341 (1st Dept.1991) (award reduced from $1,500 to $159 per transpar- ency because evidence indicated that images were generic; court distinguished prior ruling in Girard Studio Group, Ltd. v. Young & Rubicam, Inc., 147 A.D.2d 357, 536 N.Y.S.2d 790 (1st Dept.1989), permitting an award reduced from $3,000 to $1,500 per slide where evidence showed that "the lost slides represented classics from a long career").

This case presents an important question regarding the standard a federal court uses to measure the alleged excessiveness of a jury's verdict in an action for damages based on state law. We therefore granted certiorari. 516 U.S. ___ (1996).

II

Before 1986, state and federal courts in New York generally invoked the same judge-made formulation in responding to excessiveness attacks on jury verdicts: courts would not disturb an award unless the amount was so exorbitant that it "shocked the conscience of the court." See Consorti, 72 F.3d at 1012–1013 (collecting cases). As described by the Second Circuit:

"The standard for determining excessiveness and the appropriateness of remittitur in New York is somewhat ambiguous. Prior to 1986, New York law employed the same standard as the federal courts, see Matthews v. CTI Container Transport Int'l Inc., 871 F.2d 270, 278 (2d Cir.1989), which authorized remittitur only if the jury's verdict was so excessive that it 'shocked the conscience of the court.'" Id., at 1012.

See also D. Siegel, Practice Commentaries C5501:10, reprinted in 7B McKinney's Consolidated Laws of New York Ann., p. 25 (1995) ("conventional standard for altering the verdict was that its sum was so great or so small that it 'shocked the conscience' of the court").

In both state and federal courts, trial judges made the excessiveness assessment in the first instance, and appellate judges ordinarily deferred to the trial court's judgment. See, e.g., McAllister v. Adam Packing Corp., 66 A.D.2d 975, 976, 412 N.Y.S.2d 50, 52 (3d Dept. 1978) ("The trial court's determination as to the adequacy of the jury verdict will only be disturbed by an appellate court where it can be said that the trial court's exercise of discretion was not reasonably grounded."); Martell v. Boardwalk Enterprises, Inc., 748 F.2d 740, 750 (C.A.2 1984) ("The trial court's refusal to set aside or reduce a jury award will be overturned only for abuse of discretion.").

In 1986, as part of a series of tort reform measures, New York codified a standard for judicial review of the size of jury awards. Placed in CPLR § 5501(c), the prescription reads:

"In reviewing a money judgment ... in which it is contended that the award is excessive or inadequate and that a new trial should have been granted unless a stipulation is entered to a different award, the appellate division shall determine that an award is excessive or inadequate if it deviates materially from what would be reasonable compensation."

As stated in Legislative Findings and Declarations accompanying New York's adoption of the "deviates materially" formulation, the lawmakers found the "shock the conscience" test an insufficient check on damage awards; the legislature therefore installed a standard "inviting more careful appellate scrutiny." Ch. 266, 1986 N. Y. Laws 470 (McKinney). At the same time, the legislature instructed the Appellate Division, in amended § 5522, to state the reasons for the court's rulings on the size of verdicts, and the factors the court considered in complying with § 5501(c). In his signing statement, then-Governor Mario Cuomo emphasized that the CPLR amendments were meant to rachet up the review standard: "This will assure greater scrutiny of the amount of verdicts and promote greater stability in the tort system and greater fairness for similarly situated defendants throughout the State." Memorandum on Approving L. 1986, Ch. 682, 1986 N. Y. Laws, at 3184; see also Newman & Ahmuty, Appellate Review of Punitive Damage Awards, in Insurance, Excess, and Reinsurance Coverage Disputes 1990, p. 409 (B. Ostrager & T. Newman eds. 1990) (review standard prescribed in § 5501(c) "was intended to ... encourage Appellate Division modification of excessive awards").

New York state-court opinions confirm that § 5501(c)'s "deviates materially" standard calls for closer surveillance than "shock the conscience" oversight. See, e.g., O'Connor v. Graziosi, 131 A.D.2d 553, 554, 516 N.Y.S.2d 276, 277 (2d Dept.1987) ("apparent intent" of 1986 legislation was "to facilitate appellate changes in verdicts"); Harvey v. Mazal American Partners, 79 N.Y.2d 218, 225, 590 N.E.2d 224, 228, 581 N.Y.S.2d 639 (1992) (instructing Appellate Division to use, in setting remittitur, only the "deviates materially" standard, and not the "shock the conscience" test); see also Consorti, 72 F.3d at 1013 ("Material deviation from reasonableness is less than that deviation required to find an award so excessive as to 'shock the conscience.' ''); 7 J. Weinstein, H. Korn, & A. Miller, New York Civil Practice, P5501.21, p. 55–64 (1995) ("Under [§ 5501 (c)'s] new standard, the reviewing court is given greater power to review the size of a jury award than had heretofore been afforded....").

Although phrased as a direction to New York's intermediate appellate courts, § 5501(c)'s "deviates materially" standard, as construed by New York's courts, instructs state trial judges as well. See, e.g., Inya v. Ide Hyundai, Inc., 209 A.D.2d 1015, 1015, 619 N.Y.S.2d 440, 440 (4th Dept.1994) (error for trial court to apply "shock the conscience" test to motion to set aside damages; proper standard is whether award "materially deviates from what would be reasonable compensation"); Cochetti v. Gralow, 192 A.D.2d 974, 975, 597 N.Y.S.2d 234, 235 (3d Dept.1993) ("settled law" that trial courts conduct "materially deviates" inquiry); Shurgan v. Tedesco, 179 A.D.2d 805, 806, 578 N.Y.S.2d 658, 659 (2d Dept. 1992) (approving trial court's application of "materially deviates" standard); see also Lightfoot v. Union Carbide Corp. 901 F.Supp. 166, 169 (S.D.N.Y.1995) (CPLR 5501(c)'s "materially deviates" standard "is pretty well established as applicable to [state] trial and appellate courts."). Application of § 5501(c) at the trial level is key to this case.

To determine whether an award "deviates materially from what would be reasonable compensation," New York state courts look to awards approved in similar cases. See, e.g., Leon v. J & M Peppe Realty Corp., 190 A.D.2d 400, 416, 596 N.Y.S.2d 380, 389 (1st Dept.1993) ("These awards ... are not out of line with recent awards sustained by appellate courts."); Johnston v. Joyce, 192 A.D.2d 1124, 1125, 596 N.Y.S.2d 625, 626 (4th Dept.1993) (reducing award to maximum amount previously allowed for similar type of harm). Under New York's former "shock the conscience" test, courts also referred to analogous cases. See, e.g., Senko v. Fonda, 53 A.D. 2d 638, 639, 384 N. Y S. 2d 849, 851 (2d Dept.1976). The "deviates materially" standard, however, in design and operation, influences outcomes by tightening the range of tolerable awards. See, e.g., Consorti, 72 F.3d at 1013, and n. 10, 1014–1015, and n. 14.

III

In cases like Gasperini's, in which New York law governs the claims for relief, does New York law also supply the test for federal court review of the size of the verdict? The Center answers yes. The "deviates materially" standard, it argues, is a substantive standard that must be applied by federal appellate courts in diversity cases. The Second Circuit agreed. See 66 F.3d at 430; see also Consorti, 72 F.3d at 1011 ("[CPLR § 5501(c)] is the substantive rule provided by New York law."). Gasperini, emphasizing that § 5501(c) trains on the New York Appellate Division, characterizes the provision as procedural, an allocation of decision-making authority regarding damages, not a hard cap on the amount recoverable. Correctly comprehended, Gasperini urges, § 5501(c)'s direction to the Appellate Division cannot be given effect by federal appellate courts without violating the Seventh Amendment's re-examination clause.

As the parties' arguments suggest, CPLR § 5501(c), appraised under Erie R. Co. v. Tompkins, 304 U.S. 64, 82 L.Ed. 1188, 58 S.Ct. 817 (1938), and decisions in Erie's path, is both "substantive" and "procedural": "substantive" in that § 5501(c)'s "deviates materially" standard controls how much a plaintiff can be awarded; "procedural" in that § 5501(c) assigns decisionmaking authority to New York's Appellate Division. Parallel application of § 5501(c) at the federal appellate level would be out of sync with the federal system's division of trial and appellate court functions, an allocation weighted by the Seventh Amendment. The dispositive question, therefore, is whether federal courts can give effect to the substantive thrust of § 5501(c) without untoward alteration of the federal scheme for the trial and decision of civil cases.

A

Federal diversity jurisdiction provides an alternative forum for the adjudication of state-created rights, but it does not carry with it generation of rules of substantive law. As Erie read the Rules of Decision Act:

"Except in matters governed by the Federal Constitution or by Acts of Congress, the law to be applied in any case is the law of the State." 304 U.S. at 78. Under the Eric doctrine, federal courts sitting in diversity apply state substantive law and federal procedural law.

Classification of a law as "substantive" or "procedural" for Erie purposes is sometimes a challenging endeavor.[3] Guaranty Trust Co. v. York, 326 U.S. 99, 89 L.Ed. 2079, 65 S.Ct. 1464 (1945), an early interpretation of Erie, propounded an "outcome-determination" test: "Does it significantly affect the result of a litigation for a federal court to disregard a law of a State that would be controlling in an action upon the same claim by the same parties in a State court?" 326 U.S. at 109. Ordering application of a state statute of limitations to an equity proceeding in federal court, the Court said in Guaranty Trust: "Where a federal court is exercising jurisdiction solely because of the diversity of citizenship of the parties, the outcome of the litigation in the federal court should be substantially the same, so far as legal rules determine the outcome of a litigation, as it would be if tried in a State court." Ibid; see also Ragan v. Merchants Transfer & Warehouse Co., 337 U.S. 530, 533, 93 L.Ed. 1520, 69 S.Ct. 1233 (1949) (when local law that creates the cause of action qualifies it, "federal court must follow suit," for "a different measure of the cause of action in one court than in the other [would transgress] the principle of Erie"). A later pathmarking case, qualifying Guaranty Trust, explained that the "outcome-determination" test must not be applied mechanically to sweep in all manner of variations; instead, its application must be guided by "the twin aims of the Erie rule: discouragement of forum shopping and avoidance of inequitable administration of the laws." Hanna v. Plumer, 380 U.S. 460, 468, 14 L.Ed.2d 8, 85 S.Ct. 1136 (1965).

Informed by these decisions, we address the question whether New York's "deviates materially" standard, codified in CPLR § 5501(c), is outcome-affective in this sense: Would "application of the [standard] . . . have so important an effect upon the fortunes of one or both of the litigants that failure to [apply] it would [unfairly discriminate against

---

3. Concerning matters covered by the Federal Rules of Civil Procedure, the characterization question is usually unproblematic: It is settled that if the Rule in point is consonant with the Rules Enabling Act, 28 U.S.C. § 2072, and the Constitution, the Federal Rule applies regardless of contrary state law. See Hanna v. Plumer, 380 U.S. 460, 469–474, 14 L.Ed. 2d 8, 85 S.Ct. 1136 (1965); Burlington Northern R. Co. v. Woods, 480 U.S. 1, 4–5, 94 L.Ed.2d 1, 107 S.Ct. 967 (1987). Federal courts have interpreted the Federal Rules, however, with sensitivity to important state interests and regulatory policies. See, e.g., Walker v. Armco Steel Corp., 446 U.S. 740, 750–752, 64 L.Ed.2d 659, 100 S.Ct. 1978 (1980) (reaffirming decision in Ragan v. Merchants Transfer & Warehouse Co., 337 U.S. 530, 93 L.Ed. 1520, 69 S.Ct. 1233 (1949), that state law rather than Rule 3 determines when a diversity action commences for the purposes of tolling the state statute of limitations; Rule 3 makes no reference to the tolling of state limitations, the Court observed, and accordingly found no "direct conflict"); S. A. Healy Co. v. Milwaukee Metropolitan Sewerage Dist., 60 F.3d 305, 310–312 (C.A.7 1995) (state provision for offers of settlement by plaintiffs is compatible with Federal Rule 68, which is limited to offers by defendants).

citizens of the forum State, or] be likely to cause a plaintiff to choose the federal court"? Id., at 468, n. 9.

We start from a point the parties do not debate. Gasperini acknowledges that a statutory cap on damages would supply substantive law for Erie purposes.... Although CPLR § 5501(c) is less readily classified, it was designed to provide an analogous control.

New York's Legislature codified in § 5501(c) a new standard, one that requires closer court review than the common law "shock the conscience" test.... More rigorous comparative evaluations attend application of § 5501(c)'s "deviates materially" standard. ... To foster predictability, the legislature required the reviewing court, when overturning a verdict under § 5501(c), to state its reasons, including the factors it considered relevant. See CPLR § 5522(b).... We think it a fair conclusion that CPLR § 5501(c) differs from a statutory cap principally "in that the maximum amount recoverable is not set by statute, but rather is determined by case law." Brief for City of New York as Amicus Curiae 11. In sum, § 5501(c) contains a procedural instruction, ..., but the State's objective is manifestly substantive. Cf. S. A. Healy Co. v. Milwaukee Metropolitan Sewerage Dist., 60 F.3d 305, 310 (C.A.7 1995).

It thus appears that if federal courts ignore the change in the New York standard and persist in applying the "shock the conscience" test to damage awards on claims governed by New York law, " 'substantial' variations between state and federal [money judgments]" may be expected. See Hanna, 380 U.S. at 467–468. We therefore agree with the Second Circuit that New York's check on excessive damages implicates what we have called Erie's "twin aims.".... Just as the Erie principle precludes a federal court from giving a state-created claim "longer life ... than [the claim] would have had in the state court," Ragan, 337 U.S. at 533–534, so Eric precludes a recovery in federal court significantly larger than the recovery that would have been tolerated in state court.

B

CPLR § 5501(c) ... is phrased as a direction to the New York Appellate Division. Acting essentially as a surrogate for a New York appellate forum, the Court of Appeals reviewed Gasperini's award to determine if it "deviated materially" from damage awards the Appellate Division permitted in similar circumstances. The Court of Appeals performed this task without benefit of an opinion from the District Court, which had denied "without comment" the Center's Rule 59 motion. 66 F.3d at 428. Concentrating on the authority § 5501(c) gives to the Appellate Division, Gasperini urges that the provision shifts fact-finding responsibility from the jury and the trial judge to the appellate court. Assigning such responsibility to an appellate court, he maintains, is incompatible with the Seventh Amendment's re-examination clause, and therefore, Gasperini concludes, § 5501(c) cannot be given effect in federal court. Although we reach a different conclusion than Gasperini, we agree that the Second Circuit did not attend to "an essential characteristic of [the federal-court] system," Byrd v. Blue Ridge Rural Elec. Cooperative, Inc., 356 U.S. 525, 537, 2 L.Ed.2d 953, 78 S.Ct. 893 (1958), when it used § 5501 (c) as "the standard for [federal] appellate review," Consorti, 72 F.3d at 1013; see also 66 F.3d at 430.

That "essential characteristic" was described in Byrd, a diversity suit for negligence in which a pivotal issue of fact would have been tried by a judge were the case in state court. The Byrd Court held that, despite the state practice, the plaintiff was entitled to a jury trial in federal court. In so ruling, the Court said that the Guaranty Trust "outcome-determination" test was an insufficient guide in cases presenting countervailing federal interests. See Byrd, 356 U.S. at 537. The Court described the countervailing federal interests present in Byrd this way:

"The federal system is an independent system for administering justice to litigants who properly invoke its jurisdiction. An essential characteristic of that system is the manner in which, in civil common-law actions, it distributes trial functions between judge and jury and, under the influence—if not the command—of the Seventh Amendment, assigns the decisions of disputed questions of fact to the jury." Ibid. (footnote omitted).

The Seventh Amendment, which governs proceedings in federal court, but not in state court, bears not only on the allocation of trial functions between judge and jury, the issue in Byrd; it also controls the allocation of authority to review verdicts, the issue of concern here.

* * *

Byrd involved the first clause of the Amendment, the "trial by jury" clause. This case involves the second, the "re-examination" clause. In keeping with the historic understanding, the re-examination clause does not inhibit the authority of trial judges to grant new trials "for any of the reasons for which new trials have heretofore been granted in actions at law in the courts of the United States." Fed. Rule Civ. Proc. 59(a). That authority is large. See 6A Moore's Federal Practice P59.05[2], pp. 59–44 to 59–46 (2d ed. 1996) ("The power of the English common law trial courts to grant a new trial for a variety of reasons with a view to the attainment of justice was well established prior to the establishment of our Government."); see also Aetna Casualty & Surety Co. v. Yeatts, 122 F.2d 350, 353 (C.A.4 1941) ("The exercise of [the trial court's power to set aside the jury's verdict and grant a new trial] is not in derogation of the right of trial by jury but is one of the historic safeguards of that right."); Blunt v. Little, 3 F. Cas. 760, 761–762 (Case No. 1,578) (C.C. Mass. 1822) (Story, J.) ("If it should clearly appear that the jury have committed a gross error, or have acted from improper motives, or have given damages excessive in relation to the person or the injury, it is as much the duty of the court to interfere, to prevent the wrong, as in any

other case."). "The trial judge in the federal system," we have reaffirmed, "has . . . discretion to grant a new trial if the verdict appears to [the
judge] to be against the weight of the evidence." Byrd, 356 U.S. at 540.
This discretion includes overturning verdicts for excessiveness and ordering a new trial without qualification, or conditioned on the verdict
winner's refusal to agree to a reduction (remittitur). See Dimick v.
Schiedt, 293 U.S. 474, 486–487, 79 L.Ed. 603, 55 S.Ct. 296 (1935)
(recognizing that remittitur withstands Seventh Amendment attack, but
rejecting additur as unconstitutional).

In contrast, appellate review of a federal trial court's denial of a
motion to set aside a jury's verdict as excessive is a relatively late, and
less secure, development. Such review was once deemed inconsonant
with the Seventh Amendment's re-examination clause. See, e.g., Lincoln
v. Power, 151 U.S. 436, 437–438, 38 L.Ed. 224, 14 S.Ct. 387 (1894),
Williamson v. Osenton, 220 F. 653, 655 (C.A.4 1915); see also 6A Moore's
Federal Practice P59.Q8[6], at 59–167 (collecting cases). We subsequently recognized that, even in cases in which the Erie doctrine was not in
play—cases arising wholly under federal law-the question was not settled; we twice granted certiorari to decide the unsettled issue, but
ultimately resolved the cases on other grounds. See Grunenthal v. Long
Island R. Co., 393 U.S. 156, 158, 21 L.Ed.2d 309, 89 S.Ct. 331 (1968)
Neese v. Southern R. Co., 350 U.S. 77, 77, 100 L.Ed. 60, 76 S.Ct. 131
(1955).

Before today, we have not "expressly [held] that the Seventh
Amendment allows appellate review of a district court's denial of a
motion to set aside an award as excessive." Browning-Ferris Industries
of Vt., Inc. v. Kelco Disposal, Inc., 492 U.S. 257, 279, n. 25, 106 L.Ed.2d
219, 109 S.Ct. 2909 (1989). But in successive reminders that the question was worthy of this Court's attention, we noted, without disapproval,
that courts of appeals engage in review of district court excessiveness
determinations, applying "abuse of discretion" as their standard. See
Grunenthal, 393 U.S. at 159. We noted the Circuit decisions in point, id.,
at 157, n. 3, and, in Browning–Ferris, we again referred to appellate
court abuse-of-discretion review:

"[T]he role of the district court is to determine whether the jury's
verdict is within the confines set by state law, and to determine, by
reference to federal standards developed under Rule 59, whether a new
trial or remittitur should be ordered. The court of appeals should then
review the district court's determination under an abuse-of-discretion
standard." 492 U.S. at 279.

As the Second Circuit explained, appellate review for abuse of
discretion is reconcilable with the Seventh Amendment as a control
necessary and proper to the fair administration of justice: "We must give
the benefit of every doubt to the judgment of the trial judge; but surely
there must be an upper limit, and whether that has been surpassed is

not a question of fact with respect to which reasonable men may differ, but a question of law." Dagnello v. Long Island R. Co., 289 F.2d 797, 806 (C.A.2 1961) (quoted in Grunenthal, 393 U.S. at 159). All other Circuits agree. See, e.g., Holmes v. Elgin, Joliet & Eastern Ry. Co., 18 F.3d 1393, 1396 (C.A.7 1994); 11 C. Wright, A. Miller, & M. Kane, Federal Practice and Procedure § 2820, P. 209 (2d ed. 1995) ("Every circuit has said that there are circumstances in which it can reverse the denial of a new trial if the size of the verdict seems to be too far out of line."); 6A Moore's Federal Practice P59.08[6], at 59–177 to 59–185 (same). We now approve this line of decisions, and thus make explicit what Justice Stewart thought implicit in our Grunenthal disposition: "Nothing in the Seventh Amendment ... precludes appellate review of the trial judge's denial of a motion to set aside [a jury verdict] as excessive." 393 U.S. at 164 (Stewart, J., dissenting) (internal quotation marks and footnote omitted).[4]

C

In Byrd, the Court faced a one-or-the-other choice: trial by judge as in state court, or trial by jury according to the federal practice. In the the case before us, a choice of that order is not required, for the principal state and federal interests can be accommodated. The Second Circuit correctly recognized that when New York substantive law governs a claim for relief, New York law and decisions guide the allowable damages. See 66 F.3d at 430; see also Consorti, 72 F.3d at 1011. But that court did not take into account the characteristic of the federal-court system that caused us to reaffirm: "The proper role of the trial and appellate courts in the federal system in reviewing the size of jury verdicts is.... a matter of federal law." Donovan v. Penn Shipping Co., 429 U.S. 648, 649, 51 L.Ed.2d 112, 97 S.Ct. 835 (1977) (per curiam); see also Browning-Ferris, 492 U.S. at 279 ("The role of the district court is to determine whether the jury's verdict is within the confines set by state law.... The court of appeals should then review the district court's determination under an abuse-of-discretion standard.").

---

4. If the meaning of the Seventh Amendment were fixed at 1791, our civil juries would remain, as they unquestionably were at common law, "twelve good men and true," 3 W. Blackstone, Commentaries *349; see Capital Traction Co. v. Hof, 174 U.S. 1, 13, 43 L.Ed. 873, 19 S.Ct. 580 (1899) (" 'Trial by jury' in the primary and usual sense of the term at the common law and in the American constitutions ... is a trial by a jury of twelve men[.]"). But see Colgrove v. Battin, 413 U.S. 149, 160, 37 L.Ed.2d 522, 93 S.Ct. 2448 (1973) (six-member jury for civil trials satisfies Seventh Amendment's guarantee). Procedures we have regarded as compatible with the Seventh Amendment, although not in conformity with practice at common law when the Amendment was adopted, include new trials restricted to the determination of damages, Gasoline Products Co. v. Champlin Refining Co., 283 U.S. 494, 75 L.Ed. 1188, 51 S.Ct. 513 (1931), and Federal Rule of Civil Procedure 50(b)'s motion for judgment as a matter of law, see 9A C. Wright & A. Miller, Federal Practice and Procedure § 2522, pp. 244–246 (2d ed. 1995). See also Parklane Hosiery Co. v. Shore, 439 U.S. 322, 335–337, 58 L.Ed.2d 552, 99 S.Ct. 645 (1979) (issue preclusion absent mutuality of parties does not violate Seventh Amendment, although common law as it existed in 1791 permitted issue preclusion only when there was mutuality).

New York's dominant interest can be respected, without disrupting the federal system, once it is recognized that the federal district court is capable of performing the checking function, i.e., that court can apply the State's "deviates materially" standard in line with New York case law evolving under CPLR § 5501(c).[5] We recall, in this regard, that the "deviates materially" standard serves as the guide to be applied in trial as well as appellate courts in New York. ...

Within the federal system, practical reasons combine with Seventh Amendment constraints to lodge in the district court, not the court of appeals, primary responsibility for application of § 5501(c)'s "deviates materially" check. Trial judges have the "unique opportunity to consider the evidence in the living courtroom context," Taylor v. Washington Terminal Co., 133 U.S. App. D.C. 110, 409 F.2d 145, 148 (C.A.D.C.1969), while appellate judges see only the "cold paper record," 66 F.3d at 431.

District court applications of the "deviates materially" standard would be subject to appellate review under the standard the Circuits now employ when inadequacy or excessiveness is asserted on appeal: abuse of discretion. See 11 Wright & Miller, Federal Practice and Procedure § 2820, at 212–214, and n. 24 (collecting cases); see 6A Moore's Federal Practice P59.08[6], at 59–177 to 59–185 (same). In light of Erie's doctrine, the federal appeals court must be guided by the damage-control standard state law supplies, but as the Second Circuit itself has said: "If we reverse, it must be because of an abuse of discretion.... The very nature of the problem counsels restraint.... We must give the benefit of every doubt to the judgment of the trial judge." Dagnello, 289 F.2d at 806.

IV

It does not appear that the District Court checked the jury's verdict against the relevant New York decisions demanding more than "industry standard" testimony to support an award of the size the jury

---

5. JUSTICE SCALIA finds in Federal Rule of Civil Procedure 59 a "federal standard" for new trial motions in " 'direct collision' " with, and " 'leaving no room for the operation of,' " a state law like CPLR § 5501 (c) (quoting Burlington Northern R. Co., 480 U.S. at 4–5). The relevant prescription, Rule 59(a), has remained unchanged since the adoption of the Federal Rules by this Court in 1937. 302 U.S. 783. Rule 59(a) is as encompassing as it is uncontroversial. It is indeed "Hornbook" law that a most usual ground for a Rule 59 motion is that "the damages are excessive." See C. Wright, Law of Federal Courts 676–677 (5th ed. 1994). Whether damages are excessive for the claim-in-suit must be governed by some law. And there is no candidate for that governance other than the law that gives rise to the claim for relief—here, the law of New York. See 28 U.S.C. § 2072(a) and (b) ("Supreme Court shall have the power to prescribe general rules of ... procedure"; "such rules shall not abridge, enlarge or modify any substantive right"); Browning-Ferris, 492 U.S. at 279 ("standard of excessiveness" is a "matter of state, and not federal, common law"); see also R. Fallon, D. Meltzer, & D. Shapiro, Hart and Wechsler's The Federal Courts and the Federal System 729–730 (4th ed. 1996) (observing that Court "has continued since [Hanna v. Plumer, 380 U.S. 460, 14 L.Ed.2d 8, 85 S.Ct. 1136 (1965)] to interpret the federal rules to avoid conflict with important state regulatory policies," citing Walker v. Armco Steel Corp., 446 U.S. 740, 64 L.Ed.2d 659, 100 S.Ct. 1978 (1980)).

returned in this case. As the Court of Appeals recognized, see 66 F.3d at 429, the uniqueness of the photographs and the plaintiff's earnings as photographer—past and reasonably projected—are factors relevant to appraisal of the award. See, e.g., Blackman v. Michael Friedman Publishing Group, Inc., 201 A.D.2d 328, 328, 607 N.Y.S.2d 43, 44 (1st Dept. 1994); Nierenberg v. Wursteria, Inc., 189 A.D.2d 571, 571–572, 592 N.Y.S.2d 27, 27–28 (1st Dept.1993). Accordingly, we vacate the judgment of the Court of Appeals and instruct that court to remand the case to the District Court so that the trial judge, revisiting his ruling on the new trial motion, may test the jury's verdict against CLPR § 5501(c)'s "deviates materially" standard.

It is so ordered.

JUSTICE STEVENS, dissenting [omitted].

JUSTICE SCALIA, with whom the CHIEF JUSTICE and JUSTICE THOMAS join, dissenting.

Today the Court overrules a longstanding and well-reasoned line of precedent that has for years prohibited federal appellate courts from reviewing refusals by district courts to set aside civil jury awards as contrary to the weight of the evidence. One reason is given for overruling these cases: that the courts of appeals have, for some time now, decided to ignore them. Such unreasoned capitulation to the nullification of what was long regarded as a core component of the Bill of Rights—the Seventh Amendment's prohibition on appellate reexamination of civil jury awards—is wrong. It is not for us, much less for the courts of appeals, to decide that the Seventh Amendment's restriction on federal-court review of jury findings has outlived its usefulness.

The Court also holds today that a state practice that relates to the division of duties between state judges and juries must be followed by federal courts in diversity cases. On this issue, too, our prior cases are directly to the contrary.

As I would reverse the judgment of the Court of Appeals, I respectfully dissent.

* * *

NOTE

What are the implications of the decision in the principal case on whether the federal courts may apply state law standards in determining the acceptable amount when ordering remittitur?

SECTION 5. WITHDRAWING THE CASE FROM THE JURY

A. DIRECTED VERDICT

[Insert on page 895 at Section 5(A):]

Under the 1991 Amendments to the Federal Rules of Civil Procedure, a motion for a directed verdict has been renamed a "motion for judgment as a matter of law" under Rule 50(a).

[Insert on page 910 at Note (7):]

Under the 1991 Amendments to the Federal Rules of Civil Procedure, a Rule 41(b) motion to dismiss for legal insufficiency of the plaintiff's evidence should now be brought under Rule 52(c). A motion for a directed verdict pursuant to Rule 50(a) should now be called a "motion for judgment as a matter of law."

B.   JUDGMENT NOTWITHSTANDING THE VERDICT

[Insert on page 911 at Section 5(B):]

Under the 1991 Amendments to the Federal Rules of Civil Procedure, a judgment notwithstanding the verdict has been renamed a "motion for judgment as a matter of law" under Rule 50(b).

[Insert on page 915 at the NOTE ON DIRECTED VERDICT PRACTICE:]

Under the 1991 Amendments to the Federal Rules of Civil Procedure, directed verdicts and judgments notwithstanding the verdict have been renamed motions "for judgment as a matter of law" under Rule 50. Procedures have been changed to require the moving party to articulate the basis for rendering judgment.

[Insert on page 916 after the second full paragraph:]

The more flexible application, however, will likely be checked by the modifications to Rule 50 made by the 1991 Amendments to the Federal Rules of Civil Procedure. The new Rule 50(b) absolutely requires a "motion for a judgment as a matter of law" be made before the jury renders a verdict if the right to make the same motion following the return of a verdict is to be retained, see Committee Note to Proposed Rule 50.

[Insert on page 917 in lieu of the "Proposed Amendments to Rule 50":]

Since publication of the bound volume, the Supreme Court has approved the Advisory Committee's changes to Rule 50, but rejected modifications to Rule 56.

Chapter Sixteen

RES JUDICATA [FORMER ADJUDICATION]

SECTION 1. ESSENTIAL DISTINCTIONS

[Insert at page 955, in lieu of *Patterson*:]

PLANNED PARENTHOOD v. CASEY

Supreme Court of the United States, 1992.
505 U.S. 833, 112 S.Ct. 2791, 120 L.Ed.2d 674.

JUSTICE O'CONNOR, JUSTICE KENNEDY, and JUSTICE SOUTER announced the judgment of the Court and delivered the opinion of the Court with respect to Parts I, II, III, V–A, V–C, and VI, an opinion with respect to Part V–E, in which JUSTICE STEVENS joins, and an opinion with respect to Parts IV, V–B, and V–D.

I

Liberty finds no refuge in a jurisprudence of doubt. Yet 19 years after our holding that the Constitution protects a woman's right to terminate her pregnancy in its early stages, Roe v. Wade, 410 U.S. 113, 93 S.Ct. 705, 35 L.Ed.2d 147 (1973), that definition of liberty is still questioned. Joining the respondents as amicus curiae, the United States, as it has done in five other cases in the last decade, again asks us to overrule Roe. . . .

At issue in these cases are five provisions of the Pennsylvania Abortion Control Act of 1982 as amended in 1988 and 1989. 18 Pa.Cons.Stat. §§ 3203–3220 (1990). . . .   [These provisions require, among other things, a 24 hour waiting period between the provision of information about the abortion and the actual act; for a minor, the consent of one parent or a judicial bypass; for a married woman, notification of her husband. "Medical emergencies" (as defined by the Act) are exempt.]

Before any of these provisions took effect, the petitioners, who are five abortion clinics and one physician representing himself as well as a class of physicians who provide abortion services, brought this suit seeking declaratory and injunctive relief. Each provision was challenged as unconstitutional on its face. . . .

* * *

After considering the fundamental constitutional questions resolved by *Roe,* principles of institutional integrity, and the rule of stare decisis, we are led to conclude this: the essential holding of Roe v. Wade should be retained and once again reaffirmed.

* * *

III

A

The obligation to follow precedent begins with necessity, and a contrary necessity marks its outer limit. With Cardozo, we recognize that no judicial system could do society's work if it eyed each issue afresh in every case that raised it. See B. Cardozo, The Nature of the Judicial Process 149 (1921). Indeed, the very concept of the rule of law underlying our own Constitution requires such continuity over time that a respect for precedent is, by definition, indispensable. See Powell, Stare Decisis and Judicial Restraint, 1991 Journal of Supreme Court History 13, 16. At the other extreme, a different necessity would make itself felt if a prior judicial ruling should come to be seen so clearly as error that its enforcement was for that very reason doomed.

Even when the decision to overrule a prior case is not, as in the rare, latter instance, virtually foreordained, it is common wisdom that the rule of stare decisis is not an "inexorable command," and certainly it is not such in every constitutional case, see Burnet v. Coronado Oil Gas Co., 285 U.S. 393, 405–411, 52 S.Ct. 443, 446–449, 76 L.Ed. 815 (1932) (Brandeis, J., dissenting).... Rather, when this Court reexamines a prior holding, its judgment is customarily informed by a series of prudential and pragmatic considerations designed to test the consistency of overruling a prior decision with the ideal of the rule of law, and to gauge the respective costs of reaffirming and overruling a prior case. Thus, for example, we may ask whether the rule has proved to be intolerable simply in defying practical workability, Swift & Co. v. Wickham, 382 U.S. 111, 116, 86 S.Ct. 258, 261, 15 L.Ed.2d 194 (1965); whether the rule is subject to a kind of reliance that would lend a special hardship to the consequences of overruling and add inequity to the cost of repudiation, e.g., United States v. Title Ins. & Trust Co., 265 U.S. 472, 486, 44 S.Ct. 621, 623, 68 L.Ed. 1110 (1924); whether related principles of law have so far developed as to have left the old rule no more than a remnant of abandoned doctrine, see Patterson v. McLean Credit Union, 491 U.S. 164, 173–174, 109 S.Ct. 2363, 2371, 105 L.Ed.2d 132 (1989); or whether facts have so changed or come to be seen so differently, as to have robbed the old rule of significant application or justification, e.g., Burnet, supra, 285 U.S., at 412, 52 S.Ct., at 449 (Brandeis, J., dissenting).

* * *

1

Although *Roe* has engendered opposition, it has in no sense proven "unworkable," see Garcia v. San Antonio Metropolitan Transit Authority, 469 U.S. 528, 546, 105 S.Ct. 1005, 1015, 83 L.Ed.2d 1016 (1985), representing as it does a simple limitation beyond which a state law is unenforceable. While *Roe* has, of course, required judicial assessment of state laws affecting the exercise of the choice guaranteed against government infringement, and although the need for such review will remain as a consequence of today's decision, the required determinations fall within judicial competence.

2

The inquiry into reliance counts the cost of a rule's repudiation as it would fall on those who have relied reasonably on the rule's continued application. Since the classic case for weighing reliance heavily in favor of following the earlier rule occurs in the commercial context, see Payne v. Tennessee, 501 U.S. 808, ___, 111 S.Ct. 2597, ___, where advance planning of great precision is most obviously a necessity, it is no cause for surprise that some would find no reliance worthy of consideration in support of *Roe*.

While neither respondents nor their amici in so many words deny that the abortion right invites some reliance prior to its actual exercise, one can readily imagine an argument stressing the dissimilarity of this case to one involving property or contract. Abortion is customarily chosen as an unplanned response to the consequence of unplanned activity or to the failure of conventional birth control, and except on the assumption that no intercourse would have occurred but for *Roe*'s holding, such behavior may appear to justify no reliance claim. Even if reliance could be claimed on that unrealistic assumption, the argument might run, any reliance interest would be de minimis. This argument would be premised on the hypothesis that reproductive planning could take virtually immediate account of any sudden restoration of state authority to ban abortions.

To eliminate the issue of reliance that easily, however, one would need to limit cognizable reliance to specific instances of sexual activity. But to do this would be simply to refuse to face the fact that for two decades of economic and social developments, people have organized intimate relationships and made choices that define their views of themselves and their places in society, in reliance on the availability of abortion in the event that contraception should fail. The ability of women to participate equally in the economic and social life of the Nation has been facilitated by their ability to control their reproductive lives. See, e.g., R. Petchesky, Abortion and Woman's Choice 109, 133, n. 7 (rev. ed. 1990). The Constitution serves human values, and while the effect of reliance on *Roe* cannot be exactly measured, neither can the certain cost of overruling *Roe* for people who have ordered their thinking and living around that case be dismissed.

3

No evolution of legal principle has left *Roe*'s doctrinal footings weaker than they were in 1973. No development of constitutional law since the case was decided has implicitly or explicitly left *Roe* behind as a mere survivor of obsolete constitutional thinking.

It will be recognized, of course, that *Roe* stands at an intersection of two lines of decisions, but in whichever doctrinal category one reads the case, the result for present purposes will be the same. The *Roe* Court itself placed its holding in the succession of cases most prominently exemplified by Griswold v. Connecticut, 381 U.S. 479, 85 S.Ct. 1678, 14 L.Ed.2d 510 (1965), see *Roe,* 410 U.S., at 152–153, 93 S.Ct., at 726. When it is so seen, *Roe* is clearly in no jeopardy, since subsequent constitutional developments have neither disturbed, nor do they threaten to diminish, the scope of recognized protection accorded to the liberty relating to intimate relationships, the family, and decisions about whether or not to beget or bear a child. See, e.g., Carey v. Population Services International, 431 U.S. 678, 97 S.Ct. 2010, 52 L.Ed.2d 675 (1977); Moore v. East Cleveland, 431 U.S. 494, 97 S.Ct. 1932, 52 L.Ed.2d 531 (1977).

Roe, however, may be seen not only as an exemplar of *Griswold* liberty but as a rule (whether or not mistaken) of personal autonomy and bodily integrity, with doctrinal affinity to cases recognizing limits on governmental power to mandate medical treatment or to bar its rejection. If so, our cases since *Roe* accord with *Roe*'s view that a State's interest in the protection of life falls short of justifying any plenary override of individual liberty claims. Cruzan v. Director, Missouri Dept. of Health, 497 U.S. 261, 278, 110 S.Ct. 2841, ___, 111 L.Ed.2d 224 (1990). . . .

        * * *

4

We have seen how time has overtaken some of *Roe*'s factual assumptions: advances in maternal health care allow for abortions safe to the mother later in pregnancy than was true in 1973, see Akron v. Akron Center for Reproductive Health Inc., 462 U.S. 416, 429 n. 11, 103 S.Ct. 2481, 2492 n. 11, 76 L.Ed.2d 687 (1983), and advances in neonatal care have advanced viability to a point somewhat earlier. Compare *Roe,* 410 U.S., at 160, 93 S.Ct., at 730, with Webster v. Reproductive Health Services, 492 U.S. 490, 515–516, 109 S.Ct. 3040, 3055, 106 L.Ed.2d 410 (1989) (opinion of Rehnquist, C.J.); see *Akron I,* supra, 462 U.S., at 457, and n. 5, 103 S.Ct., at 2489, and n. 5 (O'Connor, J., dissenting). But these facts go only to the scheme of time limits on the realization of competing interests, and the divergences from the factual premises of 1973 have no bearing on the validity of *Roe*'s central holding, that viability marks the earliest point at which the State's interest in fetal life is constitutionally adequate to justify a legislative ban on nontherapeutic abortions. . . .

    * * *

C

. . . Our analysis would not be complete . . . without explaining why overruling *Roe*'s central holding would not only reach an unjustifiable result under principles of stare decisis, but would seriously weaken the Court's capacity to exercise the judicial power and to function as the Supreme Court of a Nation dedicated to the rule of law. To understand why this would be so it is necessary to understand the source of this Court's authority, the conditions necessary for its preservation, and its relationship to the country's understanding of itself as a constitutional Republic.

The root of American governmental power is revealed most clearly in the instance of the power conferred by the Constitution upon the Judiciary of the United States and specifically upon this Court. As Americans of each succeeding generation are rightly told, the Court cannot buy support for its decisions by spending money and, except to a minor degree, it cannot independently coerce obedience to its decrees. The Court's power lies, rather, in its legitimacy, a product of substance and perception that shows itself in the people's acceptance of the Judiciary as fit to determine what the Nation's law means and to declare what it demands.

The underlying substance of this legitimacy is of course the warrant for the Court's decisions in the Constitution and the lesser sources of legal principle on which the Court draws. That substance is expressed in the Court's opinions, and our contemporary understanding is such that a decision without principled justification would be no judicial act at all. But even when justification is furnished by apposite legal principle, something more is required. Because not every conscientious claim of principled justification will be accepted as such, the justification claimed must be beyond dispute. The Court must take care to speak and act in ways that allow people to accept its decisions on the terms the Court claims for them, as grounded truly in principle, not as compromises with social and political pressures having, as such, no bearing on the principled choices that the Court is obliged to make. Thus, the Court's legitimacy depends on making legally principled decisions under circumstances in which their principled character is sufficiently plausible to be accepted by the Nation.

The need for principled action to be perceived as such is implicated to some degree whenever this, or any other appellate court, overrules a prior case. This is not to say, of course, that this Court cannot give a perfectly satisfactory explanation in most cases. People understand that some of the Constitution's language is hard to fathom and that the Court's Justices are sometimes able to perceive significant facts or to understand principles of law that eluded their predecessors and that justify departures from existing decisions. However upsetting it may be to those most directly affected when one judicially derived rule replaces another, the country can accept some correction of error without necessarily questioning the legitimacy of the Court.

In two circumstances, however, the Court would almost certainly fail to receive the benefit of the doubt in overruling prior cases. There is, first, a point beyond which frequent overruling would overtax the country's belief in the Court's good faith.... If that limit should be exceeded, disturbance of prior rulings would be taken as evidence that justifiable reexamination of principle had given way to drives for particular results in the short term. The legitimacy of the Court would fade with the frequency of its vacillation.

That first circumstance can be described as hypothetical; the second is the point here and now. Where, in the performance of its judicial duties, the Court decides a case in such as way as to resolve the sort of intensely divisive controversy reflected in *Roe* ..., its decision has a dimension that the resolution of a normal case does not carry. It is this dimension present whenever the Court's interpretation of the Constitution calls the contending sides of a national controversy to end their national division by accepting a common mandate rooted in the Constitution.

* * *

It is true that diminished legitimacy may be restored, but only slowly. Unlike the political branches, a Court thus weakened could not seek to regain its position with a new mandate from the voters, and even if the Court could somehow go to the polls, the loss of its principled character could not be retrieved by the casting of so many votes. Like the character of an individual, the legitimacy of the Court must be earned over time. So, indeed, must be the character of a Nation of people who aspire to live according to the rule of law. Their belief in themselves as such a people is not readily separable from their understanding of the Court invested with the authority to decide their constitutional cases and speak before all others for their constitutional ideals. If the Court's legitimacy should be undermined, then, so would the country be in its very ability to see itself through its constitutional ideals. The Court's concern with legitimacy is not for the sake of the Court but for the sake of the Nation to which it is responsible.

The Court's duty in the present case is clear. In 1973, it confronted the already-divisive issue of governmental power to limit personal choice to undergo abortion, for which it provided a new resolution based on the due process guaranteed by the Fourteenth Amendment. Whether or not a new social consensus is developing on that issue, its divisiveness is no less today than in 1973, and pressure to overrule the decision, like pressure to retain it, has grown only more intense. A decision to overrule *Roe*'s essential holding under the existing circumstances would address error, if error there was, at the cost of both profound and unnecessary damage to the Court's legitimacy, and to the Nation's commitment to the rule of law. It is therefore imperative to adhere to the essence of *Roe*'s original decision, and we do so today.

* * *

SECTION 3. ISSUE PRECLUSION

D. VALID AND FINAL JUDGMENT

[Insert on page 1002, at the end of Note (4):]

Astoria Federal Savings and Loan Ass'n v. Solimino, 501 U.S. 104, 111 S.Ct. 2166, 115 L.Ed.2d 96 (1991), adds an important qualification to the rule announced in *Elliott*. In that case, plaintiff initially filed a claim under the Age Discrimination Act of 1967, 29 U.S.C.A. § 621, with the EEOC. In accordance with its regulations, the EEOC referred the matter to the state agency responsible for the disposition of age-discrimination cases. When that agency issued an adverse decision, plaintiff decided not to appeal. Instead, he refiled in federal district court. Reasoning that the findings of the state agency were preclusive on the factual issues raised in the plaintiff's claims, the district court granted defendant's motion for summary judgment. The Supreme Court disapproved this use of issue preclusion, holding that estoppel rules depend heavily on context. Since the statutory scheme at issue plainly contemplated that a federal action could be instituted after agency consideration was completed, so-called "administrative estoppel" was inappropriate.

[Insert on page 1002, after Note (5):]

(6) Does a determination made by an arbitral tribunal have preclusive effect in a subsequent court proceeding? Conversely, does a determination made by a court have preclusive effect in an arbitral proceeding? In Aufderhar v. Data Dispatch, Inc., 452 N.W.2d 648 (Minn.1990), the Supreme Court of Minnesota, in the course of holding the prior ruling by an arbitral tribunal on the issue of damages binding in a subsequent court proceeding, considered both questions (at pp. 651–653):

> [The plaintiff had obtained a determination of his damages against an uninsured motorist in arbitration. He then sued Schuck and Data Dispatch, other parties involved in the same accident, in court. These defendants argued that plaintiff was precluded from relitigating the issue of damages.]
>
> ... Most courts have considered an arbitration award to constitute a "prior adjudication" for purposes of triggering an estoppel. See, e.g., *United Food and Commercial Workers Int'l Union—Indus. Pension*

Fund v. G. Bartusch Packing Co., 546 F.Supp. 852, 855 (D.Minn.1982). We, likewise, have afforded to an arbitration award finality as to both facts and the law. *State, by Sundquist v. Minnesota Teamsters Public and Law Enforcement Employees Union Local No. 320,* 316 N.W.2d 542, 544 (Minn.1982); *Grudem Bros. Co. v. Great Western Piping Corp.,* 297 Minn. 313, 316–317, 213 N.W.2d 920, 922–23 (1973). Even in *Consolidated Freightways,* after we first observed that collateral estoppel had been applied to prevent relitigation of issues decided in other types of proceedings, which, like arbitration, are less structured and formal than traditional court actions, we further acknowledged that "arbitration is meant to be a final judgment of both law and fact." *Consolidated Freightways,* 420 N.W.2d at 613.

* * *

In this case, the "claimant" in the arbitration, and the plaintiff at trial are one and the same. Because it is clear Aufderhar was afforded "a full and fair opportunity to be heard" on the damage issue, we perceive no reason to deny the application of estoppel to prevent relitigation of that issue. To the contrary, to permit it here is entirely consistent with the public policy underlying this court's traditional encouragement of alternative forms of dispute resolution, as well as policies designed to promote judicial efficiency.

But, Aufderhar argues, to so hold runs counter to two of our cases which held that *a prior court action* did not have res judicata or collateral estoppel effect in a *later arbitration* proceeding. See *Milwaukee Mut. Ins. Co. v. Currier,* 310 Minn. 81, 245 N.W.2d 248 (1976); *Nat'l Indem. Co. v. Farm Bureau Mut. Ins. Co.,* 348 N.W.2d 748 (Minn.1984). We disagree. A close examination of each case demonstrates that the holding in neither, by analogy or otherwise, supports appellant's argument.

The issue in *Milwaukee Mutual* was whether the parties had agreed that the prior trial court adjudication would take the place of arbitration, and, therefore, had waived their contract right to arbitrate. Had they waived that right by their actions, no agreement to arbitrate would have existed resulting in lack of jurisdiction in the court to stay arbitration under Minn.Stat. § 572.09(b) (1988). We held the parties had not waived their contracted for arbitration right.

In *National Indemnity,* we expanded on that holding in a case where the right to arbitration arose by statute rather than from a contractual agreement. The dispute in *National Indemnity* related to indemnity between two insurers pursuant to Minn.Stat. § 65B.53, subd. 1 and 4 (1988). The statutes permit indemnification of a no fault automobile insurance carrier for benefits paid as a result of a collision by an at fault "commercial vehicle." We held that a judgment following a judicial proceeding did not extinguish the statutory right to arbitrate the issue because the statute bound the two insurers to arbitrate as had the insurance contract provision to arbitrate in *Milwaukee Mutual.* These issues of statutory and contractual obligations that existed in *Milwaukee Mutual* and *National Indemnity* are not involved in this case. Here, Aufderhar's right to arbitrate was created by the contract between himself and his uninsured motorist insurer—a contract to which Schuck and Data Dispatch were strangers and which afforded them no rights to participate in the arbitration. Neither case relied upon by Aufderhar supports his argument.

SECTION 5. INTERSYSTEM PRECLUSION

[Insert on page 1021 after the first paragraph in Section 5:]

(The following chart was inadvertently omitted:)

I	II	III
A: State–A	A: State	A: Federal
B: State–B	B: Federal	B: State

[Insert at page 1030, after Note (7):]

(8) Should the considerations the Court applied in *Marrese* apply to class actions, where the decision to sue on state claims in state court is made by representatives, not by the entire class? Should it make a difference if non-named class members had already brought their own suit on the federal claims in federal court? Review Matsushita Electric Industrial Co. v. Epstein, supra, page 135.

B. STATE/FEDERAL PRECLUSION

[Omit Note (5) on page 1030.]

Part VII

EFFORTS TO CONTROL DECISION MAKERS

Chapter Seventeen

APPELLATE REVIEW

SECTION 4. FINAL JUDGMENT RULE

[Insert at page 1060, as note (3):]

(3) In Behrens v. Pelletier, ___ U.S. ___, 116 S.Ct. 834, 133 L.Ed.2d 773 (1996), the Supreme Court, with Justices Breyer and Stevens dissenting, ruled that denial of a motion for summary judgment on grounds of qualified immunity was appealable under the collateral order doctrine, even though a prior denial of a motion to dismiss on that ground had been found wanting on an immediate appeal in the same case. The dissent argued that the defendant should not enjoy the benefit of immediate appellate review under the collateral order doctrine for the second time in the same case.

QUACKENBUSH v. ALLSTATE INSURANCE CO.

Supreme Court of the United States, 1996.
___ U.S. ___, 116 S.Ct. 1712, 135 L.Ed. 2d 1.

JUSTICE O'CONNOR delivered the opinion of the Court.

In this case, we consider whether an abstention-based remand order is appealable as a final order under 28 U.S.C. § 1291, and whether the abstention doctrine first recognized in Burford v. Sun Oil Co., 319 U.S. 315, 87 L.Ed. 1424, 63 S.Ct. 1098 (1943), can be applied in a common-law suit for damages.

I

Petitioner, the Insurance Commissioner for the State of California, was appointed trustee over the assets of the Mission Insurance Company and its affiliates (Mission companies) in 1987, after those companies were ordered into liquidation by a California court. In an effort to gather the assets of the defunct Mission companies, the Commissioner filed the instant action against respondent Allstate Insurance Company in state court, seeking contract and tort damages for Allstate's alleged breach of

251

certain reinsurance agreements, as well as a general declaration of Allstate's obligations under those agreements.

Allstate removed the action to federal court on diversity grounds and filed a motion to compel arbitration under the Federal Arbitration Act, 9 U.S.C. § 1 et seq. (1988 ed. and Supp. V). The Commissioner sought remand to state court, arguing that the District Court should abstain from hearing the case under Burford, supra, because its resolution might interfere with California's regulation of the Mission insolvency. Specifically, the Commissioner indicated that Allstate would be asserting its right to set off its own contract claims against the Commissioner's recovery under the contract, that the viability of these setoff claims was a hotly disputed question of state law, and that this question was currently pending before the state courts in another case arising out of the Mission insolvency.

The District Court observed that "California has an overriding interest in regulating insurance insolvencies and liquidations in a uniform and orderly manner," and that in this case "this important state interest could be undermined by inconsistent rulings from the federal and state courts." Based on these observations, and its determination that the setoff question should be resolved in state court, the District Court concluded this case was an appropriate one for the exercise of Burford abstention. The District Court did not stay its hand pending the California courts' resolution of the setoff issue, but instead remanded the entire case to state court. The District Court entered this remand order without ruling on Allstate's motion to compel arbitration.

After determining that appellate review of the District Court's remand order was not barred by 28 U.S.C. § 1447(d), see Garamendi v. Allstate Ins. Co., 47 F.3d 350, 352 (C.A.9 1995) (citing Thermtron Products, Inc. v. Hermansdorfer, 423 U.S. 336, 46 L.Ed.2d 542, 96 S.Ct. 584 (1976)), and that the remand order was appealable under 28 U.S.C. § 1291 as a final collateral order, see 47 F.3d at 353–354 (citing Moses H. Cone Memorial Hospital v. Mercury Constr. Corp., 460 U.S. 1, 74 L.Ed.2d 765, 103 S.Ct. 927 (1983)), the Court of Appeals for the Ninth Circuit vacated the District Court's decision and ordered the case sent to arbitration. The Ninth Circuit concluded that federal courts can abstain from hearing a case under Burford only when the relief being sought is equitable in nature, and therefore held that abstention was inappropriate in this case because the Commissioner purported to be seeking only legal relief. 47 F.3d at 354–356; App. to Pet. for Cert. 35a–37a (order denying petition for rehearing because Commissioner had waived any argument that this case involved a request for equitable relief).

The Ninth Circuit's holding that abstention-based remand orders are appealable conflicts with the decisions of other courts of appeals, see Doughty v. Underwriters at Lloyd's, London, 6 F.3d 856, 865 (C.A.1 1993) (order not appealable); Corcoran v. Ardra Insurance Co., Ltd., 842

F.2d 31, 34 (C.A.2 1988) (same); In re Burns & Wilcox, Ltd., 54 F.3d 475, 477, n. 7 (C.A.8 1995)(same); but see Minot v. Eckardt–Minot, 13 F.3d 590, 593 (C.A.2 1994) (order appealable under collateral order doctrine), as does its determination that Burford abstention can only be exercised in cases in which equitable relief is sought, see Lac D'Amiante du Quebec, Ltee v. American Home Assurance Co., 864 F.2d 1033, 1045 (C.A.3 1988) (Burford abstention appropriate in case seeking declaratory relief); Brandenburg v. Seidel, 859 F.2d 1179, 1192, n. 17 (C.A.4 1988) (Burford abstention appropriate in action for damages); Wolfson v. Mutual Benefit Life Ins. Co., 51 F.3d 141, 147 (C.A.8 1995) (same); but see Fragoso v. Lopez, 991 F.2d 878, 882 (C.A.1 1993) (federal court can abstain under Burford only if it is "sitting in equity"); University of Maryland v. Peat Marwick Main & Co., 923 F.2d 265, 272 (C.A.3 1991) (same); Baltimore Bank for Cooperatives v. Farmers Cheese Cooperative, 583 F.2d 104, 111 (C.A.3 1978) (same). We granted certiorari to resolve these conflicts, 516 U.S. ___ (1995), and now affirm on grounds different than those provided by the Ninth Circuit.

II

We first consider whether the Court of Appeals had jurisdiction to hear Allstate's appeal under 28 U.S.C. § 1291, which confers jurisdiction over appeals from "final decisions" of the district courts, and 28 U.S.C. § 1447(d), which provides that "an order remanding a case to the State court from which it was removed is not reviewable on appeal or otherwise."

We agree with the Ninth Circuit and the parties that § 1447(d) interposes no bar to appellate review of the remand order at issue in this case. See 47 F.3d at 352; .... As we held in Thermtron Products, Inc. v. Hermansdorfer, supra, at 345–346, and reiterated this Term in Things Remembered, Inc. v. Petrarca, 516 U.S. ___, ___ (1995) (slip op. at 3), "§ 1447(d) must be read in pari materia with § 1447(c), so that only remands based on grounds specified in § 1447(c) are immune from review under § 1447(d)." This gloss renders § 1447(d) inapplicable here: The District Court's abstention-based remand order does not fall into either category of remand order described in § 1447(c), as it is not based on lack of subject matter jurisdiction or defects in removal procedure.

Finding no affirmative bar to appellate review of the District Court's remand order, we must determine whether that review may be obtained by appeal under § 1291. The general rule is that "a party is entitled to a single appeal, to be deferred until final judgment has been entered, in which claims of district court error at any stage of the litigation may be ventilated." Digital Equipment Corp. v. Desktop Direct, Inc., 511 U.S. ___, ___ (1994) (slip op., at 4) (citations omitted). Accordingly, we have held that a decision is ordinarily considered final and appealable under § 1291 only if it "ends the litigation on the merits and leaves nothing for the court to do but execute the judgment." Catlin v. United States, 324

U.S. 229, 233, 89 L.Ed.911, 65 S.Ct. 631 (1945); (see also Digital, supra, at ___ slip op., at 3) (quoting this standard). We have also recognized, however, a narrow class of collateral orders which do not meet this definition of finality, but which are nevertheless immediately appealable under § 1291 because they " 'conclusively determine [a] disputed question' " that is " 'completely separate from the merits of the action,' " " 'effectively unreviewable on appeal from a final judgment,' " Richardson–Merrell, Inc. v. Koller, 472 U.S. 424, 431, 86 L.Ed.2d 340, 105 S.Ct. 2757 (1985) (quoting Coopers & Lybrand v. Livesay, 437 U.S. 463, 468, 57 L.Ed.2d 351, 98 S.Ct. 2454 (1978)), and "too important to be denied review," Cohen v. Beneficial Industrial Loan Corp., 337 U.S. 541, 546, 93 L.Ed. 1528, 69 S.Ct. 1221 (1949).

The application of these principles to the appealability of the remand order before us is controlled by our decision in Moses H. Cone Memorial Hospital v. Mercury Constr. Corp., 460 U.S. 1, 74 L.Ed.2d 765, 103 S.Ct. 927 (1983). The District Court in that case entered an order under Colorado River Water Conservation Dist. v. United States, 424 U.S. 800, 47 L.Ed.2d 483, 96 S.Ct. 1236 (1976), staying a federal diversity suit pending the completion of a declaratory judgment action that had been filed in state court. The Court of Appeals held that this stay order was appealable under § 1291, and we affirmed that determination on two independent grounds.

We first concluded that the abstention-based stay order was appealable as a "final decision" under § 1291 because it put the litigants " 'effectively out of court,' " 460 U.S. at 11, n. 11 (quoting Idlewild Bon Voyage Liquor Corp. v. Epstein, 370 U.S. 713, 715, n. 2, 8 L.Ed.2d 794, 82 S.Ct. 1294 (1962) (per curiam)), and because its effect was "precisely to surrender jurisdiction of a federal suit to a state court," 460 U.S. at 11, n. 11. These standards do not reflect our oft-repeated definition of finality, see supra, at 4 (citing Catlin, supra, at 233); (see, e.g., Digital, supra, at ___ slip op., at 3) (citing the Catlin definition); Lauro Lines s.r.l. v. Chasser, 490 U.S. 495, 497, 104 L.Ed.2d 548, 109 S.Ct. 1976 (1989) (same); Van Cauwenberghe v. Biard, 486 U.S. 517, 521–522, 100 L.Ed.2d 517, 108 S.Ct. 1945 (1988) (same), but in Moses H. Cone we found their application to be compelled by precedent, see 460 U.S. at 11, n. 11 ("Idlewild's reasoning is limited to cases where (under Colorado River, abstention, or a closely similar doctrine) the object of the stay is to require all or an essential part of the federal suit to be litigated in a state forum").

As an alternative to this reliance on Idlewild, we also held that the stay order at issue in Moses H. Cone was appealable under the collateral order doctrine. 460 U.S. at 11. We determined that a stay order based on the Colorado River doctrine "presents an important issue separate from the merits" because it "amounts to a refusal to adjudicate" the case in federal court; that such orders could not be reviewed on appeal from a final judgment in the federal action because the district court would be bound, as a matter of res judicata, to honor the state court's judgment; and that unlike other stay orders, which might readily be reconsidered by the district court, abstention-based stay orders of this ilk are "conclusive" because they are the practical equivalent of an order dismissing the case. 460 U.S., at 12.

The District Court's order remanding on grounds of Burford abstention is in all relevant respects indistinguishable from the stay order we found to be appealable in Moses H. Cone. No less than an order staying a federal-court action pending adjudication of the dispute in state court, it puts the litigants in this case " 'effectively out of court,' " Moses H. Cone, supra, at 11, n. 11 (quoting Idlewild Bon Voyage Liquor Corp. v. Epstein, supra, at 715, n. 2), and its effect is "precisely to surrender jurisdiction of a federal suit to a state court," 460 U.S. at 11, n. 11. Indeed, the remand order is clearly more "final" than a stay order in this sense. When a district court remands a case to a state court, the district court disassociates itself from the case entirely, retaining nothing of the matter on the federal court's docket.

The District Court's order is also indistinguishable from the stay order we considered in Moses H. Cone in that it conclusively determines an issue that is separate from the merits, namely the question whether the federal court should decline to exercise its jurisdiction in the interest of comity and federalism. See infra, at 9, 20. In addition, the rights asserted on appeal from the District Court's abstention decision are, in our view, sufficiently important to warrant an immediate appeal. See infra, at 8–9, 17–21 (describing interests weighed in decision to abstain under Burford); (cf. Digital, supra, at ___ slip op., at 15) (review under collateral order doctrine limited to those issues " 'too important to be denied review' ") (quoting Cohen, supra, at 546). And, like the stay order we found appealable in Moses H. Cone, the District Court's remand order in this case will not be subsumed in any other appealable order entered by the District Court.

We have previously stated that "an order remanding a removed action does not represent a final judgment reviewable by appeal." Thermtron Products, Inc. v. Hermansdorfer, 423 U.S. at 352–53. Petitioner asks that we adhere to that statement and hold that appellate review of the District Court's remand order can only be obtained through a petition for writ of mandamus. To the extent Thermtron would require us to ignore the implications of our later holding in Moses H. Cone, however, we disavow it. Thermtron's determination that remand orders are not reviewable "final judgments" doubtless was necessary to the resolution of that case, see 423 U.S. at 352 (posing the question whether mandamus was the appropriate vehicle), but our principal concern in Thermtron was the interpretation of the bar to appellate review embodied in 28 U.S.C. § 1447(d), see supra, at 4, and our statement concerning the appropriate procedural vehicle for reviewing a district court's remand order was peripheral to that concern.

Moreover, the parties in Thermtron did not brief the question, our opinion does not refer to Catlin or its definition of "final decisions," and our opinion nowhere addresses whether any class of remand order might be appealable under the collateral order doctrine. Indeed, the only support Thermtron cites for the proposition that remand orders are reviewable only by mandamus, not by appeal, is Railroad Co. v. Wiswall, 90 U.S. 507, 23 Wall. 507, 23 L.Ed. 103 (1875), the superannuated reasoning of which is of little vitality today, compare id., at 508 (deeming a "writ of error to review what has been done" an inappropriate vehicle for reviewing a court of appeals' "refusal to hear and decide") with Moses H. Cone, 460 U.S. at 10–11, n. 11 (holding that a stay order is appealable because it amounts to a refusal to hear and decide a case).

Admittedly, remand orders like the one entered in this case do not meet the traditional definition of finality—they do not "end the litigation on the merits and leave nothing more for the court to do but execute the judgment," Catlin, 324 U.S. at 233. But because the District Court's remand order is functionally indistinguishable from the stay order we found appealable in Moses H. Cone, see supra, at 6–7, we conclude that it is appealable, and turn to the merits of the Ninth Circuit's decision respecting Burford abstention.

III

A

We have often acknowledged that federal courts have a strict duty to exercise the jurisdiction that is Co upon them by Congress. See, e.g., Colorado River, 424 U.S. at 821 ("Federal courts have a virtually unflagging obligation ... to exercise the jurisdiction given them"); England v. Louisiana Bd. of Medical Examiners, 375 U.S. 411, 415, 11 L.Ed.2d 440, 84 S.Ct. 461 (1964) (" 'When a federal court is properly appealed to in a case over which it has by law jurisdiction, it is its duty to take such jurisdiction' ") (quoting Willcox v. Consolidated Gas Co., 212 U.S. 19, 40, 53 L.Ed. 382, 29 S.Ct. 192 (1909)); Cohens v. Virginia, 19 U.S. 264, 6 Wheat. 264, 404, 5 L.Ed. 257 (1821) (federal courts "have no more right to decline the exercise of jurisdiction which is given, than to usurp that which is not"). This duty is not, however, absolute. See Canada Malting Co. v. Paterson S.S., Ltd., 285 U.S. 413, 422, 76 L.Ed. 837, 52 S.Ct. 413 (1932) ("The proposition that a court having jurisdiction must exercise it, is not universally true"). Indeed, we have held that federal courts may decline to exercise their jurisdiction, in otherwise " 'exceptional circumstances,' " where denying a federal forum would clearly serve an important countervailing interest, Colorado River, supra, at 813 (quoting County of Allegheny v. Frank Mashuda Co., 360 U.S. 185, 189, 3 L.Ed.2d 1163, 79 S.Ct. 1060 (1959)), for example where abstention is warranted by considerations of "proper constitutional adjudication," "regard for federal-state relations," or "wise judicial administration," Colorado River, supra, at 817 (internal quotation marks omitted).

We have thus held that federal courts have the power to refrain from hearing cases that would interfere with a pending state criminal proceeding, see Younger v. Harris, 401 U.S. 37, 27 L.Ed.2d 669, 91 S.Ct. 746 (1971), or with certain types of state civil proceedings, see Huffman v. Pursue, Ltd., 420 U.S. 592, 43 L.Ed.2d 482, 95 S.Ct. 1200 (1975); Juidice v. Vail, 430 U.S. 327, 51 L.Ed.2d 376, 97 S.Ct. 1211 (1977); cases in which the resolution of a federal constitutional question might be obviated if the state courts were given the opportunity to interpret ambiguous state law, see Railroad Comm'n of Tex. v. Pullman Co., 312 U.S. 496, 85 L.Ed. 971, 61 S.Ct. 643 (1941); cases raising issues "intimately involved with [the states'] sovereign prerogative," the proper adjudication of which might be impaired by unsettled questions of state law, see Louisiana Power & Light Co. v. Thibodaux, 360 U.S. 25, 28, 3 L.Ed.2d 1058, 79 S.Ct. 1070 (1959); id., at 31 (Stewart, J., concurring); cases whose resolution by a federal court might unnecessarily interfere with a state system for the collection of taxes, see Great Lakes Dredge & Dock Co. v. Huffman, 319 U.S. 293, 87 L.Ed. 1407, 63 S.Ct. 1070 (1943); and cases which are duplicative of a pending state proceeding, see Colorado River Water Conservation Dist. v. United States, 424 U.S. 800, 47 L.Ed. 2d 483, 96 S.Ct. 1236 (1976); Pennsylvania v. Williams, 294 U.S. 176, 79 L.Ed. 841, 55 S.Ct. 380 (1935).

Our longstanding application of these doctrines reflects "the common-law background against which the statutes conferring jurisdiction were enacted," New Orleans Public Service, Inc. v. Council of City of New Orleans, 491 U.S. 350, 359, 105 L.Ed.2d 298, 109 S.Ct. 2506 (1989) (NOPSI) (citing Shapiro, Jurisdiction and Discretion, 60 N. Y. U. L. Rev. 543, 570–577 (1985)). And, as the Ninth Circuit correctly indicated, 47 F.3d at 354, it has long been established that a federal court has the authority to decline to exercise its jurisdiction when it "is asked to employ its historic powers as a court of equity," Fair Assessment in Real Estate Assn., Inc. v. McNary, 454 U.S. 100, 120, 70 L.Ed.2d 271, 102 S.Ct. 177 (1981) (Brennan, J., concurring). This tradition informs our understanding of the jurisdiction Congress has conferred upon the federal courts, and explains the development of our abstention doctrines. In Pullman, for example, we explained the principle underlying our abstention doctrines as follows:

"... The history of equity jurisdiction is the history of regard for public consequences in employing the extraordinary remedy of the injunction.... Few public interests have a higher claim upon the discretion of a federal chancellor than the avoidance of needless friction with state policies, whether the policy relates to the enforcement of the criminal law, or the administration of a specialized scheme for liquidating embarrassed business enterprises, or the final authority of a state court to interpret doubtful regulatory laws of the state. These cases reflect a doctrine of abstention appropriate to our federal system, whereby the federal courts, 'exercising a wise discretion,' restrain their authority because of 'scrupulous regard for the rightful independence of the state governments' and for the smooth working of the federal judiciary. This use of equitable powers is a contribution of the courts in furthering the harmonious relation between state and federal authority without the need of rigorous congressional restriction of those powers." 312 U.S. at 500–501 (citations omitted).

Though we have thus located the power to abstain in the historic discretion exercised by federal courts "sitting in equity," we have not treated abstention as a "technical rule of equity procedure." Thibodaux, supra, at 28. Rather, we have recognized that the authority of a federal court to abstain from exercising its jurisdiction extends to all cases in which the court has discretion to grant or deny relief. See NOPSI, supra, at 359 (mandate of federal jurisdiction "does not eliminate ... the federal courts' discretion in determining whether to grant certain types of relief"). Accordingly, we have not limited the application of the abstention doctrines to suits for injunctive relief, but have also required federal courts to decline to exercise jurisdiction over certain classes of declaratory judgments, see, e.g., Huffman, 319 U.S. at 297 (federal court must abstain from hearing declaratory judgment action challenging constitutionality of a state tax); Samuels v. Mackell, 401 U.S. 66, 69–70, 72–73, 27 L.Ed.2d 688, 91 S.Ct. 764 (1971) (extending Younger abstention to declaratory judgment actions), the granting of which is generally committed to the courts' discretion, see Wilton v. Seven Falls Co., 515 U.S. ___, ___ (1995) (slip op., at 5) (federal courts have "discretion in determining whether and when to entertain an action under the Declaratory Judgment Act, even when the suit otherwise satisfies subject-matter jurisdictional prerequisites").

Nevertheless, we have not previously addressed whether the principles underlying our abstention cases would support the remand or dismissal of a common-law action for damages. Cf. Deakins v. Monaghan, 484 U.S. 193, 202, 98 L.Ed.2d 529, 108 S.Ct. 523, and n. 6 (1988) (reserving the question whether Younger requires abstention in an action for damages); Ankenbrandt v. Richards, 504 U.S. 689, 119 L.Ed.2d 468, 112 S.Ct. 2206 (1992) (discussing, without applying, Burford abstention in damages action). To be sure, we held in Fair Assessment in Real Estate Assn., Inc. v McNary, supra, that a federal court should not entertain a § 1983 suit for damages based on the enforcement of a state tax scheme, see 454 U.S. at 115, but we have subsequently indicated that Fair Assessment was a case about the scope of the § 1983 cause of action, see National Private Truck Council, Inc. v. Oklahoma Tax Comm'n, 515 U.S. ___, ___, ___ (1995) (slip op., at 7–8), not the abstention doctrines. To the extent Fair Assessment does apply abstention principles, its holding is very limited. The damages action in that case was based on the unconstitutional application of a state tax law, and the award of damages turned first on a declaration that the state tax was in fact unconstitutional. We therefore drew an analogy to Huffman and other cases in which we had approved the application of abstention principles in declaratory judgment actions, and held that the federal court should decline to hear the action because "the recovery of damages under the Civil Rights Act first requires a 'declaration' or determination of the unconstitutionality of a state tax scheme that would halt its operation." Fair Assessment, supra, at 115.

Otherwise, we have applied abstention principles to actions "at law" only to permit a federal court to enter a stay order that postpones adjudication of the dispute, not to dismiss the federal suit altogether. See, e.g., Thibodaux, 360 U.S. at 28–30 (approving stay order); Fornaris v. Ridge Tool Co., 400 U.S. 41, 44, 27 L.Ed.2d 174, 91 S.Ct. 156 (1970) (per curiam) (directing district court to "hold its hand until the Puerto Rican Supreme Court has authoritatively ruled on the local law question in light of the federal claims" (footnote omitted)) (emphasis added); United Gas Pipe Line Co. v. Ideal Cement Co., 369 U.S. 134, 135–136, 7 L.Ed.2d 623, 82 S.Ct. 676 (1962) (per curiam) ("Wise judicial administration in this case counsels that decision of the federal question be deferred until the potentially controlling state-law issue is authoritatively put to rest"); Clay v. Sun Ins. Office Ltd., 363 U.S. 207, 212, 4 L.Ed.2d 1170, 80 S.Ct. 1222 (1960) (approving "postponement of decision" in damages suit).

Our decisions in Thibodaux and County of Allegheny. v. Frank Mashuda Co., 360 U.S. 185, 3 L.Ed.2d 1163, 79 S.Ct. 1060 (1959) illustrate the distinction we have drawn between abstention-based remand orders or dismissals and abstention-based decisions merely to stay adjudication of a federal suit. In Thibodaux, a city in Louisiana brought an eminent domain proceeding in state court, seeking to condemn for public use certain property owned by a Florida corporation. After the corporation removed the action to federal court on diversity grounds, the Federal District Court decided on its own motion to stay the case, pending a state court's determination whether the city could exercise the power of eminent domain under state law. The case did not arise within the "equity" jurisdiction of the federal courts, 360 U.S., at 28, because the suit sought compensation for a taking, and the District Court lacked discretion to deny relief on the corporation's claim. Nonetheless, the issues in the suit were "intimately involved with [the state's] sovereign prerogative." Ibid. We concluded that "the considerations that prevailed in conventional equity suits for avoiding the hazards of serious disruption by federal courts of state government or needless friction between state and federal authorities are similarly appropriate in a state eminent domain proceeding brought in, or removed to, a federal court." Ibid. And based on that conclusion, we affirmed the district court's order staying the case.

County of Allegheny was decided the same day as Thibodaux, and like Thibodaux it involved review of a District Court order abstaining from the exercise of diversity jurisdiction over a state law eminent domain action. Unlike in Thibodaux, however, the District Court in County of Allegheny had not merely stayed adjudication of the federal action pending the resolution of an issue in state court, but rather had dismissed the federal action altogether. Based in large measure on this distinction, we reversed the District Court's order. See 360 U.S. at 190; Thibodaux, 360 U.S., at 31 (Stewart, J., concurring) ("In Mashuda, the Court holds that it was error for the District Court to dismiss the complaint" (emphasis added)).

We were careful to note in Thibodaux that the District Court had only stayed the federal suit pending adjudication of the dispute in state court. Unlike the outright dismissal or remand of a federal suit, we held, an order merely staying the action "does not constitute abnegation of judicial duty. On the contrary, it is a wise and productive discharge of it. There is only postponement of decision for its best fruition." Id., at 29. We have thus held that in cases where the relief being sought is equitable in nature or otherwise discretionary, federal courts not only have the power to stay the action based on abstention principles, but can also, in otherwise appropriate circumstances, decline to exercise jurisdiction altogether by either dismissing the suit or remanding it to state court. By contrast, while we have held that federal courts may stay actions for damages based on abstention principles, we have not held that those principles support the outright dismissal or remand of damages actions.

One final line of cases bears mentioning. Though we deal here with our abstention doctrines, we have recognized that federal courts have discretion to dismiss damages actions, in certain narrow circumstances, under the common-law doctrine of forum non conveniens. The seminal case recognizing this authority is Gulf Oil Corp. v. Gilbert, 330 U.S. 501, 91 L.Ed. 1055, 67 S.Ct. 839 (1947), in which we considered whether a Federal District Court sitting in diversity in New York could dismiss a tort action for damages on the grounds that Virginia provided a more appropriate locale for adjudicating the dispute. Id., at 503. We conceded that the application of this doctrine should be "rare," id., at 509, but also held that the exercise of forum non conveniens is not limited to actions in equity:

"This Court, in recognizing and approving it by name has never indicated that it was rejecting application of the doctrine to law actions which had been an integral and necessary part of [the] evolution of the doctrine. Wherever it is applied in courts in other jurisdictions, its application does not depend on whether the action is at law or in equity." Id., at 505, n. 4 (citations omitted).

The dispute in Gulf Oil was over venue, not jurisdiction, and the expectation was that after dismissal of the suit in New York the parties would refile in federal court, not the state courts of Virginia. This transfer of venue function of the forum non conveniens doctrine has been superseded by statute, see 28 U.S.C. § 1404(a); Piper Aircraft Co. v. Reyno, 454 U.S. 235, 253, 70 L.Ed.2d 419, 102 S.Ct. 252 (1981), and to the extent we have continued to recognize that federal courts have the power to dismiss damages actions under the common-law forum non conveniens doctrine, we have done so only in "cases where the alternative forum is abroad." American Dredging Co. v. Miller, 510 U.S. 443, 449, n. 2 (1994); see, e.g., Piper, 454 U.S., at 265–269 (dismissal of wrongful death action).

The fact that we have applied the forum non conveniens doctrine in this manner does not change our analysis in this case, where we deal with the scope of the Burford abstention doctrine. To be sure, the abstention doctrines and the doctrine of forum non conveniens proceed from a similar premise: In rare circumstances, federal courts can relinquish their jurisdiction in favor of another forum. But our abstention doctrine is of a distinct historical pedigree, and the traditional considerations behind dismissal for forum non conveniens differ markedly from those informing the decision to abstain. Compare American Dredging, supra, at 448–449 (describing "multifarious factors," including both public and private interests, which might allow a district court to dismiss a case under doctrine of forum non conveniens) with Burford, 319 U.S. at 332–333 (describing "federal-state conflict" that requires a federal court to yield jurisdiction in favor of a state forum). Federal courts abstain out of deference to the paramount interests of another sovereign, and the concern is with principles of comity and federalism. See, e.g., ibid.; Younger, 401 U.S. at 44–45. Dismissal for forum non conveniens, by contrast, has historically reflected a far broader range of considerations, see Piper, 454 U.S. at 241, 257–262 (describing the interests which bear on form non conveniens decision); Gulf Oil, 330 U.S. at 508–509 (same), most notably the convenience to the parties and the practical difficulties that can attend the adjudication of a dispute in a certain locality, see Piper, supra, at 257–259 (evidentiary problems, unavailability of witnesses, difficulty of coordinating multiple suits); Gulf Oil, supra, at 511 (availability of witnesses, need to interplead Virginia corporation, location of evidence).

B

With these background principles in mind, we consider the contours of the Burford doctrine. The principal issue presented in Burford was the "reasonableness" of an order issued by the Texas Railroad Commission, which granted "a permit to drill four oil wells on a small plot of land in the East Texas oil field." 319 U.S., at 317.

Due to the potentially overlapping claims of the many parties who might have an interest in a common pool of oil and the need for uniform regulation of the oil industry, Texas endowed the Railroad Commission with exclusive regulatory authority in the area. Texas also placed the authority to review the Commission's orders in a single set of state courts, "to prevent the confusion of multiple review," id., at 326, and to permit an experienced cadre of state judges to obtain "specialized knowledge" in the field, id., at 327. Though Texas had thus demonstrated its interest in maintaining uniform review of the Commission's orders, the federal courts had, in the years preceding Burford, become increasingly involved in reviewing the reasonableness of the Commission's orders, both under a constitutional standard imposed under the Due Process Clause, see, e.g., Railroad Comm'n of Tex. v. Rowan & Nichols Oil Co., 310 U.S. 573, 577, 84 L.Ed. 1368, 60 S.Ct. 1021 (1940), and under state law, which established a similar standard, see Burford, 319 U.S. at 317, 326.

Viewing the case as "a simple proceeding in equity to enjoin the enforcement of the Commissioner's order," id., at 317, we framed the question presented in terms of the power of a federal court of equity to abstain from exercising its jurisdiction:

"Although a federal equity court does have jurisdiction of a particular proceeding, it may, in its sound discretion, whether its jurisdiction is invoked on the ground of diversity of citizenship or otherwise, 'refuse to enforce or protect legal rights, the exercise of which may be prejudicial to the public interest,' for it 'is in the public interest that federal courts of equity should exercise their discretionary power with proper regard for the rightful independence of state governments in carrying out their domestic policy.' While many other questions are argued, we find it necessary to decide only one: Assuming that the federal district court had jurisdiction, should it, as a matter of sound equitable discretion, have declined to exercise that jurisdiction here?" Id., at 317–318 (footnote omitted) (quoting United States ex rel. Greathouse v. Dern, 289 U.S. 352, 360, 77 L.Ed. 1250, 53 S.Ct. 614 (1933) and Pennsylvania v. Williams, 294 U.S. at 185).

Having thus posed the question in terms of the District Court's discretion, as a court sitting "in equity," to decline jurisdiction, we approved the District Court's dismissal of the complaint on a number of grounds that were unique to that case. We noted, for instance, the difficulty of the regulatory issues presented, stating that the "order under consideration is part of the general regulatory system devised for the conservation of oil and gas in Texas, an aspect of 'as thorny a problem as has challenged the ingenuity and wisdom or legislatures.'" 319 U.S., at 318 (quoting Rowan, supra at 579). We also stressed the demonstrated need for uniform regulation in the area, 319 U.S., at 318–319, citing the unified procedures Texas had established to "prevent the confusion of multiple review," id., at 325–326, and the important state interests this uniform system review was designed to serve, id., at 319–320. Most importantly, we also described the detrimental impact of ongoing federal court review of the Commission's orders, which review had already led to contradictory adjudications by the state and federal courts. Id., at 327–328, 331–332.

We ultimately concluded in Burford that dismissal was appropriate because the availability of an alternative, federal forum threatened to frustrate the purpose of the complex administrative system that Texas had established.

* * *

... Ultimately, what is at stake is a federal court's decision, based on a careful consideration of the federal interests in retaining jurisdiction over the dispute and the competing concern for the "independence of state action," Burford, 319 U.S. at 334, that the State's interests are paramount and that a dispute would best be adjudicated in a state forum. See NOPSI, 491 U.S. at 363 (question under Burford is whether adjudication in federal court would "unduly intrude into the processes of state government or undermine the State's ability to maintain desired uniformity"). This equitable decision balances the strong federal interest in having certain classes of cases, and certain federal rights, adjudicated in federal court, against the State's interests in maintaining "uniformity in the treatment of an 'essentially local problem,'" 491 U.S. at 362 (quoting Alabama Pub. Serv. Comm'n, supra, at 347), and retaining local control over "difficult questions of state law bearing on policy problems of substantial public import," Colorado River, supra, at 814. This balance only rarely favors abstention, and the power to dismiss recognized in Burford represents an "'extraordinary and narrow exception to the duty of the District Court to adjudicate a controversy properly before it.'" Colorado River, supra, at 813 (quoting County of Allegheny, 360 U.S., at 188).

C

We turn, finally, to the application of Burford in this case. As in NOPSI, see 491 U.S. at 363, the federal interests in this case are pronounced, as Allstate's motion to compel arbitration under the Federal Arbitration Act implicates a substantial federal concern for the enforcement of arbitration agreements. See Mitsubishi Motors Corp. v. Soler Chrysler–Plymouth, Inc., 473 U.S. 614, 631, 87 L.Ed.2d 444, 105 S.Ct. 3346 (1985) (FAA reflects "emphatic federal policy in favor of arbitral dispute resolution"); cf. Moses H. Cone, 460 U.S. at 25–26 (in deciding whether to defer to state court adjudication under the Colorado River doctrine, "the presence of federal-law issues must always be a major consideration weighing against surrender"). With regard to the state interests, however, the case appears at first blush to present nothing more than a run-of-the-mill contract dispute. The Commissioner seeks damages from Allstate for Allstate's failure to perform its obligations under a reinsurance agreement. What differentiates this case from other diversity actions seeking damages for breach of contract, if anything, is the impact federal adjudication of the dispute might have on the ongoing liquidation proceedings in state court: The Commissioner claims that any recovery by Allstate on its setoff claims would amount to an illegal "preference" under state law. This question appears now to have been conclusively answered by the California Supreme Court, see Prudential Reinsurance Co. v. Superior Court of Los Angeles Cty., 3 Cal.4th 1118, 842 P.2d 48 (1992) (permitting reinsurers to assert setoff claims in suits filed by the Commissioner in the Mission insolvency), although at the time the District Court ruled this question was still hotly contested.

The Ninth Circuit concluded that the District Court's remand order was inappropriate because "Burford abstention does not apply to suits seeking solely legal relief." 47 F.3d at 354. Addressing our abstention cases, the Ninth Circuit held that the federal courts' power to abstain in certain cases is "located ... in the unique powers of equitable courts," and that it derives from equity courts' " 'discretionary power to grant or withhold relief.' " 47 F.3d at 355 (quoting Alabama Pub. Serv. Comm'n v. Southern R. Co., 341 U.S. at 350–351). The Ninth Circuit's reversal of the District Court's abstention-based remand order in this case therefore reflects the application of a per se rule: "The power of federal courts to abstain from exercising their jurisdiction, at least in Burford abstention cases, is founded upon a discretion they possess only in equitable cases." 47 F.3d at 355–356.

To the extent the Ninth Circuit held only that a federal court cannot, under Burford, dismiss or remand an action when the relief sought is not discretionary, its judgment is consistent with our abstention cases. We have explained the power to dismiss or remand a case under the abstention doctrines in terms of the discretion federal courts have traditionally exercised in deciding whether to provide equitable or discretionary relief, see supra, at 9–11, 14, and the Commissioner appears to have conceded that the relief being sought in this case is neither equitable nor otherwise committed to the discretion of the court. See App. to Pet. for Cert. 35a–37a (order denying petition for rehearing). In those cases in which we have applied traditional abstention principles to damages actions, we have only permitted a federal court to "withhold action until the state proceedings have concluded," Growe, 507 U.S. at 32; that is, we have permitted federal courts applying abstention principles in damages actions to enter a stay, but we have not permitted them to dismiss the action altogether, see supra, at 11–14.

The per se rule described by the Ninth Circuit is, however, more rigid than our precedents require. We have not strictly limited abstention to "equitable cases," 47 F.3d at 356, but rather have extended the doctrine to all cases in which a federal court is asked to provide some form of discretionary relief. See Huffman, 319 U.S. at 297; Samuels, 401 U.S. at 69–70, 72–73; supra, at 11. Moreover, as demonstrated by our decision in Thibodaux, see supra, at 12–14, we have not held that abstention principles are completely inapplicable in damages actions. Burford might support a federal court's decision to postpone adjudication of a damages action pending the resolution by the state courts of a disputed question of state law. For example, given the situation the District Court faced in this case, a stay order might have been appropriate: the setoff issue was being decided by the state courts at the time the District Court ruled, see Prudential Reinsurance Co., supra, and in the interest of avoiding inconsistent adjudications on that point, the District Court might have been justified in entering a stay to await the outcome of the state court litigation.

Like the Ninth Circuit, we review only the remand order which was entered, and find it unnecessary to determine whether a more limited abstention-based stay order would have been warranted on the facts of this case. We have no occasion to resolve what additional authority to abstain might be provided under our decision in Fair Assessment, see supra, at 11–12. Nor do we find it necessary to inquire fully as to whether this case presents the sort of "exceptional circumstance" in which Burford abstention or other grounds for yielding federal jurisdiction might be appropriate. Under our precedents, federal courts have the power to dismiss or remand cases based on abstention principles only where the relief being sought is equitable or otherwise discretionary. Because this was a damages action, we conclude that the District Court's remand order was an unwarranted application of the Burford doctrine. The judgment is affirmed.

It is so ordered.

JUSTICE SCALIA, concurring. [Omitted.]

JUSTICE KENNEDY, concurring. [Omitted.]

Chapter Eighteen

REPRISE: ALTERNATIVE METHODS OF CIVIL DISPUTE RESOLUTION, PARTICULARLY ARBITRATION

SECTION 3. VOLUNTARY ARBITRATION

B. ARBITRABILITY

1. AS DETERMINED BY THE ARBITRATION AGREEMENT

[Insert on page 1118, before *Sharon Steel Corp.*:]

FIRST OPTIONS OF CHICAGO, INC. v. KAPLAN

Supreme Court of the United States, 1995.
514 U.S. 938, 115 S.Ct. 1920, 131 L.Ed.2d 985.

JUSTICE BREYER delivered the opinion of the Court.

In this case we consider two questions about how courts should review certain matters under the federal Arbitration Act, 9 U.S.C. § 1 et seq. (1988 Ed. and Supp. V): (1) how a district court should review an arbitrator's decision that the parties agreed to arbitrate a dispute, and (2) how a court of appeals should review a district court's decision confirming, or refusing to vacate, an arbitration award.

I

The case concerns several related disputes between, on one side, First Options of Chicago, Inc., a firm that clears stock trades on the Philadelphia Stock Exchange, and, on the other side, three parties: Manuel Kaplan; his wife, Carol Kaplan; and his wholly owned investment company, MK Investments, Inc. (MKI), whose trading account First Options cleared. The disputes center around a "workout" agreement, embodied in four separate documents, which governs the "working out" of debts to First Options that MKI and the Kaplans incurred as a result of the October 1987 stock market crash. In 1989, after entering into the agreement, MKI lost an additional $1.5 million. First Options then took control of, and liquidated, certain MKI assets; demanded immediate payment of the entire MKI debt; and insisted that the

Kaplans personally pay any deficiency. When its demands went unsatisfied, First Options sought arbitration by a panel of the Philadelphia Stock Exchange.

MKI, having signed the only workout document (out of four) that contained an arbitration clause, accepted arbitration. The Kaplans, however, who had not personally signed that document, denied that their disagreement with First Options was arbitrable and filed written objections to that effect with the arbitration panel. The arbitrators decided that they had the power to rule on the merits of the parties' dispute, and did so in favor of First Options. The Kaplans then asked the Federal District Court to vacate the arbitration award, see 9 U.S.C. § 10 (1988 Ed., Supp. V), and First Options requested its confirmation, see § 9. The court confirmed the award. Nonetheless, on appeal the Court of Appeals for the Third Circuit agreed with the Kaplans that their dispute was not arbitrable; and it reversed the District Court's confirmation of the award against them. 19 F.3d 1503 (1994).

We granted certiorari to consider two questions regarding the standards that the Court of Appeals used to review the determination that the Kaplans' dispute with First Options was arbitrable. 513 U.S. ___, 115 S.Ct. 634, 130 L.Ed.2d 539 (1994). First, the Court of Appeals said that courts "should independently decide whether an arbitration panel has jurisdiction over the merits of any particular dispute." 19 F.3d, at 1509 (emphasis added). First Options asked us to decide whether this is so (i.e., whether courts, in "reviewing the arbitrators' decision on arbitrability," should "apply a de novo standard of review or the more deferential standard applied to arbitrators' decisions on the merits") when the objecting party "submitted the issue to the arbitrators for decision." Pet. for Cert. i. Second, the Court of Appeals stated that it would review a district court's denial of a motion to vacate a commercial arbitration award (and the correlative grant of a motion to confirm it) "de novo." 19 F.3d, at 1509. First Options argues that the Court of Appeals instead should have applied an "abuse of discretion" standard. See Robbins v. Day, 954 F.2d 679, 681–682 (C.A.11 1992).

II

The first question—the standard of review applied to an arbitrator's decision about arbitrability—is a narrow one. To understand just how narrow, consider three types of disagreement present in this case. First, the Kaplans and First Options disagree about whether the Kaplans are personally liable for MKI's debt to First Options. That disagreement makes up the merits of the dispute. Second, they disagree about whether they agreed to arbitrate the merits. That disagreement is about the arbitrability of the dispute. Third, they disagree about who should have the primary power to decide the second matter. Does that power belong primarily to the arbitrators (because the court reviews their arbitrability decision deferentially) or to the court (because the court makes up its mind about arbitrability independently)? We consider here only this third question.

Although the question is a narrow one, it has a certain practical importance. That is because a party who has not agreed to arbitrate will normally have a right to a court's decision about the merits of its dispute (say, as here, its obligation under a contract). But, where the party has agreed to arbitrate, he or she, in effect, has relinquished much of that right's practical value. The party still can ask a court to review the arbitrator's decision, but the court will set that decision aside only in very unusual circumstances. See, e.g., 9 U.S.C. § 10 (award procured by corruption, fraud, or undue means; arbitrator exceeded his powers); Wilko v. Swan, 346 U.S. 427, 436–437, 74 S.Ct. 182, 187–188, 98 L.Ed. 168 (1953) (parties bound by arbitrator's decision not in "manifest disregard" of the law), overruled on other grounds, Rodriguez de Quijas v. Shearson/American Express, Inc., 490 U.S. 477, 109 S.Ct. 1917, 104 L.Ed.2d 526 (1989). Hence, who—court or arbitrator—has the primary authority to decide whether a party has agreed to arbitrate can make a critical difference to a party resisting arbitration.

We believe the answer to the "who" question (i.e., the standard-of-review question) is fairly simple. Just as the arbitrability of the merits of a dispute depends upon whether the parties agreed to arbitrate that dispute, see, e.g., Mastrobuono v. Shearson Lehman Hutton, Inc., 514 U.S. ___, ___, 115 S.Ct. 1212, 1216, 131 L.Ed.2d 76 (1995); Mitsubishi Motors Corp. v. Soler Chrysler–Plymouth, Inc., 473 U.S. 614, 626, 105 S.Ct. 3346, 3353, 87 L.Ed.2d 444 (1985), so the question "who has the primary power to decide arbitrability" turns upon what the parties agreed about that matter. Did the parties agree to submit the arbitrability question itself to arbitration? If so, then the court's standard for reviewing the arbitrator's decision about that matter should not differ from the standard courts apply when they review any other matter that parties have agreed to arbitrate. See AT & T Technologies, Inc. v. Communications Workers, 475 U.S. 643, 649, 106 S.Ct. 1415, 1418, 89 L.Ed.2d 648 (1986) (parties may agree to arbitrate arbitrability); Steelworkers v. Warrior & Gulf Navigation Co., 363 U.S. 574, 583, n. 7, 80 S.Ct. 1347, 1353, n. 7, 4 L.Ed.2d 1409 (1960) (same). That is to say, the court should give considerable leeway to the arbitrator, setting aside his or her decision only in certain narrow circumstances. See, e.g., 9 U.S.C. § 10. If, on the other hand, the parties did not agree to submit the arbitrability question itself to arbitration, then the court should decide that question just as it would decide any other question that the parties did not submit to arbitration, namely independently. These two answers flow inexorably from the fact that arbitration is simply a matter of contract between the parties; it is a way to resolve those disputes—but only those disputes—that the parties have agreed to submit to arbitration. See, e.g., AT & T Technologies, supra, at 649, 106 S.Ct., at 1418; Mastrobuono, supra, at ___, and n. 9, 115 S.Ct., at 1216–1217, and n. 9;

Allied–Bruce Terminix Cos. v. Dobson, 513 U.S. ___, ___, 115 S.Ct. 834, 837–838, 130 L.Ed.2d 753 (1995); Mitsubishi Motors Corp., supra, at 625–626, 105 S.Ct., at 3353.

We agree with First Options, therefore, that a court must defer to an arbitrator's arbitrability decision when the parties submitted that matter to arbitration. Nevertheless, that conclusion does not help First Options win this case. That is because a fair and complete answer to the standard-of-review question requires a word about how a court should decide whether the parties have agreed to submit the arbitrability issue to arbitration. And, that word makes clear that the Kaplans did not agree to arbitrate arbitrability here.

When deciding whether the parties agreed to arbitrate a certain matter (including arbitrability), courts generally (though with a qualification we discuss below) should apply ordinary state-law principles that govern the formation of contracts. See, e.g., Mastrobuono, supra, at ___, and n. 9, 115 S.Ct., at 1219, and n. 9; Volt Information Sciences, Inc. v. Board of Trustees of Leland Stanford Junior Univ., 489 U.S. 468, 475–476, 109 S.Ct. 1248, 1253–1254, 103 L.Ed.2d 488 (1989); Perry v. Thomas, 482 U.S. 483, 492–493, n. 9, 107 S.Ct. 2520, 2526–2527, n. 9, 96 L.Ed.2d 426 (1987); G. Wilner, 1 Domke on Commercial Arbitration s 4:04, p. 15 (rev. ed. Supp.1993) (hereinafter Domke). The relevant state law here, for example, would require the court to see whether the parties objectively revealed an intent to submit the arbitrability issue to arbitration. See, e.g., Estate of Jesmer v. Rohlev, 241 Ill.App.3d 798, 803, 182 Ill.Dec. 282, 286, 609 N.E.2d 816, 820 (1993) (law of the State whose law governs the workout agreement); Burkett v. Allstate Ins. Co., 368 Pa.Super. 600, 608, 534 A.2d 819, 823–824 (1987) (law of the State where the Kaplans objected to arbitrability). See generally Mitsubishi Motors, supra, at 626, 105 S.Ct., at 3353.

This Court, however, has (as we just said) added an important qualification, applicable when courts decide whether a party has agreed that arbitrators should decide arbitrability: Courts should not assume that the parties agreed to arbitrate arbitrability unless there is "clea[r] and unmistakabl[e]" evidence that they did so. AT & T Technologies, supra, at 649, 106 S.Ct., at 1418–1419; see Warrior & Gulf, supra, at 583, n. 7, 80 S.Ct., at 1353, n. 7. In this manner the law treats silence or ambiguity about the question "who (primarily) should decide arbitrability" differently from the way it treats silence or ambiguity about the question "whether a particular merits-related dispute is arbitrable because it is within the scope of a valid arbitration agreement"—for in respect to this latter question the law reverses the presumption. See Mitsubishi Motors, supra, at 626, 105 S.Ct., at 3353 (" '[A]ny doubts concerning the scope of arbitrable issues should be resolved in favor of arbitration' ") (quoting Moses H. Cone Memorial Hospital v. Mercury Constr. Corp., 460 U.S. 1, 24–25, 103 S.Ct. 927, 941, 74 L.Ed.2d 765 (1983)); Warrior & Gulf, supra, at 582–583, 80 S.Ct., at 1352–1353.

But, this difference in treatment is understandable. The latter question arises when the parties have a contract that provides for arbitration of some issues. In such circumstances, the parties likely gave at least some thought to the scope of arbitration. And, given the law's permissive policies in respect to arbitration, see, e.g., Mitsubishi Motors, supra, at 626, 105 S.Ct., at 3353, one can understand why the law would insist upon clarity before concluding that the parties did not want to arbitrate a related matter. See Domke § 12.02, p. 156 (issues will be deemed arbitrable unless "it is clear that the arbitration clause has not included" them). On the other hand, the former question—the "who (primarily) should decide arbitrability" question—is rather arcane. A party often might not focus upon that question or upon the significance of having arbitrators decide the scope of their own powers. Cf. Cox, Reflections Upon Labor Arbitration, 72 Harv.L.Rev. 1482, 1508–1509 (1959), cited in Warrior & Gulf, 363 U.S., at 583, n. 7, 80 S.Ct., at 1353, n. 7. And, given the principle that a party can be forced to arbitrate only those issues it specifically has agreed to submit to arbitration, one can understand why courts might hesitate to interpret silence or ambiguity on the "who should decide arbitrability" point as giving the arbitrators that power, for doing so might too often force unwilling parties to arbitrate a matter they reasonably would have thought a judge, not an arbitrator, would decide. Ibid. See generally Dean Witter Reynolds Inc. v. Byrd, 470 U.S. 213, 219–220, 105 S.Ct. 1238, 1241–1242, 84 L.Ed.2d 158 (1985) (Arbitration Act's basic purpose is to "ensure judicial enforcement of privately made agreements to arbitrate").

On the record before us, First Options cannot show that the Kaplans clearly agreed to have the arbitrators decide (i.e., to arbitrate) the question of arbitrability. First Options relies on the Kaplans' filing with the arbitrators a written memorandum objecting to the arbitrators' jurisdiction. But merely arguing the arbitrability issue to an arbitrator does not indicate a clear willingness to arbitrate that issue, i.e., a willingness to be effectively bound by the arbitrator's decision on that point. To the contrary, insofar as the Kaplans were forcefully objecting to the arbitrators deciding their dispute with First Options, one naturally would think that they did not want the arbitrators to have binding authority over them. This conclusion draws added support from (1) an obvious explanation for the Kaplans' presence before the arbitrators (i.e., that MKI, Mr. Kaplan's wholly owned firm, was arbitrating workout agreement matters); and (2) Third Circuit law that suggested that the Kaplans might argue arbitrability to the arbitrators without losing their right to independent court review, Teamsters v. Western Pennsylvania Motor Carriers Assn., 574 F.2d 783, 786–788 (1978); see 19 F.3d, at 1512, n. 13.

First Options makes several counterarguments: (1) that the Kaplans had other ways to get an independent court decision on the question of arbitrability without arguing the issue to the arbitrators (e.g., by trying to enjoin the arbitration, or by refusing to participate in the arbitration and then defending against a court petition First Options would have brought to compel arbitration, see 9 U.S.C. § 4); (2) that permitting parties to argue arbitrability to an arbitrator without being bound by the result would cause delay and waste in the resolution of disputes; and (3) that the Arbitration Act therefore requires a presumption that the Kaplans agreed to be bound by the arbitrators' decision, not the contrary. The first of these points, however, while true, simply does not say anything about whether the Kaplans intended to be bound by the arbitrators' decision. The second point, too, is inconclusive, for factual circumstances vary too greatly to permit a confident conclusion about whether allowing the arbitrator to make an initial (but independently reviewable) arbitrability determination would, in general, slow down the dispute resolution process. And, the third point is legally erroneous, for there is no strong arbitration-related policy favoring First Options in respect to its particular argument here. After all, the basic objective in this area is not to resolve disputes in the quickest manner possible, no matter what the parties' wishes, Dean Witter Reynolds, supra, at 219–220, 105 S.Ct., at 1241–1242, but to ensure that commercial arbitration agreements, like other contracts, " 'are enforced according to their terms,' " Mastrobuono, 514 U.S., at ___, 115 S.Ct., at 1214 (quoting Volt Information Sciences, 489 U.S., at 479, 109 S.Ct., at 1256), and according to the intentions of the parties, Mitsubishi Motors, 473 U.S., at 626, 105 S.Ct., at 3353. See Allied–Bruce, 513 U.S., at ___, 115 S.Ct., at 837. That policy favors the Kaplans, not First Options.

We conclude that, because the Kaplans did not clearly agree to submit the question of arbitrability to arbitration, the Court of Appeals was correct in finding that the arbitrability of the Kaplan/First Options dispute was subject to independent review by the courts.

III

We turn next to the standard a court of appeals should apply when reviewing a district court decision that refuses to vacate, see 9 U.S.C. § 10 (1988 Ed., Supp. V), or confirms, see § 9, an arbitration award. Although the Third Circuit sometimes used the words "de novo" to describe this standard, its opinion makes clear that it simply believes (as do all Circuits but one) that there is no special standard governing its review of a district court's decision in these circumstances. Rather, review of, for example, a district court decision confirming an arbitration award on the ground that the parties agreed to submit their dispute to arbitration, should proceed like review of any other district court decision finding an agreement between parties, i.e., accepting findings of fact that are not "clearly erroneous" but deciding questions of law de novo. See 19 F.3d, at 1509.

One Court of Appeals, the Eleventh Circuit, has said something different. Because of federal policy favoring arbitration, that court says that it applies a specially lenient "abuse of discretion" standard (even as to questions of law) when reviewing district court decisions that confirm (but not those that set aside) arbitration awards. See, e.g., Robbins v. Day, 954 F.2d, at 681–682. First Options asks us to hold that the Eleventh Circuit's view is correct.

We believe, however, that the majority of Circuits is right in saying that courts of appeals should apply ordinary, not special, standards when reviewing district court decisions upholding arbitration awards. For one thing, it is undesirable to make the law more complicated by proliferating review standards without good reasons. More importantly, the reviewing attitude that a court of appeals takes toward a district court decision should depend upon "the respective institutional advantages of trial and appellate courts," not upon what standard of review will more likely produce a particular substantive result. Salve Regina College v. Russell, 499 U.S. 225, 231–233, 111 S.Ct. 1217, 1221–1222, 113 L.Ed.2d 190 (1991). The law, for example, tells all courts (trial and appellate) to give administrative agencies a degree of legal leeway when they review certain interpretations of the law that those agencies have made. See, e.g., Chevron U.S.A. Inc. v. Natural Resources Defense Council, Inc., 467 U.S. 837, 843–844, 104 S.Ct. 2778, 2781–2782, 81 L.Ed.2d 694 (1984). But, no one, to our knowledge, has suggested that this policy of giving leeway to agencies means that a court of appeals should give extra leeway to a district court decision that upholds an agency. Similarly, courts grant arbitrators considerable leeway when reviewing most arbitration decisions; but that fact does not mean that appellate courts should give extra leeway to district courts that uphold arbitrators. First Options argues that the Arbitration Act is special because the Act, in one section, allows courts of appeals to conduct interlocutory review of certain antiarbitration district court rulings (e.g., orders enjoining arbitrations), but not those upholding arbitration (e.g., orders refusing to enjoin arbitrations). 9 U.S.C. § 16 (1988 Ed., Supp. V). But that portion of the Act governs the timing of review; it is therefore too weak a support for the distinct claim that the court of appeals should use a different standard when reviewing certain district court decisions. The Act says nothing about standards of review.

We conclude that the Court of Appeals used the proper standards for reviewing the District Court's arbitrability determinations.

IV

Finally, First Options argues that, even if we rule against it on the standard-of-review questions, we nonetheless should hold that the Court of Appeals erred in its ultimate conclusion that the merits of the Kaplan/First Options dispute were not arbitrable. This factbound issue is beyond the scope of the questions we agreed to review.

The judgment of the Court of Appeals is affirmed.

NOTES

(1) Is the Court's observation that "ordinary state-law principles that govern the formation of contracts" should determine whether the parties agreed to arbitrate correct? Should not federal principles be decisive? And should those principles not take account of the federal bias in favor of arbitration?

(2) Once it has been established that there is a valid arbitration agreement binding between some parties, does it necessarily follow that the court may decide independently which additional parties are bound by that agreement? And, under the usual arbitration clause declaring arbitrable disputes arising under or in connection with the agreement, does not the clause clearly and unmistakably evidence the parties' intention that the reach of the arbitration clause, and the question of whether it has been waived for that matter, be reserved for the arbitrators? On these questions, see Smit, H., The Arbitration Clause: Who Determines Its Validity and Its Personal and Subject Matter Reach, 6 Am.Rev.Int'l Arb. ___ (1995).

DOCTOR'S ASSOCIATES, INC. v. DISTAJO

United States Court of Appeals, Second Circuit, 1995.
66 F.3d 438.

José A. Cabranes, Circuit Judge: *

This case is about forum-shopping, by one and all. Doctor's Associates, Inc. ("DAI") is the national franchisor of Subway sandwich shops. DAI and its franchisees entered into standard franchise agreements, which required them to arbitrate all contractual disputes in Bridgeport, Connecticut, under Connecticut law. When problems did arise, however, neither side invoked the arbitration clause. First, DAI directed its wholly owned real-estate leasing companies to bring summary eviction proceedings against the franchisees in local state courts. The franchisees, in turn, scrambled to obtain judgments against DAI in local state courts.

When DAI found itself faced with state court claims around the country, it sought shelter in the arbitration clause of its franchise agreements. Accordingly, it petitioned the federal district court in Connecticut to compel arbitration under the Federal Arbitration Act. Before the district court could act, some of the franchisees won state court judgments against DAI. But DAI eventually convinced the district court to enjoin the franchisees from pursuing their state actions—even from enforcing judgments already entered—and to send the parties to Bridgeport to resolve their disputes around the arbitral table. On appeal, we are presented with several questions relating to the Federal Arbitration Act: (1) whether a district court has subject matter jurisdiction over a petition to compel arbitration where there is complete diversity among all the parties to the arbitration agreement (all of whom are joined as parties in the petition), but where other, nondiverse parties

---

* Some footnotes omitted, others renum-   bered.

have been joined as defendants in a parallel state action involving the same underlying dispute; (2) whether the district court should have accorded preclusive effect to various state court judgments entered in Alabama, Illinois, and North Carolina courts; (3) whether an arbitration clause is void for "lack of mutuality" under Connecticut law if it requires only one party to submit disputes to arbitration; (4) whether a party to an arbitration agreement waives its right to compel arbitration when it litigates substantial issues through an alter ego; and (5) whether a district court or an arbitrator should decide whether a party was fraudulently induced to assent to an arbitration agreement.

The district court found complete diversity, refused to accord preclusive effect to the state court judgments, found that the arbitration clause did not lack mutuality, held that DAI had not waived its right to arbitrate regardless of whether its leasing affiliates, which brought the court proceedings, were its alter egos, and left the question of fraudulent inducement to the arbitrators. As discussed below, we affirm in part and reverse in part.

I. FACTS

Doctor's Associates, Inc. ("DAI"), a Florida corporation, is the national franchisor of "Subway" sandwich shops. DAI entered into identical franchise agreements with each of the defendant franchisees (the "Franchisees"). Each agreement contains an identical arbitration clause, which provides that any claim arising out of or relating to the franchise agreement must be arbitrated in Bridgeport, Connecticut, under the Commercial Arbitration Rules of the American Arbitration Association. According to the arbitration clause, no party may take legal action against the other in connection with the franchise agreement without first attempting to arbitrate the dispute.[1]

DAI requires each franchisee to sublease its premises from one of several real-estate leasing companies that are wholly owned by DAI. Each sublease contains a "cross-default" provision, whereby any breach of the franchise agreement by the franchisee constitutes a breach of the sublease.[2] According to the deposition testimony of one of its own

---

1. The arbitration clause provides as follows:

Any controversy or claim arising out of or relating to this contract or the breach thereof shall be settled by Arbitration in accordance with the Commercial Arbitration Rules of the American Arbitration Association at a hearing to be held in Bridgeport, Connecticut and judgment upon an award rendered by the Arbitrator(s) may be entered in any court having jurisdiction thereof. The commencement of arbitration proceedings by an aggrieved party to settle disputes arising out of or relating to this contract is a condition precedent to the commencement of legal action by either party. The cost of such a proceeding will be borne equally by the parties.

2. The cross-default provision reads in relevant part as follows: If at any time during the term of this Sublease, Sublessee shall default in the performance of any of the terms, covenants or conditions of the aforesaid Franchise Agreement ... Sublessor, at its option, may terminate this lease ... and upon such termination, Sublessee shall quit and surrender the leased premises to Sublessor....

officers, DAI wanted its leasing affiliate to be the franchisees' sublessor, to obtain greater leverage over them in the event of a dispute.

A.   *The District Court Proceedings in Doctor's Associates,*
Inc. v. Distajo (Nos. 94–9207, 94–9209, 94–9293)

From 1991 through 1993, various disputes arose between DAI and the several franchisees. DAI never filed any demands for arbitration, despite its claims that the franchisees had breached the franchise agreements. Instead, DAI directed its leasing companies to invoke the cross-default provisions of the subleases, and to institute eviction proceedings in state courts against each franchisee.

In response to these eviction proceedings, each of the franchisees filed a state court action claiming, inter alia, fraud and breach of contract by DAI, its leasing companies, and several of DAI's officers and agents.

According to the franchisees, DAI uses this subleasing arrangement to circumvent the arbitration clause in the franchise agreements. They argue that the leasing companies are mere shells, or alter egos, of DAI. It is undisputed that the leasing companies are wholly owned by DAI, that they have no assets or net income, and that DAI decides when the leasing companies will file eviction proceedings. Pursuant to the sublease, the franchisee must pay rent directly to the actual landlord; no rent is paid to the leasing company. According to the franchisees, DAI has taken the position that the arbitration clause in the franchise agreement is not binding on its leasing companies, because they are not parties to that agreement. The franchisees claim also that the leasing companies have asserted the right to proceed with eviction lawsuits against the franchisees even if the franchisees file arbitration demands against DAI. Thus, DAI allegedly brought eviction lawsuits through its leasing companies to pressure its franchisees into resolving disputes, but invokes the arbitration clause to protect itself against litigation initiated by the franchisees.

DAI responded to each state lawsuit brought by the franchisees by serving a demand for arbitration pursuant to the franchise agreement. When the franchisees refused to arbitrate their disputes, DAI filed petitions to compel arbitration, pursuant to the Federal Arbitration Act, 9 U.S.C. § 4, in the United States District Court for the District of Connecticut. All sixteen cases were eventually consolidated before Chief Judge Peter C. Dorsey. Before the district court ruled on DAI's petitions, the state courts in Alabama, Illinois, and North Carolina entered judgments in favor of the franchisees in Cases 1–12 and 15–16.

In the district court, DAI contended that the franchisees were bound by the franchise agreement to submit any disputes with DAI to arbitration in Bridgeport, Connecticut, before instituting judicial proceedings. The franchisees responded by seeking dismissal of DAI's petitions on several grounds, including, inter alia: (1) lack of subject matter jurisdiction, due to incomplete diversity of the parties; and (2) collateral estoppel, based on the intervening state court judgments. The district court rejected each of these contentions in a ruling dated September 29, 1994. The district court simultaneously rejected DAI's motion to enjoin the franchisees from pursuing parallel state court proceedings, on the grounds that the requested injunction did not fall within any of the narrow exceptions to the Anti–Injunction Act, 28 U.S.C. § 2283.

On November 10, 1994, the district court granted DAI's petitions to compel arbitration. In doing so, the court rejected several defenses raised by the franchisees, including the following: (1) that the arbitration clause was void for lack of mutuality; (2) that DAI had waived arbitration by virtue of its leasing companies' prosecution of eviction lawsuits; and (3) that DAI had fraudulently misrepresented the scope of the arbitration clause in the franchise agreement. The court held that the arbitrators, not the court, should determine whether the leasing companies were "alter egos" of DAI, and then address the question whether DAI had fraudulently misrepresented the scope of the arbitration agreement.

When the franchisees continued to pursue their state court actions, DAI obtained a temporary restraining order from the district court on November 22, 1994, preventing them from participating in the parallel state proceedings. On December 14, 1994, the district court entered a preliminary injunction, barring the Distajo franchisees from seeking enforcement of their Illinois judgment. Doctor's Assocs., Inc. v. Distajo, 870 F.Supp. 34 (D.Conn.1994). The court concluded that injunctive relief was "not inappropriate" under the Anti–Injunction Act, 28 U.S.C. § 2283, because continued state litigation would "impair the integrity of the order of arbitration." In granting DAI's motion, the court rejected the franchisees' argument that an intervening judgment entered in favor of the Distajo franchisees by an Illinois state court on October 24, 1994, was "final" for res judicata purposes and would preclude entry of the injunction under the full faith and credit statute, 28 U.S.C. § 1738.

All of the franchisees filed timely appeals from the district court's order of September 29, 1994, denying their motions to dismiss, and the order of November 10, 1994, compelling arbitration. All of the franchisees except those from Alabama (Cases 8–12) also appeal from the court's December 9, 1994, order entering the preliminary injunction.

B. The District Court Proceedings in Doctor's Associates, Inc. v. Bickel (No. 94–7183)

The proceedings in the Bickel case differ somewhat from those cases consolidated under the Distajo rubric. On December 16, 1994, the Bickels filed a complaint in Illinois state court against DAI, its leasing company, its development agent, and three DAI officers. DAI responded by filing a petition to compel arbitration in the United States District Court for the District of Connecticut on January 20, 1995, and moved to enjoin the Bickels from prosecuting their state court action. On February 7, 1995, the Illinois court entered a default judgment against DAI. On February 13, 1995, Chief Judge Dorsey granted both DAI's petition to compel arbitration and its motion for a preliminary injunction, while permitting DAI to move the Illinois court to vacate the default judgment on the basis of defective service of process. The district court entered a written order embodying the Bickel injunction on May 9, 1995, but did not order DAI to post a bond.

The Bickels appeal from the court's order of May 9, 1995, granting DAI's petition to compel arbitration and entering the preliminary injunction.

II. DISCUSSION

"When reviewing a district court's determination of its subject matter jurisdiction, we review factual findings for clear error and legal conclusions de novo." In re Vogel Van & Storage, Inc., 59 F.3d 9, 11 (2d Cir.1995). We also review de novo the district court's decision to compel arbitration. Collins & Aikman Prods. Co. v. Building Systems, Inc., 58 F.3d 16, 19 (2d Cir.1995).

A. Subject Matter Jurisdiction

Section 4 of the Federal Arbitration Act ("FAA"), 9 U.S.C. §§ 1–16, confers jurisdiction on district courts to hear petitions to enforce arbitration agreements, but only to the extent that the court would otherwise have jurisdiction over the dispute. The statute provides as follows: "A party aggrieved by the alleged ... refusal of another to arbitrate under a written agreement for arbitration may petition any United States district court which, save for such agreement, would have jurisdiction under Title 28, in a civil action ... of the subject matter of a suit arising out of the controversy between the parties, for an order directing that such arbitration proceed in the manner provided for in such agreement." 9 U.S.C. § 4 (emphasis added). As the Supreme Court has explained, "[t]he Arbitration Act is something of an anomaly in the field of federal-court jurisdiction. It creates a body of federal substantive law establishing and regulating the duty to honor an agreement to arbitrate, yet it does not create any independent federal-question jurisdiction under 28 U.S.C. § 1331 (1976 ed., Supp. V) or otherwise. Section 4 provides for an order compelling arbitration only when the federal district court would have jurisdiction over a suit on the underlying dispute; hence, there must be diversity of citizenship or some other independent basis for federal jurisdiction before the order can issue." Moses H. Cone Memorial Hosp. v. Mercury Constr. Corp., 460 U.S. 1, 25 n. 32, 103 S.Ct. 927, 941 n. 32, 74 L.Ed.2d 765 (1983).

The parties seem to agree that the only possible basis for federal subject matter jurisdiction in this case would be diversity of citizenship. 28 U.S.C. § 1332. It is a long-settled rule that in order to invoke diversity jurisdiction, the petitioner must show "complete diversity"—

that is, that it does not share citizenship with any defendant. C.T. Carden v. Arkoma Assocs., 494 U.S. 185, 187, 110 S.Ct. 1015, 1017, 108 L.Ed.2d 157 (1990); Strawbridge v. Curtiss, 7 U.S. (3 Cranch) 267, 267, 2 L.Ed. 435 (1806), overruled on other grounds, 43 U.S. (2 How.) 497, 555, 11 L.Ed. 353 (1844); Curley v. Brignoli, Curley & Roberts Assocs., 915 F.2d 81, 84 (2d Cir.1990), cert. denied, 499 U.S. 955, 111 S.Ct. 1430, 113 L.Ed.2d 484 (1991). DAI is a Florida corporation with its principal place of business in Florida. The franchisees are residents of Alabama, Illinois, Massachusetts, North Carolina, and Pennsylvania.

The franchisees argue that there is not complete diversity of citizenship here. According to the franchisees, the "controvers[ies] between the parties" to which the FAA refers involve not only DAI, but also DAI's development agents—some of whom share the same citizenship with certain franchisees. None of those agents was a party to the franchise agreement; none has been joined as a party in the present proceeding. These local DAI agents, the franchisees contend, are "indispensable parties" to the present federal action, as evidenced by the fact that the affiliates are named defendants in the franchisees' state actions. In other words, the franchisees argue that their state court actions are the "suit[s] arising out of the controversy between the parties" hypothesized by the FAA. If so, then the citizenship of all the parties in the state actions determines whether there is complete diversity in the federal action to compel arbitration. Because these agents cannot be joined without destroying diversity, the franchisees argue that the district court should have dismissed the petitions to compel.

DAI responds that the "suit arising out of the controversy between the parties" is DAI's action to compel arbitration—not the parallel state action—and that DAI's affiliates are not "indispensable parties" to the federal action. Accordingly, DAI argues that we should look at the citizenship only of the parties named in the petition to compel, when determining whether there is diversity jurisdiction. Prudential–Bache Sec., Inc. v. Fitch, 966 F.2d 981, 988 (5th Cir.1992) ("jurisdiction for a petition to compel arbitration [must] be determined from the face of the petition"). DAI offers a textual argument and a policy argument to support its position. First, it notes that the FAA asks whether the district court would have jurisdiction over a suit arising out of a controversy "between the parties." The phrase "the parties" most sensibly refers to those persons who are parties to the arbitration agreement—and who therefore can be named in the petition to compel arbitration. Second, DAI argues that the FAA would be fatally undermined if "the parties" described in § 4 could be expanded to include persons who had not signed the arbitration clause but who allegedly were involved in the "underlying controversy." If such a rule were adopted, a party resisting arbitration could defeat federal jurisdiction simply by suing someone from the same state, plus the party seeking to compel arbitration, in a separate state lawsuit. Diversity would be destroyed simply by claiming that the local defendants in the parallel action were "indispensable parties" to the petition to compel.

We agree with DAI. The "parties" to which § 4 of the FAA refers are the parties to the petition to compel. As with any federal action, diversity of citizenship is determined by reference to the parties named in the proceeding before the district court, as well as any indispensable parties who must be joined pursuant to Rule 19 of the Federal Rules of Civil Procedure. Where joinder of a party would destroy subject matter jurisdiction, the court must dismiss the action if that party is "indispensable" to the litigation. Fed.R.Civ.P. 19(b); Fluent v. Salamanca Indian Lease Auth., 928 F.2d 542, 548 (2d Cir.) (finding dismissal proper where indispensable party was Indian tribe that enjoyed sovereign immunity from suit), cert. denied, 502 U.S. 818, 112 S.Ct. 74, 116 L.Ed.2d 48 (1991). But individuals who are not parties to the arbitration agreement cannot be "indispensable" parties under Rule 19(b) if they do not meet either of the threshold tests of Rule 19(a). That provision only requires joinder of a party if (1) the court cannot afford "complete relief" to those already joined, in the absence of that party, and (2) the unjoined party has an interest in the litigation and his absence may either impede his ability to protect that interest or subject the already-joined parties to a risk of inconsistent obligations—which often means the risk of piecemeal litigation. Neither condition is satisfied in the present case. First, the district court can grant all the relief sought by DAI in this case—an order compelling arbitration—regardless of whether DAI's development agents (nonparties to the arbitration agreement) are present. Second, the other consideration set forth in Rule 19(a)—possible prejudice resulting from piecemeal litigation—is overcome in this context by the FAA's strong bias in favor of arbitration. Indeed, the Supreme Court has categorically stated that the FAA requires courts to enforce an arbitration agreement "notwithstanding the presence of other persons who are parties to the underlying dispute but not to the arbitration agreement." Moses H. Cone, 460 U.S. at 20, 103 S.Ct. at 939. A district court should not consider the citizenship of strangers to the arbitration contract, since they are not "parties" [to] the suit arising out of the controversy within the meaning of the FAA.

Accordingly, we hold that the district court was correct in looking only to the citizenship of the parties in the action before it—that is, DAI and the franchisees, who signed the arbitration agreement—to determine whether there was complete diversity. Because the parties conceded at oral argument that DAI and the franchisees are completely diverse, we affirm the district court's finding that it possessed subject matter jurisdiction pursuant to 28 U.S.C. § 1332 and 9 U.S.C. § 4.

B. *Preclusive Effect of State Court Judgments*

The franchisees claim that the district court should have accorded full faith and credit to the various state court judgments that found the arbitration clause unenforceable in cases involving DAI and various of the defendant franchisees.

The full faith and credit statute, 28 U.S.C. § 1738, provides that "[state] judicial proceedings ... shall have the same full faith and credit in every court within the United States ... as they have by law or usage in the courts of such State ... from which they are taken." Accordingly, a federal court must "give preclusive effect to state-court judgments whenever the courts of the State from which the judgments emerged would do so." Allen v. McCurry, 449 U.S. 90, 96, 101 S.Ct. 411, 415, 66 L.Ed.2d 308 (1980); Valley Disposal, Inc. v. Central Vermont Solid Waste Management Dist., 31 F.3d 89, 98 (2d Cir.1994).

The parties agree that the question, therefore, is whether the various state court judgments (one in Alabama, eight in Illinois, and one in North Carolina) would be accorded preclusive effect under Alabama, Illinois, or North Carolina law, respectively. We address each state's law in turn.

1. *The Alabama Judgment (Case # 8)*

During October 1993, DAI's real-estate leasing company and its equipment leasing company filed suit against franchisee John McCrary in the Circuit Court of Talladega County, Alabama. In December 1993, McCrary filed a counterclaim against those DAI affiliates, and added DAI and its Alabama development agents as cross-claim defendants. On January 25, 1994, DAI and its affiliates filed a motion to dismiss the counterclaims and cross-claims or, in the alternative, to stay the Alabama case pending arbitration. DAI claims that it withdrew that motion after filing its petition to compel arbitration in the district court in Connecticut on March 8, 1994. On June 28, 1994, McCrary filed in the Alabama court a "Motion to Determine Non–Arbitrability of Issues."

On July 7, 1994, the Alabama Circuit Court ruled that the arbitration clause was void and unenforceable "for any of the following independent reasons": (1) lack of mutuality; (2) fraudulent inducement; (3) waiver by DAI of the right to invoke the arbitration clause; and (4) invalidity of the clause under Alabama law prohibiting all arbitration agreements, since the agreement lacked a sufficient "interstate nexus" to permit application of the FAA (which preempts state laws invalidating arbitration clauses affecting interstate commerce). The court also held that the issues raised in McCrary's counterclaim fell outside the scope of the arbitration clause. The Alabama court then expressly found "no just reason for delay" and accordingly directed that final judgment be entered in favor of McCrary.

DAI subsequently filed a motion for reconsideration, which the Alabama court denied on September 28, 1994. McCrary represents to this court that DAI subsequently appealed these orders to the Alabama Supreme Court. (The parties have been barred from proceeding with that appeal pursuant to the preliminary injunction entered by the district court on December 9, 1994.)

In an order entered September 29, 1994, denying McCrary's motion to dismiss, the district court declined to give preclusive effect to this Alabama judgment. The court reasoned that because a motion to reconsider the judgment was still pending in state court, there was not yet a final judgment on the merits. Thus, principles of res judicata and collateral estoppel would not apply.

On appeal, DAI concedes that the Alabama ruling was indeed "final" for the purposes of preclusion. Under Alabama law, an order entered upon less than all of the claims presented in an action is a final, appealable order if "the judge makes an express determination that there is no just reason for delay...." Goza v. Everett, 365 So.2d 658, 659 (Ala.1978). "Alabama courts, like federal courts, generally apply the same test of finality for purposes of preclusion as they do for appealability." Stone v. Williams, 970 F.2d 1043, 1055 (2d Cir.1992), cert. denied, ___ U.S. ___, 113 S.Ct. 2331, 124 L.Ed.2d 243 (1993); see also First Ala. Bank of Montgomery, N.A. v. Parsons Steel, Inc., 825 F.2d 1475, 1480 (11th Cir.1987) (interpreting Alabama law), cert. denied sub nom. McGregor v. First Ala. Bank of Montgomery, 484 U.S. 1060, 108 S.Ct. 1015, 98 L.Ed.2d 980 (1988). Because the Circuit Court of Talladega County expressly found that its decision was final and that there was no reason for delay, its July 7, 1994, order was immediately appealable and thus would be accorded preclusive effect under Alabama law as of that date.

DAI urges this court nevertheless to disregard the Alabama judgment, for three reasons. First, DAI argues that the Supreme Court's decision in Allied–Bruce Terminix Cos. v. Dobson, ___ U.S. ___, 115 S.Ct. 834, 130 L.Ed.2d 753 (1995), overturned the interstate commerce analysis that provided the Alabama court's fourth rationale for voiding the arbitration clause. The Supreme Court's decision, DAI contends, constitutes an "intervening change in the applicable legal context," Staten Island Rapid Transit Operating Auth. v. ICC, 718 F.2d 533, 543 (2d Cir.1983), that requires a federal court not to accord preclusive effect to the Alabama decision. See Restatement (Second) of Judgments § 28(2) (1980). Even if Allied–Bruce did undermine one rationale supporting the Alabama court's judgment, however, the Supreme Court's decision did not affect the alternate grounds set forth by the court for voiding the arbitration clause. Because the legal context has not shifted at all in these other areas, we cannot reexamine the Alabama judgment.

Second, DAI contends that it was not afforded a "full and fair opportunity to litigate" the arbitration claims in the Alabama court. See Milltex Indus. Corp. v. Jacquard Lace Co., 922 F.2d 164, 168 (2d Cir.1991); Stone, 970 F.2d at 1056. DAI assigns error to three aspects of the procedure followed in the Alabama court, each of which we reject:

(1) DAI complains that it was not afforded the right to file a brief in response to McCrary's "Motion to Determine the Non–Arbitrability of the Issues." But as DAI conceded at oral argument before this court, nothing in the record indicates that it ever sought to file such a brief, much less that the Alabama court prevented it from filing one. Absent any evidence to the contrary, we accept the statement in the written order of the Alabama court that "[b]oth sides have thoroughly briefed the issues and provided factual evidence in support of their respective positions." (2) DAI also claims that it was not afforded "meaningful oral argument." Because DAI does not claim that oral argument was completely denied, we dismiss the argument out of hand. This court has held that "[o]ral argument is not a necessary component of due process in all circumstances." Zaluski v. INS, 37 F.3d 72, 73 (2d Cir.1994); see also FCC v. WJR, The Goodwill Station, Inc., 337 U.S. 265, 276, 69 S.Ct. 1097, 1103, 93 L.Ed. 1353 (1949) ("Certainly the Constitution does not require oral argument in all cases where only insubstantial or frivolous questions of law, or indeed even substantial ones, are raised."). Courts have broad discretion to determine how much, if any, oral argument is appropriate in a given case. We will not second-guess the Alabama court's allocation of its time. (3) Finally, DAI argues that the Alabama court drastically misapplied the law. This argument is nothing more than an invitation for this court to revisit the merits of the Alabama court's judgment—precisely what the full faith and credit statute tells us not to do. See Charles Koen & Assocs. v. City of Cairo, 909 F.2d 992, 1000 n. 8 (7th Cir.1990) ("The full faith and credit statute does not permit federal courts to reassess the merits of state court judgments."). "Lower federal courts are not superior to state courts." Lion Bonding & Sur. Co. v. Karatz, 262 U.S. 77, 90, 43 S.Ct. 480, 484, 67 L.Ed. 871 (1923); see also District of Columbia Court of Appeals v. Feldman, 460 U.S. 462, 482, 103 S.Ct. 1303, 1314, 75 L.Ed.2d 206 (1983) ("[A] United States District Court has no authority to review final judgments of a state court in judicial proceedings."). If DAI is dissatisfied with the judgment of the Alabama trial court, it should take an appeal.

Third, DAI argues that there was no motion properly before the Alabama court that would permit it to decide the arbitrability issue. That is, DAI claims that it had already withdrawn its own motion to compel arbitration under § 3 of the FAA, and that McCrary's own "Motion to Determine the Non–Arbitrability of the Issues" was unauthorized, considering that McCrary had never sought a declaratory judgment in his complaint. According to DAI, the Alabama opinion is therefore purely "advisory," and is not entitled to preclusive effect under state law. This argument fails for two reasons. First, the Alabama court clearly believed that DAI's motion to dismiss had been submitted for decision, since it denied that motion on the merits. Second, Stamps v. Jefferson County Board of Education, 642 So.2d 941, 944 (Ala.1994), which DAI cites, does not support the proposition that a declaratory judgment is merely "advisory" if such relief was not specifically request-ed in the complaint. All the Alabama Supreme Court stated in Stamps was that "[a]ctions or opinions are denominated 'advisory,' . . . where the judgment sought would not constitute specific relief to a liti-gant. . . ." 642 So.2d at 944 (quoting Edwin M. Borchard, Declaratory Judgments 34 (1934)) (emphasis deleted). In that case, a group of teachers had sued their employer and sought a judicial declaration that their work duties subjected them to prosecution by a state agency. The court held that such a declaratory judgment would be purely advisory because the prosecutorial agency had not been joined as a party, and thus would not be bound by the decision. Id. But DAI is a party in the Alabama action, and is bound by the state court judgment. Because the declaratory judgment finding the arbitration clause to be unenforceable provides "specific relief" to McCrary against DAI, as required by Stamps, it cannot be brushed aside as an "advisory" opinion.

For these reasons, we hold that the district court should have accorded full faith and credit to the Alabama judgment. Accordingly, we reverse the district court orders denying McCrary's motion to dismiss and compelling him to pursue arbitration. On remand, we direct the district court to dismiss DAI's petition to compel McCrary to arbitrate. Although McCrary did not appeal from the December 9, 1994 order entering the preliminary injunction, we nevertheless exercise our pen-dent appellate jurisdiction in the interests of judicial economy to vacate the injunction. See Golino v. City of New Haven, 950 F.2d 864, 868 (2d Cir.1991) ("[W]here we have jurisdiction to consider some questions on appeal, we may exercise our discretion to take pendent jurisdiction over related questions."), cert. denied sub nom. Lillis v. Golino, ___ U.S. ___, 112 S.Ct. 3032, 120 L.Ed.2d 902 (1992).

2. *The Illinois Judgments (Cases 1–6, 15–16, DAI v. Bickel)*

Eight groups of Illinois franchisees filed complaints against DAI, its leasing companies, and DAI's two co-owners, and their cases were eventually consolidated before the Circuit Court of Madison County, Illinois. On October 24, 1994, the Illinois court granted the franchisees' motion for summary judgment, declaring the arbitration clause void and unenforceable on several grounds. The court stated that its decision was a "final and appealable order and judgment under Illinois Supreme Court Rule 304(a) in that there is no just reason for delaying either the enforcement of or the appeal from this judgment and order."

DAI represented to the district court that it had filed a motion for reconsideration in the Illinois court, and that the possibility of appeal remained open. Reasoning that a judgment subject to appeal was not final under Illinois law, the district court refused to accord preclusive effect to the Illinois court's decision. The district court relied on Pelon v. Wall, 262 Ill.App.3d 131, 135, 199 Ill.Dec. 546, 634 N.E.2d 385 (2d

Dist.1994), which held that "[f]or res judicata purposes, a judgment is not final until the possibility of appellate review has been exhausted."

The Bickels also filed a complaint against DAI and others in the Circuit Court of Madison County, on December 16, 1994. DAI failed to enter an appearance in Madison County within the prescribed time, so the Illinois court entered a default judgment in favor of the Bickels on February 7, 1994. In its judgment, the Illinois court declared the arbitration clause void and unenforceable, and scheduled a hearing on damages for April 4, 1995. On February 13, 1995, however, the district court ruled that for the purposes of issue preclusion, the Illinois judgment obtained by the Bickels was no more final than the judgment obtained by the other franchisees in Madison County. Accordingly, the district court granted DAI's petition to compel arbitration and enjoined the Bickels from continuing their Illinois litigation. The injunction contained an exception, however, which permitted DAI to move the Illinois court to set aside its default judgment.

The Illinois Supreme Court has held that an Illinois judgment is not final, and thus not entitled to preclusive effect, until the time for appeal has expired. Ballweg v. City of Springfield, 114 Ill.2d 107, 113, 102 Ill.Dec. 360, 499 N.E.2d 1373 (1986) ("For purposes of applying the doctrine of collateral estoppel, finality requires that the potential for appellate review must have been exhausted."); Relph v. Board of Educ., 84 Ill.2d 436, 442, 50 Ill.Dec. 830, 420 N.E.2d 147 (1981) (holding that an appellate court's mandate to remand with instructions for further proceedings establishes the law of the case, but does not constitute a final judgment entitled to res judicata effect—partially because the trial court's further proceedings are subject to subsequent appeal, and partially because the appellate court's mandate is subject to review by the Illinois Supreme Court); see also People v. Condon, 246 Ill.App.3d 74, 76, 185 Ill.Dec. 932, 615 N.E.2d 802 (2d Dist.1993) (holding that judgment is not final for purposes of preclusion until the potential for appellate review has been exhausted).

The franchisees respond by citing Illinois Founders Insurance Co. v. Guidish, 248 Ill.App.3d 116, 120, 187 Ill.Dec. 845, 618 N.E.2d 436 (1st Dist.1993), where it was said that "[t]he pendency of an appeal has no effect on the finality of the order appealed from. Under certain circumstances, the pendency of an appeal can affect the enforceability of a judgment ... but not its finality. More to the point, a final judgment can serve as the basis to apply the doctrines of res judicata and collateral estoppel even though the judgment is being appealed."

The Illinois Appellate Court's statement in Guidish is clearly at odds with the Illinois Supreme Court's categorical statements in Ballweg and Relph. See Prymer v. Ogden, 29 F.3d 1208, 1213 n. 2 (7th Cir.) (discussing, but declining to resolve, conflict in authority), cert. denied, ___ U.S. ___, 115 S.Ct. 665, 130 L.Ed.2d 599 (1994). Despite the best efforts of the franchisees to distinguish Ballweg and Relph, we must follow the rulings of the Illinois Supreme Court.

We hold that the district court correctly refused to accord preclusive effect to the Illinois judgments.

3. *North Carolina (Case # 7)*

In April 1993, Michael Johnson filed a complaint against DAI and several affiliated individuals in the General Court of Justice, Superior Court Division, in Gaston County, North Carolina. Johnson alleged, inter alia, fraud, breach of contract, and conversion. DAI replied by filing two motions. First, it moved to stay the lawsuit pending arbitration. Second, it moved to dismiss Johnson's complaint, on the grounds that he had waived his right to challenge the arbitration agreement by previously participating in arbitration proceedings with DAI. Johnson, in turn, claimed that the arbitration clause was unenforceable on several grounds, including (1) that it lacked mutuality and (2) that he had been fraudulently induced into executing the arbitration agreement.

On May 3, 1994, the North Carolina court denied both of DAI's motions. In its written order, the court explicitly addressed only the issues raised in DAI's motion to dismiss: it held that Johnson's "limited participation in the arbitration proceedings did not constitute a waiver of his right to challenge the enforceability of the arbitration clause." With respect to DAI's first motion, however, the court did not explain why it denied the stay, nor did it make any findings of fact or conclusions of law regarding the arbitration clause.

Johnson argues that the North Carolina court must have relied on one of the rationales offered by Johnson (lack of mutuality or fraudulent inducement) even though the court did not specify which one. In North Carolina, however, collateral estoppel only precludes the relitigation of issues that were actually and necessarily decided in the earlier action. King v. Grindstaff, 284 N.C. 348, 200 S.E.2d 799, 805 (1973). The party invoking the benefit of collateral estoppel (here, Johnson) bears the burden of establishing what was in fact determined by the prior judgment. Thomas M. McInnis & Assocs., Inc. v. Hall, 318 N.C. 421, 349 S.E.2d 552, 557 (1986). Even if one of the issues raised by Johnson— mutuality or fraudulent inducement—was necessarily decided by the state judge, it is impossible to ascertain which issue was actually decided. We therefore hold that the judgment of the Gaston County court would not be accorded preclusive effect under North Carolina law with respect to the validity of the arbitration clause.

Accordingly, we affirm the district court's decision not to accord full faith and credit to the judgment against DAI obtained by Johnson in the North Carolina court.

C. The Franchisees' Challenges to the Arbitration Clause

1. Mutuality

The franchisees argue that the arbitration clause is void for lack of mutuality, in that it requires a franchisee to submit all controversies to arbitration but reserves to DAI (through its leasing companies) the right to seek summary eviction against the franchisees. The district court rejected this argument, finding no lack of mutuality: If the leasing companies were separable entities, then "the arbitration clause will be enforceable only as to DAI and the [franchisees], obliging them to arbitrate, thus establishing mutuality." If, on the other hand, the leasing companies were indistinguishable from DAI, then they too would be bound to arbitrate. Either way, the court reasoned, mutuality was not an issue.

We agree that mutuality is not an issue, but for different reasons. Preliminarily, we note that the parties have not offered any reason why we should not apply the choice-of-law clause in the franchise agreements, which indicates that Connecticut law applies. Connecticut courts, however, have not addressed the precise question whether an arbitration clause may be void for "lack of mutuality."

The term "mutuality" can refer to several different concepts in contract law. Although it is unclear whether the franchisees are referring to "mutuality of obligation" or "mutuality of remedy," both doctrines are largely dead letters. The doctrine of "mutuality of obligation" requires a valid contract to be based on an exchange of reciprocal promises. 1A Arthur L. Corbin, Corbin on Contracts § 152, at 3 (1963). As applied to arbitration clauses, that rule has been restated to mean that "the consideration exchanged for one party's promise to arbitrate must be the other party's promise to arbitrate." Hull v. Norcom, Inc., 750 F.2d 1547, 1550 (11th Cir.1985) (interpreting New York law). But "mutuality of obligation" has been largely rejected as a general principle in contract law, as well as in the arbitration context. The latest Restatement of Contracts provides that "[i]f the requirement of consideration is met, there is no additional requirement of . . . 'mutuality of obligation.' " Restatement (Second) of Contracts § 79 (1979). Option contracts, for example, are unquestionably valid under this modern rule despite their lack of "mutuality of obligation." That is, one party's promise to honor a future offer to purchase an item is valid if supported by the other party's present payment of a sum of money. The promise to accept the offer need not be supported by a reciprocal promise to make that offer. The New York Court of Appeals essentially adopted the Second Restatement position in a case involving a challenge to an arbitration clause which bound only one of the parties to arbitrate. In Sablosky v. Edward S. Gordon Co., 73 N.Y.2d 133, 137, 538 N.Y.S.2d 513, 516, 535 N.E.2d 643, 645 (1989), the court held that "[i]f there is consideration for the entire agreement that is sufficient; the consideration supports the arbitration option, as it does every other obligation in the agreement. . . . Since it is settled that the validity of an arbitration agreement is to be determined by the law applicable to contracts generally . . . there is no reason for a different mutuality rule in arbitration cases."

Most courts facing this issue have arrived at the same conclusion. See, e.g., Wilson Elec. Contractors, Inc. v. Minnotte Contracting Corp., 878 F.2d 167, 168 (6th Cir.1989); Becker Autoradio U.S.A., Inc. v. Becker Autoradiowerk GmbH, 585 F.2d 39, 47 (3d Cir.1978); W.L. Jorden & Co. v. Blythe Indus., 702 F.Supp. 282, 284 (N.D.Ga.1988); Willis Flooring, Inc. v. Howard S. Lease Constr. Co. & Assocs., 656 P.2d 1184, 1185 (Alaska 1983) ("As one clause in a larger contract, the [arbitration] clause is binding to the same extent that the contract as a whole is binding."); LaBonte Precision, Inc. v. LPI Indus. Corp., 507 So.2d 1202, 1203 (Fla.Dist.Ct.App.1987); Kalman Floor Co. v. Jos. L. Muscarelle, Inc., 196 N.J.Super. 16, 481 A.2d 553 (1984), aff'd for reasons stated below, 98 N.J. 266, 486 A.2d 334 (1985). Contra Stevens/Leinweber/Sullens, Inc. v. Holm Dev. & Management, Inc., 165 Ariz. 25, 795 P.2d 1308, 1313 (Ct.App.1990); R.W. Roberts Constr. Co. v. St. Johns River Water Management Dist., 423 So.2d 630, 633 (Fla.Dist. Ct.App.1982).

It has been argued that, according to the Supreme Court's decision in Prima Paint Corp. v. Flood & Conklin Manufacturing Co., 388 U.S. 395, 403–04, 87 S.Ct. 1801, 1805–06, 18 L.Ed.2d 1270 (1967), an arbitration clause is separable from its underlying contract, and therefore must be supported by separate consideration. Stevens, 795 P.2d at 1312–13. In Prima Paint, the Court held that a claim of fraud in the inducement of an underlying contract must be left to the arbitrators, but that a claim of fraud in the inducement of the arbitration clause should be decided by the court. Prima Paint, 388 U.S. at 403–04, 87 S.Ct. at 1805–06. In reaching this conclusion, the Court endorsed the result reached by our court in Robert Lawrence Co. v. Devonshire Fabrics, Inc., 271 F.2d 402 (2d Cir.1959) (Medina, J.), cert. granted, 362 U.S. 909, 80 S.Ct. 682, 4 L.Ed.2d 618, cert. dismissed for mootness, 364 U.S. 801, 81 S.Ct. 27, 5 L.Ed.2d 37 (1960). In Robert Lawrence, we described the FAA as distinguishing between "the entire contract between the parties on the one hand and the arbitration clause of the contract on the other," 271 F.2d at 409—the latter being described as a "separable part of the contract." Id. at 410. At one point in Robert Lawrence, we speculated that "we would suppose that generally where the arbitration provision of the contract is sufficiently broad to encompass the issue of fraud, the mutual promises to arbitrate would form the quid pro quo of one another and constitute a separable and enforceable part of the agreement. We do not decide this point, however, as it is not necessarily before us."

Id. at 411. This passage, one might argue, indicates that an arbitration clause must be treated as a contract supported by independent consideration. For the following reasons, however, we reject this characterization.

First, of course, we clearly labelled our statement in Robert Lawrence as dicta. Second, though we suggested that mutual promises to arbitrate could constitute sufficient consideration to support an arbitration agreement, we did not exclude the possibility that other consideration could support the agreement. Third, we indicated only that arbitration clauses are "separable" from void or voidable provisions of a contract—not that they are independent contracts. Although we consider an arbitration clause separately for the limited purpose of evaluating a claim of fraudulent inducement, we do not do so for all purposes. For example, when determining the parties' intent in the arbitration clause, we must read the contract as a whole. Mastrobuono v. Shearson Lehman Hutton, Inc., ___ U.S. ___, ___, 115 S.Ct. 1212, 1217, 131 L.Ed.2d 76 (1995) (quoting Restatemetn (Second) of Contracts § 202(2) (1979)). State law generally governs the determination of whether the parties agreed to arbitrate a certain matter, First Options of Chicago, Inc. v. Kaplan, ___ U.S. ___, ___, 115 S.Ct. 1920, 1924, 131 L.Ed.2d 985 (1995), and Connecticut courts "construe the contract as a whole" and consider "all relevant provisions ... when determining the intent of the parties." White v. Kampner, 229 Conn. 465, 641 A.2d 1381, 1385 (1994).

Wilson Electrical Contractors, Inc. v. Minnotte Contracting Corp., 878 F.2d 167, 169 (6th Cir.1989), rejected the contention that under Prima Paint, "an arbitration clause is an independent contract that is separable from the main contract in which it is found and therefore must have all of the essential elements of a contract, including consideration." As the Wilson court pointed out, more recent decisions of the Supreme Court have consistently emphasized that the FAA is grounded in a strong federal policy favoring arbitration. Id. at 169. A doctrine that required separate consideration for arbitration clauses might risk running afoul of that policy. In any event, because the franchisees make no claim that the underlying contract was the result of fraud, we have no occasion to consider the arbitration clause in isolation from the larger contract. Accordingly, we need not decide whether the arbitration clause must be supported by independent consideration.

The doctrine of "mutuality of remedy" affords no greater relief for the franchisees. That rule, which provides generally that a "plaintiff shall not get specific enforcement unless the defendant could also have obtained it," 5A Arthur L. Corbin, Corbin on Contracts § 1181, at 336 (1964), is also defunct. See, e.g., Sablosky, 73 N.Y.2d at 137, 538 N.Y.S.2d 513, 535 N.E.2d 643 ("Mutuality of remedy is not required in arbitration contracts."). As explained in the latest Restatement, "the law does not require that the parties have similar remedies in case of breach, and the fact that specific performance or an injunction is not available to one party is not a sufficient reason for refusing it to the other party. The rationale of the supposed requirement of "mutuality of remedy" is to "make sure that the party in breach will not be compelled to perform without being assured that he will receive any remaining part of the agreed exchange from the injured party. It is therefore enough if adequate security can be furnished." Restatement (Second) of Contracts § 363 cmt. c (1979).

In view of Connecticut's strong policies favoring arbitration, see, e.g., White v. Kampner, 229 Conn. 465, 471, 641 A.2d 1381, 1384 (1994); Garrity v. McCaskey, 223 Conn. 1, 7, 612 A.2d 742, 746 (1992), we believe that the Connecticut courts would conclude that "where the agreement to arbitrate is integrated into a larger unitary contract, the consideration for the contract as a whole covers the arbitration clause as well." W.L. Jorden & Co., 702 F.Supp. at 284. The franchisees do not contest that the franchise agreement as a whole is supported by consideration. Absent a failure of consideration, in this instance, we cannot invalidate the agreement in whole or in part.

2.   *Waiver of Right to Pursue Arbitration*

The district court held that regardless of whether the leasing companies were DAI's alter egos, DAI had not waived its right to compel arbitration under the franchise agreement. On the one hand, if the leasing companies were not DAI's alter egos, then their pursuit of eviction proceedings against the franchisees could not be imputed to DAI. On the other hand, even if the leasing companies were DAI's alter egos, DAI nevertheless invoked its arbitration rights as soon as it was named a party in the various state court actions commenced by the franchisees. Somewhat opaquely, the court held that DAI "cannot be held to have waived a right of arbitration by an after-the-fact holding that it is the alter ego of the leasing companies." We disagree.

There is no authority to support the notion that a party is liable for acts of its alter ego only if a court has previously found that an alter ego relationship exists. As we have explained in the context of contractual liability, "it is clear that the consequence of applying the alter ego doctrine is that the corporation and those who have controlled it without regard to its separate entity are treated as but one entity, and ... the acts of one are the acts of all." Fisser v. International Bank, 282 F.2d 231, 234 (2d Cir.1960) (holding parent corporation bound to arbitrate, where its alter ego instrumentality signed arbitration agreement); see also Interocean Shipping Co. v. National Shipping & Trading Corp., 523 F.2d 527, 539 (2d Cir.1975) (holding that company may be compelled to arbitrate even if not party to agreement containing arbitration clause, where company is alter ego of another party that clearly is subject to arbitration), cert. denied, 423 U.S. 1054, 96 S.Ct. 785, 46 L.Ed.2d 643 (1976). We believe that this principle applies with equal force in the present context. If DAI and its leasing companies should be treated as one and the same, then the initiation of eviction proceedings by the leasing companies must be imputed to DAI.

There remain two further questions: (1) whether the district court or the arbitrators should determine the waiver issue, and (2) what standard should be used by the appropriate decisionmaker. As to the first question, we note that the defense of waiver is generally referable to the arbitrators in cases involving petitions to compel under § 4 of the FAA—with one important exception which we shall shortly explain. In World Brilliance Corp. v. Bethlehem Steel Co., 342 F.2d 362 (2d Cir. 1965), we squarely held that issues of waiver, like issues of fraud in the inducement of the entire contract, were properly resolved by the arbitrators, not the district court. Id. at 364–65. In reaching this conclusion, we pointed out that § 2 of the FAA makes an arbitration agreement enforceable " 'save upon such grounds as exist at law or in equity for the revocation of any contract.' " Id. at 364 (quoting 9 U.S.C. § 2). Waiver, we explained, does not constitute a ground for "revocation" of a contract within the meaning of § 2, and thus is not a basis for invalidating an arbitration contract. Id. Likewise, we explained that under § 4, a court is required to grant a petition to compel arbitration except where a question of fact exists as to (1) "the making of the arbitration agreement" or (2) the "failure, neglect, or refusal of another [i.e., the respondent to the § 4 petition] to arbitrate." Id. at 364–65 (quoting 9 U.S.C. § 4 (emphasis added)). Because acts by the petitioner constituting waiver of the right to arbitrate did not fall within either of these enumerated categories, a district court cannot refuse to order arbitration under § 4 on a theory of waiver. Id. at 365. We reaffirmed this restrictive interpretation of § 4 in Trafalgar Shipping Co. v. International Milling Co., 401 F.2d 568, 571 (2d Cir.1968), where we held that most questions regarding the defense of laches should be decided "by the arbitrators, not the courts." In that case, we repeated that "[t]he only issues which the court is authorized to consider on a motion to compel arbitration are ones which pertain to 'the making of the arbitration agreement or the failure, neglect, or refusal to perform the same,' " id. at 571, and that the latter phrase referred to the failure of the respondent in a § 4 action to submit to arbitration, id. at 572.

Our decision in World Brilliance did not call into question, however, a parallel line of cases that considers waiver to be an equitable defense to a stay application under § 3 of the FAA, which a court is empowered to consider. Section 3 authorizes a court to stay proceedings pending arbitration, "providing the applicant for the stay is not in default in proceeding with such arbitration." 9 U.S.C. § 3. For example, in Kulukundis Shipping Co. v. Amtorg Trading Corp., 126 F.2d 978 (2d Cir.1942), a defendant sought to amend his answer nine months into the litigation and two months before trial, raising for the first time the defense that the case was arbitrable. Id. at 986. We construed the defendant's motion to amend as an application for a § 3 stay of proceedings. Id. at 986 n. 29. We explained that the proviso in § 3—that a stay shall be granted "providing the applicant for the stay is not in default in proceeding with such arbitration"—referred to a party "who, when requested, has refused to go to arbitration or who has refused to proceed with the hearing before the arbitrators once it has commenced." Id. at 989. We also noted with approval that, in other courts, "[a] plaintiff who brought suit on a contract, without seeking to avail himself of its arbitration clause, has been held to have waived his rights thereunder, so that he could not subsequently, after a long delay, ask the court, under Section 3, to stay the action pending arbitration." Id. We also indicated our agreement with a Fourth Circuit decision finding waiver of the right to arbitrate by a counterclaim defendant who participated at length in litigation, but on the eve of trial moved for a stay under § 3 of the FAA. Id. (describing Radiator Specialty Co. v. Cannon Mills, Inc., 97 F.2d 318 (4th Cir.1938)). The defendant in Kulukundis did not waive its right to arbitrate, we held, because it had not pursued litigation as extensively as had the parties in these other cases. 126 F.2d at 989.

We again equated a waiver of the right to arbitrate with a "default in proceeding with such arbitration" under § 3 in Robert Lawrence, 271 F.2d at 412; see Carcich v. Rederi A/B Nordie, 389 F.2d 692, 696 (2d Cir.1968) (deciding waiver issue where defendant moved for stay). The Court of Appeals for the District of Columbia Circuit apparently took the same view, when it explained that "[t]he right to arbitration, like any other contract right, can be waived. A party waives his right to arbitrate when he actively participates in a lawsuit or takes other action inconsistent with that right. Once having waived the right to arbitrate, that party is necessarily 'in default in proceeding with such arbitration.'" Cornell & Co. v. Barber & Ross Co., 360 F.2d 512, 513 (D.C.Cir.1966) (per curiam).

Yet some of our cases have also recognized that a court may consider a waiver defense to § 4 actions to compel arbitration as well as to § 3 stay applications—seemingly in derogation of our holding in World Brilliance. For example, in Chatham Shipping Co. v. Fertex Steamship Corp., 352 F.2d 291, 293–94 (2d Cir.1965), the petitioner had filed a complaint alleging breach of a contract but then filed a § 4 petition and moved to dismiss the first complaint, before the defendant had even filed an answer. We rejected the respondent's defense of waiver on the merits, even though World Brilliance had been decided only seven months earlier. In Demsey & Associates, Inc. v. S.S. Sea Star, 461 F.2d 1009, 1017 (2d Cir.1972), where a defendant in a contract action pleaded arbitration "as an affirmative defense" after trial had been completed, we did not construe it as seeking either a § 3 stay or a § 4 order compelling arbitration. We held that the defendant's failure to raise the arbitration issue until after filing cross-claims, participating in discovery, and going to trial on the merits constituted waiver of its right to arbitrate. Id. The court did not discuss its authority for reaching the waiver issue—possibly because the defendant had neither sought a stay under § 3, nor petitioned the court to compel arbitration under § 4. Id. Yet in all of the cases cited in Demsey, except Chatham, the court decided the waiver issue only where a defendant, deep into the litigation, sought a stay of judicial proceedings under § 3 of the FAA. Id. at 1017–18.

Any distinction between § 3 and § 4 actions—never fully explicated—submerged even more deeply by the time this court decided Sweater Bee by Banff, Ltd. v. Manhattan Industries, Inc., 754 F.2d 457 (2d Cir.), cert. denied, 474 U.S. 819, 106 S.Ct. 68, 88 L.Ed.2d 55 (1985). That case involved a defendant who, only after obtaining an adverse ruling on a motion to dismiss pursuant to Rule 12(b)(6) of the Federal Rules of Civil Procedure, sought both a § 3 stay and a § 4 order compelling arbitration. 754 F.2d at 459. Citing Demsey, we stated that "[t]he rule of this circuit . . . is that the litigation of substantial issues going to the merits may constitute a waiver of arbitration," id. at 461, and proceeded to decide the waiver issue. Shortly thereafter, we faced a similar case involving a defendant who sought to sever certain claims from ongoing litigation and petitioned the court to compel arbitration of those claims under § 4 of the FAA. Rush v. Oppenheimer & Co., 779 F.2d 885, 886 (2d Cir.1985). We made it clear that "waiver of the right to compel arbitration due to participation in litigation may be found only when prejudice to the other party is demonstrated," id. at 887, and again decided the waiver issue. Finally, in Kramer v. Hammond, 943 F.2d 176 (2d Cir.1991), we held that a party bringing a petition to compel under § 4 had waived his right to arbitration by engaging in prior litigation in state courts, not in the district court.[1] Id. at 180. Again, the parties did not raise and we did not discuss why this issue was for the courts rather than the arbitrators to resolve.

It would appear that the waiver defense has slowly been transformed from a statutorily mandated inquiry in § 3 cases—whether the "applicant for the stay is . . . in default in proceeding with such arbitration"—into a broader equitable defense in § 4 cases. This trend has its limits, however, and another of our decisions suggests how the equitable waiver defense may be reconciled with our holdings in World Brilliance. In Prudential Lines, Inc. v. Exxon Corp., 704 F.2d 59 (2d Cir.1983), we reaffirmed the holdings of World Brilliance and Trafalgar that a waiver defense, like a laches defense, was "an arbitrable issue." Id. at 67. We

---

1. Prior to our decision in Kramer, all of the cases in which we reached the issue of waiver involved substantial litigation on the merits in the district court which was asked to grant the § 3 stay, not in other state or federal courts. Our decisions to rule on the waiver issue, rather than to refer the question to the arbitrators, could have been explained as exercises of the federal courts' inherent power to deal with abusive litigation practices in their courtrooms. See, e.g., Chambers v. NASCO, 501 U.S. 32, 44–45, 111 S.Ct. 2123, 2132–33, 115 L.Ed.2d 27 (1991) ("A primary aspect of [a court's] discretion [to exercise its inherent powers] is the ability to fashion an appropriate sanction for conduct which abuses the judicial process."). . . .

noted that in the cases where the court itself decided the issue of waiver, the "party had previously participated in court proceedings to litigate the same dispute." Id. at 67 n. 8. We therefore distinguished between cases where the waiver defense was based on prior litigation by the party seeking arbitration—when the court should decide the issue of waiver— and those when the defense was based on other actions. It may be that the modern evolution of our waiver doctrine does not correspond precisely to our understanding of the FAA thirty years ago. Yet we are bound to abide by our most recent precedent. Cf. Commodity Futures Trading Commission v. Dunn, 58 F.3d 50, 54 (2d Cir.1995) (holding that a panel of Court of Appeals may not "disregard the reasoning of a decision [of a prior panel] because an entirely different line of reasoning was available").

Clearly, the present case falls squarely within the parameters of Kramer v. Hammond, where the party invoking arbitration (DAI) was allegedly involved in prior litigation in state courts. Pursuant to the distinction we drew in Prudential Lines, and consistent with Kramer, we hold that the issue of DAI's waiver of arbitration is for the district court to resolve on remand. The factual contentions to be resolved include whether the leasing companies were mere alter egos of DAI. If DAI was responsible for the eviction proceedings, it must then be determined whether prosecution of those eviction actions constituted litigation of "substantial issues going to the merits." Sweater Bee, 754 F.2d at 461. This inquiry will require a determination of whether, in fact, the particular eviction proceedings were based on the cross-default provisions of the subleases. If the alleged violations of the subleases were premised on violations of the franchise agreement (which DAI was contractually bound to resolve through arbitration) then DAI did litigate substantial issues going to the merits, and the only remaining question will be whether the franchisees suffered prejudice from the eviction proceedings. See, e.g., Cotton v. Slone, 4 F.3d 176 (2d Cir.1993) (finding prejudice where defendant failed to pursue interlocutory appeal from denial of motion to compel, and instead fully litigated arbitrable issues on the merits in the district court); Com–Tech Assocs. v. Computer Assocs. Int'l, Inc., 938 F.2d 1574, 1576–77 (2d Cir.1991) (finding prejudice where defendant's extensive litigation before raising issue of arbitration forced plaintiffs to litigate arbitrable claims, and caused considerable expense and delay).

Accordingly, we reverse the district court's order rejecting the franchisees' waiver argument, and remand for further proceedings.

3. *Fraudulent Misrepresentation*

The franchisees argue that DAI fraudulently misrepresented to them that arbitration was a condition precedent to the institution of legal action by either party to the franchise agreement. They argue that DAI had, in reality, reserved the right to bring summary eviction actions against the franchisees through its leasing companies. The franchisees also claim that DAI failed to disclose that it had a custom and practice of bringing summary eviction proceedings and other legal proceedings for alleged violations of the franchise agreement. The district court held that these allegations would be pertinent only if the leasing companies were indeed DAI's alter egos. Both the alter ego and fraudulent-inducement issues, the court concluded, should properly be left to the arbitrators. This was error.

In Prima Paint, 388 U.S. at 403–04, 87 S.Ct. at 1805–06, the Supreme Court stated that "if the claim is fraud in the inducement of the arbitration clause itself—an issue which goes to the 'making' of the agreement to arbitrate—the federal court may proceed to adjudicate it." See also Scherk v. Alberto–Culver Co., 417 U.S. 506, 519 n. 14, 94 S.Ct. 2449, 2457 n. 14, 41 L.Ed.2d 270 (1974) (citing Prima Paint for the proposition that "an arbitration or forum-selection clause in a contract is not enforceable if the inclusion of that clause in the contract was the product of fraud or coercion"). As this court has explained, if the "arbitration clause was induced by fraud, there can be no arbitration; and if the party charging this fraud shows there is substance to his charge, *there must be a judicial trial of that question* before a stay can issue." Robert Lawrence, 271 F.2d at 411.

The franchisees allege that they were fraudulently induced to assent to the arbitration clause—not to the rest of the contract. Accordingly, under Prima Paint, the district court had to reach the fraudulent inducement issue before deciding whether to compel arbitration. Resolution of the fraud issue, in turn, will require an answer to the antecedent question of whether the leasing companies were DAI's alter egos.

We therefore reverse the district court's determination that the arbitrators rather than the court should decide the alter-ego and fraudulent-inducement questions. On remand, the district court must resolve these issues.

III. Conclusion

1. We affirm the district court's decision that it had subject matter jurisdiction over all of DAI's petitions to compel arbitration, because there was complete diversity between the parties to the arbitration clause.

2. We reverse the district court's holding that the Alabama court's judgment in the McCrary case (Case # 8) was not entitled to full faith and credit. That judgment had preclusive effect under Alabama law, and thus barred DAI from seeking to enforce its arbitration agreement with McCrary. We therefore reverse the district court's denial of franchisee McCrary's motion to dismiss DAI's motion to compel and its order granting DAI's petition to compel McCrary to arbitrate. In the exercise of our pendent appellate jurisdiction, we vacate the preliminary injunction barring McCrary from pursuing his Alabama state court

claims against DAI. We direct the district court, on remand, to dismiss with prejudice DAI's motion to compel McCrary to arbitrate.

3. We affirm the district court's holding that the Illinois courts' judgments in Cases 1–6, 15–16, and DAI v. Bickel were still subject to appeal, and thus under Illinois law were not entitled to preclusive effect. We therefore affirm the district court's denial of those franchisees' motions to dismiss.

4. We affirm the district court's holding that the North Carolina judgment in the Johnson case (Case # 7) was not entitled to full faith and credit. That judgment would not be accorded preclusive effect under North Carolina law, because the court's written order does not indicate what issues were actually decided. We therefore affirm the district court's denial of the Johnson franchisees' motion to dismiss.

5. We affirm the district court's holding that "mutuality" was not at issue, but on different grounds. We hold that where consideration supports a contract as a whole, an arbitration clause in that contract is not void for lack of consideration.

6. We reverse the district court's holding that DAI did not waive its right to petition to compel arbitration, and remand for further proceedings. We hold that if the leasing companies were mere alter egos of DAI, their pursuit of eviction proceedings based on violations of the franchise agreements could constitute waiver of DAI's right to demand arbitration.

7. We reverse the district court's decision to defer to the arbitrators on the question of whether DAI fraudulently induced the franchisees to enter into the arbitration agreement. On remand, the district court shall decide this issue.

8. Because the district court should have decided the alter ego, waiver and fraudulent-inducement issues, we reverse its order granting DAI's motion to compel arbitration in all cases and remand for further proceedings. We also reverse its entry of preliminary injunctions against all of the franchisees—including, in the exercise of our pendent appellate jurisdiction and in the interests of judicial economy, the Alabama franchisees.

9. Finally, because we reverse the district court's orders entering the preliminary injunctions, we need not address the franchisees' contention that those orders violated the Anti–Injunction Act.

NOTES

(1) Once it has been decided that an arbitration agreement was entered into, should it not be left to the arbitrators to determine (at least in the first instance) whether there was fraud in the inducement of the arbitration agreement?

(2) Should a court, when confronted with a plea that the arbitration agreement had previously been ruled unenforceable, decide the binding effect of the prior determination itself or refer the issue to the arbitrators?

(3) Who decides (at least in the first instance) whether a unilateral arbitration clause is enforceable: the court or the arbitrators? Does the principal case involve a unilateral arbitration clause? Did the arbitration clause purport to give DAI the right to seek arbitration of its eviction claims?

(4) Does the court or do the arbitrators decide whether the arbitration clause was waived?

[Insert on page 1124, as Note (4):]

(4) In Allied–Bruce Terminix Companies, Inc. v. Dobson, 513 U.S. 265, 115 S.Ct. 834, 130 L.Ed.2d 753 (1995), the Supreme Court, with Justices Scalia and Thomas dissenting, ruled that a contract between an Alabama homeowner and the local Alabama franchise of Terminix was a transaction "involving commerce" within the meaning of Section 2 of the Federal Arbitration Act. It therefore ruled arbitrable a dispute arising from that contract, even though an Alabama statute ruled predispute arbitration agreement invalid. The Court ruled that so long as the contract in fact involved commerce, it was irrelevant that the parties did not contemplate an interstate commerce connection.

[Insert on page 1131, after Note (6):]

(7) Gilmer v. Interstate/Johnson Lane Corp., 500 U.S. 20, 111 S.Ct. 1647, 114 L.Ed.2d 26 (1991). Gilmer was a securities representative registered with the New York Stock Exchange which required him to abide by the NYSE Rules. Rule 347 of these Rules provides for arbitration of any controversy arising out of a registered representative's employment or termination of employment. Gilmer was discharged. He brought suit in the district court alleging that he had been discharged in violation of the Federal Age Discrimination in Employment Act of 1967. The question of whether Gilmer's claim was arbitrable under the Federal Arbitration Act was raised for the first time in the Supreme Court by *amici curiae*. The Supreme Court nevertheless decided it and held the claim arbitrable.

D. THE AWARD AND ITS ENFORCEMENT

[Insert on page 1135, at the end of the page:]

NOTE ON RES JUDICATA IN ARBITRATION

Arbitral awards may also be given conclusive effect in ordinary litigation. Conversely, court judgments may be given conclusive effect in arbitration. On these aspects, see p. 189 of this Supplement; Shell, Res Judicata and Collateral Estoppel Effects of Commercial Arbitration, 35 UCLA L.Rev. 623 (1988); Hayford & Peeples, Commercial Arbitration in Evolution: An Assessment and Call For Dialogue, 10 Ohio St.J. on Disp.Resol. 343 (1995).

APPENDIX

[Insert on page 1143, as Note (1):]

NOTES

(1) On the *Burnham* case, See Wald, The Left–For–Dead Fiction of Corporate "Presence": Is it Revived by Burnham? 54 La.L.Rev. 189 (1993); Daleiden, The Aftermath of Burnham v. Superior Court: A New Rule of Transient Jurisdiction? 32 Santa Clara L.Rev. 989 (1992).

†